The Art of Champa

Jean-François Hubert

Text: Jean-François Hubert
Translation: Anna Allanet

Layout:
Baseline Co Ltd
127-129A Nguyen Hue Boulevard,
District 1, Ho Chi Minh City

François Devos for all photographs.

ISBN 1-85995-975-X

Printed in China

Acknowledgments

My thanks go first of all to my editor, Jean-Paul Manzo who enthusiastically accepted my project, and to Eliane de Sérésin who had the task of seeing it get done. May they find here the expression of my deep gratitude.
Particular mention is due to François Devos, photographer, who agreed to accompany me to places that were often picturesque, to take magnificent photos.

Thanks also to all those without whom, for one reason or another,
this work would not have come into existence:

Sophie Allard-Latour
Philippe Damas
Dominique Darbois
Jean-Luc Enguehard
Michel Inguimberty
Jean-Paul Morin
Cang Nguyen
Eric Pouillot
Richard Prevost
Nicholas Scheeres
Lan Tran
Marc Vartabedian
Jean Volang
Anna Zweede

Finally, my very special thanks go to Joëlle Loiret, whose professional eye and sense of form and content are only equalled by her patience and tenacity.

The Art of Champa

Jean-François Hubert

Contents

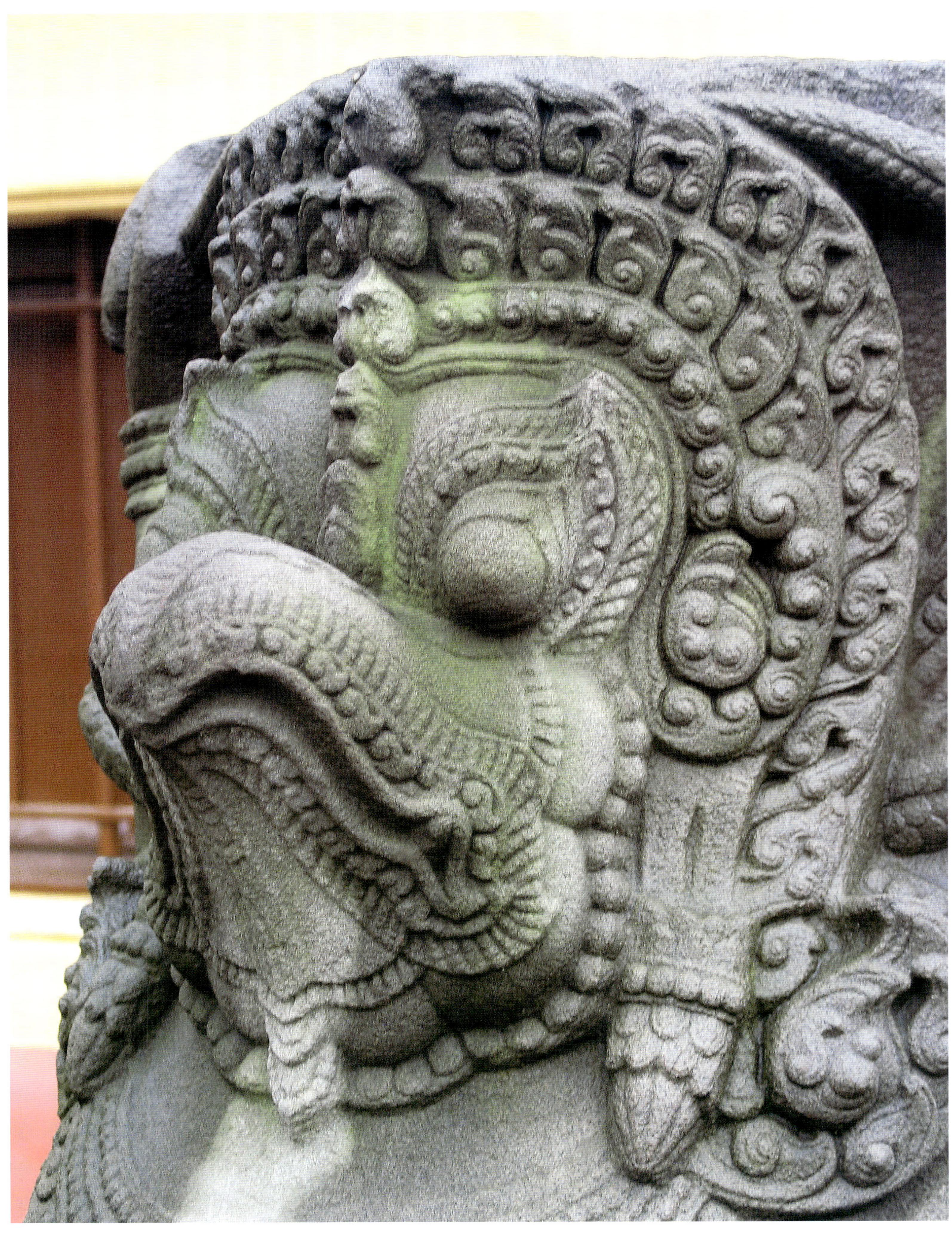

Introduction

Evoking Champa means glorifying death, sanctifying remnants, magnifying clues, singing the praises of mourning, and reconstructing history. Champa only exists now in the memories of a diminishing collection of living people who desire eternal life, in a half-audible melody – necessarily exotic – that is hummed by a few disquieted spirits.

Yet, in defiance of time, held in compassion by it, wreaking revenge on the injustice of the inevitable... Cham statues bear witness to this civilisation that was swallowed up in the meanders of history, profane child of the divine work of destruction.

Civilisations die, but all are fecund. They leave in our collective memory those fundamental notions, impossible to articulate, which are irresolutely infinite and unattainably absolute.

Perhaps, however, the Cham civilisation is a little more lost to us than others: death is not a state of being but a discourse, and Champa has long lacked orators and an audience. Still, what a gesture! A mysterious birth, a stateless ideal, a glorious decadence, a death announced in the name of impossible otherness. Champa is five hundred years of mystery, a thousand of destruction, and three hundred of being forgotten.

The most efficient approach to its rediscovery was to capture its vestiges, its abandoned towers, its forgotten sculptures, its sublime sites where the divine wanders; a pleasant task for the willing traveller, armed with the learned indications of the great ancients and attentive to the unbiased attraction of discovery. Examining a statue, carrying out an authentication, is to interrogate condensed history. All the statues illustrated in this book were closely examined, measured, inspected, and authenticated. All from private collections, often heretofore unpublished, they bring new blood to the observation: in art, nothing is more dangerous than inbred models and limited fields of vision.

Cham art in general and Cham sculpture in particular is profoundly original. It was rediscovered by the French and has now been repossessed by the Vietnamese at the beginning of the twenty-first century.

Profoundly original because even if a few stylistic comparisons can be made, origins referred to, or influences noted, Cham sculpture differs from all other schools of sculpture – past or present.

Rediscovered by the French during the period of French administration in Indochina (which included Vietnam) in the second half of the nineteenth century, its scientists and explorers supported by the government of the day. Explorers, supported by architects, epigraphists and archaeologists not only garnered a unique fund of knowledge, combining documentation and commentary, but also carried out the major work of conserving

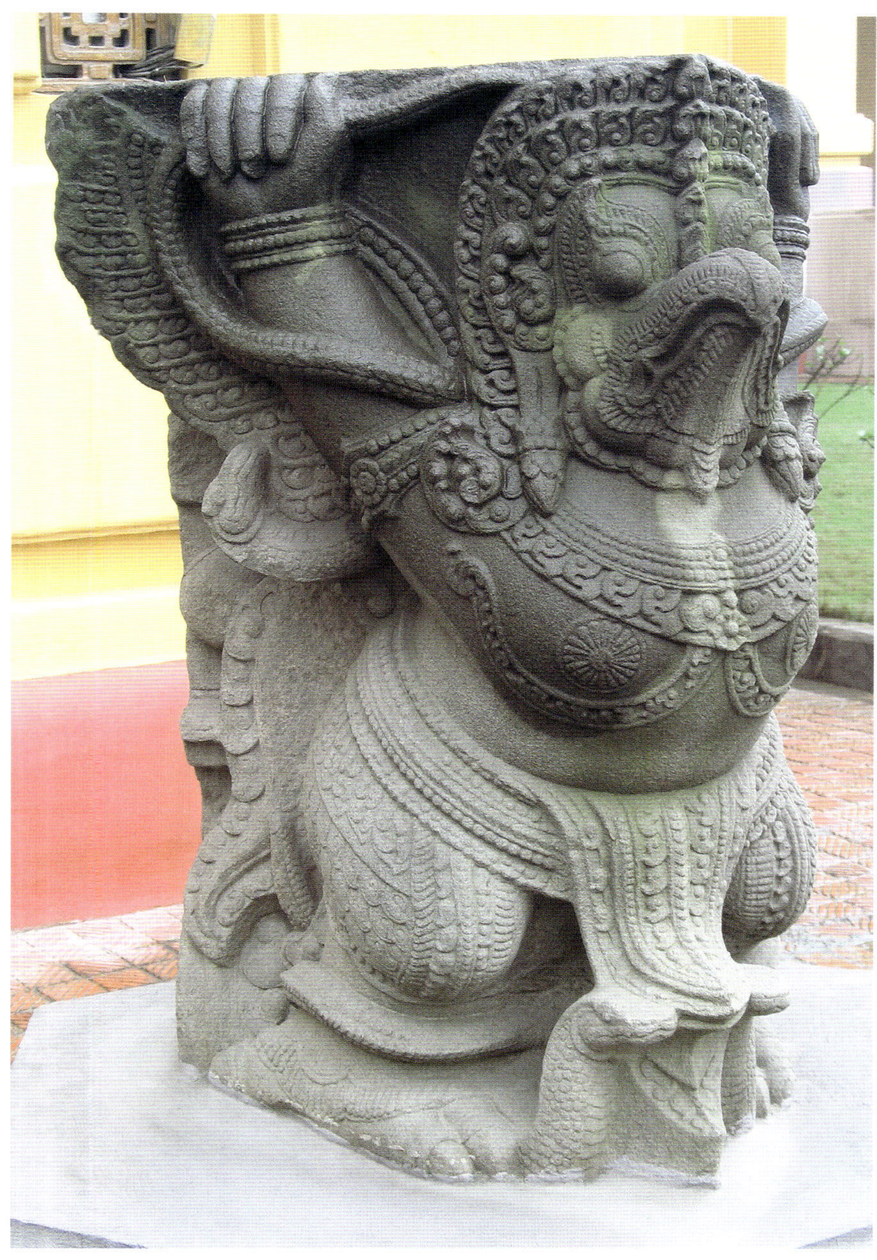

Previous Page

1. *Sandstone Garuda in the Thâp-Mam style* (12th Century) standing in front of the Vietnam History Museum (Hanoi) (detail).

2. *Sandstone Garuda in the Thâp-Mam style* (12th Century), standing in front of the Vietnam History Museum (Hanoi).

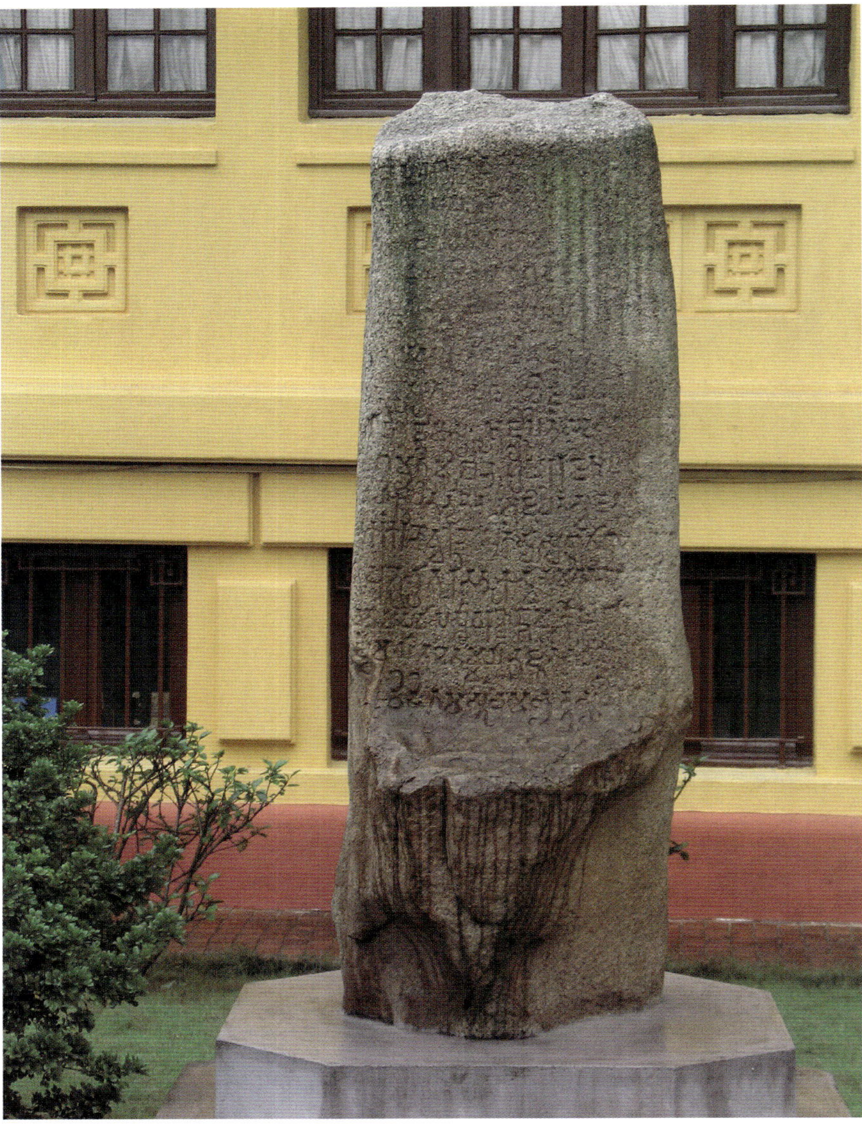

3. *Vo-Canh Inscription Standing in front of the Vietnam History Museum (Hanoi).* Dated from the 3rd and 4th Century, it remains pivotal in much research although its being of Cham origin is uncertain.

Following Page
4. *Vo-Canh Inscription,* standing in front of the Vietnam History Museum (Hanoi). (detail).

Cham sites. In a world where the use of French is declining, it is not insignificant to note that French remains the language of reference for the study of Cham art: no precise reference, no serious study could – even today – escape from the detailed examination and attentive reading of documents drawn from the best sources, all written in French, over the last five hundred years.

These documents have been repossessed today by the Vietnamese because they have been able, after the demands of years of war, to interest themselves in an art that, for many, remains foreign. After all, in the collective conscience that cements a nation, the Chams were, consciously, the enemy to the south, those who pillaged the north, and who, after Chinese occupation until the tenth century, appeared as the obstacle to an "expansion to the south" (Nam Tien) that the north's demographic growth rendered inevitable. Subconsciously, the Chams were also a source of guilt for the majority Kinh, having irreversibly destroyed a local culture that was over a thousand years old, reducing a people to assimilation. Roughly 100,000 Chams still live in Vietnam, listed in the inventory of fifty-four minorities in the country, living mainly near Phan Rang and Phan Ri, or near Chau Doc, all in the southern part of modern Vietnam.

The repossession of Cham culture is now flourishing: the care given to new publications, the valorising and restoration of sites, and the efficient archaeological digs, are all indications of a national realisation and of a true will to reclaim Cham heritage which, today, is incontestably Vietnamese.

However, it would be incorrect to inscribe Cham art in general and Cham sculpture in particular in an exclusively Franco-Vietnamese historical relationship or in an isolated national policy. Cham sculpture has long won over an international audience. Certainly, the first museums to exhibit it were founded in Vietnam under French influence. It is essentially the *Ecole française d'Extreme-Orient* (EFEO) (French School of the Far East) to which the mission to conserve historic monuments in Indochina was conferred, and the creation of the first museums is due. The school's buildings first housed, as early as 1899 in Saigon, a few stones brought back from the ruins in My Son. Then a few sculptures left for Hanoi between 1900 and 1905 and, little by little, through pieces gathered fortuitously or during organised digs, true museum collections were constituted. The dates of the actual creation of these museums are earlier but we have chosen to list here their definitive installation: the Louis Finot Museum in Hanoi (inaugurated in 1933), the Henri Parmentier Museum (1936) in Tourane-Danang, the Khai Dinh Museum in Hue (1923), the Blanchard de la Brosse Museum in Saigon (1929). Bit by bit foreign museums found it possible to assemble collections of quality, for example, the Cleveland Museum of Art, Cleveland, the Metropolitan Museum in New York and Brooklyn in the USA,

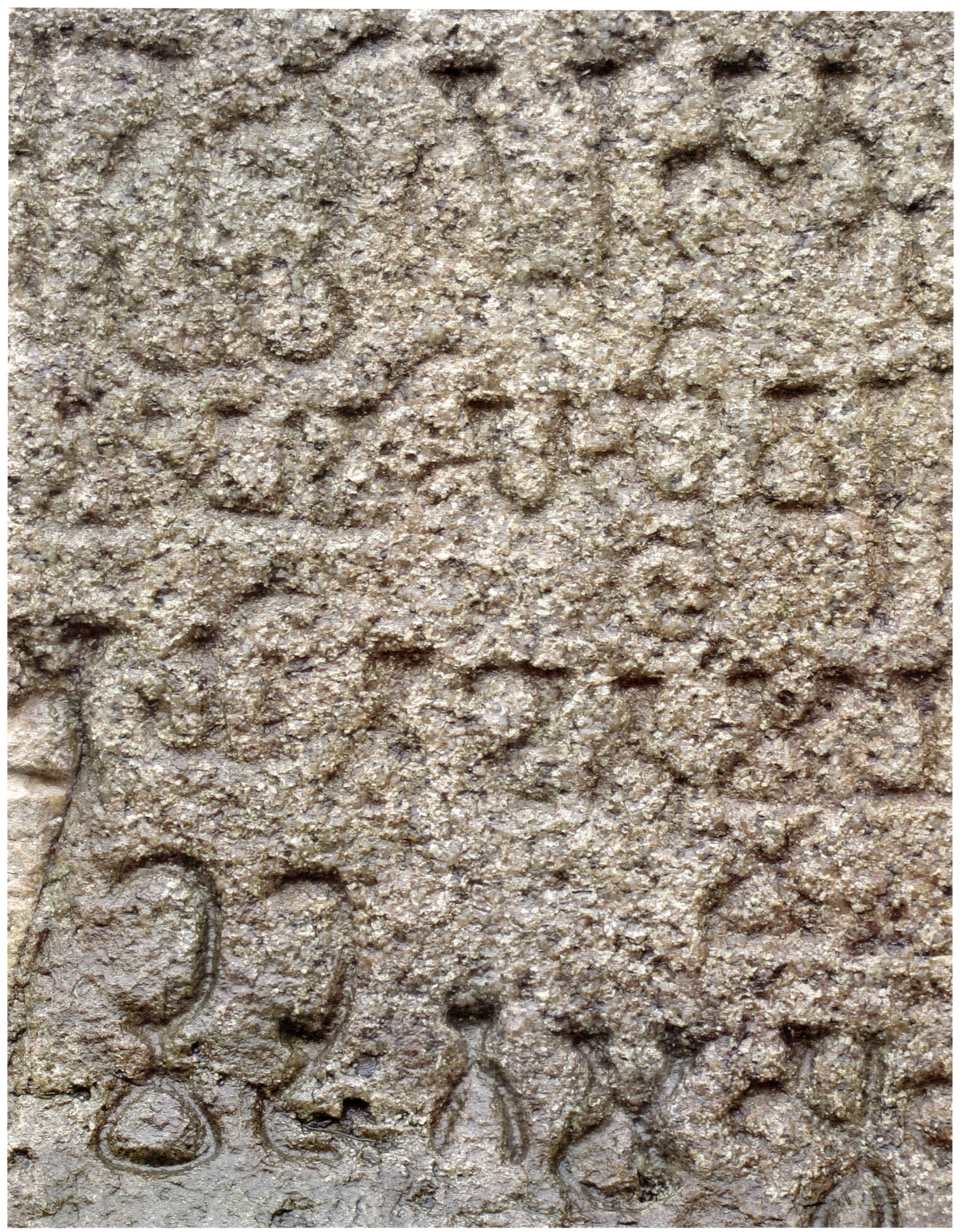

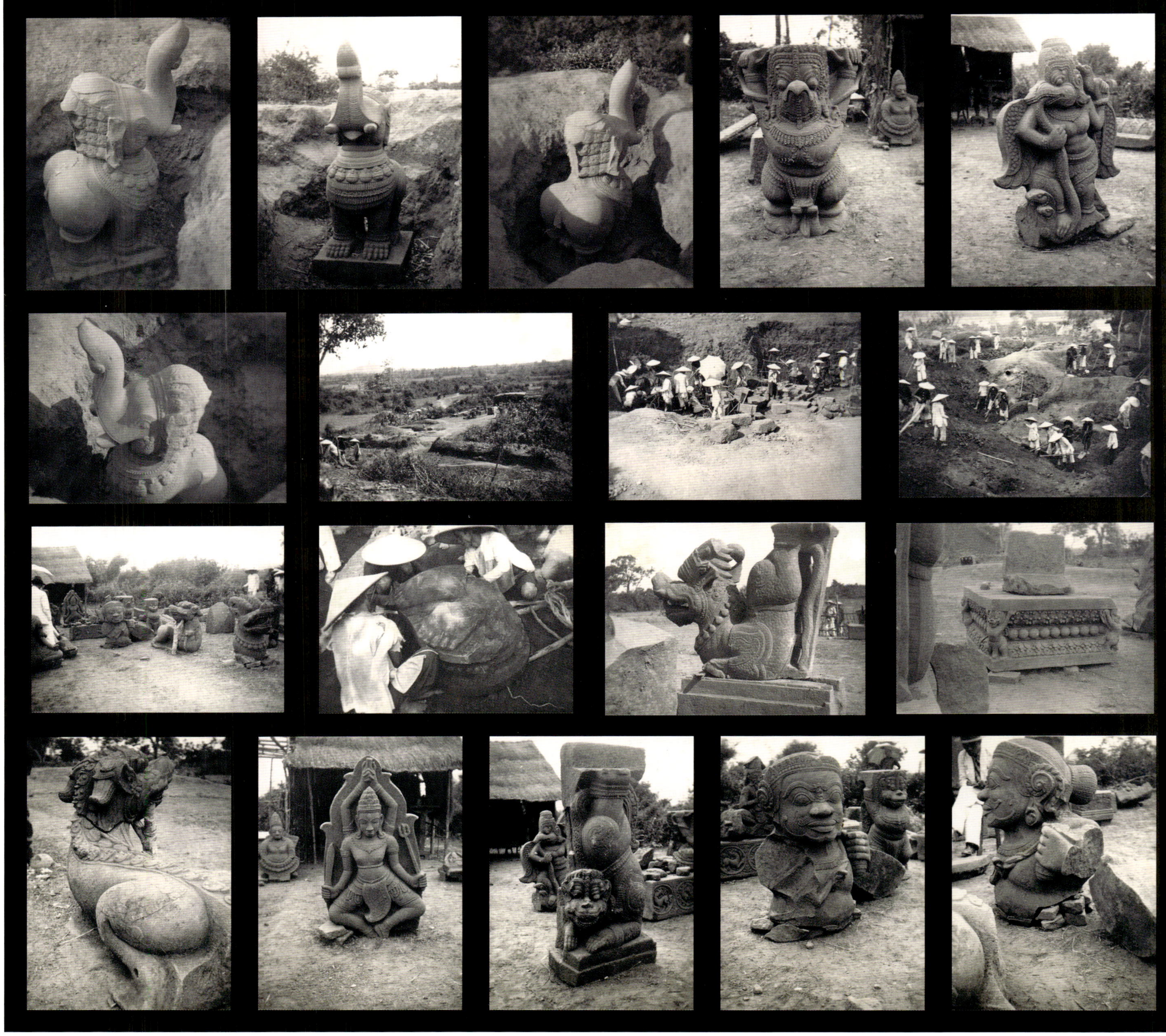

Museum Rietberg in Switzerland, Guimet in Paris, and Labit in Toulouse.

Not only epigraphists, architects, archaeologists, and translators but also hobbyists have provided knowledge of the Cham civilisation, its temples and, in particular, its sculpture. Below, category by category, these illustrious innovators are listed with a brief overview of their contributions.

The first group to recall is that of epigraphists: specialists whose science concerns the study and knowledge of inscriptions. Firstly, it must be noted the following learned men all contributed significantly to the current understanding of this ancient culture. However, there are limitations that this science has in the identification and dating of Cham art:

Auguste Barth (1834-1916), trained as an expert on India and wrote the founding charter of the FEEL in 1901; Georges Maspero (1872-1942), was an administrator in Indochina but is often confused with his brilliant brother, the linguist Henri (1883-1945); Louis Finot (1864-1935), archivist and palaeographer, Sanskrit expert, and director of the EFEO; Paul Pelliot (1878-1945); Henri Parmentier (1871-1949); Georges Coedes (1886-1969), who published his first article on epigraphy in the EFEO bulletin at the age of eighteen in 1904, and who had perfect mastery, in addition to Cham, of Sanskrit and Khmer among other languages; Paul Mus (1909-1960), an expert on India, specialist on the spread of Hinduism throughout India and South-East Asia, and who was interested above all in the natural, and beneficial, confrontation of Hindu and indigenous elements in the elaboration of the Cham religion.

Unfortunately, all the work of collecting and translating inscriptions is of little help in the study and the dating of Cham sculptures. If there are, today, about 230 officially tallied inscriptions from the fourth to the fifteenth centuries, in Sanskrit, ancient Cham, or in both languages, only about one hundred of these inscriptions have truly been studied. Mainly inscribed on stelae, they contain information concerning boundaries or religious events, but are of little use in dating the temples. Firstly, stelae may have been moved from one temple to another, and, secondly, it is not always easy to know whether the date on the stelae is that of the temple's inauguration or of the start of its construction which, given the length of time that building could take, limits the precision of possible dating.

Architect Henri Parmentier, notably in this category as well, was a graduate of the *Ecole des Beaux Arts* in Paris and hired by the EFEO at its creation. Between 1902 and 1908, he uncovered the main Cham sites (though not all, as is too often believed), publishing the related findings in his majestic two-volume book *Descriptive Inventory of the Cham Monuments of Annam* in 1909 and 1918. He uncovered the monuments of My Son and Dong Duong in

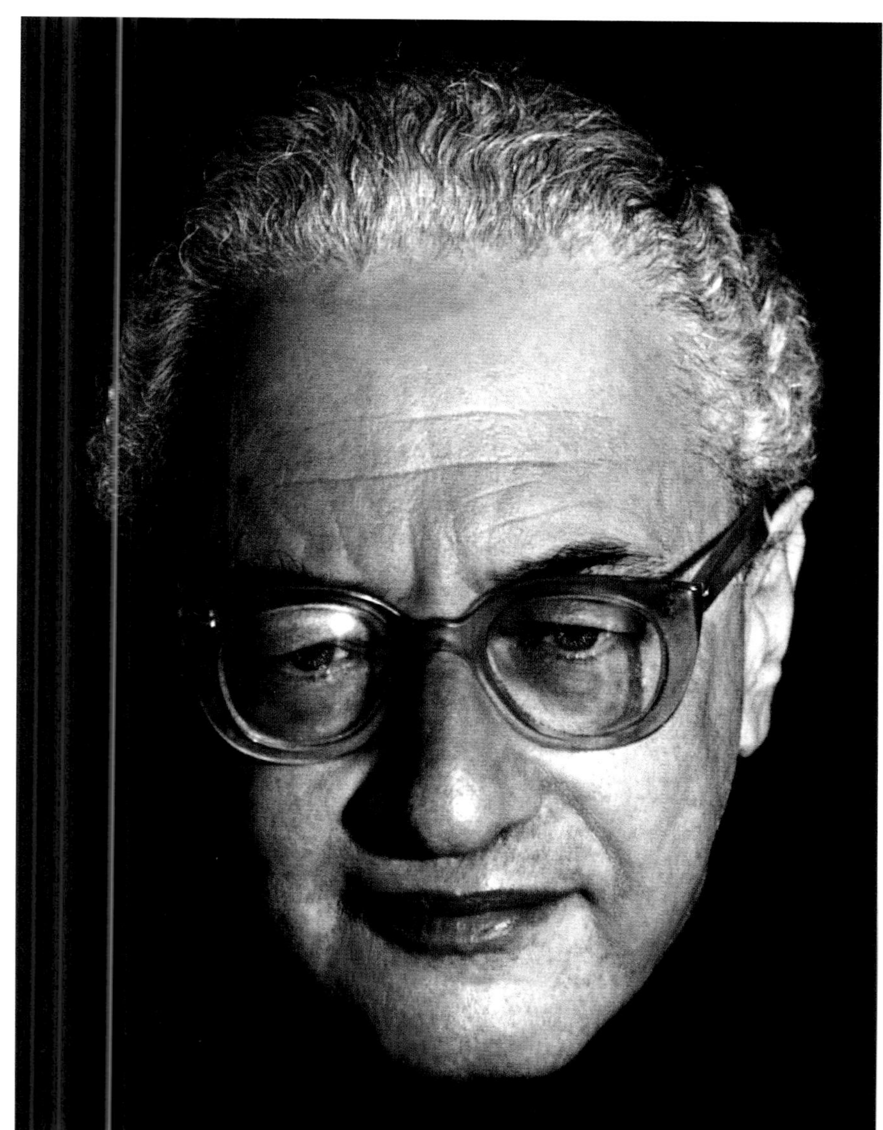

Previous Page
5. Cham archeological Thâp-Mam digs, 1933.

6. Portrait of Philippe Stern, 1953.

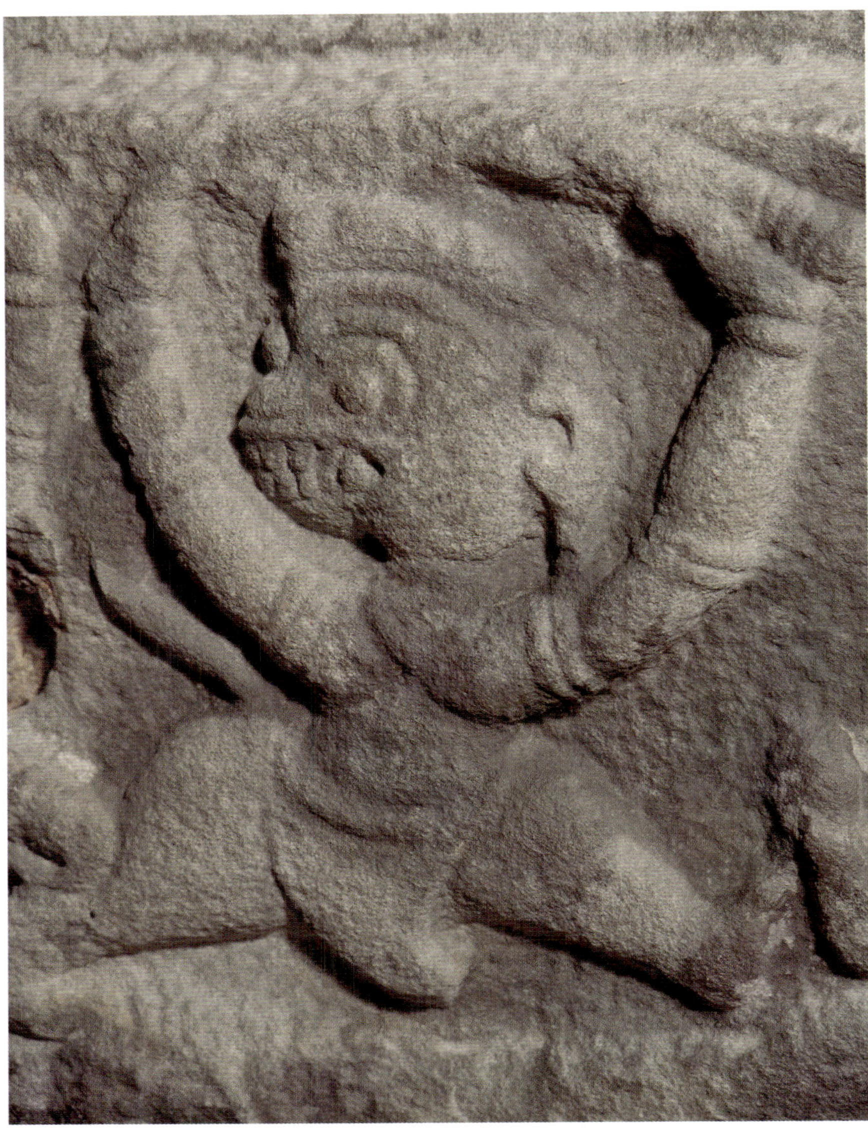

7. *Frieze of monkeys*, Bas-relief, Sandstone, length 64 cm, Thâp-Mam style, 11th - 12th Century (detail).

Following Page
8. *Frieze of monkeys*, Bas-relief, Sandstone, length 64 cm, Thâp-Mam style, 11th - 12th Century.

1902 and 1903, those of Po Klaung Garai in 1908 and the Po Nagar in Nha Trang between 1906 and 1909. We owe the creation, in 1918, of the Cham Museum in Da Nang (formerly Tourane) to him; the museum was given his name after its enlargement in 1936. Jean-Yves Claeys (1896-1979), was another architect who graduated from the *Ecole des Beaux-Arts* in Paris as well as the *Ecole des Arts Decoratifs* in Nice. An employee of the Public Works administration in Indochina, he became a member of the EFEO in 1927, then curator of the monuments of Annam. He dedicated his work not only to Cham architecture but also to archaeology, notably to uncovering the Thâp-Mam site in 1934-35 after working on Tra Kieu in 1920.

Parmentier and Claeys not only uncovered monuments buried in vegetation but also drew up precise lists that catalogued, for the purpose of protection, statues and inscriptions for the museums of the EFEO and carried out several digs in the immediate surroundings of the main monuments.

It was common to amalgamate the responsibilities of the archaeologist and museum curator into a single role during the first half of the twentieth century

Philippe Stern (1875-1979), was the director of the Guimet Museum in Paris, and corresponding member of the EFEO as of 1930. Putting observation before theorisation, he set out a method of dating that became the reference: He "based…his analyses on a rigorous and comparative study of the evolution of specific motifs that decorated arcatures, pilasters, friezes, small columns, *pièces d'accent* and other architectural elements."

In 1936, with his protégé Gilberte de Coral-Rémusat, in the course of his single mission to Asia, he visited – in addition to Cambodia, of course – the most important monuments of Champa. Following his providential re-dating of the Bayon in Angkor, which he made younger by taking it out of the ninth century and placing it in the twelfth, against the authorised and authoritarian opinion of the Finot-Parmentier-Goloubew trio, he proposed, first for Cham architecture and then for its sculpture, dating that created a solid precedent, even if it was to be subsequently completed and modified.

Jean Boisselier (1912-1996) took up the task later. After his studies at the *Ecole des Beaux-Arts* and at the *Ecole du Louvre* in Paris, he joined the EFEO in 1949. Having been made scientific head as of 1953 of the conservation work at Angkor, this formidable erudite analyst stimulated research for dozens of years, as much for Thai or Cham art as for that of the Khmer. His work in the analysis, identification and dating of Cham sculpture remains completely fundamental. This is true even if the master showed a certain reticence at the end of his life toward certain discoveries or rediscoveries. For example, he denied the discoveries at An My in 1982, despite their importance in allowing the confirmation of the existence of an early style of sculpture.

The contemporary Vietnamese school has, in recent years, brought a great deal to the knowledge of art from Champa. Ngo Van Doanh, Tran Ky Phuong and Pham Thuy Hop have, through their knowledge of the field, their immediate and renewed access to new archaeological discoveries, and their familiarity with Vietnamese sociology, also contributed to the renaissance of knowledge of Cham art. Po Dharma and Pierre-Bernard Lafont, in France, also participate in this process.

Finally, there are those who, though strictly amateurs, collected more than they studied, and were often the source of great rivers

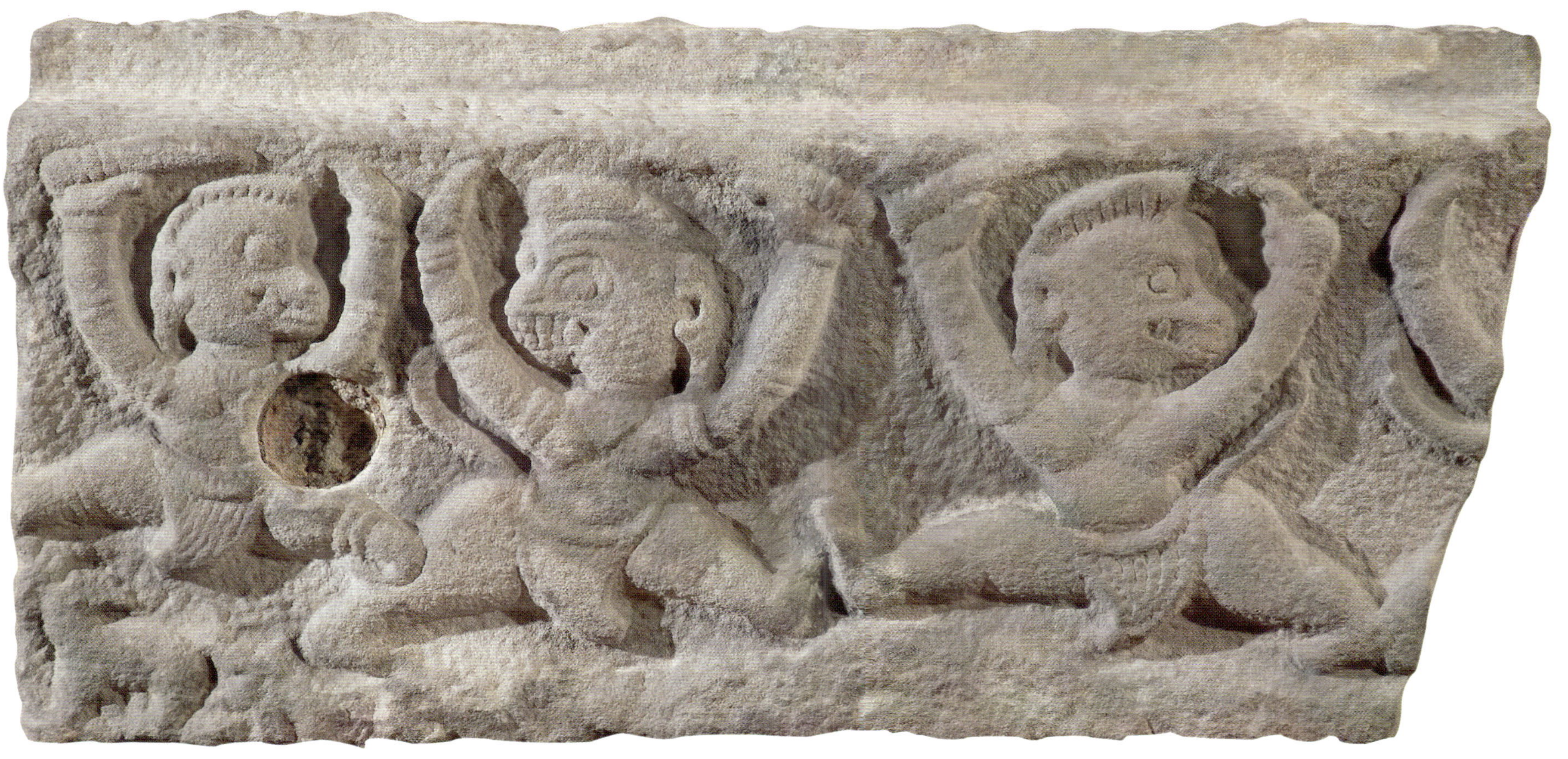

of knowledge. Charles Lemire (1839-1912), French resident of Quang Nam, compiled a collection between 1886 and 1892, which he kept in the "Cham Garden" in Da Nang (Tourane) until 1891-1892. Camille Paris, postal agent in Indochina first, then colonist, Father Cadière and Father Durand, Prosper d'Odend'hal, and Doctor Albert Sallet all efficiently contributed to the composition of a collection in the Cham museum in Da Nang (Tourane), not to forget Doctor Morice, who is discussed in more detail later. The Vietnamese collector Vu Kim Loc from Ho Chi Minh City is part of the process today. His collection, patiently assembled and mainly devoted to Cham metals, primarily jewellery and religious artefacts, is described in a very interesting book (see bibliography) written in collaboration with the eminent Vietnamese archaeologist Le Xuan Diem. The study of Cham art in general and Cham sculpture in particular needs such renewed initiatives to make headway.

The above piece comes from the collection of Doctor Claude-Albert Morice (1845-1877) who, after graduating from the Military School of Health in Lyons, became a doctor in the French Navy and spent his first period in Vietnam from 1872 to 1874 during which he devoted himself to his passion, natural history.

He collected numerous specimens and samples of the country's fauna and flora and sent them to the Museum of Natural History in Lyons; he also made the history and languages of Vietnam his passion.

During his second sojourn, that was cut short by his untimely death, he was a doctor attached to the consulate in Thi Nay near the city of Qui Nhon, a region that was Cham and where the architectural traces of ancient Champa were abundant. Morice became particularly interested in the statuary of what was the heart of the ancient kingdom of Vijaya, finally conquered in 1471 under the rule of Le Thanh Tong by the Viets during the *Nam Tien* ('March to the South').

He gathered – in the spirit of the times which saw more a scientific desire to assemble elements of documentation than to constitute a true art collection – a group of statues. Some were complete, others broken, having decorated the Cham temples and fallen from their brick structures as they gradually sank into the ground. Habitually, these stones were left untouched by the Viets, who feared the vengeful spirits of Cham gods.

No one knew what had happened to Doctor Morice's collection until Robert Stenuit, founding director in 1970 of GRASP (*Groupe de recherche archeologique sous-marine post-medievale)* (Research group for submarine post-Medieval archaeology) and the discoverer, notably, in 1976 of the Witte Leeuw (1), learned, thanks to documentary research, that a French *Messageries Maritimes* boat, the *Mekong*, sank on 17 June 1877 close to the coast of Somalia. The boat had left Saigon for Marseille and apparently contained Doctor Morice's Cham collection.

The *Illustration,* in its 21 July 1877 issue, related the tragic incident: the sinking steamboat was depicted with sixty-six passengers and 180 officers and crew reaching, thanks to longboats, with more or less difficulty, the shore that was luckily close by.

To locate with precision the place where the boat had sunk, Stenuit, for three long years, consulted numerous archives, notably those of the *Messageries Maritimes* and the former Protectorate of Aden; he studied manuscripts and maps and decided to set up an expedition to recover the statues. He was financed by two Americans from Pennsylvania, Mr. Edwards and his son.

On 9 October 1995 a boat sailing from Djibouti reached the site north of Somalia. Of course, the crew knew that the shipment had been pillaged at the time of the wreck by the Somalians in exchange for sparing the lives of the survivors and camels to carry them to the north coast. However, Stenuit was practically sure that the Cham stone pieces, due to their weight and their minimal interest for local inhabitants, had remained in the sunken ship. For the submarine archaeologists, the problem appeared simple to resolve: here was a sunken ship whose structure corresponds to that of the *Mekong* and its orientation on the sea floor as described in the *Illustration* (stern to the south, prow to the north). The search, carried out with the help of a magnetometer placed in a longboat christened *Docteur Morice* in homage to the Frenchman, resulted in the identification of a wreck among eight potential ships, the area being somewhat of a marine graveyard. The inscription *Messageries imperials* (Imperial Transport) on plates brought up to the surface confirmed the successful identification. In this way, statue after statue, eighteen pieces in all, were brought up. However, Robert Stenuit was dissatisfied; the number was insufficient, as his initial estimation based on his knowledge of the list of pieces expedited foresaw at least ten other pieces. In fact, better exploitation of archives allowed him, upon his return to France, to learn that a first shipment, sent before the shipwreck, had reached Marseille and then Lyons. After some difficulties and thanks to an astonishing intuition, Stenuit located the ten missing statues at the Museum of Natural History in Lyons, where they had joined the zoological and botanical samples sent back to his home town years earlier by the doctor from Lyon.

To quote a lovely remark of Stenuit's, these pieces he found stacked in a hallway at the museum, had been "buried rather than swallowed by sea". A plain label mentioned for one of them: "Head of monster. Sandstone. Origin unknown. Cham art, 13th – 14th centuries. Received in 1933. MGL 2415".

The pieces collected during Robert Stenuit's expedition, including these, were separated in a sale at Christie's in Amsterdam (2). The catalogue lists fourteen numbers for thirteen complete pieces and seven fragments.

The twofold interest of Stenuit's search is, first, it facilitated dating certain Cham pieces more precisely (3) and, second, it challenged certain commonly accepted pedigrees as a result of its other lesson. Steinuit's "expedition" shows that the search for the origins of pieces is always tricky, particularly concerning Cham art; the Natural History Museum label bears witness: dated 1933, the arrival of the piece was much earlier (1877). Luckily, certain public documents permitted the truth to be established. What would it have meant if the facts had been left to faulty individual memories, adding confusion as generations went by, between Khmer and Cham or Indian art, all seen under the banner of an abusively generic "Far East"?

(1) The *Witte Leeuw* ("White Lion"), returning from the Dutch East Indies, was sent to the bottom by two Portuguese caraques on 2 June 1613, off the coast of today's Jamestown (Saint Helena).

(2) *Indian, Himalayan and Southeast Asian Art*, Christie's Amsterdam, 31 October 2000, pp.96-103.

(3) For example, No. 197 in the catalogue of Christie's sale datable from the Thâp-Mam style, 12th century, allows a happy comparison with No. 175 reproduced in *Le musee de sculpture Cam de Dà Nang* (The Da Nang Museum of Cham Sculpture) (Editions de l'AFAO, Paris 1997, p.168). The comparison of the two heads of Kala, the first supporting a divinity, the second alone, removes all doubt concerning the piece in the Da Nang Museum, very probably found in Tra Kieu and put in the museum in 1918. If stylistic differences remain, the overall economy common to the two pieces and the very slight probability of forgeries at Morice's time, are so many arguments in favour of the authenticity of the Da Nang piece.

Following Page

9. Andre Maire (1898-1984), *The Tra-Kieu Buddha*, 1956.
Charcoal and chalk on paper, 65 cm x 50 cm, Signed and dated at bottom left.

Two years before his final return to France, the French artist, who was a teacher at the School of Architecture of Dalat at the time, went on with his work based on an imaginative and poetic reinterpretation of reality. Here, a Cham elephant from the 10th Century, probably drawn at the museum in Tourane, is incarnated in a temple, itself inhabited by a large Buddha (seen from the back), possibly a reminiscence of Dong Duong...

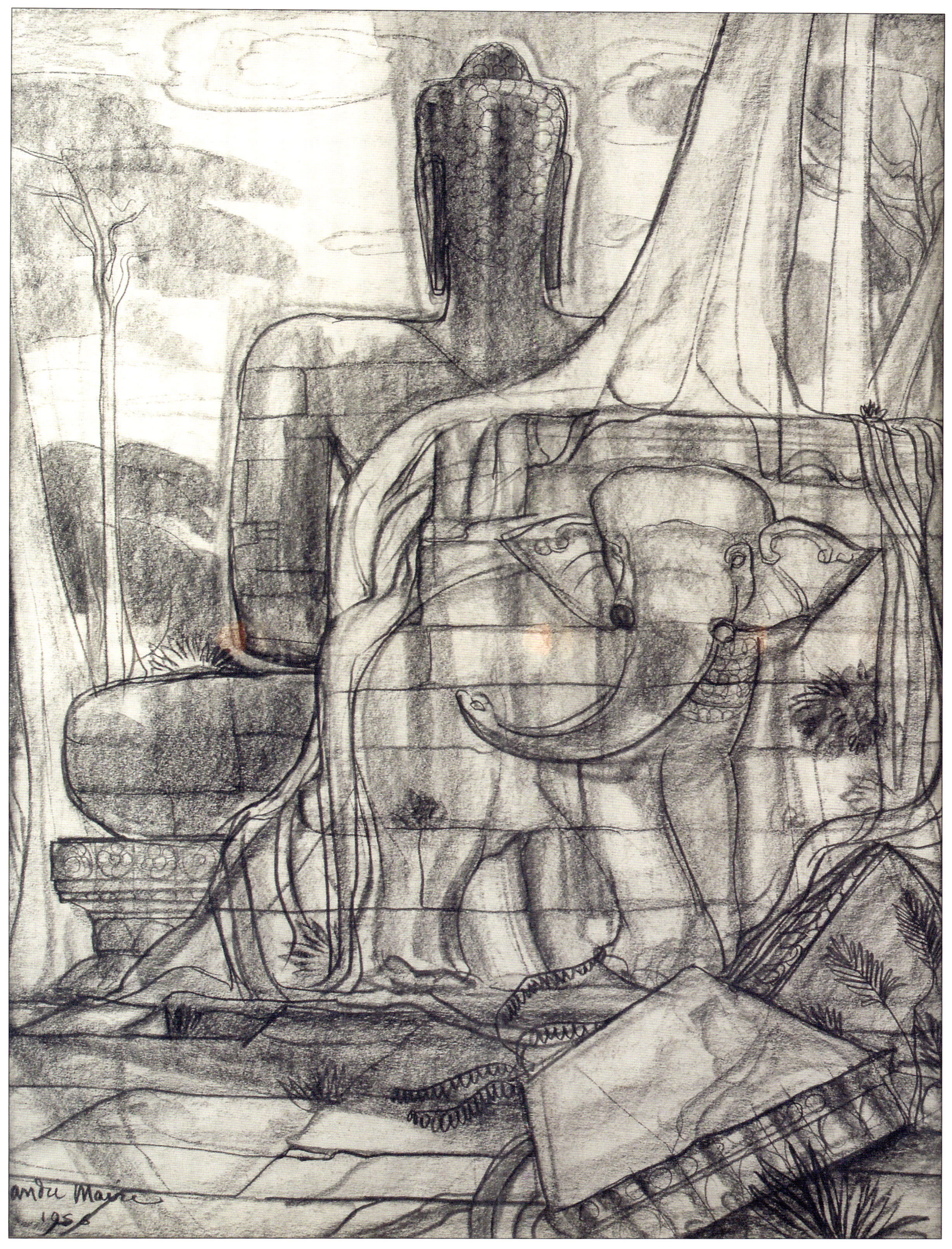

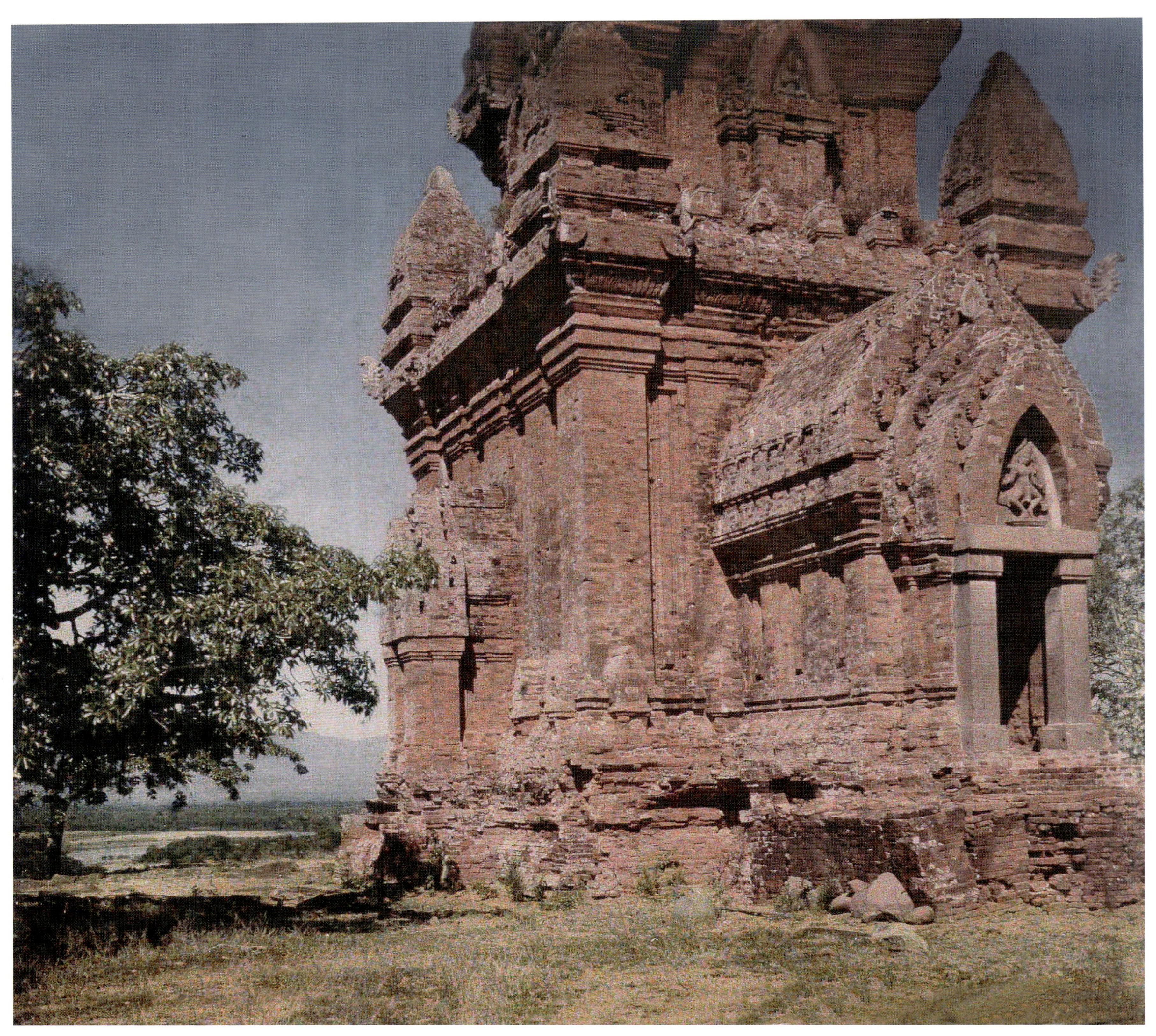

10. *The Cham Temple of Po Klaung Garai*, c. 1920.

Following Page
11. *Collection in the main room of the Cham Museum in Tourane*, 1922.

The History of Champa

Someone visiting Vietnam today, exploring Phan Thiet, Phan Ri and Phan Rang or even Chau Doc, coming across people who are sometimes curiously dressed, would find it difficult to believe that they, the Chams, occupied practically two thirds – in length – of modern Vietnam. In the tenth century, the Khmer Empire and Champa were the main powers of continental South-east Asia, while, to the north, Dai Viet was nothing but a very young kingdom after having been a province of the Chinese Empire for over a thousand years.

Our sources for knowledge of the history of Champa are both textual and archaeological.

For one, there are Chinese and Vietnamese texts (the Annals), the accounts of travellers (from Chinese and Arab to Occidental missionaries and Marco Polo), Cham manuscripts (notably those kept at the Inventory of Archives at the Asiatic Society of Paris), epigraphy (about 210 inscribed stones – written between the fourth and fifteenth centuries at times in Sanskrit, at times in old Cham, sometimes in both languages – have been recorded). Many of them are still waiting to be translated, a complicated task, as it requires a real knowledge of the general history of the country that pure linguists do not have.

There are also archaeological vestiges, the original Cham towers, from Hoa Lai to Chien Dan, from My Son to Po Klaung Garai and so many others, still with us despite the ravages of time and the terrible destruction due principally to the second Vietnam war.

Then one could add to these sources the memory of the Vietnamese Chams, eighty thousand in the provinces of Binh Thuan and Ninh Thuan in central Vietnam, fifteen thousand in Ho Chi Minh City (Saigon) and Chau Doc (An Giang province) close to the Cambodian border, as well as their hundred and fifty thousand "fellow citizens" in Cambodia who survived the barbaric Khmer Rouge. The Chams of central Vietnam are of Brahmanical heritage (Ahirs, or Kaphia or Chuh, Chams), the others follow a particular Muslim cult (Bani Chams). To these two groups must be added the three hundred thousand inhabitants of the High Plateaus who belong to the Austro-Asian language group (Mnongs, Naas and Stiengs) or the Austronesian language group (Jarais, Rhades, Churus, Ra-glais) who participated wholly in Champa's history, the inhabitants of the plains – those called the Chams – evidently not having been the only inhabitants of the Cham country.

Champa appears in Chinese texts as of the second century. It spread over territories that stretched from north to south, from the Gate of Annam (Hoanh So'n) practically to Ho Chi Minh City

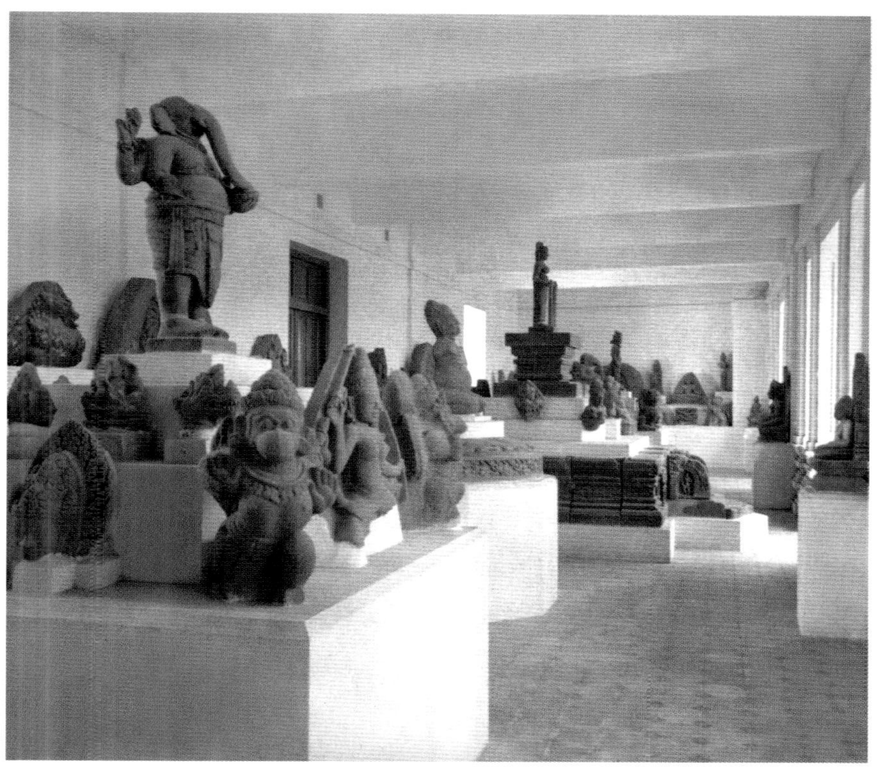

(Baigaur in Cham) between the eighth and tenth centuries, and it reached west as far as the Mekong, as witnessed by the Khmer site in Laos, Vat Phu, the stele of Vat Luang Kau or the Prasat Damrei Krap of Mount Kulen in Cambodia, or the expedition led by Doudart de Lagrée that, going through Bassac in 1883 noted that the peoples there still remembered the Chams.

If written proof of the early presence of Chams on the High Plateaus were needed, one could refer to the inscriptions of the Kon Klor temple in the valley of Bla near Kontum that have been dated to 914, that mention the construction by a local chief by the name of Mahindravarman of a sanctuary dedicated to the god Mahindra-Lokesvara, or to other inscriptions such as those of the Yang Prong temple (late thirteenth-early fourteenth centuries), or to the temple of Yang Mum (late fourteenth-early fifteenth centuries)...

The history of the Champa, its beginnings remaining incompletely understood, is made of victories and defeats but also of an inexorable destiny that, of a brilliant and complex civilisation, left only crumbling temples – structures of great originality that are difficult to apprehend – and a decimated and dispersed people. The Chinese Annals report an uprising in 192 AD of people living south of the Chinese command post in Renan (Nhat Nam in Vietnamese), today's Hue, who founded a state called Lin Yi that began by

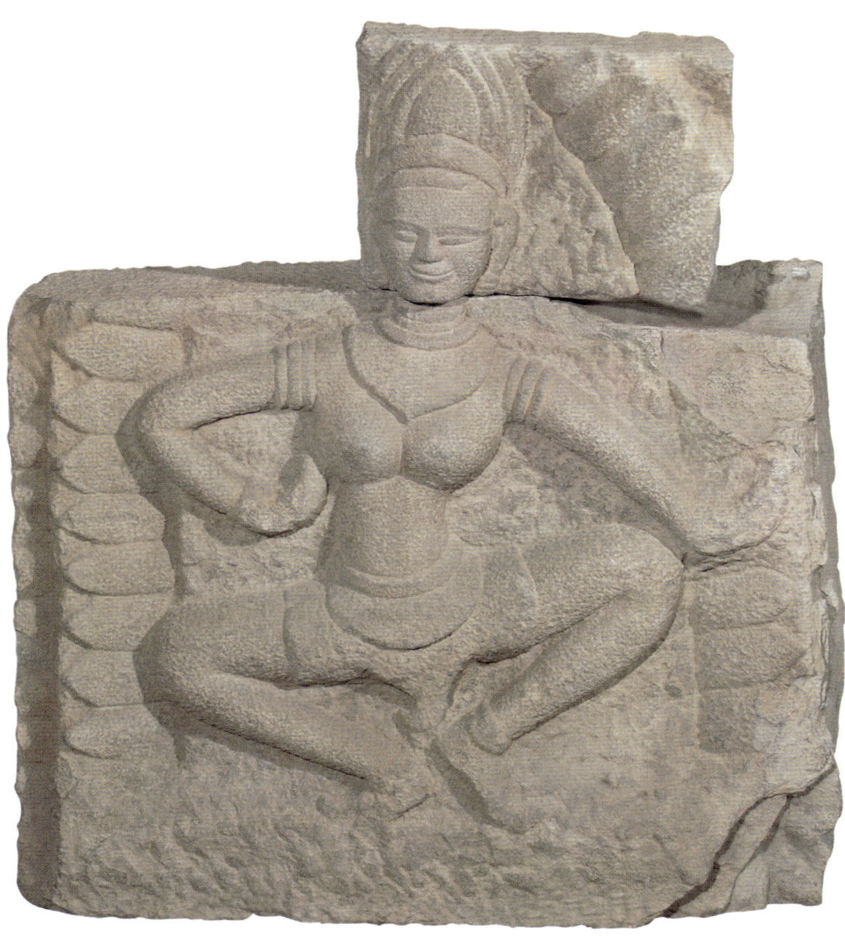

12. *Dancer*, High-relief, Sandstone, Height 84 cm, Thâp-Mam style, 12th - 13th Century.

enlarging toward the north to the Gate of Annam and later encompassed Hindu principalities toward the south. From 192 to 758 the texts always used the term Lin Yi; only in 758 did the name "Huan Wang" come into use. In 875, the entity was designated as "Chiem Thanh", the Sino-Vietnamese transcription of Champapura or "City of the Chams".

Epigraphy offers two inscriptions in Sanskrit, one dated to 658 that was found in central Vietnam in Quang Nam (C96, stele found near My Son E6), the other dated to 668 that was found in Cambodia (the Kdei Ang inscription), that use the term "Champa" for the first time. A description of primitive Lin Yi, its religion, its language or languages, its inhabitants – this all remains under study.

What is better known is the history of the country from the eighth century to, on one hand, the end of Hindu Champa in 1471 when Vijaya fell, and, on the other hand, the period from 1471 to 1832: a slow irregular decline that, from the loss of Kauthara to the annihilation of Panduranga, led to the historically exact conclusion that Champa, as a state, no longer existed. From 1832 on, it was thus part of the conquering, structured, Vietnamese nation, inscribed in frontiers that barely changed until our times with the integration of the Mekong delta.

In the eighth century, then, Champa stretched from the Gate of Annam in the north to the Donnai basin in the south. Probably organised as a confederate state, it was divided into what seem to be principalities, consisting of alluvial plains scored by mountain chains plunging into the sea, called, from north to south, Indrapura, Amaravati, Vijaya, Kauthara and Panduranga. The history of Champa is not only that of the Viet-Cham couple: The country had relations with China of which it was a vassal, to which it paid a tribute and to which it sent ambassadors; with Cambodia, which rapidly (as of the ninth century) became warlike as they did with the Malay world, principally Java, or with the Dai Viet. All these relations were multiple: belligerent, commercial but also matrimonial and, above all, unstable. From the eighth to the fifteenth centuries, Cham civilisation was mainly Hindu (without forgetting Buddhism – essentially in sculpture – from the end of the ninth and the beginning of the tenth centuries), which is to say that it borrowed from India its cults, principally that of Shiva, its language, Sanskrit, its social structure (four classes) and its concept of royalty. An aristocratic elite guaranteed the political, economic and social systems. As for the population, it was composed of farmers, pioneers in aquatic rice cultivation (the variety of rice with a short growth cycle – 100 days – that was born in Champa acted as an important factor in agricultural progress once introduced to southern China in the thirteenth century); merchants who exported sandalwood, cinnamon, rhinoceros horns, elephant tusks; ceramic artisans, specialists in glazing especially from the twelfth to the fifteenth centuries as witnessed by the productions of Go Sanh whose site is near An Nhon, but also sailors who, from the two great ports Tai Chiem (Hoi An region) and Thai Nai (in Binh Dinh) traded or pirated them depending on the period and the demand…

It goes without saying that this social framework was continuously weakened from top to bottom by the various offensive or defensive combats that the Chams had to wage. The first were against the Chinese who tried several times to enlarge their empire toward the south from conquered Annam ("the pacified south" was the highly condescending Chinese name for the Vietnam of those times) and who, to do this, undertook battles that were often victorious. For example, we know that about 446, Tra Kieu, the Cham capital, was devastated by the Chinese general Tan Hezhi who pillaged statues of gold worth a total of 100,000 taels of pure gold, or about 3.6 tons of metal… The second were against the Javanese who destroyed the Po Nagar temple in Nha

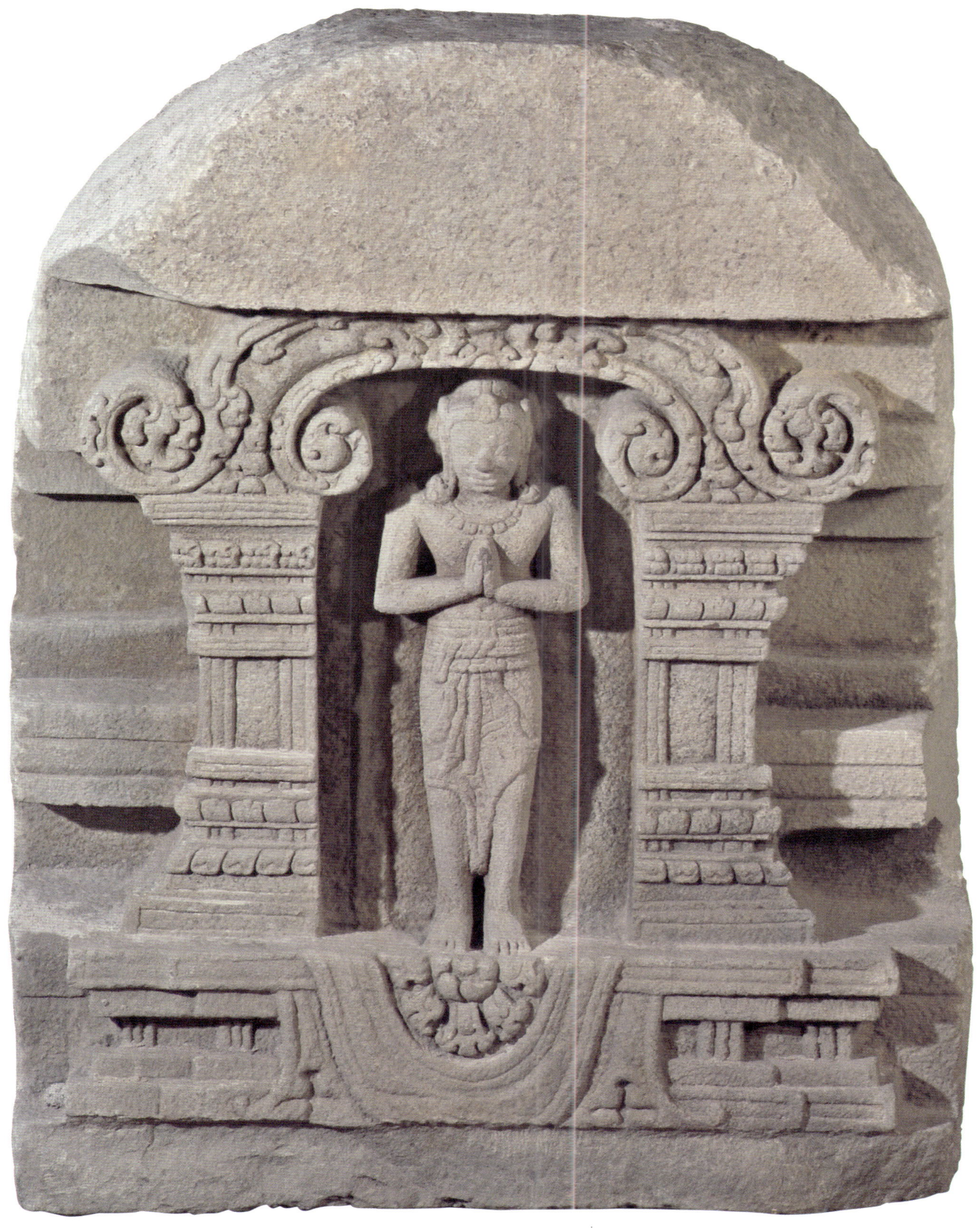

13. *Brahman*, High-relief, Sandstone, Height 72 cm, My Son E1 style, 7th - 8th Century.

A Brahman is a member of the highest of the four classes ("varna", meaning "colour" in Sanskrit) of Brahmanical India. Priests responsible for sacrifices are chosen from this class. Granted numerous privileges, they devoted themselves to the study of the Vedas and other sacred texts as well as to religious ceremonies. This sculpture is one of the elements of a pedestal that, given the size of the blocks, must have been the support for either a monumental linga (such as the one in the centre of the My Son E1 temple) or a no less monumental divinity. The niche occupied by the Brahman has a threshold decorated with a rosette and garlands. Notice the wide, lowered arcature topped by a rosette and completed by mouldings. The Brahman is in anjali and wearing a sampot that hangs very low (almost to his ankles) and held by two belts. The mukhuta is shaped like a hood with a diadem bearing three large rosettes. The long ears are enhanced with jewellery.

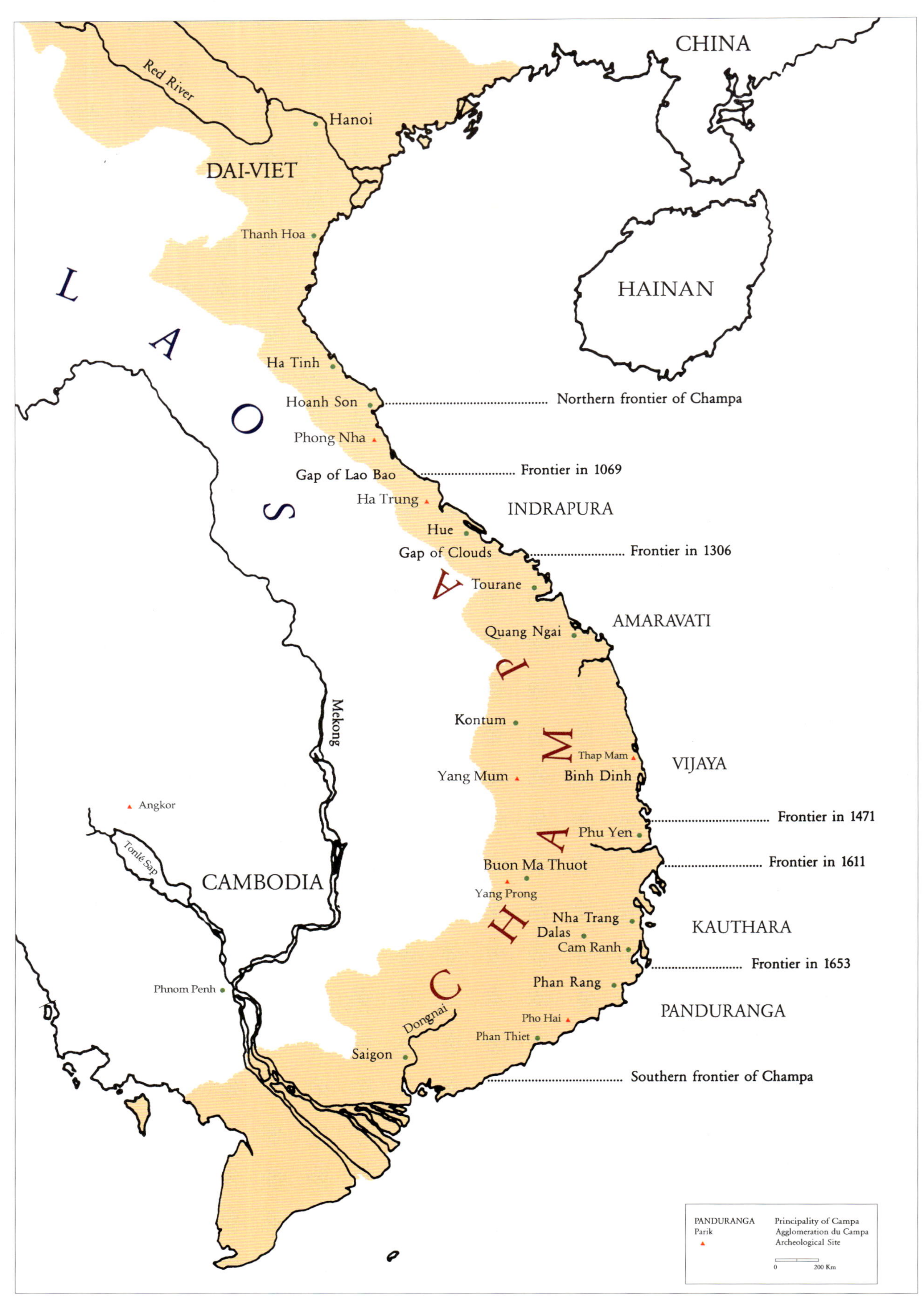

14. *Map of Champa indicating archeological sites.*

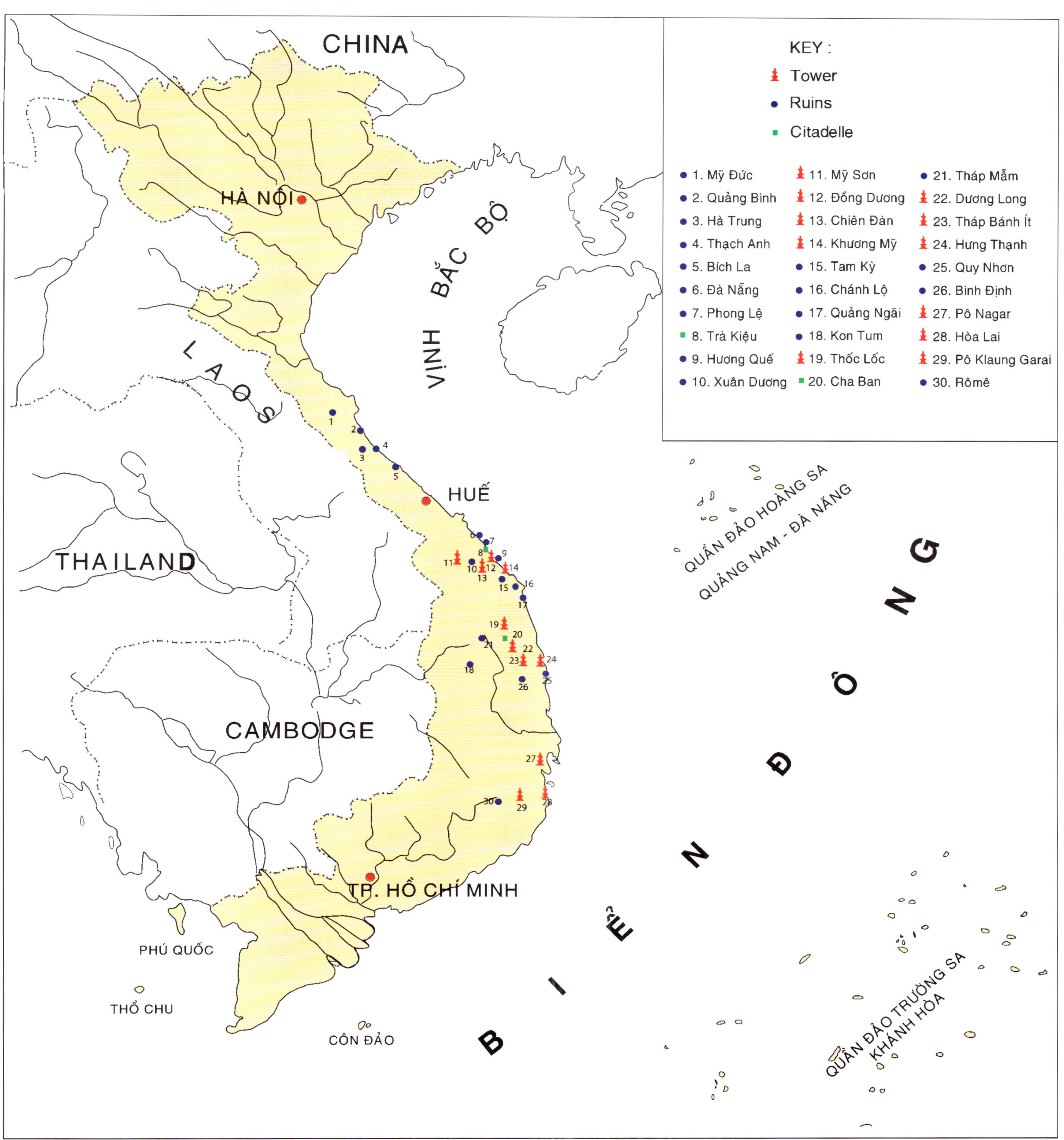

15. *The principal Cham sites* (towers, ruins …)

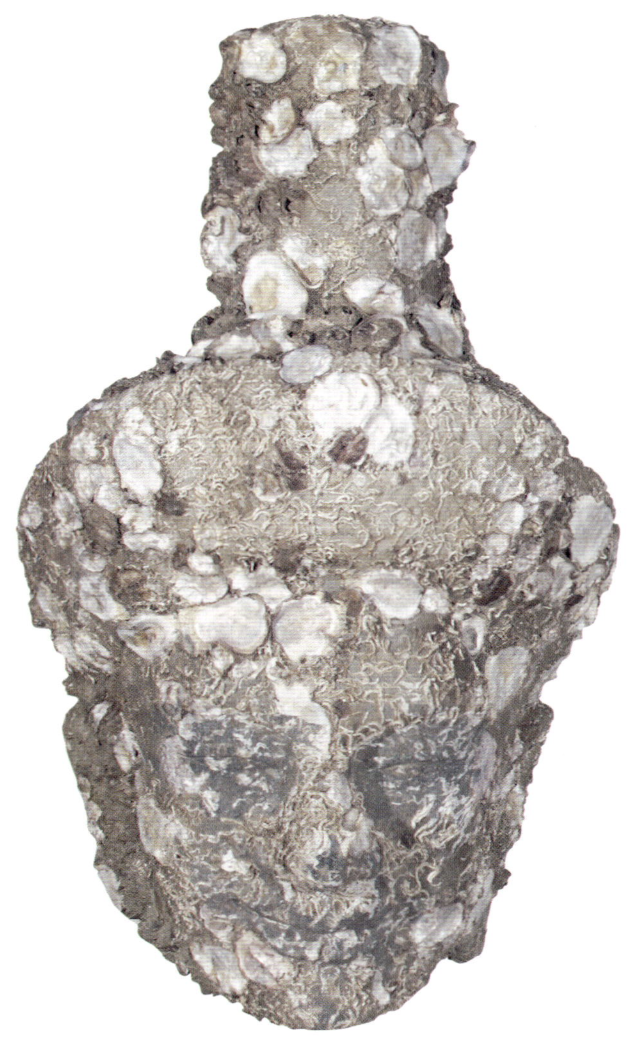

Trang in 774 and another temple near Vira Pura (the "heroic city"), meaning probably near Phan Rang in the south in 787. But what were only attempts became, as of the tenth century due to the unendurable population increase of the north, a slow but steady devastating southerly push, which culminated in the annihilation of Hindu Champa as witnessed by the destruction of Vijaya by the Dai Viet in 1471.

In fact, in the year 1000, given the threat of the tyrannical Dai Viet who were independent after gaining freedom from Chinese occupation, the Chams moved their capital city, leaving Indrapura (destroyed in 982) for Vijaya, much further south, in the territory that is today the province of Binh Dinh. What followed were only battles, most often lost. In 1044, the Viets took Vijaya and killed the monarch; in 1068 they captured the Cham king Rudravarman III who, a year later, exchanged his freedom for lands that became, under the reign of the Viet sovereign Ly Thanh Tong, the provinces ("chau" in Viet) Dia Ly, Ma Linh and Bo Chinh, definitely amputating the kingdom of Champa of its northern part.

The Chams also regularly had to fight the Khmers, defeated in 1074 and 1080, but victorious in 1145 when they took Vijaya. Combat between Khmers and Chams carried on for, all told, almost 150 years (from 1074 to 1220).

Other than the Viets, Khmers, and Javanese, the Chams were subjected to Mongol assaults: in 1238 Sagatou, coming out of conquered China (the Mongols had installed the Yuan dynasty there that ruled China until the arrival of the Mings in 1368), decided to invade Champa. Refusing any confrontation, the Chams took refuge in the mountains where, for two years, they waited for the occupiers to withdraw. If to all this are added the fratricide struggles of the second half of the twelfth century between the allied principalities of Amaravati and Panduranga and that of Vijaya, it is easy to understand the fragility in which Champa found itself at the beginning of the fourteenth century. But does the fragility of a state justify the frivolity of a sovereign? Can passionate love take the place of politics? In 1306, the sovereign Jaya Simhavarman III proposed to the king of Dai Viet – who accepted the offer – the provinces of O and Li in return for the hand of his daughter, princess Huyen Tran; thus, the entire region between the Lao Bao col and the Col of Clouds, between Hue and Tourane became – peacefully, for once – Vietnamese territory. It must be added that this Cham sovereign died less than a year after the arrival of the princess and that this territory, despite several attempts, was never recovered. All to the contrary: as of 1307, the names of districts were changed and O became Thuan ("submission") and Li became Hoa ("transformation"). Gentle omens... Nevertheless, a respite of several dozens of years was offered by another monarch, Che Bong Nga, who, having come to the throne about 1360, undertook a whole series of successful military campaigns that brought him as far as the capture of Thang Long (today's Hanoi) and allowed him to deal with all the Viet counterattacks and even kill their king, Tran Due Tong, who unwisely attacked Vijaya in 1377, the year that the Chams recaptured Thang Long. In 1380, Nghe An, Dien Chau and Thanh Hoa were pillaged. In 1382, 1383 and 1389, Che Bong Nga accumulated victories and raids, until he was killed by the Viets in 1390. His successor, Jaya Simhavarman Sri Harijatti, was unable to maintain his hold over the region north of the Col of Clouds that he reconquered. At the end of his reign in 1400, the decadence of Champa was already inscribed. At the northern frontier, Dia Viet mobilised enormous military forces. Within the borders, Sanskrit culture, an indispensable support for both Hinduism and Mahayanism, was not renewed and died out (the last Sanskrit inscription in Champa can be dated to 1252) as regular and direct relations that Champa kept with India were interrupted by Muslim invasions of India at the end of the twelfth century. In addition, and this is a classic historical fact, the Hindu elite that held its legitimacy in the gods no longer inspired the confidence of their inferiors since concretely the Khmers, the Chinese and above all the Vietnamese appeared in the long term as superior warriors, due to their victories, and therefore in the eyes of the Chams (ruled and even rulers) as the representatives of better political systems. As of

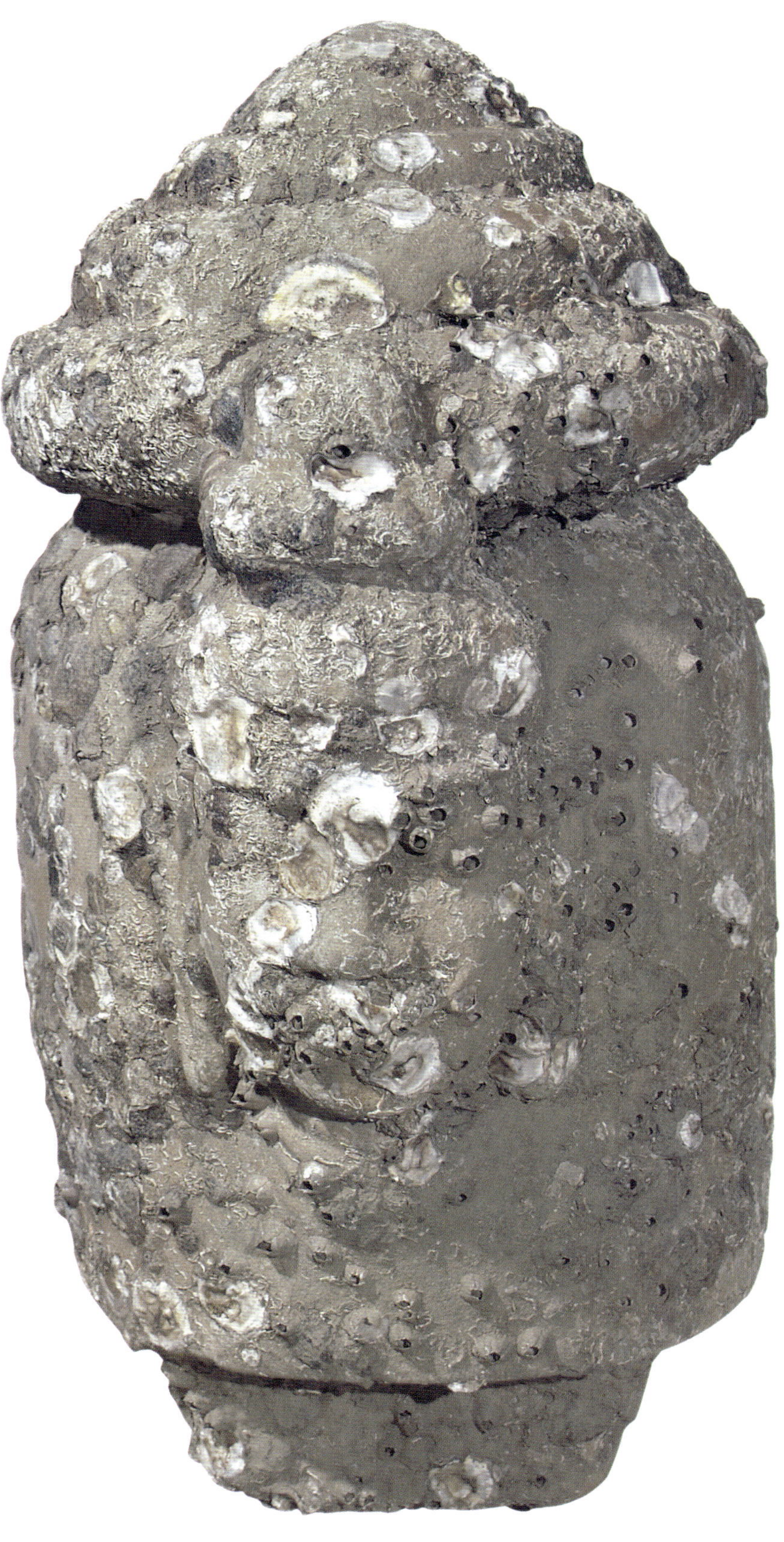

Previous Page
16. *Head of Vishnu*, Sandstone, height 25 cm, Khmer art, 9th - 10th Century.

17. *Mukhalinga*, Sandstone, height 48 cm (without tenon), Preangkorian art, 7th Century.

Both works are covered in marine concretions. The most recent is unique in Cham sculpture, while the older one manifests a similar inspiration, (cf p. 53)

the beginning of the fifteenth century, the Viets took the principality of Amaravati (that, today, is the south of Quang Nam and the north of Quang Ngai). In 1471, having got over one more Chinese invasion in 1407 and its subsequent devastating occupation – the Chinese destroyed everything that had any element of "Vietnaminity" – and having suspended their "Nam Tien", the Viets recaptured the principality, in far more drastic fashion: the Cham capital Vijaya was conquered by King Le Thanh Tong who razed the city, beheaded 40,000 people, deported 30,000, and imposed on the Chams what the Chinese had done to the Viets sixty years earlier by systematically wiping out all traces of "Chamity". In 1471, the Chinese world imposed itself locally on the Hindu world that had dominated the eastern part of Indochina since the fourth century AD. It was in Vijaya, that year, that the frontier marker between the Chinese world and the Indian world was established in the name "Indo-China".

The disappearance of Hindu Champa was more than just nominal: the Viets, faithful to their soldier-farmer concept, cultivating the land that one protects and protecting the land that one cultivates, preferred to ensure the stability of a conquered territory before invading another; therefore, the occupation stopped at the Cu Mong col whereas victorious troops had already reached Mount Thac Bi, considerably further south. A military chief in Vijaya, Bo Tri Tri, became the vassal of Dai Viet and was given responsibility for Kauthara, Panduranga and all of the related west (the High Plateaus); the limits of a new Cham kingdom were defined, whose sovereign even obtained the investiture of the Chinese emperor in 1478.

However, while this new kingdom was labelled Cham, if the former system is taken into consideration, it was no longer Hindu. On the contrary, ideologically it rested on a very complex base that drew from the animism of southern peoples supplemented by later Indian additions and, from the seventeenth century, Islam, the religion of the Prophet that, although it was present in the region as from the twelfth century, only truly took root then in the ports and cities. As we will see, it is obvious that classic Cham statuary was no longer of the same type as well as growing rarer from the sixteenth century on. But changing style does not mean no longer existing: the Chams were not only not annihilated but rebelled against the Nguyen, princes of the south, in conflict with the Trinh, princes of the north, all under the supposed authority of the late Le sovereigns. In 1594, they also assisted the sultan of Johore to combat the Portuguese from Malacca. However, the Nguyen soon crushed Cham ambitions. In 1611, the entire northern part of Kauthara to Cape Varela was conquered, transformed into the frontier province Tran Bien and populated with 30,000 prisoners, former partisans of the Trinh. The Nguyen refused to pay the taxes due the Le for the territories that the Nguyen controlled and they also refused to pay homage. The submission of Champa thereby

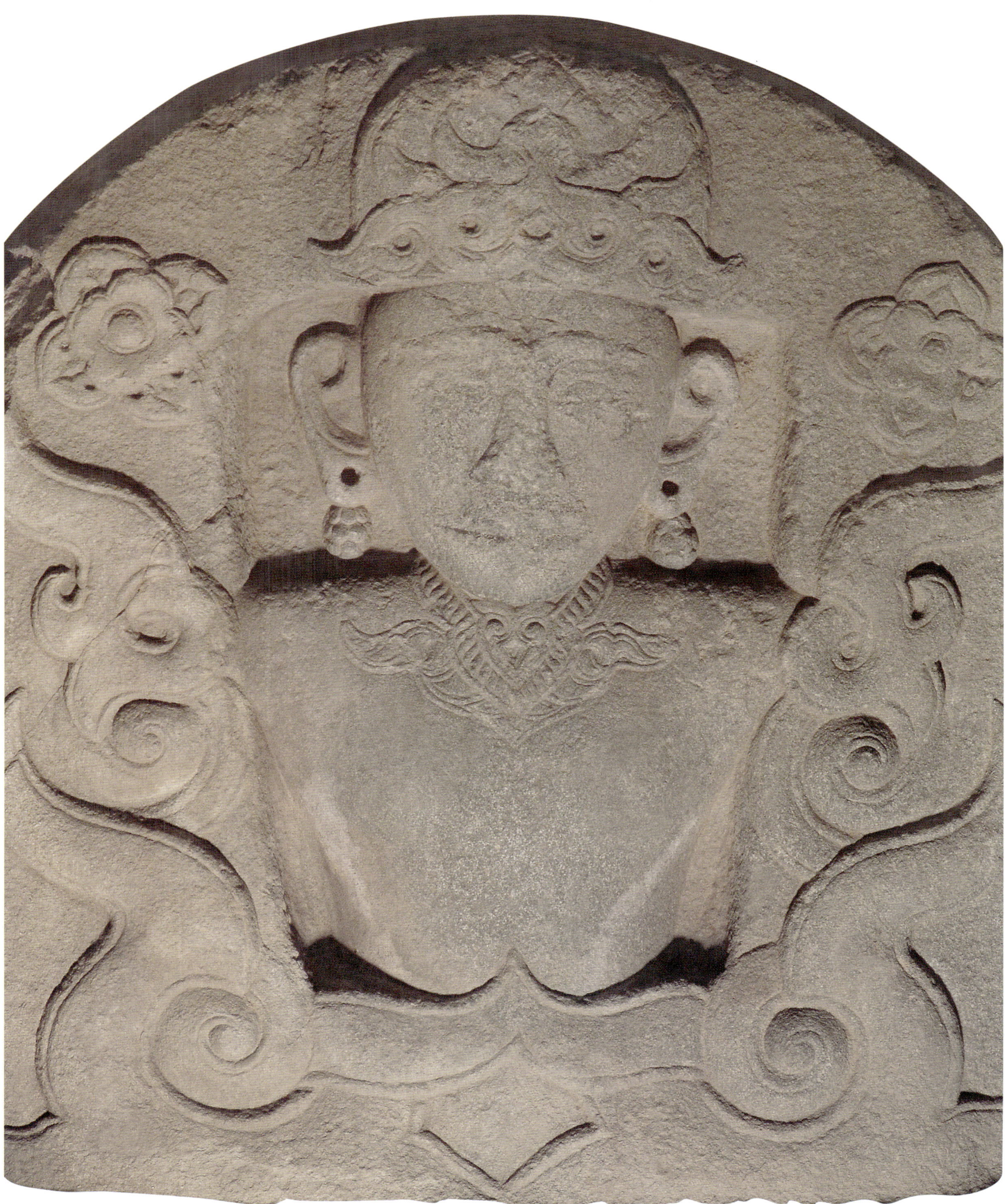

became a source of legitimacy: entrusted with a real "mandate from the heavens", they added new territories and vassals. Later, in 1653, the frontier was drawn in the Cam Ranh region after a war in which the Cham king Po Nraup committed suicide; only a single of the five original provinces, Panduranga, remained Cham. It was progressively broken up: the Nguyen, beginning in the second half of the seventeenth century, took over a part of what still was at that time the Khmer delta; in 1658 the region that today is Bien Hoa was occupied and for the first time the Viet danger thus came from the south as well, meaning that any attempt by the Champs at reconquest ran the risk of being strangled. In 1692 an endeavour to win back what had been Kauthara by the king Po Saut was severely repressed by the Nguyen: Panduranga was turned into a Viet county named Binh Thuan of which, cleverly, the administration was entrusted to the brother of the defeated king though with a Viet mandarin title. This therefore marked the end of Champa as an independent country. However, following a Cham revolt the next year, the Nguyen lord re-established Panduranga with full rights. The monarchy was restored, with a nominated king, Po Saktiraydaputih, who owed an annual tribute to the Nguyens. This slowly but surely progressively rubbed out Champa or what was left of it; judicial exception was granted to the Viets who lived in the country: the Binh Thuan prefecture administrated them directly, even within the borders of Panduranga. This privilege of jurisdiction as well as administration led, within the Cham country, to the existence of an increasing number of zones where the Chams were bereft of rights since Viet immigration to lands left uncultivated – won and lost by the Chams or simply purchased by the Viets – meant that the political, economic, social and therefore cultural influence of the Viets rapidly increased, at the expense of the Chams'. Po Dharma even used the expression "real puzzle" to describe the Panduranga of his day.

From the end of the eighteenth century until 1832, the Chams withered away more and more quickly. First, the Tay-Son revolted against the Nguyen in 1771 which turned Panduranga-Champa into the favoured battleground, as it was of strategic interest to the two opponents. Until 1801, fighting raged, with its accompanying devastation. Then, despite the remittance of a small autonomous zone between the bay of Cam Ranh, the region of Ba-ria and high Dong-nai that was given to Po Sau Nun Can, brother in arms of the emperor Gia Long (formerly Nguyen Anh who had bested the Tay-Son in 1802) the final blow was dealt by the son and successor (1820) of Gia Long, Emperor Minh Menh. He chose one of his henchmen to govern this zone and thereby regained control of it little by little, even in the face of opposition by Le Van Duyet, a faithful follower of Gia Long and viceroy of Gia Dinh Thanh. At his death in 1832, Minh Menh eradicated all remaining opposition, encompassed Panduranga in his hegemony and tied it administratively to the circumscriptions of An Phuoc and Hoa Da in the Binh Thuan province.

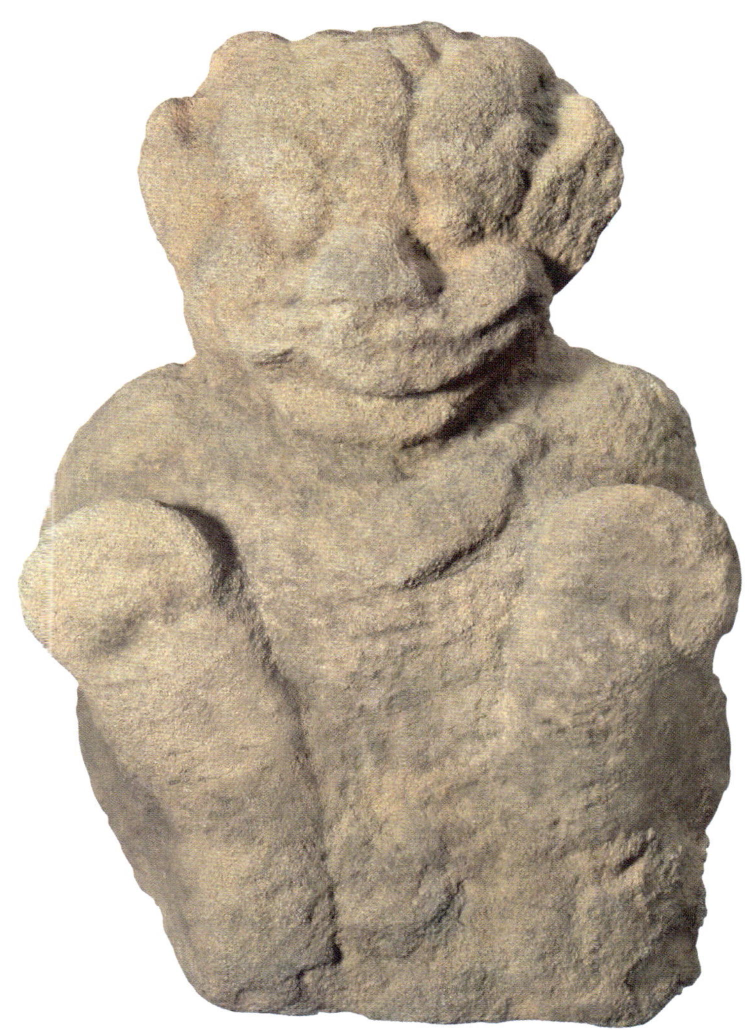

Previous Page
18. *Kut* Sandstone, height 80 cm, Yang Mum style, ca. 15th Century (detail).

19. *Sitting Lion*, Nearly free-standing, sandstone, height 30 cm, Chien Dan Style, 10th - 11th Century.

In 1832 Champa was at its definitive end, although there were a few tragically repressed outbursts such as that of 1833-34 during the Holy War (jihad) led by the Muslim religious dignitary, the Katip Suma, and that of the fight for independence of Ja Thak Va, to which his death in 1835 put an end.

Then began, after the one set off by the fall of Vijaya, the second decline of the Chams. This time, not only the elite but the entire population was concerned. Everything, under Viet auspices, had to disappear, including habitations: the Chams were dispersed in hamlets belonging to Viet villages and only later identified as one of the 54 minorities of the Viet country…

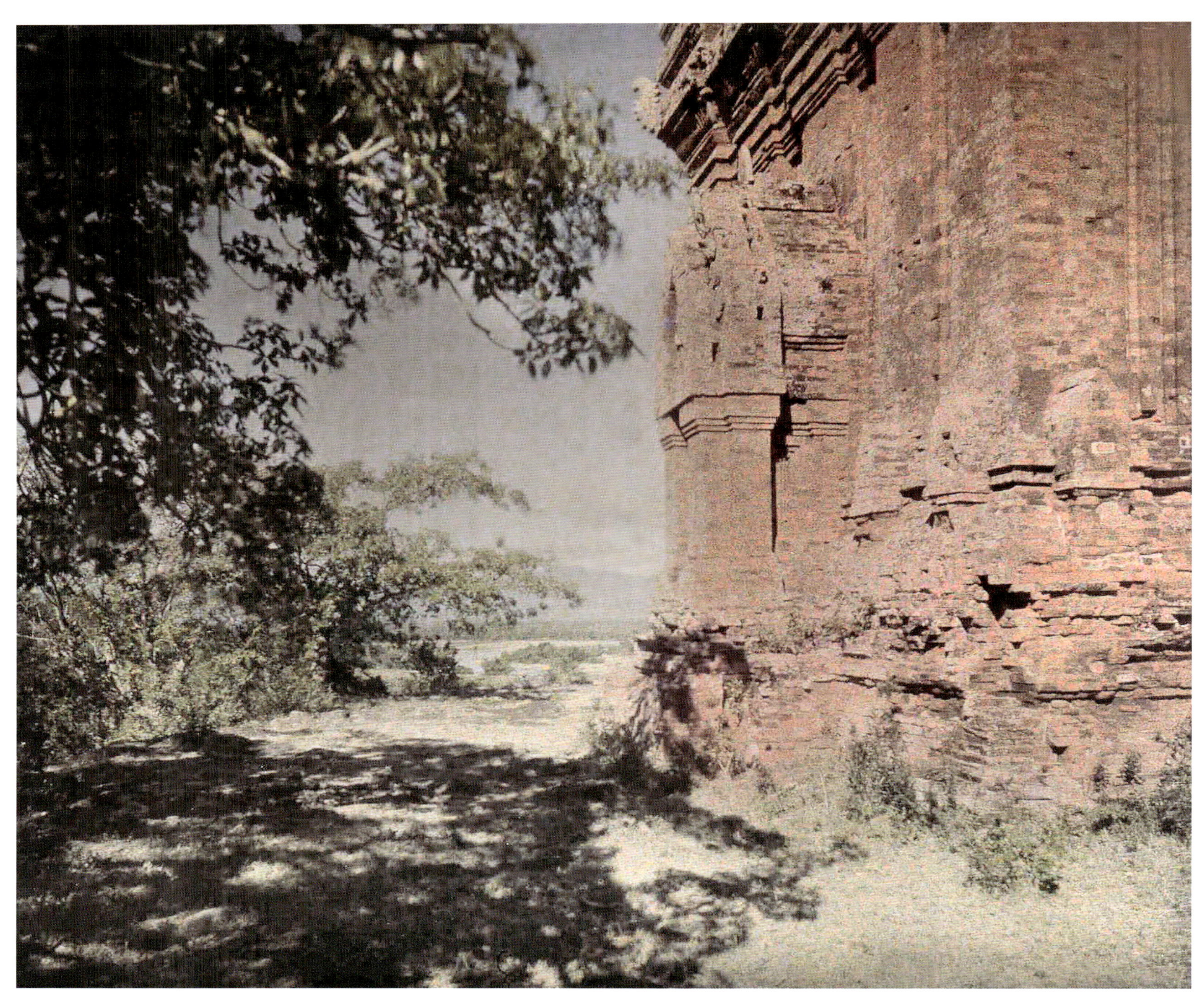

20. *The Cham Temple of Po Klaung Garai*, c. 1920.

Following Page

21. *An example of a possible reutilisation of Cham stone* (basis of the pole of a house...).

Cham Architecture

To approach Cham architecture, one must first identify its ruins. "Pillaged and sacked over and over again at the time of their splendour, then left for centuries to the weather of different seasons and the depredations of men, nothing remains today of the arrangements of the temples." (Maspero)

This assessment, made by Georges Maspero at the beginning of the twentieth century, sets out the devastation undergone by the Chams, notably through their monuments – attributes of their power and repository of their wealth. In the chronology at the back of this text are given the various dates of successive destructions, tied to confrontations with their immediate neighbours. Numerous and violent civil wars also gnawed for years at the interior of Cham territory, its people and monuments.

Furthermore, to these destructions by warfare must be added, for one, the passage of time that has lead to the sinking and dislocation of structures – most often due to unstable ground that supported the temple's tower, the "kalan" – that in turn brought about the fall of sculptures set in the frame of bricks, and, for another, subsequent use of the temples as mines by people who came to help themselves to easily accessible building material (bricks, stones) for their new structures. The Viets having almost completely replaced the Chams during Nam Tien, these temples retained absolutely no religious significance.

The recent war also tragically affected Cham monuments. When Parmentier inventoried the My Son site at the beginning of the twentieth century, he counted seventy towers or temples. Up to 1945, the EFEO carried out major renovation work on these sacred buildings. Today, only about twenty remain: the disastrous effect of the war is obvious. Perhaps the American bombing in 1969 was the most ill fated, destroying at My Son groups A and A' that included nineteen structures, among which the splendid and magnificent A1 Tower, on the pretext that a Viet-Cong transmitter was installed there. Jean Boisselier used the A1 Tower to refine his progressive dating of the Khoung My and Tra Kieu styles within the style of My Son A1.

It is thus still very difficult today to truly describe Cham architecture. We are therefore brought to present an overall schema that can serve to describe a sort of "ideal" type.

In Cham architecture, two types of arrangements of sites can be found:

Either an architectural triplet, composed of three parallel towers dedicated respectively to Brahma, Shiva and Vishnu, as for example at Chien Dan (north of Tam Dy), Khuong My (south of Tam Ky), Duong Long (Tay Son), Hung Thanh (Qui Nhon), and Hoa Lai (Phan Rang);

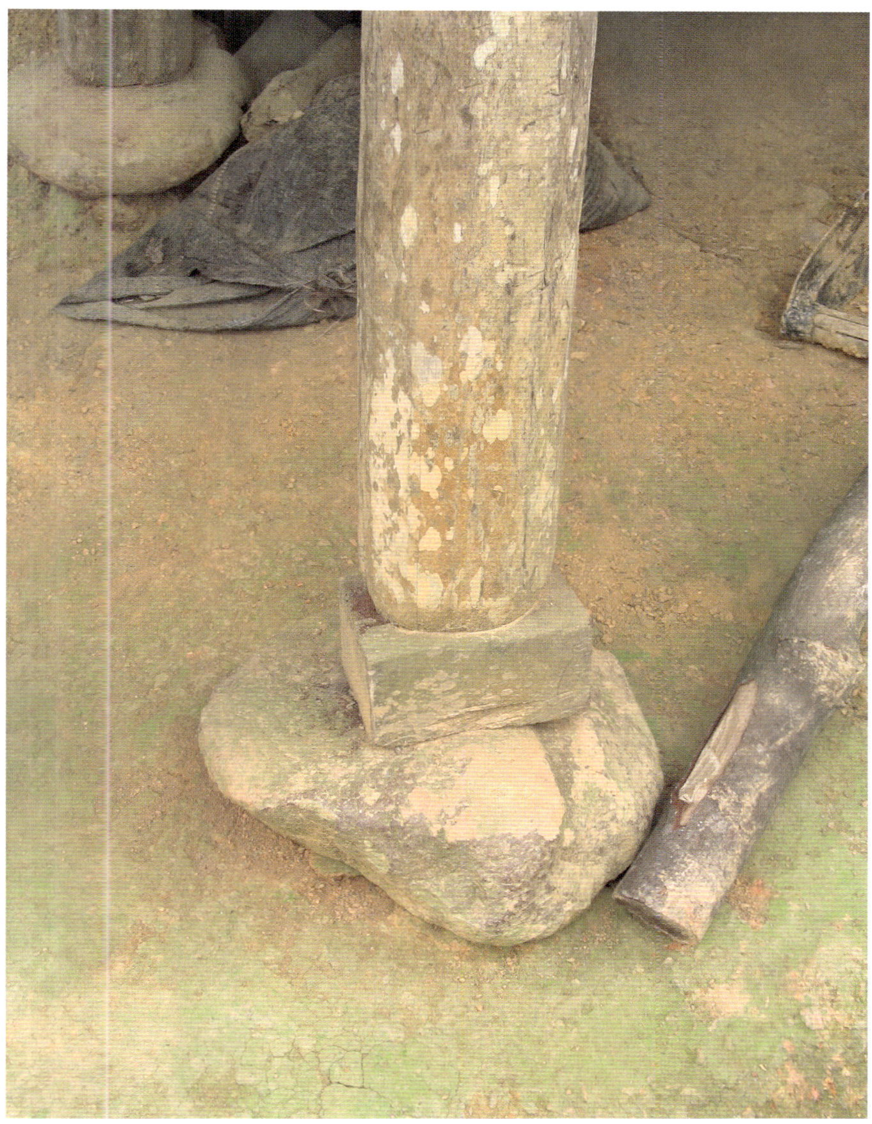

or a central tower dedicated to Shiva, as for example at Dong Duong (Thang Binh), My Son A1 (Duy Xuyen), or at the "Ba Tower" (Nha Trang).

It seems that the first sets of towers, chronologically, were the "three parallel towers" devoted to the three gods. Then, about the ninth century, the balance was disrupted and Shiva was raised to the highest rank, although a penchant for Shiva was already discernable in the system of three parallel towers, as the one dedicated to Shiva was always the highest. It can also be noted that, if this observation seems valid, it means that numerous rearrangements were made over the centuries, keeping only the core structure.

Originally, according to the Indian notion that informed the erection of these temples, the Cham temple was a Mount Meru in miniature, or more precisely its summit or summits, represented by the step-pyramid structure, each level repeating the previous one on a smaller scale. One can suppose that the central mountain range – an essential aspect of Cham geography – exercised figurative authority over the Cham temple. The "linga towers" can be explained as circular with a rounded, bulbous top in the shape of a linga (rather than a pointed, pyramidal one) as at Bang An (Quang Nam).

GENERAL THEORETICAL PLAN OF A CHAM TEMPLE

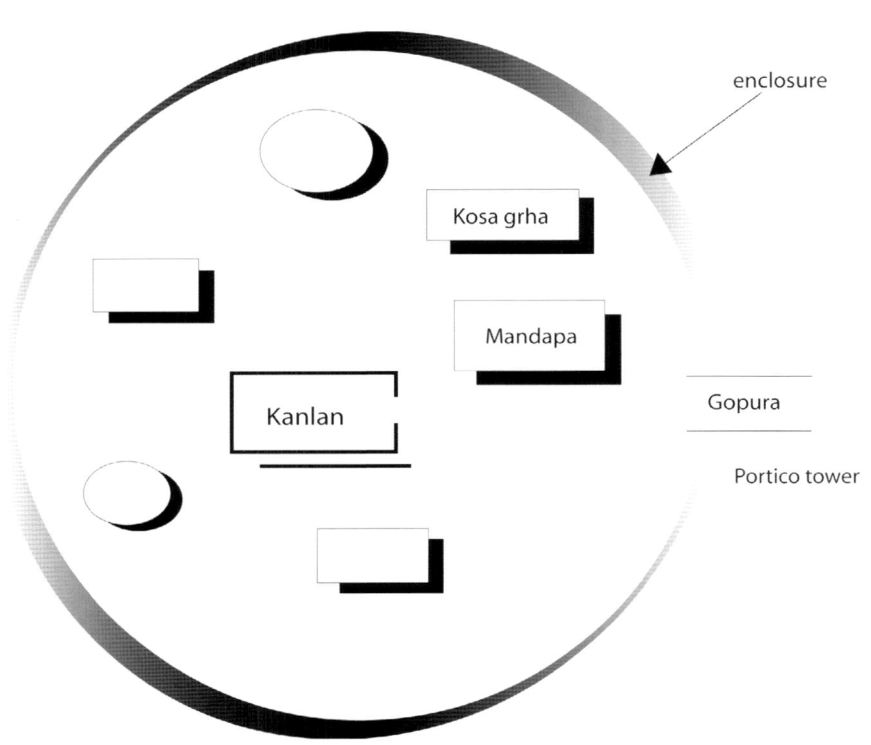

The main temple, "kalan" in Cham, is surrounded by towers and ancillary structures, inside an enclosure wall. It usually opens toward the rising sun; that is to say the east (except at My Son where some kalans open to the west while, still at My Son, the famous A1 kalan opens to both the east and the west.

In Cham architecture, secondary towers with their curved roofs shaped like boats, are very typical of the architecture of South-east Asia, as at My Son or Po Klong Garai.

CROSS-SECTION OF A TYPICAL KALAN

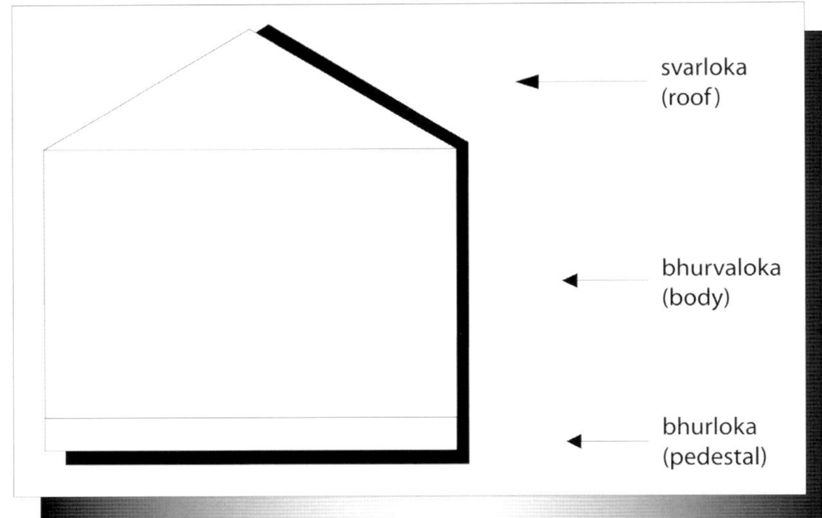

The kalan is comprised, from bottom to top, of a square pedestal (the bhurloka) that symbolises the material world, a main body, also square (the bhurvaloka) that is the symbol of the premonitory world and a pointed roof (the svarloka), symbol of the spiritual world.

Inside the kalan is the main statue or linga itself, resting on a snanadroni, a very shallow recipient with a spout (or somasutra) which points north. The various liquids used for ablutions, of either the statue or the linga, run off into the snanadroni (called "yoni" in the case of a linga) and are carried by the somasutra out of the kalan where they are collected by worshippers who consider them sacred.

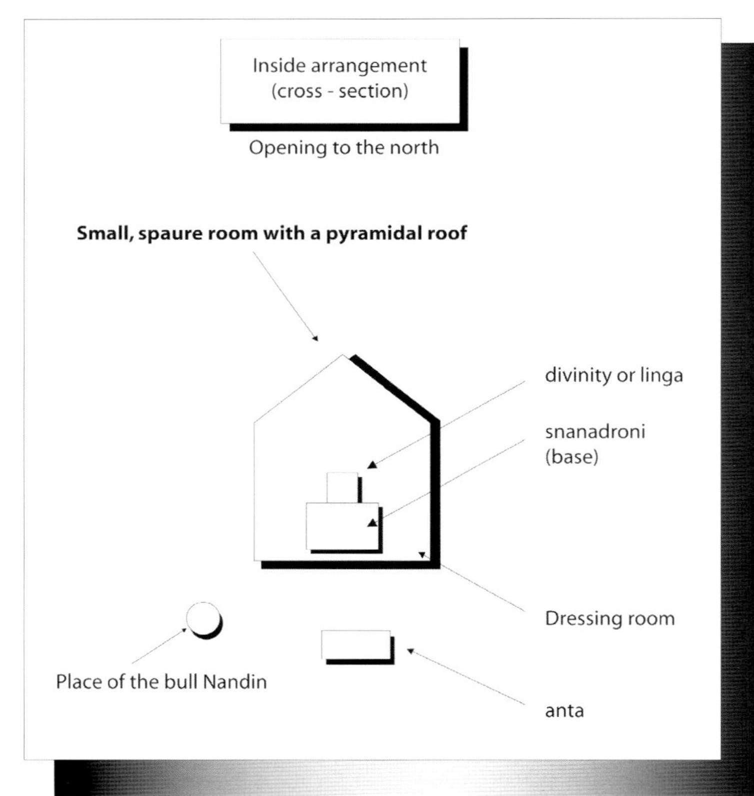

The tower or "kalan" is dedicated to the worship of kings and their protective gods. The small, square room is used by officiants, and not the worshippers, who circle the divinity-snanadroni complex, except in the case of Buddhist temples like Dong Duong because the altar there is against the west wall.

Coming out of the kalan itself, one enters a vestibule where, to the left, is the bull Nandin, always lying with his head toward the divinity-snanadroni or the linga-yoni set. Once across this vestibule, one reaches the entrance door, flanked to the right and left by pilasters that are often covered with inscriptions. Facing the kalan is a gopura, a portico tower that is oriented east-west.

The mandapa ("pavilion" in Sanskrit), a long building made of bricks with several windows and two doors oriented east-west, is the place of meditation and prayer preceding the ritual ceremony in the kalan.

Three types of mandapa can be found as shown in the diagram below:

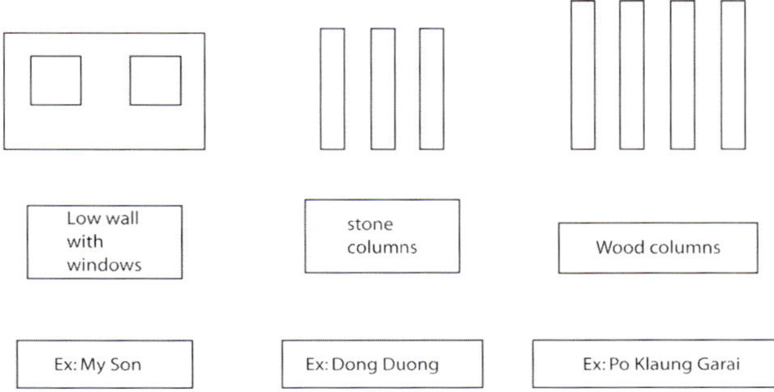

In front of the kalan-tower is the kosa grha, storage for ceremonial objects, with a door facing the north and windows with an east-west orientation. This building, also brick, has a curved roof shaped like a boat.

The gopura (portico tower) and surrounding wall are also made of brick. Outside the wall one can find a stela tower, while inside the enclosure there are small temples consecrated to either the divinity's favourites or the dikpalaka.

Generally, in the course of time, other towers with devotional purposes were added: to increase the power of the god, later towers, which are higher, came to encircle the original one. Thus, on the terrain of My Son, it has been confirmed (if all later degradations are forgotten) that the A1 tower that dates from the tenth century is higher and has more impact than the E1 tower from the seventh century.

All Vietnamese authors believe that Cham builders, in order to lay the parallel-piped bricks (measuring 30 x 20 x 10 cm each and baked at low temperatures) that make up all of these structures, used a resin (Dipterocapus Alatus Roxb) that was boiled and then mixed with lime (from the calcination of seashells) and brick powder. It should be noted that the stone (sandstone), other than serving to sculpt the divinities described above, was used for the side-posts, pilasters, lintels and cornerstones. The Cham temple, therefore, definitely had a brick shell on which stone elements were placed.

Each temple has a founding myth, bijective with founding Hindu myths. The temple is a reflection of the universe, but also of the god. For example, in a temple dedicated to Shiva, the linga is Shiva's soul and the temple is his body.

The temple is, as mentioned earlier, Mount Meru, the axis of the world and of Jambudvipa, the mythical continent that India and nations under Indian influence identify India with. However, in Champa one does not find the image of the ocean ringing Jambudvipa in mythical Indian divine cosmology, such as the pool (for example, in India) or a round tower (as in Cambodia).

Thus the temple is the gods body, but also the universe over which the god rules. This universe welcomes gods that will serve the main god. The first servant, who is also a god or – more precisely – goddess, is the god's wife. In the most widespread case of Shivaist temples in Champa, this wife is Parvati, situated in a chapel close to the main temple. Nandin, Ganesha and Skanda carry out their services in annexes that are isolated from each other.

The puja ("worship" in Sanskrit) designates any ceremony during which a god is venerated. In theory, it follows rules written in the shastras ("rule" or "precept" in Sanskrit) and the agamas ("tradition"); these vary over time and place. By retaining a minimum number of practices known throughout the Indian world, though, a basic schema can be defined – certainly after the fact – that may apply to any Cham divinity. In any case, worship is not a temporary undertaking.

First, the statue is installed in the temple. It is purified by priests with incense and camphor while they sing the sacred syllables, musical parcels of cosmic power: mantras. (In Sanskrit, "man" means "think".) The mantra associated with Shiva is "hrim". Next, the priests invite the god to descend into his image (made of stone or metal). He is then installed by the rites of infusing breath and opening the eyes. At the end of the rites, the god is thanked for his passage into his image.

After this, once installed in the temple, the divinity is feted several times per day (at dawn and dusk, sometimes at noon and midnight as well). The celebrant, purified, rings a bell to wake the sleeping god, and anoints the statue with oil, camphor, flowers, sandalwood paste, but also, especially for the linga, with milk and water that are later gathered in the somasutra of the yoni.

This localised cult is only practiced on sculptures that, once installed, are never moved. Fixed, these must be distinguished from mobile sculptures, used in processions or for private devotion.

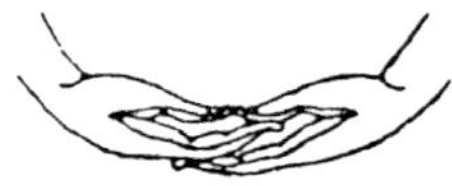

Dhyani Mudra (meditation)

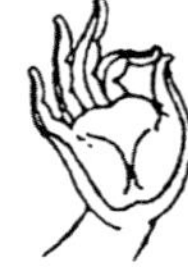

Vitarka Mudra (education)

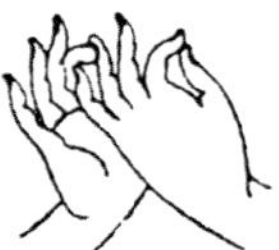

Dharmacakra Mudra
(set in motion by the wheel of the Doctrine)

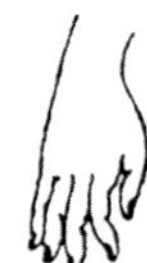

Bhumisparsa Mudra (the earth is a witness)

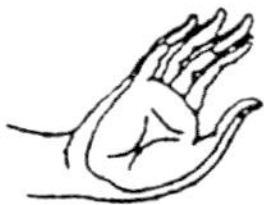

Abhaya Mudra (absence of fear)

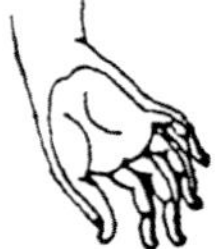

Varada Mudra (fulfillment of vows)

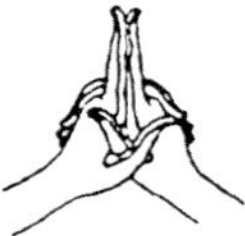

Uttarabodhi Mudra (supreme illumination)

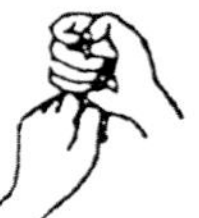

Mudra of supreme wisdom

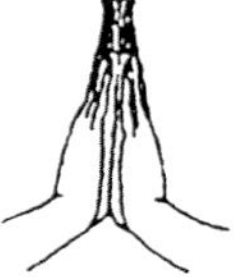

Anjali Mudra (hail and veneration)

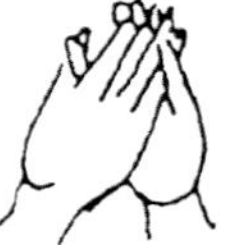

Vajrapradama Mudra (Unshakable faith)

22. *The ten principles of Mudra*, Dictionnaire de la sagesse orientale. Bouddhisme, Hindouisme, Taoïsme, Zen. Robert Laffont, coll. Bouquins, 1989.

Gods and their representation

Cham sculpture was essentially the expression, direct or indirect, of the Indian, Brahman or Buddhist pantheon as interpreted locally. One must speak of interpretation because, although the "score" was imposed, the sculpture was anything but a copy of the Indian model; rather, it was truly taken on by local artists who expressed their own sensitivity through their renditions. This re-creation was constant, having taken place over almost a thousand years; each new statue coming to enrich the previous ones. Before identifying with precision the themes illustrated, there are a few general remarks that need to be made, pointing out the characteristics of these types of sculptures.

A rapid comparison of Cham and Indian sculpture, in its different schools, brings to light a few of the main currents in the former.

As a rule, Cham sculpture is primarily Shivaist and represents the god Shiva in a condensed fashion; it seems to hold feminine divinities as secondary; it is modest: no sexes are shown except in a fanciful manner for monkeys or lions; it is peaceful: no scenes of horror, no gods with violent forms – no Bhairava or Kali. Even in the case of armed secular figures, the question can be asked: are they warriors or acrobats? There are no sophisticated divinities as in Tibet, for example. Finally, Cham sculpture remained stable through the centuries and while styles evolved, divinities or animals, for example, followed a constant thematic thread.

We know that the Hindu trinity, the Trimurti, found a place in Indian philosophy as of 500 BCE: progressively, the influence of the Vedas lessened to the benefit of, notably, the Puranas (Sanskrit: "Antiquities"), the collection of legends and ritual practices attributed to the sage Vyasa that underlie new beliefs, in which fervent devotion and detachment became the dominant values. In Champa, this trinity had a hierarchy: the spirit of Shiva is omnipresent in Cham sculpture. However, his different representations are limited in comparison with Indian creations. The same is true for Vishnu and Brahma, in addition to these gods being represented far less often. Besides the usual Shiva, one can certainly find mukhalinga and Nataraja, but will search in vain for Ardhanarishvara, Bhairava, Brikshatana, Dakshinamurti, Ekapada, Gangadhara, Kamari, Lingodbhavamurti, Sharabha, Tripurantaka, even Harihara (present in Khmer art), the many complex forms of Shiva that one comes across in the original Indian model. Practically, Shiva, the "gracious" in Sanskrit, the destructive god in the Brahman triad, is found represented either standing still, with two arms and three eyes of which one is central, or dancing, with four arms. In the second case, he is called "Nataraja" (in Sanskrit, "god of the dance") or, more commonly, "Natesha" ("lord of the dance" in Sanskrit), both these names designating all the dancing forms of Shiva.

Other than the god himself, one regularly encounters his symbol, the linga ("sign" in Sanskrit) that can be expressed in different forms; namely, mukhalinga ("sign with a face"), jatalinga ("sign with a chignon"), but the most frequently is represented as follows:

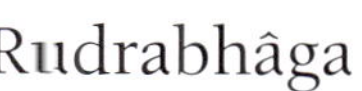

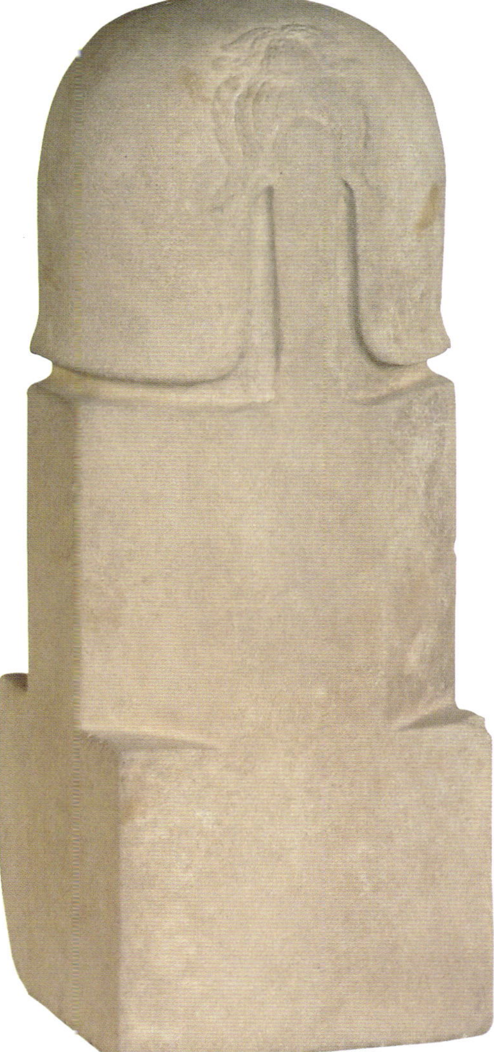

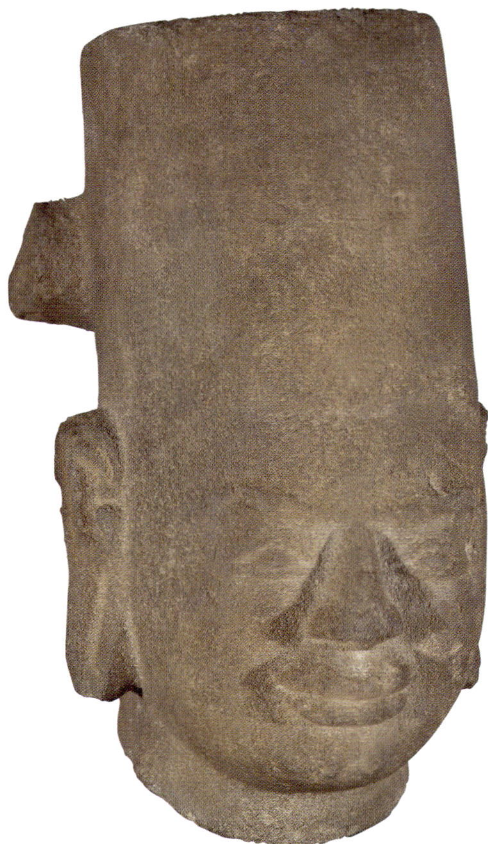

The god's entourage consists of Uma or Parvati, his consort (Sanskrit: "sakti"), the bull Nandin, his mount, but also Ganesha, his son, who can be identified by his elephant head and – very rarely – Skanda, his other son. Each and every one has his own history, legitimacy and constitutes the essential element of a perfectly ordered religious system.

Vishnu, "he who penetrates all" in Sanskrit, is in the Brahman triad, with Shiva and Brahma; he whose task it is to ensure the perpetuity of the world between the time of its creation by Brahma and its destruction by Shiva. Four-handed Shiva is generally represented with a disk and a conch shell (upper hands), a sledgehammer and a small ball (lower hands), and he may be riding his mount Garuda. His spouse, his "sakti", is Lakshmi or Sri, born from the churning of the ocean of milk.

Vishnu also incarnates various avatars (Sanskrit: "descent") to fight the demons (the Asura) who combat the gods. These avatars are not random, but are organised according to a succession that is unchangeable in cosmic time: among these avatars, let us cite only Rama for the moment, the hero of the Ramayana and Buddha of whom, though it is often forgotten, representations are also found in Brahmanism.

Brahma is present, but more rarely, in Cham iconography. Graced with four heads (three, in fact, as the back one cannot physically exist in a high or low relief seen straight on). His consort, Sarasvati, is more difficult to identify for her part, often iconographically similar to Uma or Lakshmi.

Buddhism in Cham sculpture finds far less expression than Brahmanism. It is essentially, but not exclusively, illustrated in the Dong Duong style (ninth and tenth centuries), where Buddhas and bodhisattvas are present, although Chinese Annals already evoked in the Linyi era Hinayana ("small vehicle") Buddhist monks. The Buddhist iconography used is classic: monastic clothing, "usnisha" (bump on the skull) and sometimes "urna" (tuft of hair between the eyebrows). On the contrary, bodhisattvas, characteristic of the Mahayana, are found much more often, also dateable from the Dong Duong period: Avalokitesvara wears the image of the Buddha Amitabha in his hair. Prajnaparamita sometimes seems to be Avalokitesvara's companion; as he does, she wears Amitabha in her hair. Vajrapani, with the Vajra ("diamond lightning") as his main attribute, is also found. Buddhism does not seem ever to have been the state religion in Champa, but more the personal inclination of the sovereign. When he founded Dong Duong during the second half of the ninth century, King Indravarman II rendered homage to Laksmindra Lokesvara, the other name for Avalokitesvara, but also – in the foundation stela – to Shiva Bhadresvara and thereby explicitly to Shivaism. This syncretism can equally be identified in the second stela at Dong Duong, which informs us that Haradevi, queen and widow of the king Pramabuddhaloka, had Hindu images mounted. Let us simply remember that Hara is another name for Shiva.

In addition to these divinities, Brahman or Buddhist, one encounters other representations, secondary, but shared by the two religions, such as certain animals (lion, naga, deer or gazelle) or the gods of directions (dikpalaka). The latter are placed essentially in the courtyards of temples and more rarely on slabs placed on entablatures or on door lintels, among them, Indra, perched on his mount, the elephant Airavata, or Vayu on his mount, the horse. The dvarapala are also present, these guardians of the doors of temples that are always in pairs, one looking benevolent, the other terrifying.

Animals can also be part of the statuary of a temple: lions (as they were imagined, since the Chams could not have seen such an animal as no lions lived in Champa), elephants that are very realistic as they were native to Champa, Garuda, Naga ("snakes"), and monkeys, among others.

Finally, one must add the characters of the main Indian epics (the Ramayana and the Mahabharata) such as Rama, Sugriva, and Hanuman, who, having left the anonymity of the species, incarnated as the heroes of the most famous epics of Indian history.

We must note that it can be difficult to identify not only certain divinities themselves, but also the register (religious or decorative) to which they belong.

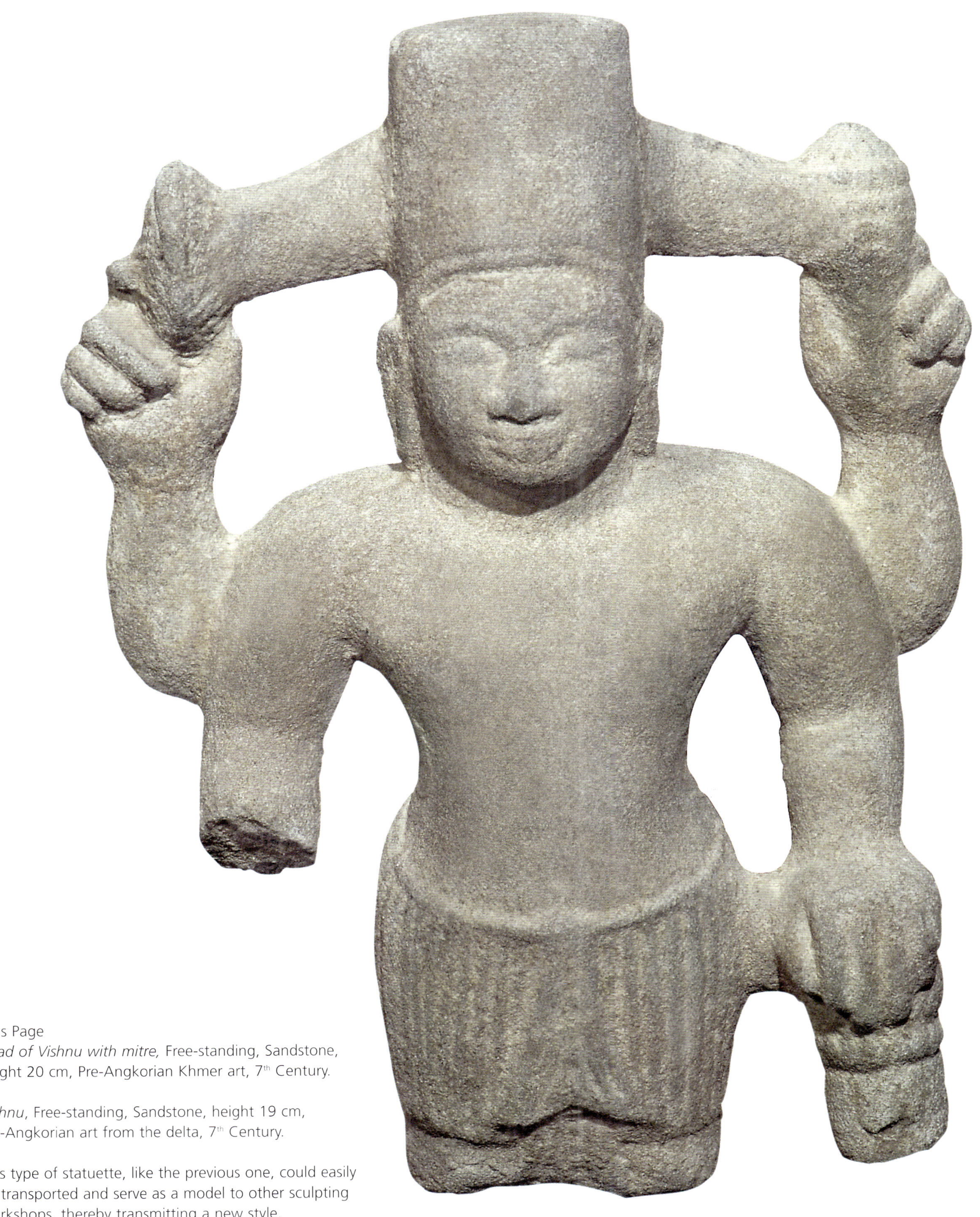

Previous Page

23. *Head of Vishnu with mitre,* Free-standing, Sandstone, height 20 cm, Pre-Angkorian Khmer art, 7th Century.

24. *Vishnu*, Free-standing, Sandstone, height 19 cm, Pre-Angkorian art from the delta, 7th Century.

This type of statuette, like the previous one, could easily be transported and serve as a model to other sculpting workshops, thereby transmitting a new style.

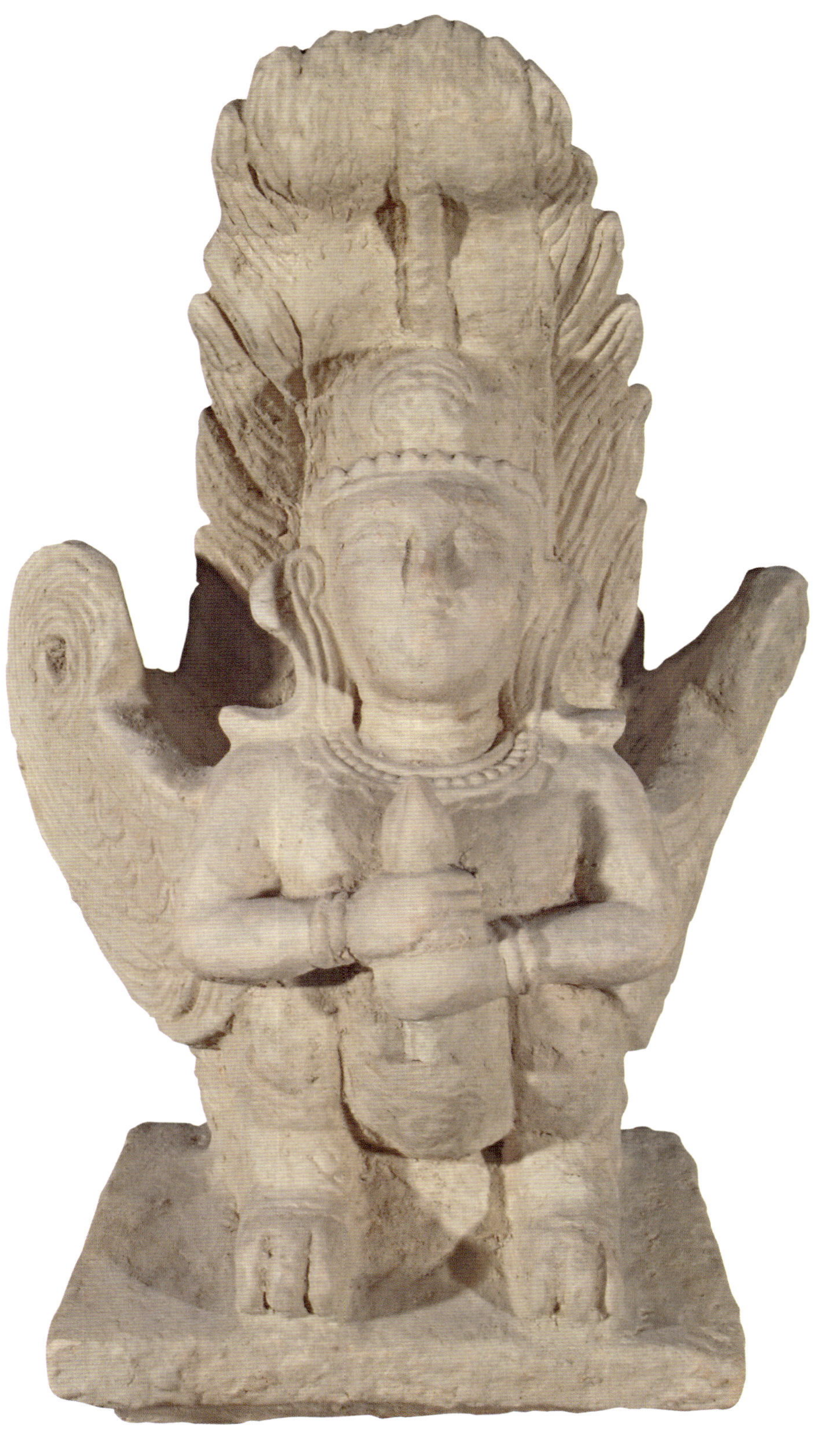

25. *Kinnari*, Free-standing, Clay, height 39 cm,
Vietnamese art from the Ly dynasty, 11th - 12th Century.

Following Page
26. *Vishnu*, Free-standing, Sandstone, height 25cm, 6th Century.

All of these sculptures were made in different forms and in diverse materials.

Classically, they can be categorised as free-standing, high-relief or bas-relief. A free-standing piece is a sculpture that one can walk around in order to admire the sculptor's work. A high-relief is a sculpture with a very prominent relief but cannot be detached from its background. Finally, a bas-relief is a sculpture that is not very prominent, placed on a uniform background.

In practice, things are more complex: there are practically free-standing pieces, when a sculpture is equipped with a back tenon, and the distinction between high-relief and bas-relief can appear impossible and the choice arbitrary.

The materials used for sculpture are mostly sandstone or brick or, much more rarely, terra cotta. In jewellery making, gold, silver, gilded silver, bronze and all sorts of alloys were favoured. The abundance of high quality sandstone explains why most statues found are made of stone. Certainly, we have seen with what voracity invaders seized – in order to melt them down – sculptures made of precious metals such as gold and silver, but this disappearance due to pillaging cannot hide the fact that stone was the principal material of Cham statuary. As an example, it is only through a lack of schist that neighbouring Thailand gave priority to clay, laterite, bronze, and not for a supposed preference to model rather than to cut directly into stone.

It will be immediately noticed that not a single sculptor's name has come down through the ages. As is most often the case in ancient Asia, the sculptor remained anonymous. The Cham statue was an act of faith that went beyond individualised creation. Sculpting a statue was a religious act, an expression of cultural fervour that transfigured its creator. Cham sculptors carved a concentrate of the divine; the supernatural that imbues the sculpture was transported into the temple. Worshippers prayed to the god himself who had descended into his representation. Thus one understands the necessary capitulation of the sculptor to religious norms, which contain so many stylistic obligations. One also comprehends better the lasting expression of these representations: at least dozens of years, if not hundreds, for certain styles, such as in Thâp-Mam. In addition, one realises more clearly how a drastic change in style equated to a veritable cultural revolution. One grasps why a sculpture is by definition a political, economic, social and cultural cross-section of an era as well.

The quarries of Champa provided sandstone with a variety of colours and grains. It was almost always grey, in different tones, although the patina the stone acquired over time or the vermilion colouring given by being buried in the earth over long periods coloured by cinnabar, can make an identification of the original colour difficult. The grain of Cham sandstone is fairly rough, appearing lumpy at times, especially if the sculptures come from the

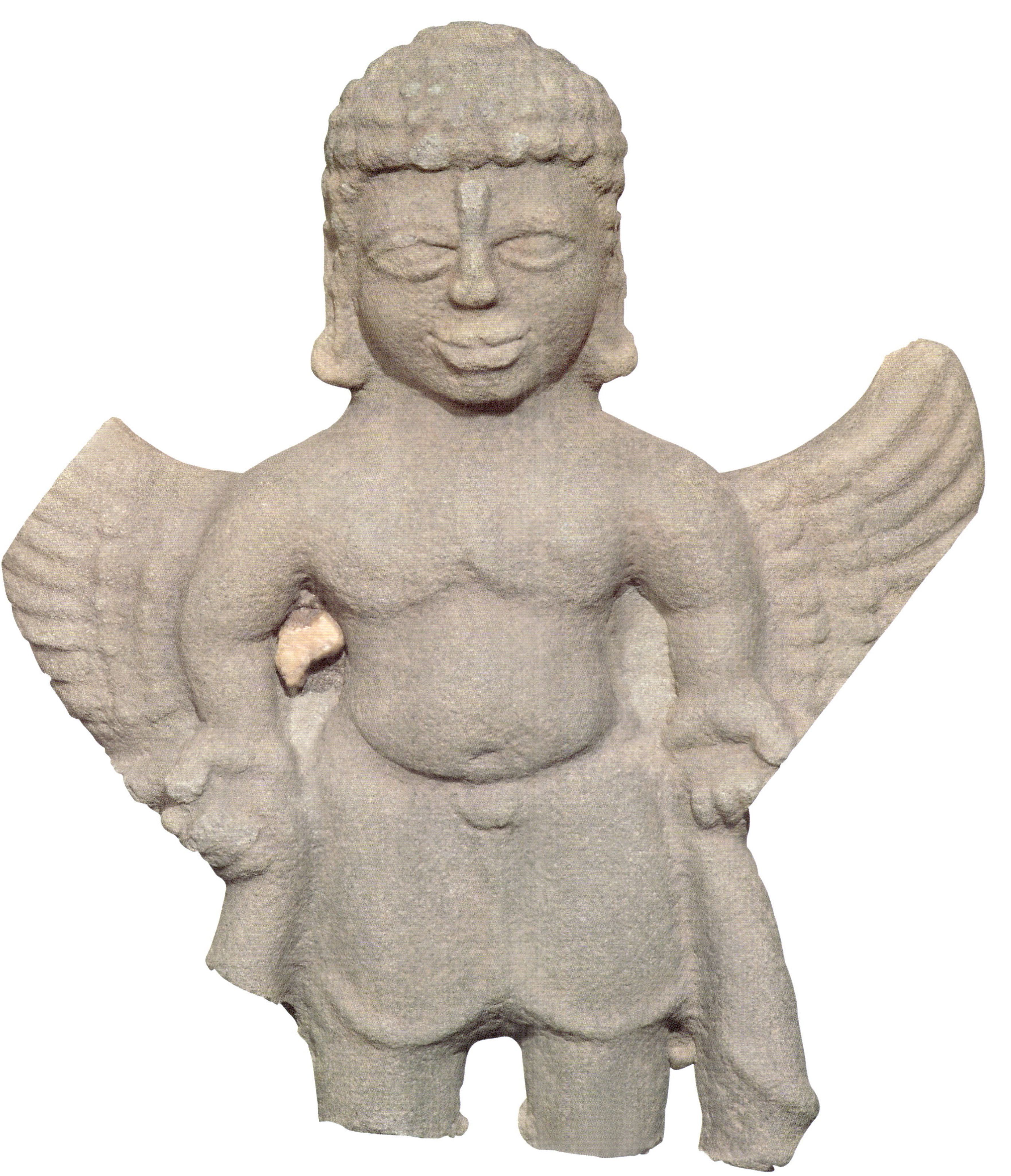

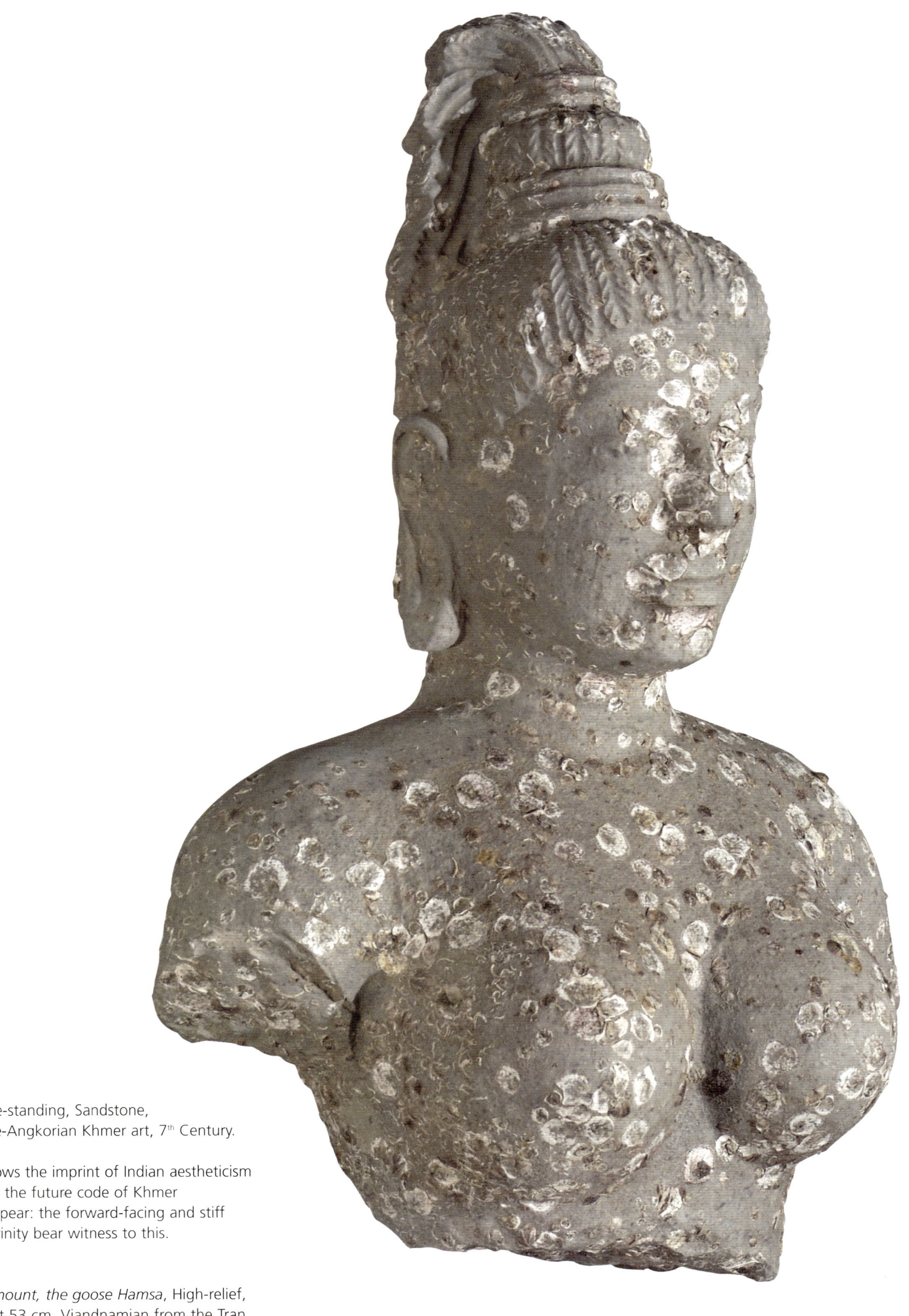

27. *Bust of Uma*, Free-standing, Sandstone, height 52 cm, Pre-Angkorian Khmer art, 7th Century.

This work still shows the imprint of Indian aestheticism but indications of the future code of Khmer representation appear: the forward-facing and stiff aspects of the divinity bear witness to this.

Following Page
28. *Brahma and his mount, the goose Hamsa*, High-relief, Sandstone, height 53 cm, Viandnamian from the Tran dynasty, 13th Century.

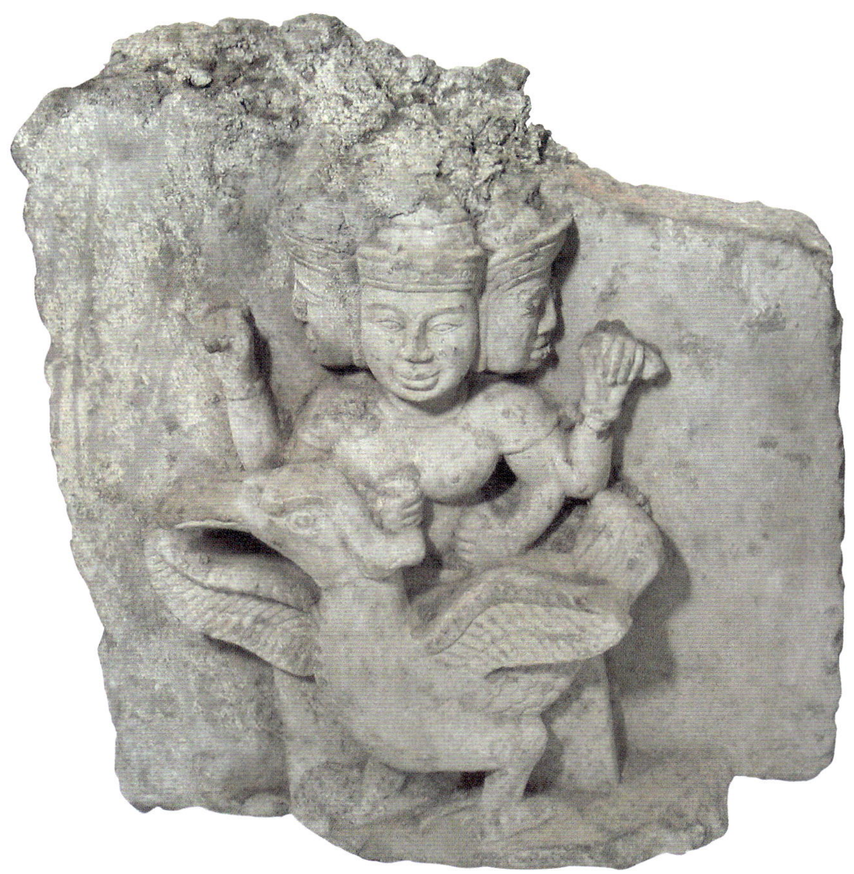

Tam Ky region, but can also be very fine, such as that of the pieces of the My Son E1 style or, much later, those of the Yang Mum style. It is paradoxical to observe that, spanning 700 years, the same grain unites sculptors that are otherwise so far apart stylistically. One can understand how difficult dating these works was at the beginning of the twentieth century.

The sculptor proceeded to cut directly, following imposed iconography. Two technical imperatives did limit his creativity, however: first, the volume of the block of stone he was given to use and, next, the balance of the statue itself. Observation shows that no monumental sculpture was created. The biggest are hardly more than two metres tall. For example, note the dvarapala of Dong Duong, one of which is trampling a buffalo, the other a bear, kept in the Da Nang museum and measuring 2.15 and 2.18 metres respectively. The balance of a statue and, in a sense, its stability, was ensured by the creation of reinforcements, mainly at the ankles, in the form of blocks of stone left compact. Note the Cham sculptor never used supporting arches that can be found, for example, in the art of its "chronological neighbours" in Funan or Cambodia.

We can suppose that the inspiring iconography, besides through texts, was propagated by the importation of statuettes that could be easily transported (see p.33 and 35). But one mustn't forget that Cham sculptors were also inspired by their environment: corporal appearance and clothing were those of the people around them; nature became a model for decorative motifs. From all of that, the Cham sculptor made his own original art, in which respect was always interwoven with fantasy. For him, disorder was order without power.

The different sources of inspiration for Cham sculpture have been, in our opinion, too systematically linked with obvious foreign influences. Whereas it seems evident that, via Funan, Champa received Indian influence, searching for stylistic elements in Dai Co Viet or China seems far-fetched. Of course, coincidences can be found, the motif that any artist has to create not being infinitely multipliable. One can observe imprints that are both decorative and ideological but, in the case of the Viet, precisely in the opposite direction: the terra cotta kinnari (p.34) or the stone Brahma (p.37) are elements from Viet buildings that bear witness to this. One can more seriously identify in Khmer lands and in Java as well, representations in common, without an influence in the true sense of the word being identifiable. From neighbouring Khmers, one can very schematically outline a notable influence on the art of Sambor Prei Kuk, explained by the family ties of Isanavarman I. Some influences after the twelfth century can also be noticed that are attributed to warfare between the two peoples. But the influence is two-directional. Thus, it is undeniable that the Prasat Damrei Krap in Cambodia is the work of a Cham master. Equally, contributions by the Thâp-Mam style to that of the Bayon can be identified.

However, it is especially with Java that one is led to evoke certain similarities; yet, one must beware of oversimplification. Certainly, yesterday as today, "Champa" is geographically the maritime passage between China and Indonesia. But does that suffice to see anything more than analogies in the following elements? Busts with hair in large curls from Cung Son (in Phu Yen province) are very close to those of Chandi Bima on the Dieng plateau in Java. It is sometimes difficult to identify as Cham the small bronze Mahayanist statues from the eighth and ninth centuries found in Vietnam, but astonishingly Javanese in style. Architecturally, the Hoa Lai group is related to Javanese temples in general, but does noting false doors with vertical divisions – which only existed in Indonesia – allow the comparison to be taken even further? Certain occasional similarities between Java and Tra Kieu have often been raised from a sculptural point of view. But none of this appears convincing. Once again, this poses the problem of over-bearing importance being given to literature and the positioning of historical narratives as instruments of technical analysis. We indeed know by an inscription, that of Nhan Bieu, that the Cham prince Rajadvara went to Java twice at the beginning of the tenth century. Also, texts tell us that in 1292, Champa assisted Madjapahit to resist a Mongol invasion from the sea, that Jaya Simhavarman III, the Cham sovereign, married a Javanese princess and, that in 1318, the Cham prince Che Nan took refuge on Java. Is this enough to prove true ties, that themselves would serve as foundations for sculptural similarities? We do not think so.

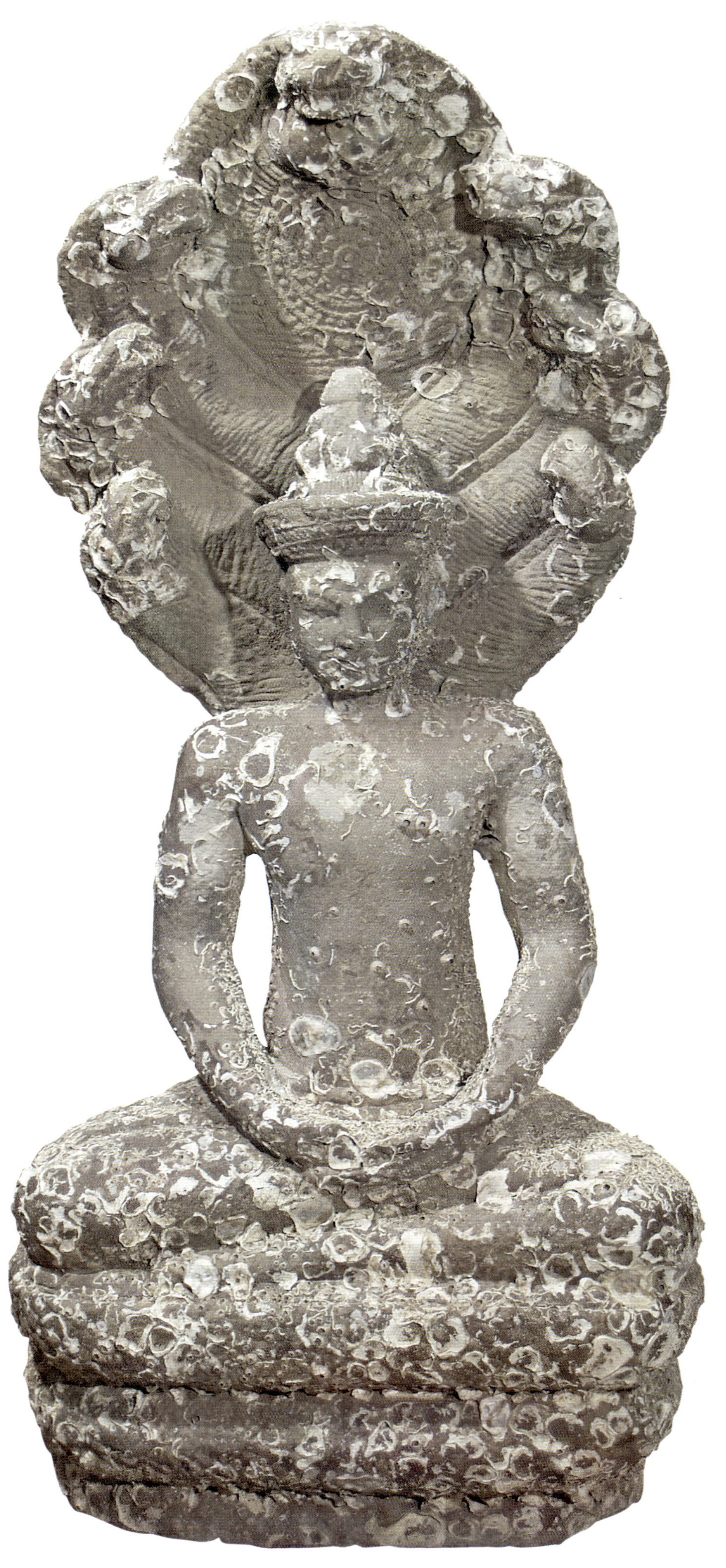

Styles and the dating of sculptures

In art, dating is much more difficult than iconographical identification. It even happens that, through laxity or insufficient experience with the object, the latter, though certainly in a scholarly way, is invoked as a servile tool for the former. This is a dangerous practice: "You have a solution. Always the same one: iconography. One step further, it calms your anxieties and answers all your questions." (Daniel Arasse, *On n'y voit rien* [We see nothing], *Descriptions*, p.32). Unluckily, the iconographical tool seems to have been overused. It is striking to notice that the term "patina" is wholly unknown to most authors. And yet this is the key to dating. A stone, a bronze, have a patina imposed by the passage of time, that situates the object in it. This patina has technical components that predispose, intellectually, the object's dating.

To precisely date Cham sculptures, to propose the characteristics of particular styles, was the task that, as of the beginning of the twentieth century, French specialists took upon themselves.

It was due to Henri Parmentier and his *Descriptive Inventory of Cham Monuments in Annam* (whose publication, begun in 1912, was completed in 1918), but above all, Philippe Stern and his remarkable *The Art of Champa (former Annam) and its Evolution* published in 1942 and Jean Boisselier (*Statuary of Champa*, 1963) that a general but often-contested dating system was established. It goes without saying that more recent discoveries, in particular in 1982 (on the An My site) not only allowed some of these datings to be made more precise, improved or even contradicted, but also made it possible to determine that they needed to be moved back in time, and to place them regionally (Tran Ky Phuong, Ngo Van Doanh). The An My site, in the Tam Ky district, Quang Nam province, notably delivered several remarkable sculptures (linga-yoni, dikpala, etc.) that Vietnamese archaeologists date from the first half of the tenth century. In addition, in 1987-88, numerous new Cham sites were identified, either on the plain (Tuy Phuoc and An Nhon districts) or on the high plateaux (Gia Lai, Kontum). Parmentier's classification no longer has any didactic value. On the other hand, in terms of iconography and dating, the work of Stern and that of Boisselier remain the reference.

Let us briefly recall how these men formulated their reasoning and their conclusions. Parmentier began with a principle: "Between two undated forms of art, the most perfect one is the oldest." His observation, in the field, of temples and Cham sculptures brought him, guided by this principle, to divide Cham art into two periods. The first, called "primary", stretches from the seventh to the tenth centuries, and is itself divided into three "arts" that can overlap chronologically: "primitive" art of the seventh to tenth centuries,

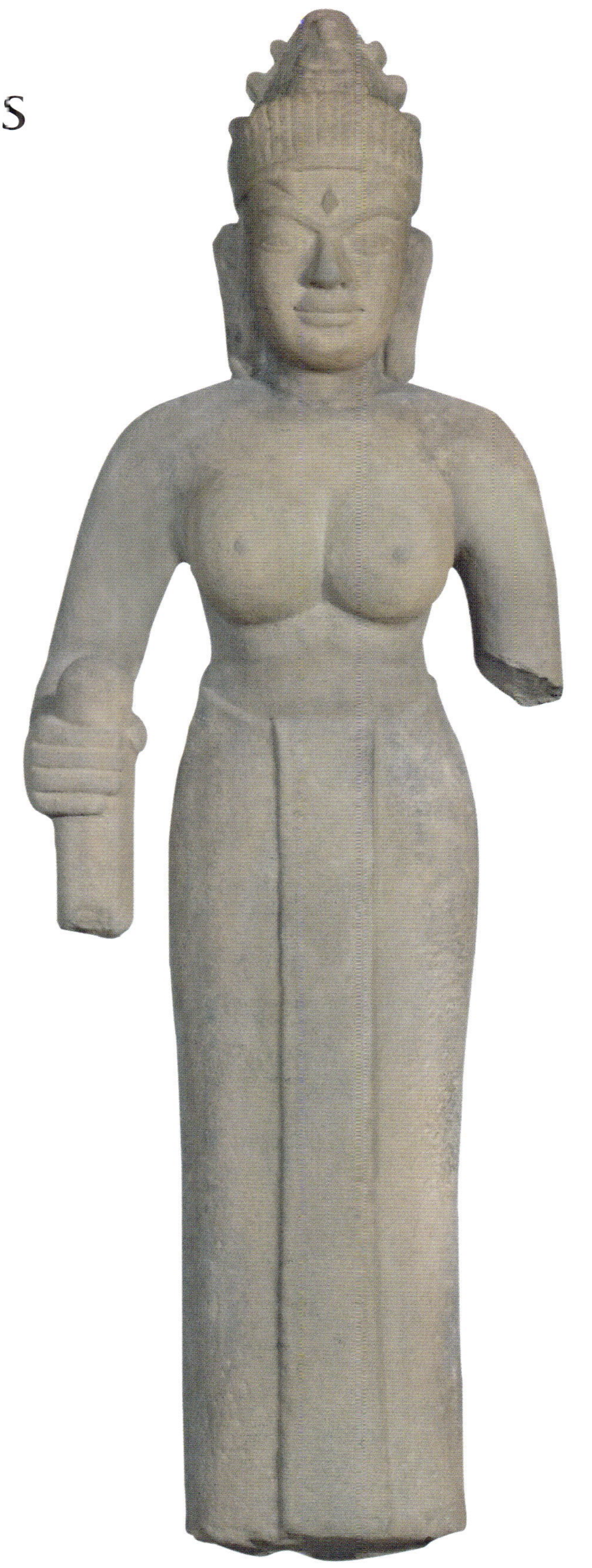

Previous Page
29. *Buddha protected by the serpent Mucilinda*, Sandstone, height 88 cm,
Angkorien Art, 11th - 12th Century.
Typical to Khmer, this image is unique in Cham sculpture.

30. *Tara*, Free-standing, Sandstone, height 94 cm,
Dong Duong style, 9th - 10th Century.
The divinity is standing, sculpted in the round rather than leaning against a stele. She wears a representation of Amitabha in her hair. Both arms (one is broken today) gripped two vertical staffs that served as supports. She is dressed in a sarong with vertical folds, her breasts are heavy and rounded. Her face is the archetype of the Dong Duong style.

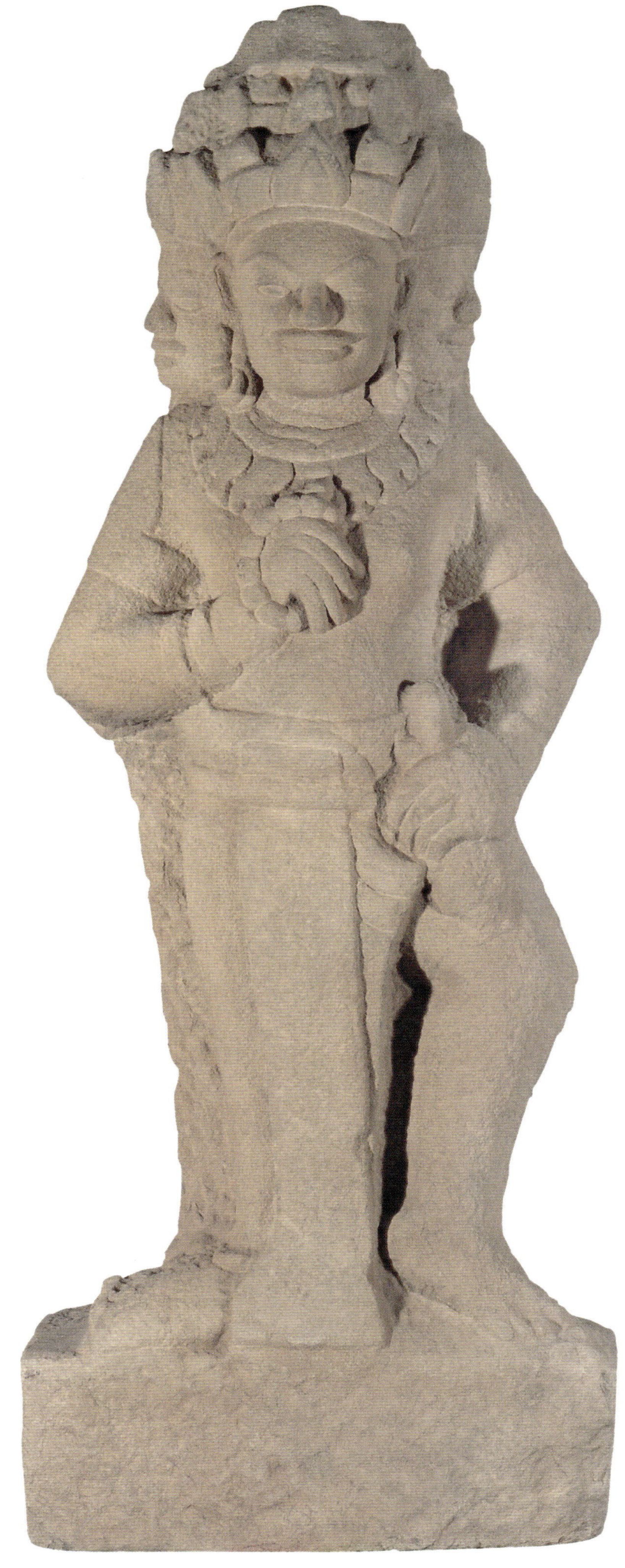

31. *Brahma*, High-relief, Sandstone, height 100 cm, Tra Kiêu style, 10th Century.

It is very rare to represent God in Cham statuary, which essentially gives precedent to representations of Shiva. Usually reproduced in the round with four heads, this god, due to the technique of High-relief, only has three. He is holding a meditation rosary and the urn for alms.

Following page
32. *Brahma,* High-relief, Sandstone, height 100 cm, Tra Kiêu style, 10th Century (detail).

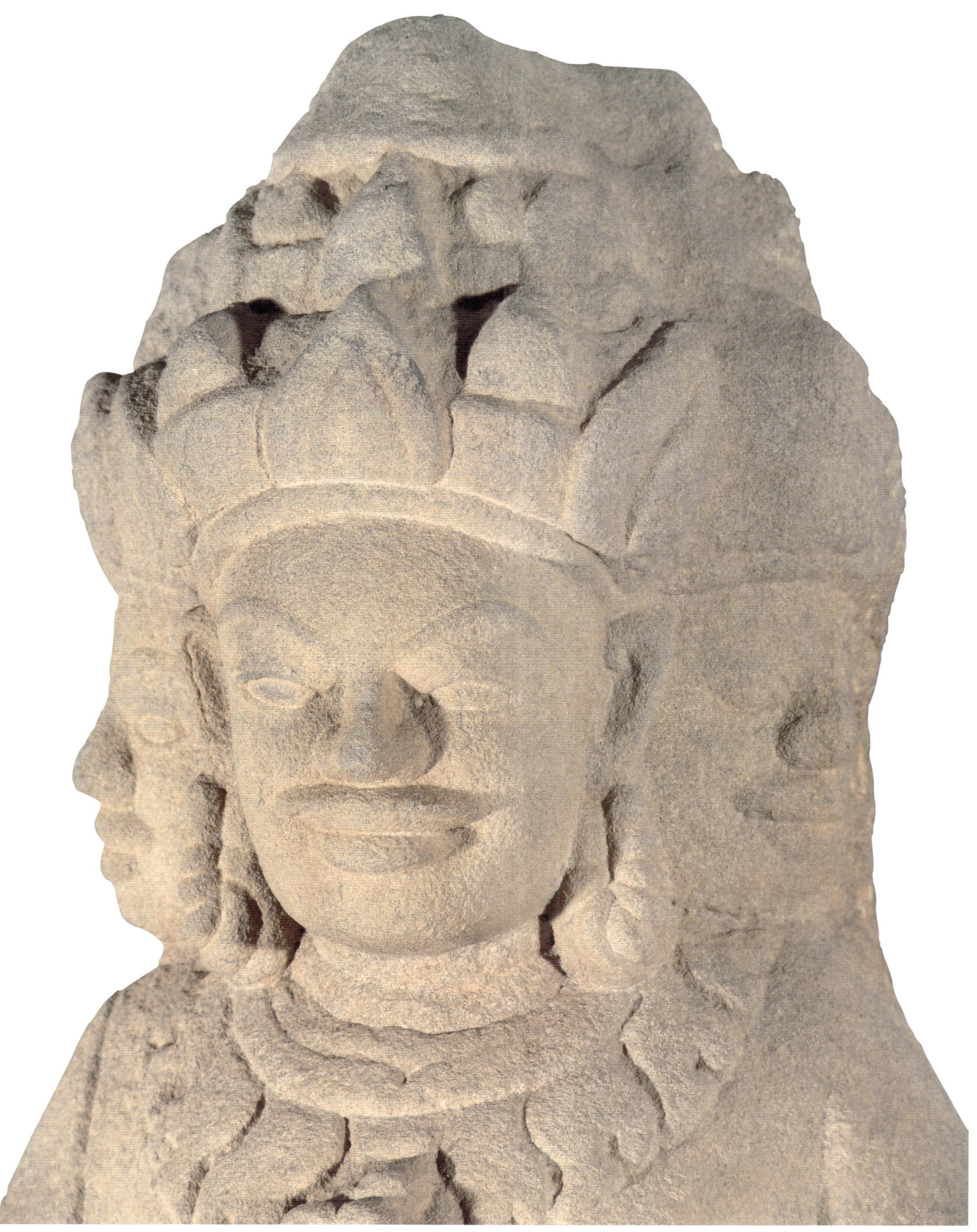

illustrated notably by My Son A1; "cubic" art from the seventh to ninth centuries, as at Hoa Lai, and "mixed" art, in the tenth century, as at Dong Duong. The second period, called "secondary", can here again be separated into "classic" art of the eleventh century, such as at the Silver Towers, "derived" art, in the twelfth to seventeenth centuries, as at Po Klaung Garai, and "pyramidal" art, from the tenth to fourteenth centuries, as at Po Nagar in Nha Trang.

To make these classifications, Parmentier gave precedence to his training as an architect, which led him to date buildings rather than sculptures. The general shape of the edifice, its elements (base, pilasters, *pièces d'accent*, false doors, etc.), and certain elements of decoration (foliated scrolls, lotus flowers) serve as the basis for this stylistic and chronological classification.

Gilberte de Coral Remusat (1903 – 1943), "free attaché" (1931) to the conservation of the Indo-Chinese museum at the Trocadero in Paris, then "attaché" (1934) to the Guimet Museum (Paris) and correspondent for the French School of the Extreme Orient, contested, as early as 1932, Parmentier's work. She essentially affirmed that the central tower at Dong Duong had to be classified between "cubic" art and the art of My Son A1. She identified in this manner four other styles: Tra Kieu (seventh and eighth centuries), Dong Duong (eighth to tenth centuries), "classical" and Binh Ding styles (post tenth century), and, finally, the "late" style. Coral-Remusat's classification is no longer taken into consideration today, but she managed to "dust off" the material and offered a wide window of study to Philippe Stern.

Stern specifies, as of page two of his book, his project:

AVANT-PROPOS

Nous désirions depuis longtemps appliquer à l'art cham la méthode de recherches par évolution des motifs qui nous avait permis de fixer la chronologie de nombreux édifices khmèrs. Les documents photographiques réunis à Paris, avant notre mission de 1935-1936, étaient malheureusement insuffisants pour permettre un travail de cet ordre. Grâce à l'« *Inventaire descriptif des monuments čams de l'Annam* » (1) de M. Parmentier, nous avons cependant voulu, avant de partir et sur le bateau qui nous emmenait vers l'Indochine, tenter un premier essai dans cette voie. Il ne nous était pas désagréable, avouons-le, d'arriver en Annam avec une étude en formation et quelques résultats déjà acquis. Mais, surtout, un panorama des diverses possibilités chronologiques était pour nous nécessaire. Examiner les monuments sans hypothèses préalables, c'est, croyons-nous, — et l'expérience l'a prouvé — aller au-devant d'un échec. Trop d'observations sont possibles, trop de photographies intéressantes peuvent être prises; même en multipliant pages de notes et clichés, on a toutes chances d'omettre la constatation essentielle qui éclairera l'évolution si on ne sait pas, par avance, les éléments qu'il est nécessaire d'analyser, les détails qu'il convient de noter et de photographier. Il faut, en somme, arriver devant l'édifice *en sachant exactement les questions qu'on doit lui poser*; prêt d'ailleurs, dans la multiplicité des hypothèses de travail, à rejeter aussitôt celles pour lesquelles les réponses reçues seraient non seulement négatives mais seulement hésitantes. C'est, pensons-nous, parce que nous avons agi ainsi que nous avons rapporté notes et photographies indispensables au présent travail.

***

Still, after the identification of detailed architectural markers, their classification and the establishment of an architectural chronology, Stern comes – in the appendix of his short text – to a major reserve (p. 11):

APPENDICE

La sculpture chame et son évolution.

Si nous plaçons la sculpture en appendice, c'est que les résultats qu'apporte son étude nous semblent plus fragiles que ceux fournis par l'examen des édifices et du décor architectural. La sculpture chame se présente à nous d'une manière assez bizarre. A trois styles d'architecture correspondent, avec évidence, trois styles de sculpture : le nombre des pièces trouvées, le lieu des découvertes, les détails de décoration nous donnent des certitudes. Nous connaissons ainsi la sculpture du style de Dông-dzu'o'ng, celle du style du Binh-dinh, celle du style tardif. Pour les autres styles, la répartition de la statuaire et des bas-reliefs dépend de l'époque où nous croirons devoir placer les sculptures de Tra-kiêu qui, par leur nombre et leur valeur, sont peut-être les plus importantes de l'art cham. Elles étaient considérées jusqu'ici comme les plus anciennes du Champa et fixées au VIIe siècle en correspondance avec le style dit primitif (style de Mi-so'n A-1). Mais notre chronologie transporte le style de Mi-so'n A-1 vers le Xe siècle. Il semble que *la sculpture de Tra-kiêu* doive suivre ce mouvement, *rester contemporaine du style de Mi-s'on A-1 et devenir ainsi postérieure au style de Dông-dzu'o'ng*. Nous tentons de l'établir et c'est *la partie la plus importante de cette étude sur la sculpture chame* (voir p. 75 à 79). Un certain nombre de nettes présomptions convergent dans ce sens et paraissent presque atteindre à la certitude. Si le style de Tra-kiêu est ainsi ramené au Xe siècle, peu de sculptures du style ancien et du style de Hoa-lai seraient parvenues jusqu'à nous. Nous manquons d'ailleurs de données pour reconnaître les œuvres de ces périodes. Nous ne pouvons en identifier qu'un très petit nombre, Parmi les sculptures qui restent d'époque indécise, plusieurs ont chance d'appartenir à cette époque ancienne, mais aucun indice précis ne nous permet de l'assurer.

It is thus by taking up again, in part, the method that had worked so well in his study of Khmer monuments, that Stern approached the study of Cham temples. For him, here again, two main elements must serve to establish an evolution: the arcature and the pilaster. The word "arcature" must be understood to include "the arch of doors and false doors, the great arches of the edifice's body, those of the superstructure, those finally on the applied ornaments that decorate the bases of the pilasters and bases. The pilasters are those which decorate the walls of the monuments." To these two elements, Stern added others that, for him, completed in order of importance, his study: "the frieze of garlands under the cornice, the small column, the cornice, the *pièces d'accent*, the corner fascia, the lintel, and finally certain decorations that only existed in ancient times, or that only appeared at a late period."

He thus reached the date of the temples as his final result, and inferred the date of the art statuary itself. He thus proposed, on one hand a constitution of styles, on the other a chronological classification of the same. Examining essentially the vestiges of My Son, Phu Hai, Hoa Lai, Po Dam, Dong Duong, Khuong My, Nha Trang (Po Nagar), Binh Lam, Thap Ba, Thap Nhan, Hung Thanh, Canh Thien, Tho Loc, Thu Thien, Bang An, Po Klaung Garai, Yang Mum and Po Rome, he proposed seven styles that came one after the other from the eighth to the sixteenth centuries. The following table enumerates these styles, with the names of vestiges associated with each one by Stern.

	STYLE	NAME OF VESTIGES
I	My Son E1 Style	My Son E-1
	(or "antique" style)	My Son F-1
	(Seventh-eighth century)	Phu Hai
II	Hoa Lai Style	Hoa Lai
	(Eighth-ninth centuries)	Po Dam
		My Son F-1
		My Son C-7
		My Son A-13
III	Dong Duong Style	Dong Duong
	(Ninth century)	My Son A-10
		My Son B-4
IV	My Son A1 Style	My Son A-1
	(Tenth century)	My Son B-2
		My Son B-3
		My Son B-5
		My Son B-6
		My Son B-8
		My Son C-1
		My Son C-2
		My Son C-3
		My Son C-4
		My Son C-5
		My Son C-6
		My Son D-1
		My Son D-2
		My Son D-4
		Khuong My
		North-west towers at Po Nagar Nha Trang
V	Po Nagar Nha Trang Style	Kalan Po Nagar, Nha Trang
	(or intermediate style between	Binh Lam
	My Son A1 and Binh Dinh)	Thap Bac
	(Eleventh-twelfth centuries)	Thap Nhan
		Chien Dan
		My Son B-1
		My Son E-4
		My Son K
VI	Binh Dinh Style	Duong Long
	(Twelfth-thirteenth centuries)	Hung Thanh
		Canh Tien
		Thoc Loc
		Thu Thien
		South tower Po Nagar, Nha Trang
		Bang An
		My Son G
		My Son H
VII	Po Klaung Garai Style	Po Klaung Garai
	(or late style)	Yang Mum
	(Fourteenth-Sixteenth centuries)	Po Rome

We can note that Stern, as in the case of the Khmer temples, chose, for his styles, eponymous temples that he saw as the most characteristic of the style identified. We thus understand that these denominations lock up research somewhat, as they scorn later discoveries that might better illustrate a pre-named style. In this way, Stern and Boisselier did not know the true wealth of the Chien Dan temple, definitely brought to light in the early 1980s.

Jean Boisselier, for his part, completed, by adding to it and making it more specific, Stern's dating. We can but briefly, as the dimensions of this book dictate, summarise the combined contribution of these two authors.

The first verifiable style is that of My Son E1, which begins at the start of the seventh century and continues into the eighth. Its main characteristics, like those of the pediment of the eponymous temple are: the originality of the theme (the creation of the world with Vishnu coming out of Brahma's navel), the sobriety of its treatment, the very low arch (i.e. whose height is less than half of its width), wide and decorated with separated flowers on a plain background. The second is that of Dong Duong (late ninth, early tenth centuries) with heads of divinities or laymen that are original: narrow foreheads, limited by two peaks of hair that come down to the prominent eyebrows presented in a continuous line, wavy and going upward toward the hair; long eyes, with thin eyelids; wide noses that are aquiline in profile; an unsmiling mouth (the smile will only come later) with thick lips having turned-up corners and short chins.

Next comes the My Son A1 style, that can be chronologically divided into the Khuong My style (first half of the tenth century) and the Tra Kieu (second half of the tenth century) with a "sub-style" referred to as Chanh Lo (late tenth to first half of the eleventh centuries).

In all these styles flourish soft poses and faces, beautiful jewellery and richness in themes. It should be noted that with the Chanh Lo style, there was a pronounced evolution toward a simplification of jewellery, a new composition of the kirita-mukuta, a new composition of clothing – the turned up edge and the pocket-like draping having disappeared – with a new body position in which the back is arched and previous jutting hips are gone and the obliteration on the face of the half-smile and the "fundamental question"; finally, a return to traditional facial features: large lips, wide nose, eyebrow ridges in strong relief. If it be necessary to speak once again of a return of/to the past, the Chanh Lo style could furnish convincing arguments.

Then followed the Thâp-Mam style, at the end of the eleventh to the fourteenth centuries. It was, at one and the same time, Baroque in its elaborate decoration, and by the imaginative expression of its divinities, centred more on Vishnu than previous ones. In Thâp-Mam faces, the features are thick, the lips fleshy, the eyebrows are clearly in relief, the pupils are not drawn, the nose is hooked, the

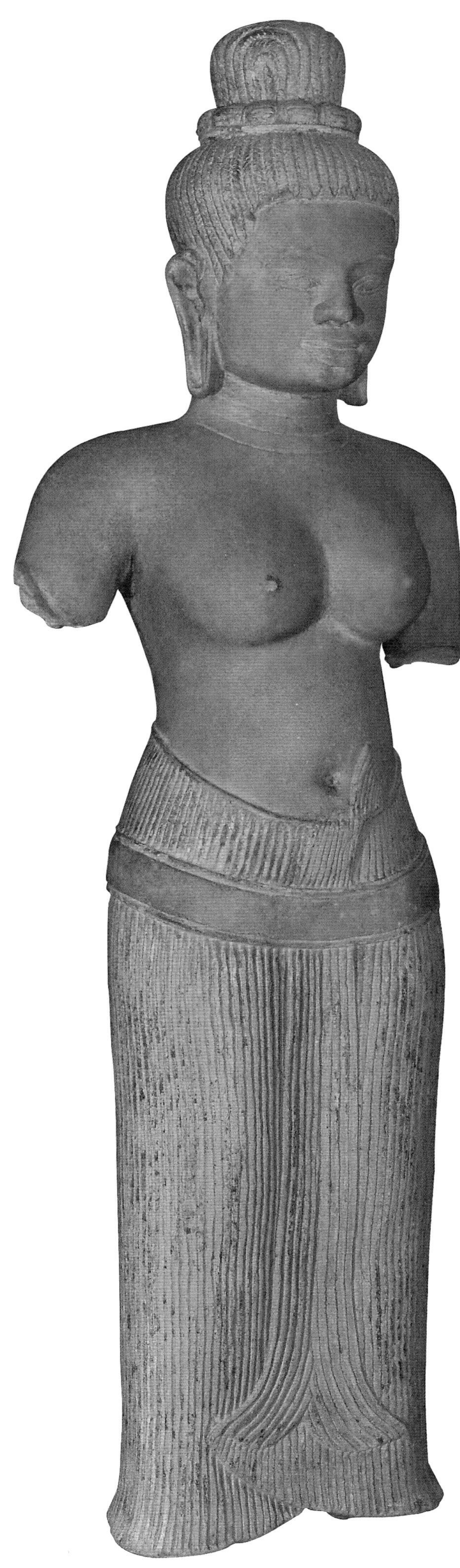

jata (Sanskrit: "chignon") is decorated with a band of parallel braids and the earlobe is horizontal. The dvarapala busts show eyes that are slightly bulging, a pouting lower lip, obvious neck tendons, dilated nostrils, a beard, moustache and eyebrows that seem to be lying on the face more than belonging to it and subtle "make-up". The motif that bears the name Thâp-Mam, a sort of curled up snail in relief with a point toward the top also allows, especially in borders, to date sculptures. It was about this style, which is so surprising, that Boisselier asked himself if it was a question "of a decadent piece of work or [one at the] summit of art pushed to its limits". One might well consider this a translation of the whole of the author's ambiguity about Cham art.

Finally, the Yang Mum style (fourteenth and fifteenth centuries): heads with long faces, a thin nose, half-closed semi-circular eyes, eyebrows that hardly touch with very strongly accentuated double curves, stylised ears, a beard – when one is present – cut into a point and a drooping moustache with slightly raised edges. The diadem band has no pearls and consists of a single row of jewels. The ear pendants are simple rings. The general silhouette is modified as the legs have a tendency to disappear and be replaced by a base. The Yang Mum Shiva, kept in the Da Nang Museum, is an excellent example of the quality of this style and the probable influence of the high plateaux, a part of Champa. Last but not least, the kut that may only express, finally, symbols sculpted into a simple stela, continue to intrigue. The kut conjures up the deceased and does not seem contrary to Boisselier's affirmation, to correspond to an "increasing ignorance of technique" but, on the contrary, to an interesting stylisation in which purity manifests respect for the god. But the end of the fifteenth century saw the imposition of a modification in the nature of Cham statuary: the 1471 defeat brought about not only the physical elimination of the elites but a loss of all holy places as well (My Son, Tra Kieu, Dong Duong). The Hindu spring had run dry. In what was left of Champa, new religious forms found expression, the cultural reserve of the autochtons flourished anew: animism came back strongly and many genies (the Yan) were worshipped. As of the end of the sixteenth century, a twofold religious supplement took root: on one hand, statues conserved from previous periods became the object of new cults, Hinduism having been erased from people's memories, and, on the other hand, Islam, present sporadically in the region as of the twelfth century, took hold in the ports of Champa-Panduranga.

The second fact does not seem to have influenced statuary. On the contrary, the first, if it did not influence styles themselves, which remained frozen, brought another use for them: divinities were left in their physical integrity, but re-christened with the names of the

33. *Uma*, Sandstone, height 72.5 cm, Khmer art from Baphuon, 11th Century. Whilst Cham Art was developing on the other side of the border, a high-quality sculpture was also being established in the Khmer region; a splendid example of the subtle art created by the Baphuon.

newly proclaimed heroes, be they leaders or genies. Three examples can be given:

For one, Po Yan Ina Nagar. This goddess, worshipped in Nha Trang, is supposed to have been born from sea foam and clouds. She is the creator of the earth and at the hierarchical summit of all supernatural beings; however, from the statuary point of view, it is simply a question of a Bhagavati ("she who is blessed"), Sakti of Shiva or Vishnu, perhaps dating from the tenth or eleventh century. However preposterous this may appear, none of today's worshippers of the divinity could say that she was of Brahman origin.

Secondly, Po Klan Garai, the mythical king who taught human beings to build dams on the rivers in the Kauthara and Panduranga plains. Here again, it is a question of a mukhalinga, purely Brahman, and therefore deviated from his first function.

Finally, Po Rome, king from 1627 to 1651, the unifier. He was the object at one and the same time of a local cult (Cham jat) and an Islamic cult (Cham bani); once again, our Po Rome was originally a Shivaist idol.

We can give one other example of the integration of Islam into the Cham pantheon – within the theoretical limits in representation of a monotheistic religion – by noting that Allah became a local divinity named Po Uvalvah.

Identified, dated, and interpreted: Cham sculpture has long concentrated erudition. Nevertheless, some questions persist. Identifying styles is an honourable mission, but making do with expressions such as "continuation of" or failing to integrate certain spontaneous innovations by labelling them "aberrations" is not constructive. Cham sculpture, perhaps more than any other school of Asian sculpture, privileges the unexpected.

The unexpected is surprising; essentially, it must not baffle. We are but in the earliest stages of a knowledge of Cham sculpture. Certainly, massive destruction, to which we have often referred, will unfortunately limit the material needed to deepen this knowledge, but the risk of making pat judgments through sententious remarks is being forced to recant them. Let us illustrate this by returning to the writing of Jean Boisselier and notably to the text that he entrusted for the exhibit "Kingdoms of Vietnam" held in Paris in 1995 and that is integrally included in the catalogue, *The Museum of Cham Sculpture in Da Nang*, published in 1997. Emmanuel Guillon, his spiritual heir, specifies that Jean Boisselier "somewhat considered [this text] as his testament in the matter". We can therefore infer that Jean Boisselier delivered the quintessence of his thinking within it. Nevertheless, without modifying an iota of the solemn admiration that we have for Boisselier's work, we must go back to certain sentences – taken at

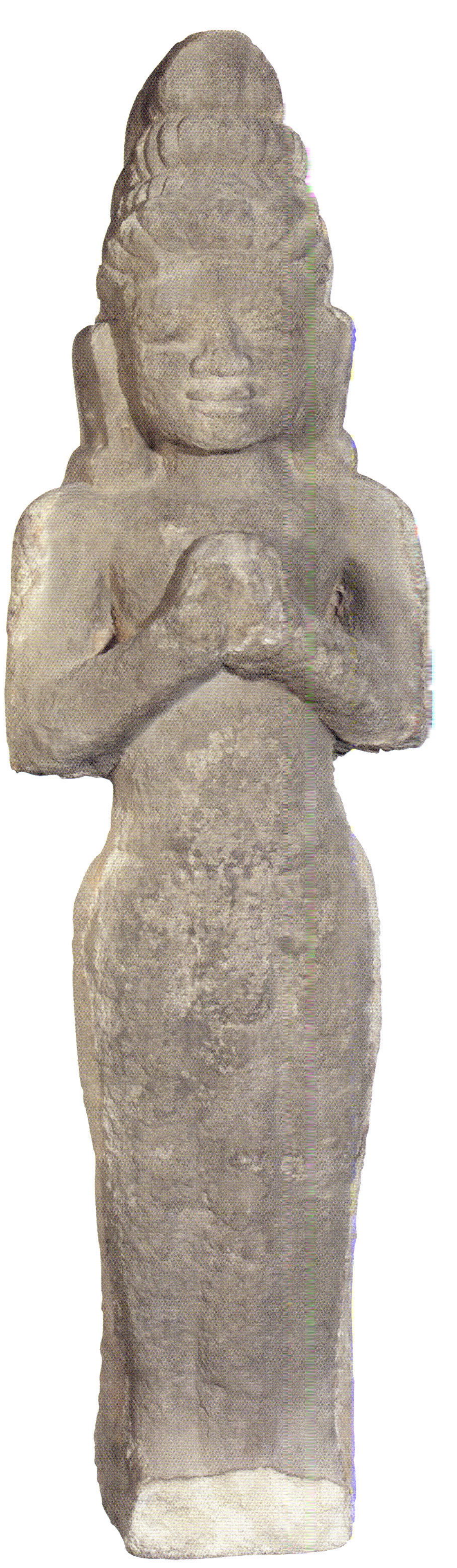

34. *Figure*, High-relief, Sandstone, height 82 cm, Chien Dan style, 10th - 11th Century.

The person is in anjalimudra, a gesture of adoration and veneration.

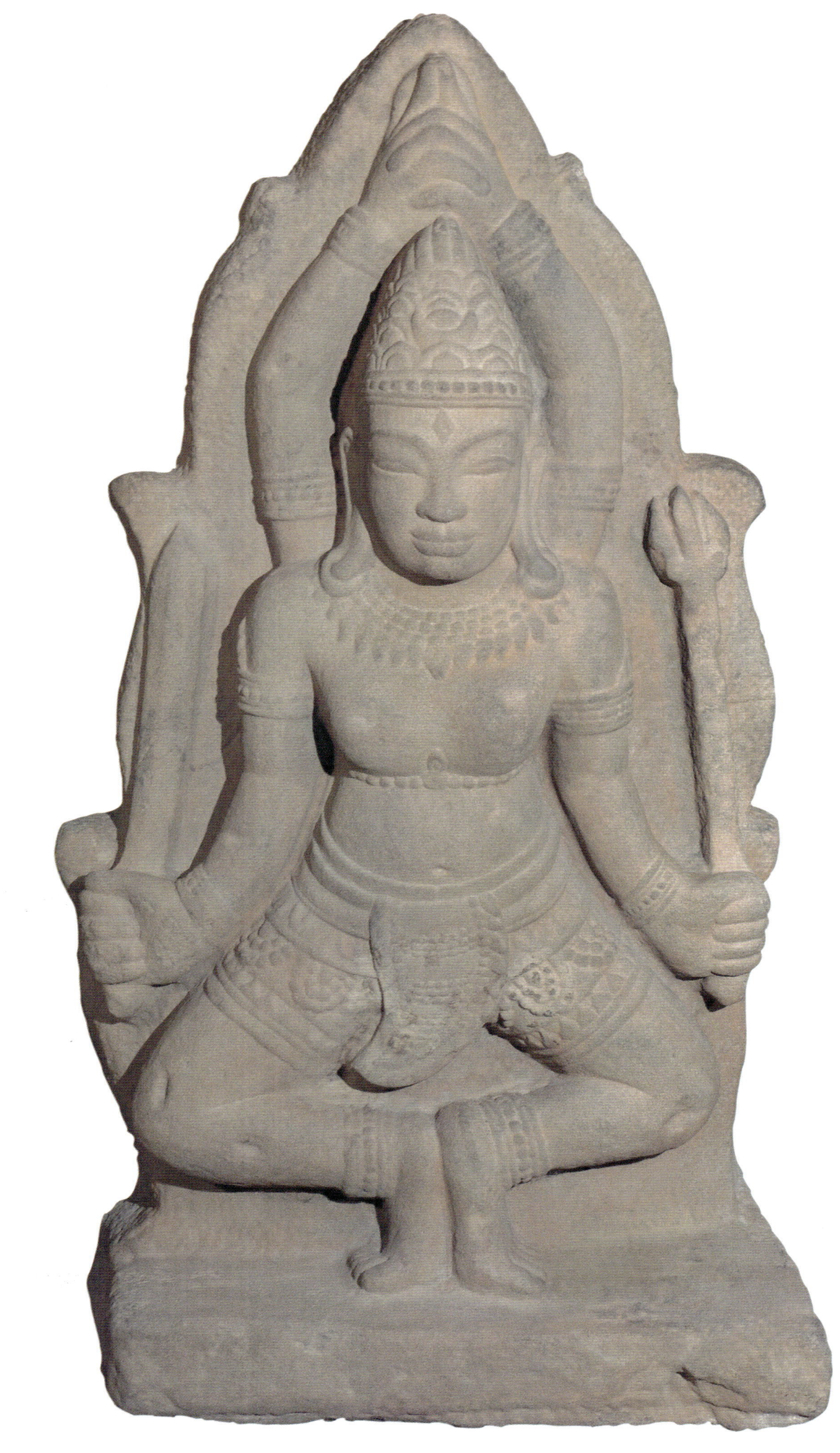

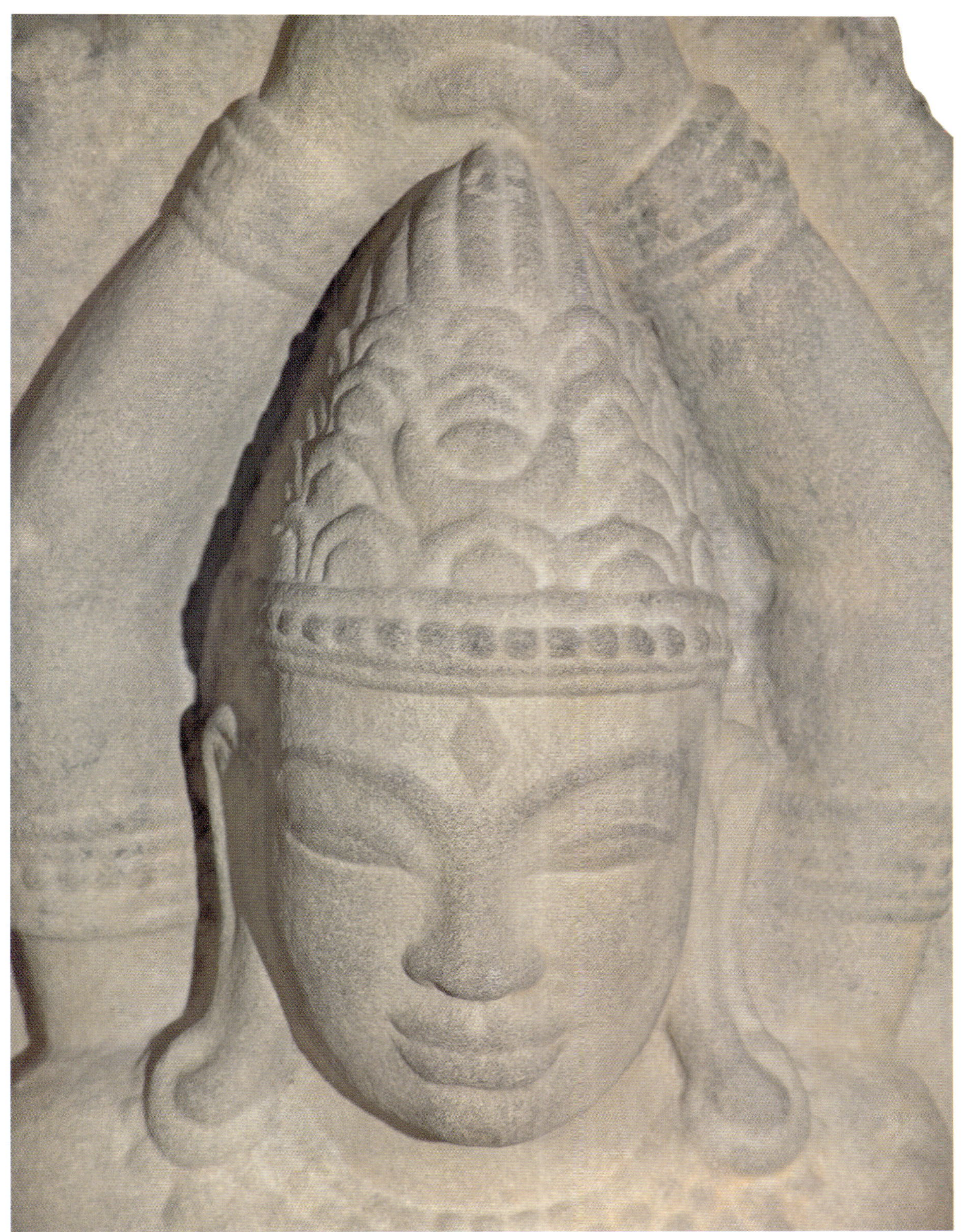

Previous Page

35. *Shiva dancing*, High-relief, Sandstone, height 104 cm, Thâp-Mam style, 12th Century.

The "beneficial" holds a lance in his lower right hand, and a trident in the lower left. A crescent moon in inserted into his hairstyle. A third eye decorates his forehead. The two upper arms join above the head, hands linked. They are mechanically superposed on the shoulders without being their natural prolongation. Dancing is shown by the bent thighs, the raised feet joined at the tops, the toes supporting the body weight, the parallel forearms. Rich dress (clothing, jewellery) can be noted. The divinity is leaning against a chevet nimbé.

36. *Shiva dancing*, High-relief, Sandstone, height 104 cm, Thâp-Mam style, 12th Century (detail).

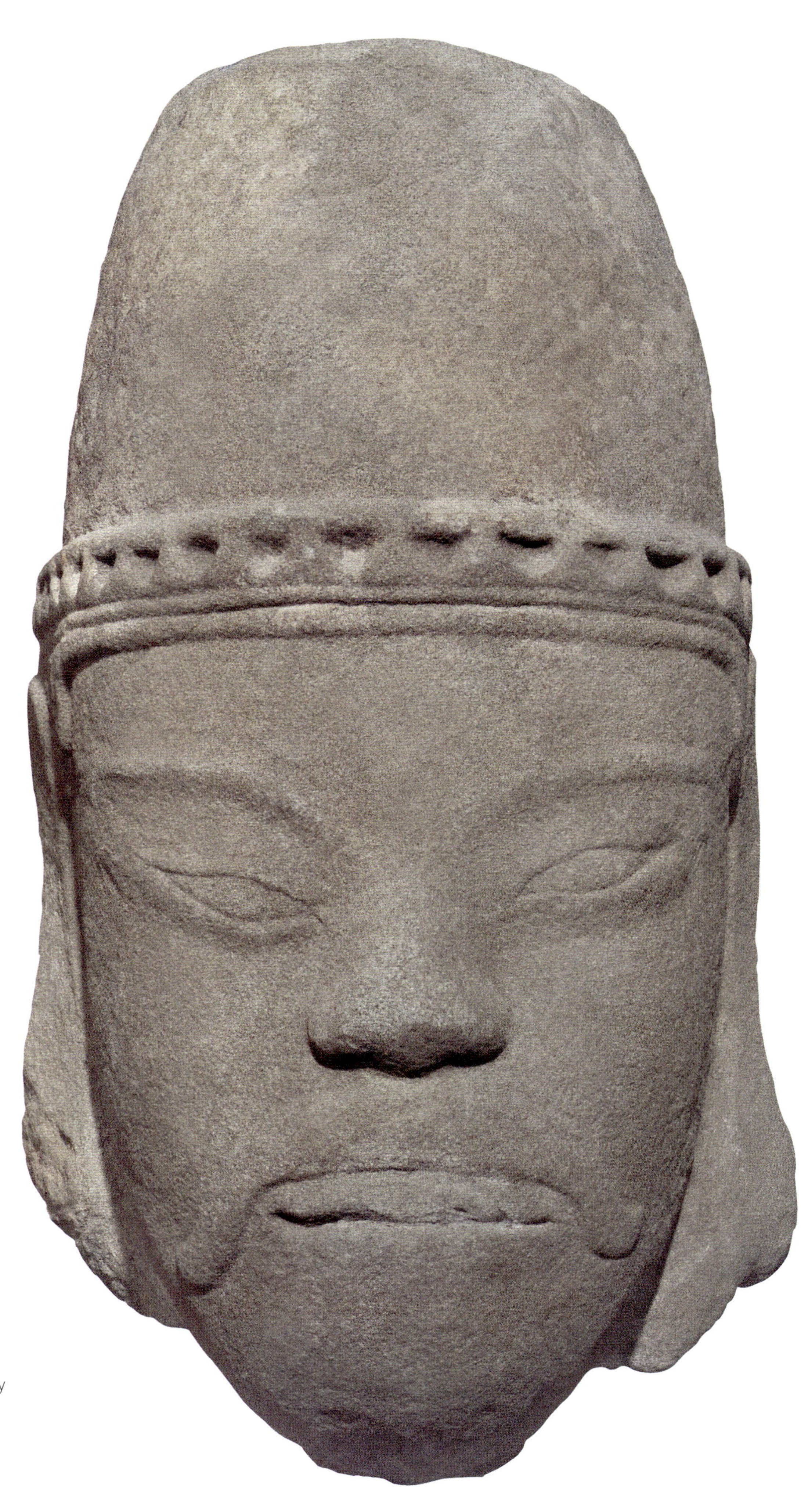

37. *Head of Dvarapala*, Nearly free-standing, Sandstone, height 35 cm, Yang Mum style, 15th Century.

The guardian has a long face and wears a mitre with a concentric lower frieze. His features recall the "terrible" side of the guardian; therefore, this is Mahakala. The "benevolent" double would be a Nandisvara. Generally, the guardians carry the emblems of the divinities that they protect.

Following Page
38. *Vishnu mitré*, Nearly free-standing, sandstone, height 25 cm, Thâp-Mam Style, 12th - 13th Century.

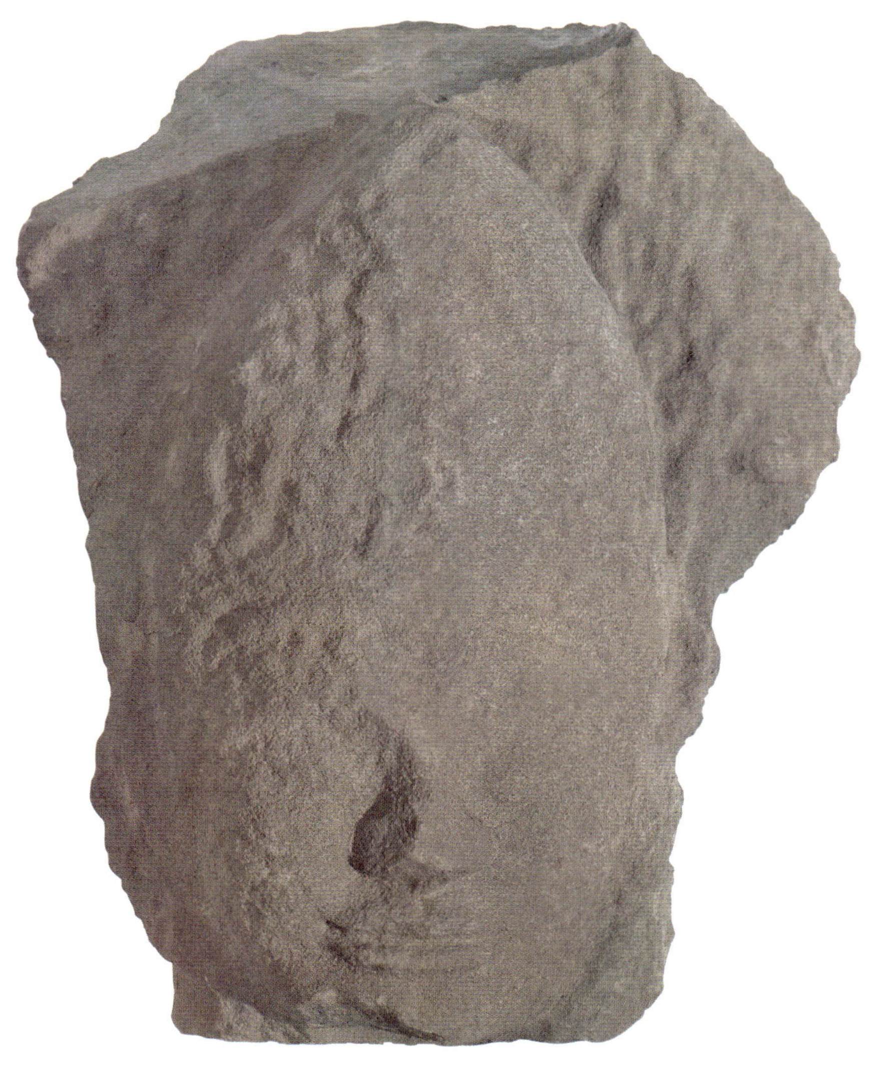

random – that we find leave room for criticism. For the sake of clarity, these sentences will not be situated in this text, but in the bibliography. Thus, Boisselier, for example, judges Cham sculptures "as much the most authentic masterpieces as the most bastardised idols of all of South-east Asia." "Bastardised"; this is an insulting adjective. Sometimes the error is more serious. "The idols first and foremost were made in high-relief and attached to stelae whereas the guardians of sanctuaries and other dvarapala continued for a long time to be sculpted as free-standing pieces". This is incorrect. The first guardians recorded (from the sixth and seventh centuries) are in high-relief.

Boisselier pays homage to the My Son E1 style (eighth century), even using the term "true masterpieces". Nevertheless, his dogmatic will to freeze the characteristics of style might lead to an absurd affirmation. Thus, for a Shiva that he cites, he brings his students to speak of "the continuation of the My Son E1 style" (eighth century) but especially to notice that that "the chignon, the jata, however, has a third braid, which will only appear two centuries later; this may then be a copy of an older statue that hoped to perpetuate the characteristics of the model." Reading this sentence allows us to imagine the difficult position in which Emmanuel Guillon, editor of this notice, found himself and we pay him homage for his fidelity; still, the argument does not seem efficient.

As well, on the subject of the Dong Duong style, Boisselier writes that this school of sculpture "happily considered as the most profoundly original, is the only one that clearly shows the influence of Chinese iconography while the resistance of Champa to all influence from the north is constant and notorious". This sentence holds its own contradiction. How can an influence be identified that – the author says so himself in the second part of his sentence – was refused? And how is it possible not to propose a logical influence, one that simple examination of the sculptures proves, from the south: from Funan first and its Khmer descendants afterwards?

Boisselier then wants to limit the intellectual expression of the Cham artist. He evokes "faces whose features are exaggerated, stylised in a manner that is practically outrageous". So be it. And then? Also, he notes, about the Thâp-Mam style, "attitudes that are often unlikely were often chosen." Unlikelihood has a right to exist in art. He further notes a "long and painful artistic decline" that does not seem to conform to reality at all. The works of the Yang Mum style are, in our opinion, stupefyingly powerful and original.

More seriously, when he adds to the styles suggested by Stern, the Khuong My (tenth century), he makes the following elucidation: "Khuong My sculptures, fairly numerous, are either a transition between Dong Duong art and the art of My Son A1 and Tra Kieu, or works that are comparable on all points to the latter, clearly establishing the bridging position of Khuong My." Let us admit that by reading these words alone, it becomes obvious that the Khuong My style cannot exist autonomously, in a defined manner, and therefore is unusable in precise dating.

In addition, Boisselier writes that in the tenth century, "External contributions, mostly Indonesian, marked the iconography of the Garuda, makara, dirti-mukha and that even Chinese or Sino-Vietnamese influence seems to appear in the Tra Kieu for the first time in Indianised South-east Asia." Nothing in the facts corroborates these affirmations.

For the purpose of simplification and in respect for the future of this research, this text uses the following chronology:

6th – 7th centuries:	Primary style
7th – 8th centuries:	My Son E1 style
9th – 10th centuries:	Dong Duong style
10th century:	Tra Kieu style
10th – 11th centuries:	Chien Dan style
11th – 13th centuries:	Thâp-Mam style
14th – 15th centuries:	Yang Mum style.

Each of these styles groups the characteristics listed above, thereby constituting standard models that can be accompanied by variations.

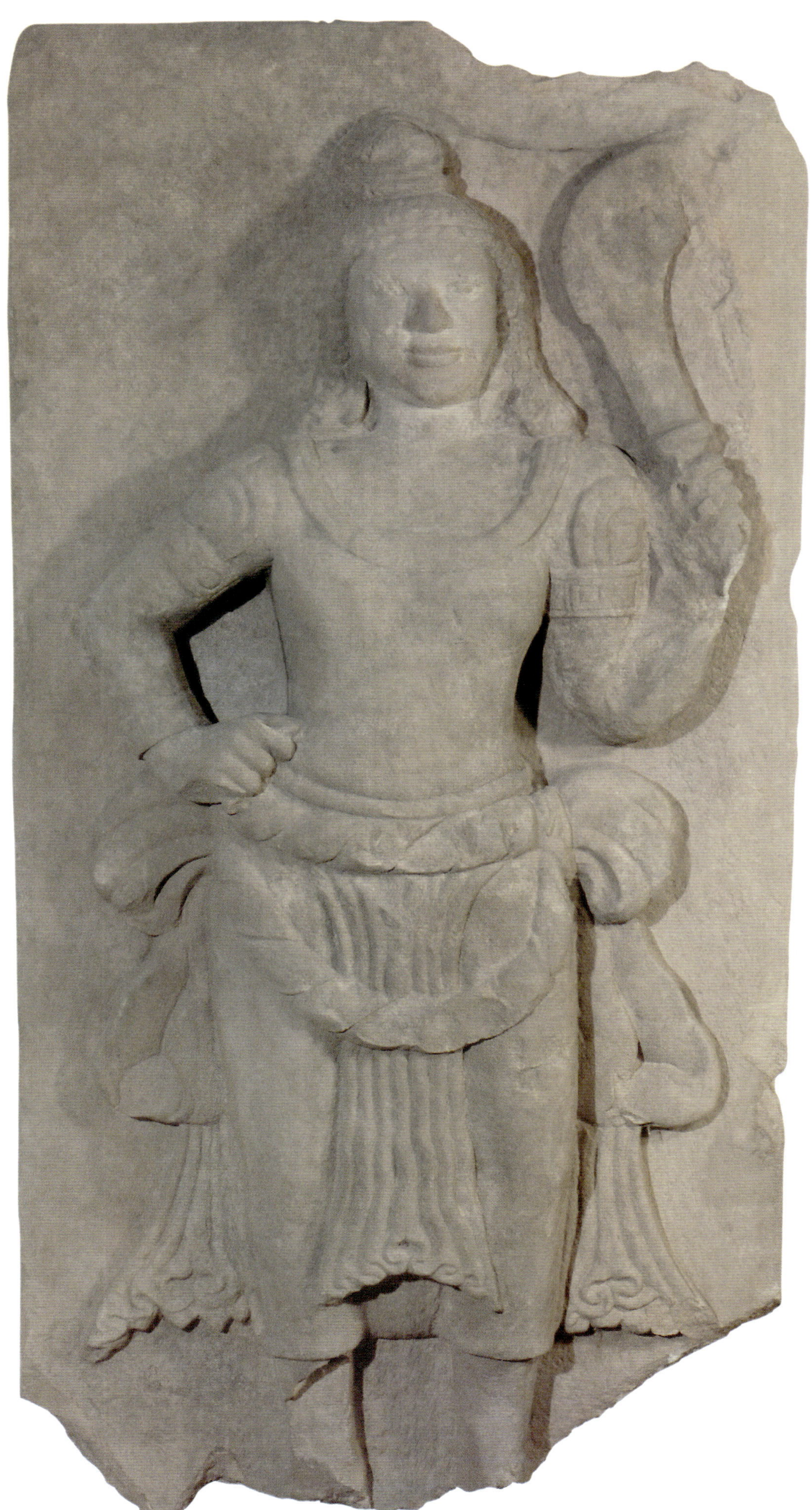

39. *Dvarapala*, High-relief, Sandstone, height 160 cm, Primary style, 6th - 7th Century.

Following Page

40. *Dvarapala*, High-relief, Sandstone, height 144 cm, Primary style, 6th - 7th Century.

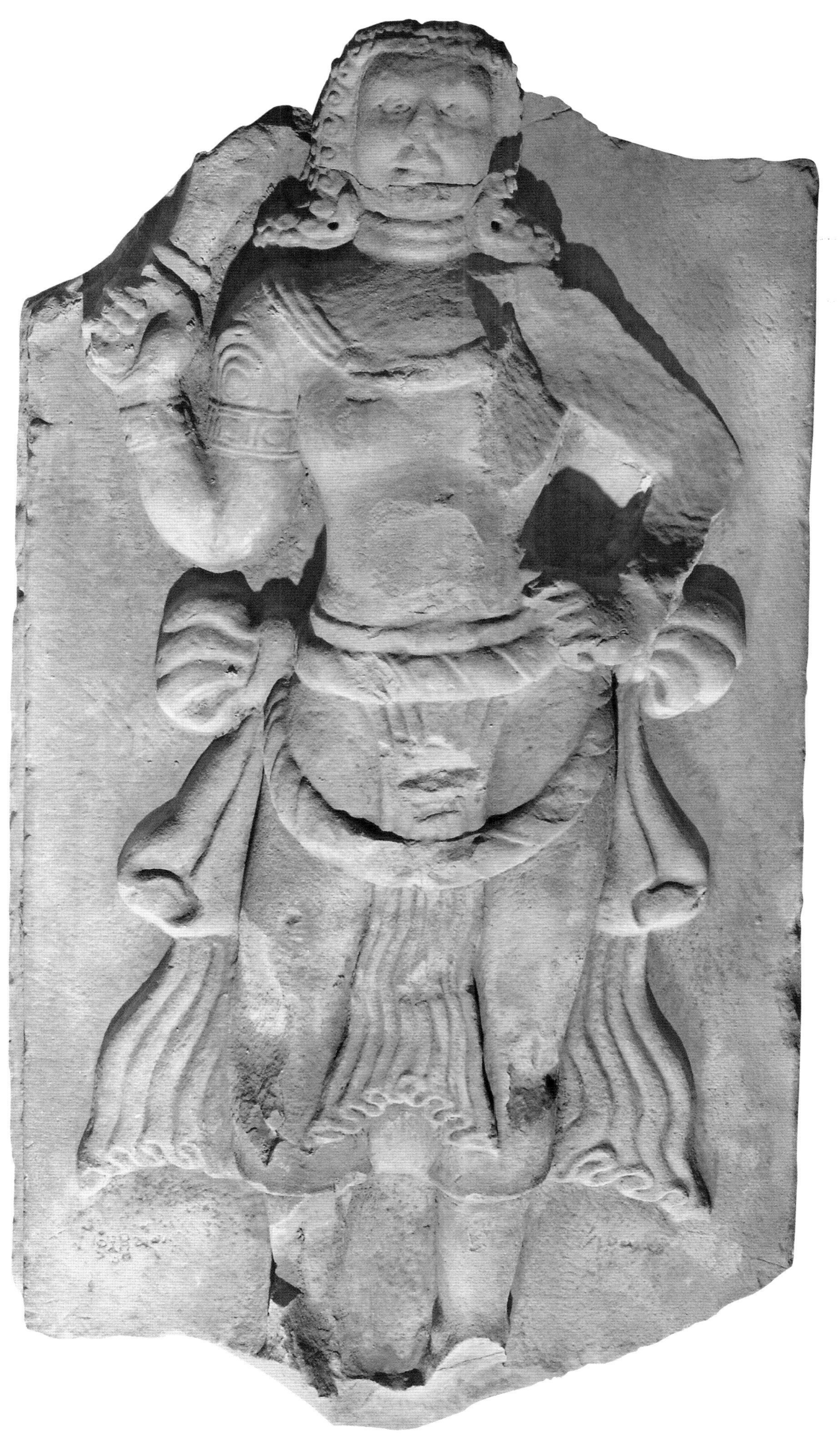

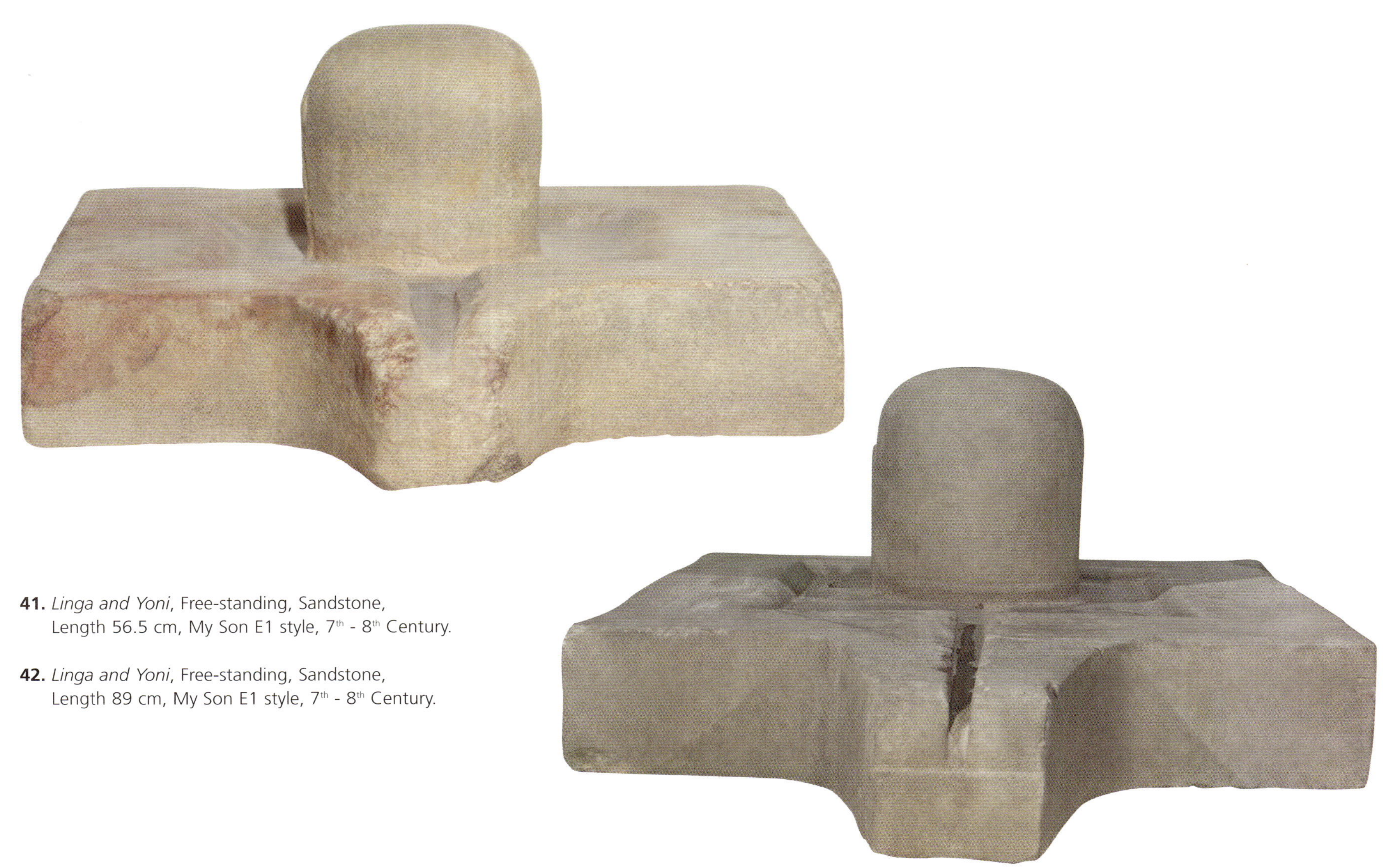

41. *Linga and Yoni*, Free-standing, Sandstone, Length 56.5 cm, My Son E1 style, 7th - 8th Century.

42. *Linga and Yoni*, Free-standing, Sandstone, Length 89 cm, My Son E1 style, 7th - 8th Century.

The linga, symbol of Shiva, is interpreted in various ways in Cham art. A typology can be established according to the shape and possible ornamentation.

The "standard" linga has three parts with, from bottom to top, a prismatic lower section with a square base, an octagonal middle section and a cylindrical domed top section. Each of these sections is defined by a Sanskrit name: Brahmabhaga, Vishnubhaga and Rudrabhaga, in reference to the founding gods of the Brahman trinity. "Standard" linga is used, because linga with single sections (Rudrabhaga) do exist, as do linga with two sections (lacking either the Brahmabhaga or the Vishnubhaga).

Some of the linga are sculpted, or simply etched with a single face (ekalinga) or multiple faces, or with a dividing line (never very realistic in Cham art) called the jatalinga.

The yoni, a horizontal stone, represents manifest energy. The linga, when associated with the yoni, symbolises the male and female energies of Shiva and his creative and destructive functions. This symbol, absent from the Vedas, is purely a creation of Indian-Hindu thought transmitted to the entire sphere of influence and notably to Champa.

The linga must constantly be kept wet by the faithful. They accomplish their task by pouring a liquid onto it that is usually water but can also be milk, butter, even honey and flowers at times. The somasutra, or groove in the yoni, always points northward. It allows the liquids of homage to drain away to the outside of the sanctuary.

A three-part linga either has three equal parts or has parts that are divided according to certain proportions. The respective dimensions of the sections vary depending on the texts referred to. Thus, a linga venerated by Brahmans must have, from the bottom, three parts that proportionally correspond to 4, 5, 6 or 7, 7, 8. For the Ksathrya, the proportion must be 5, 6, 7 or 5, 5, 6; for the Vaishya, 6, 7, 8 or 4, 4, 5 and for the Shudra 7, 8, 9 or 3, 3, 4.

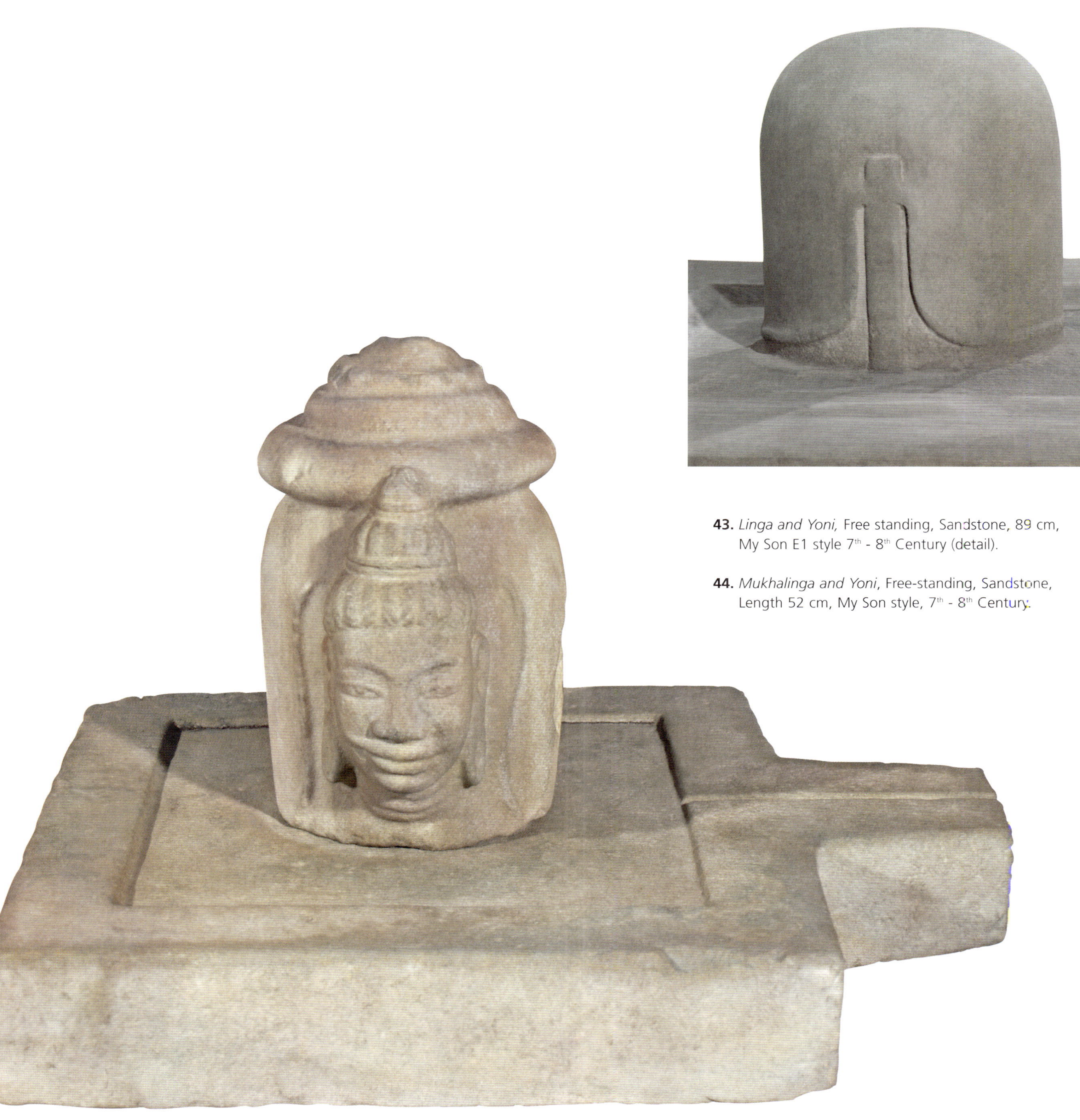

43. *Linga and Yoni,* Free standing, Sandstone, 89 cm, My Son E1 style 7th - 8th Century (detail).

44. *Mukhalinga and Yoni*, Free-standing, Sandstone, Length 52 cm, My Son style, 7th - 8th Century.

The linga, equipped with a quadrangular tenon 5 cm long, can be removed.

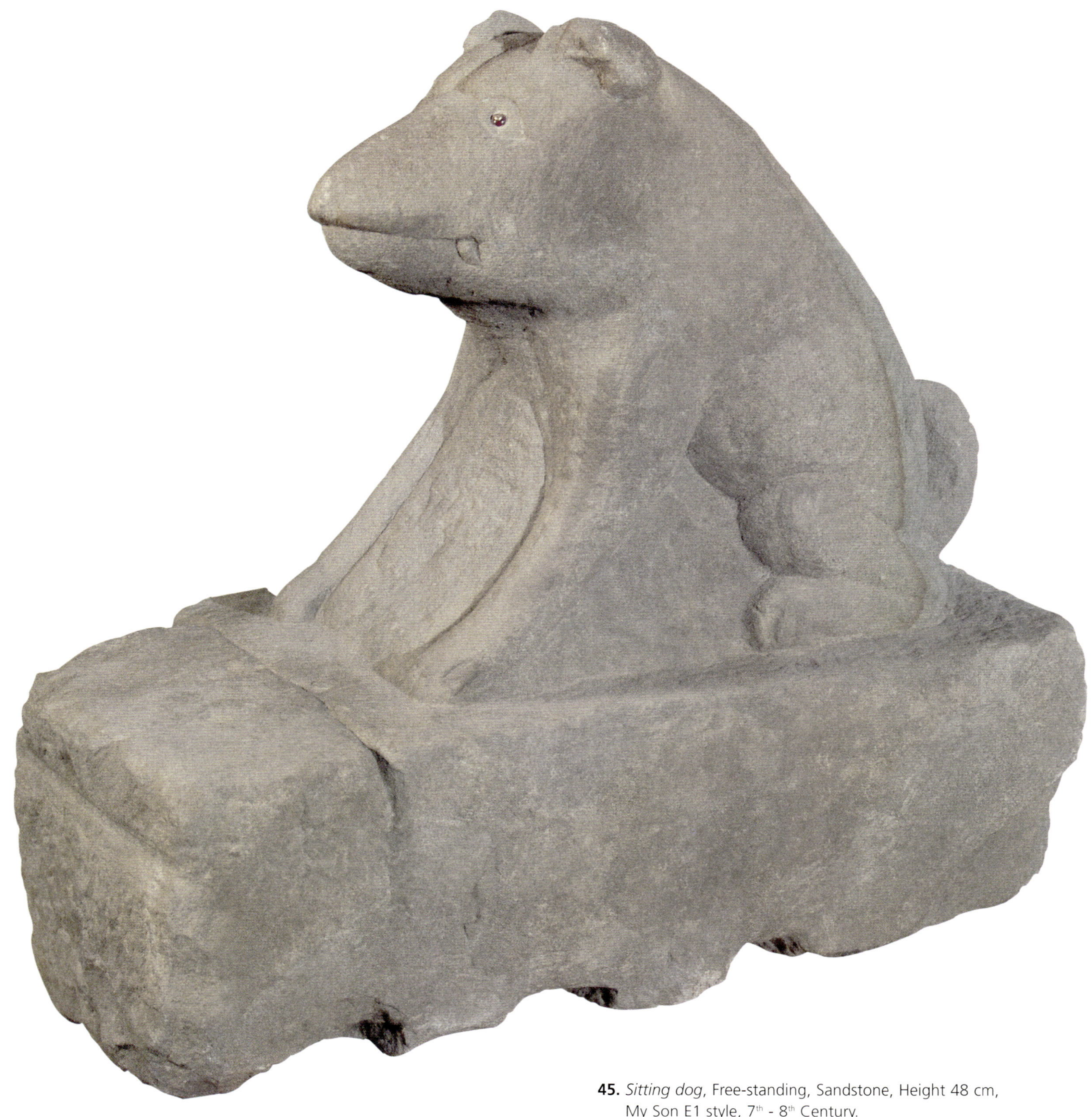

45. *Sitting dog*, Free-standing, Sandstone, Height 48 cm, My Son E1 style, 7th - 8th Century.

Following Page
46. *Sitting dog*, Free-standing, Sandstone, Height 48 cm, My Son E1 style, 7th - 8th Century (detail).

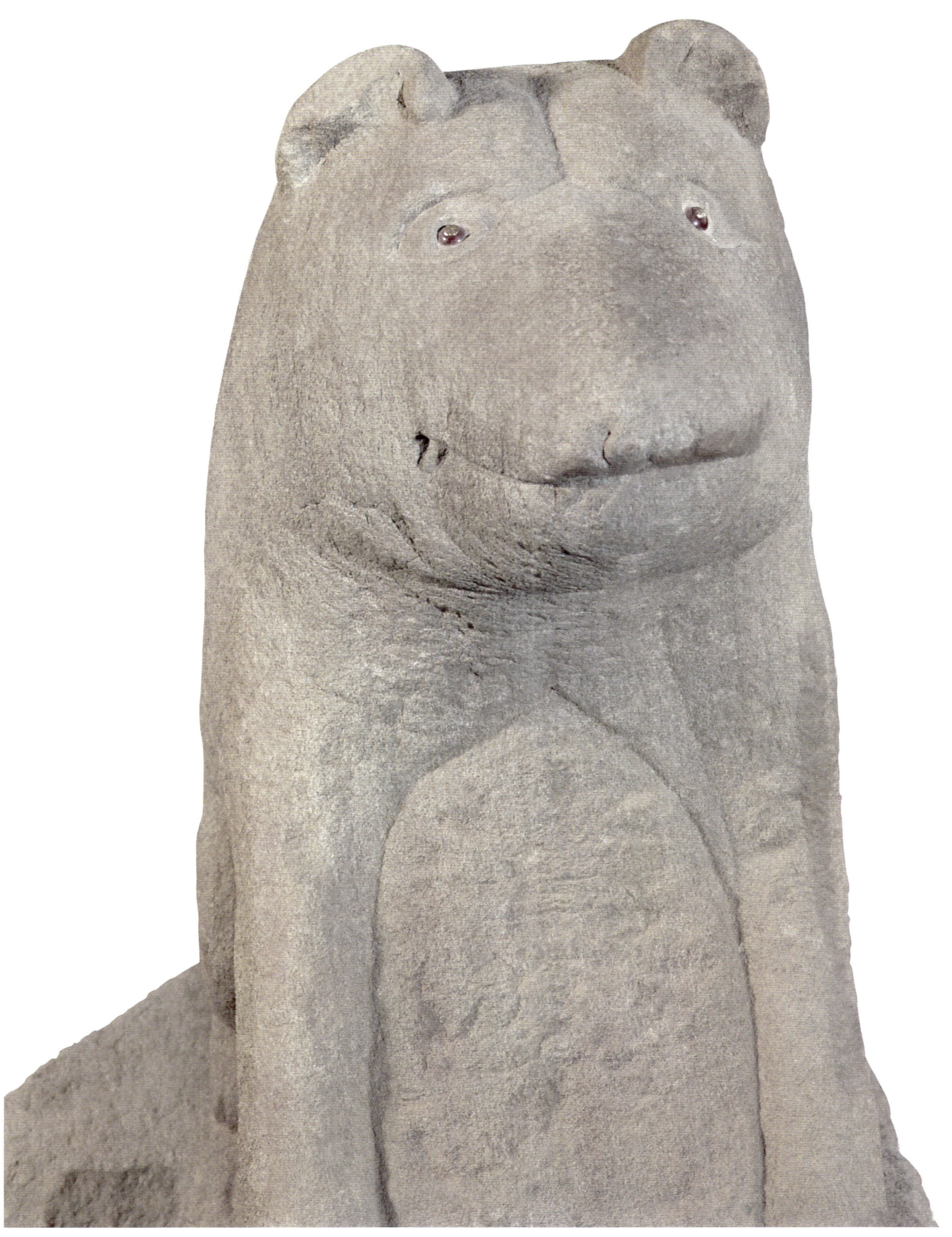

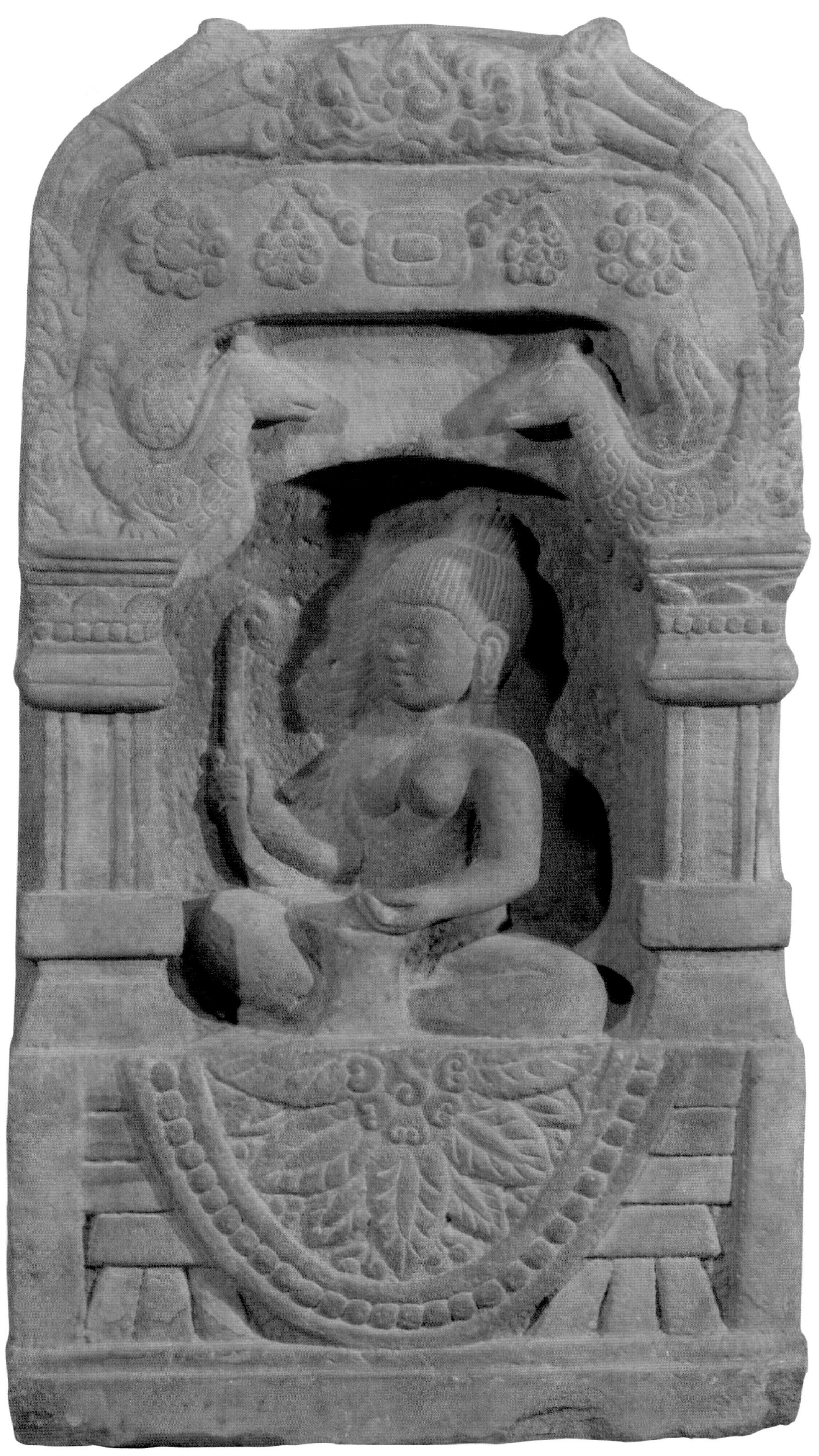

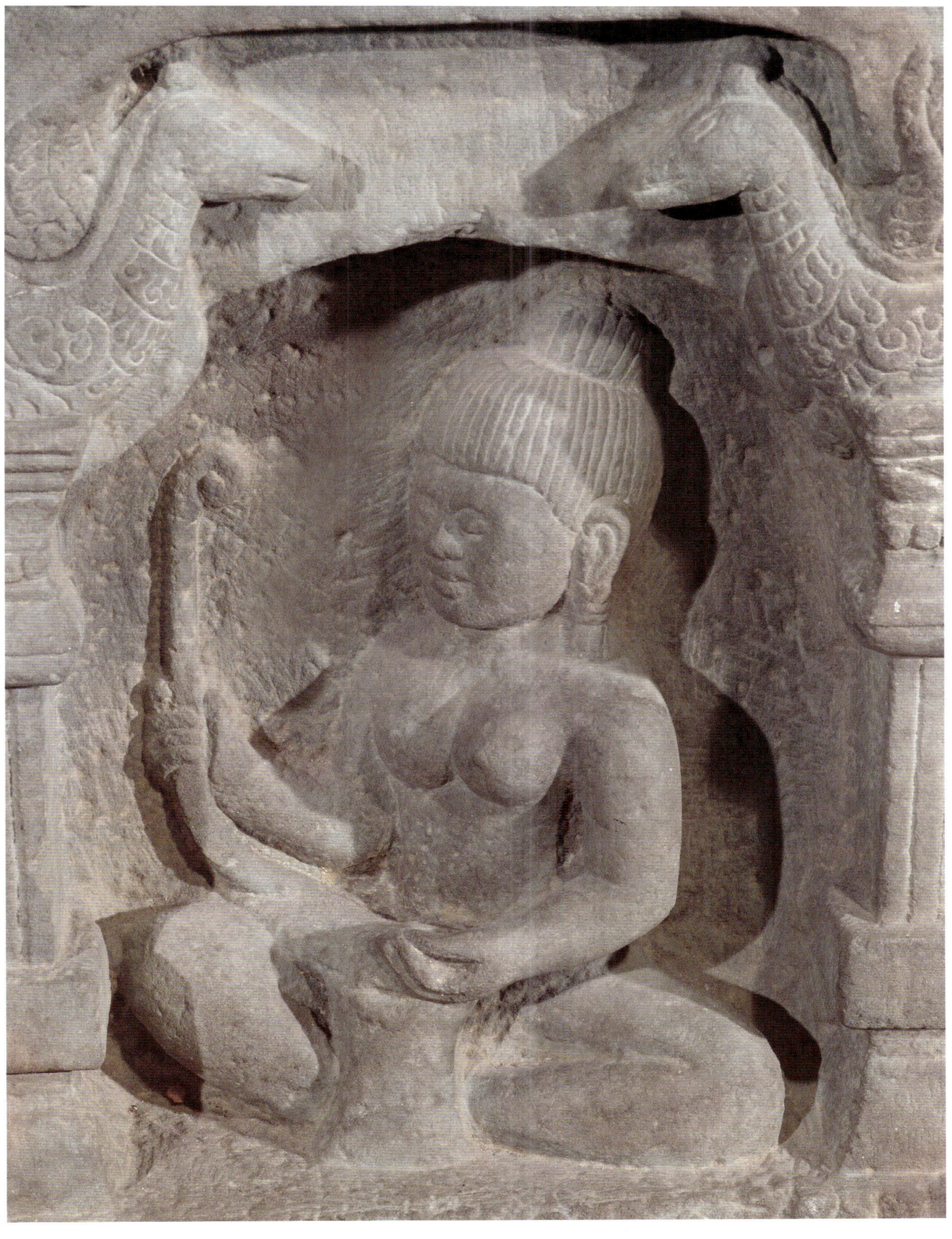

Previous Page
47. *Rama* High-relief, Sandstone, Height 75 cm,
My Sơn E1 style, 7th - 8th Century.

48. *Rama* High-relief, Sandstone, Height 75 cm,
My Sơn E1 style, 7th - 8th Century (detail).

Rama, the "charming" in Sanskrit is an avatar of Vishnu. Hero of Ramayana, his weapon is the the bow.

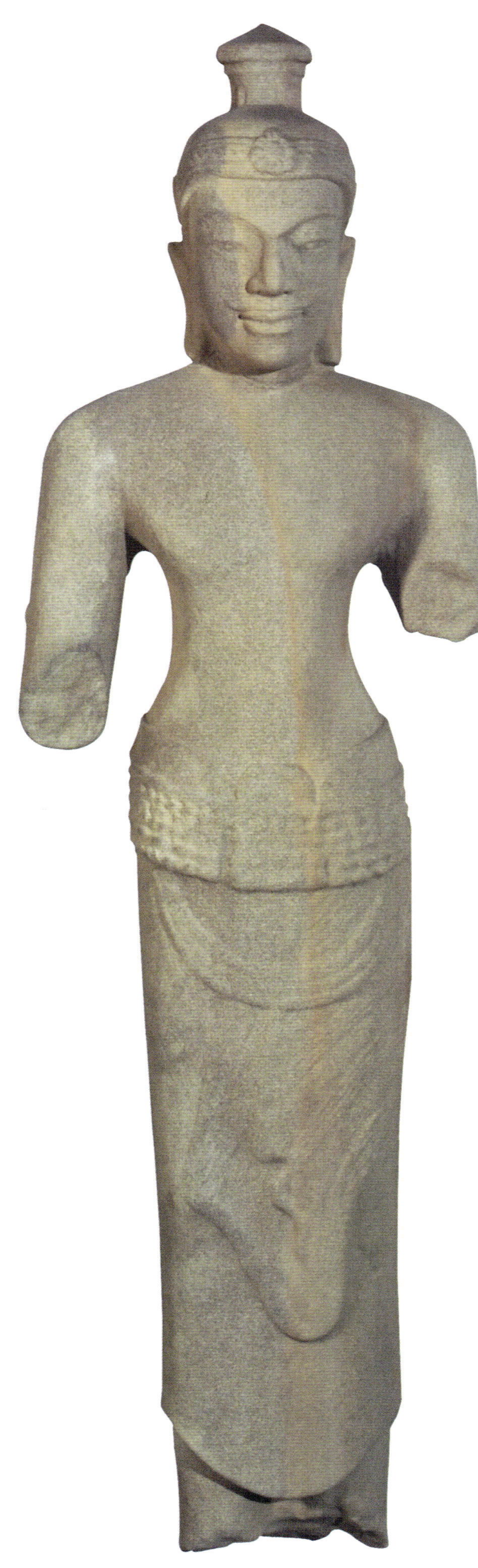

The god is identifiable by the eye in his forehead. The hair is worn like a skullcap topped by a ringed, octagonal, vertical element and held in place by a diadem with three large rosettes. The face has heavy lips and a rather imposing moustache. The nose is straight and the eyebrows touch. The pupils are noticeably raised. The clothing, held by two belts, hangs very low. It is notably by comparing this style of dress to that found on figures on the tympani of My Son E1 and My Son C1 that it is evident that dating from the eighth century should be retained.

49. *Shiva*, Free-standing, Sandstone, height 78 cm, My Son E1 style, 8th Century.

Following Page
50. *Garuda*, High relief, Sandstone, Height 110 cm, My Son E1 style, 7th - 8th Century.

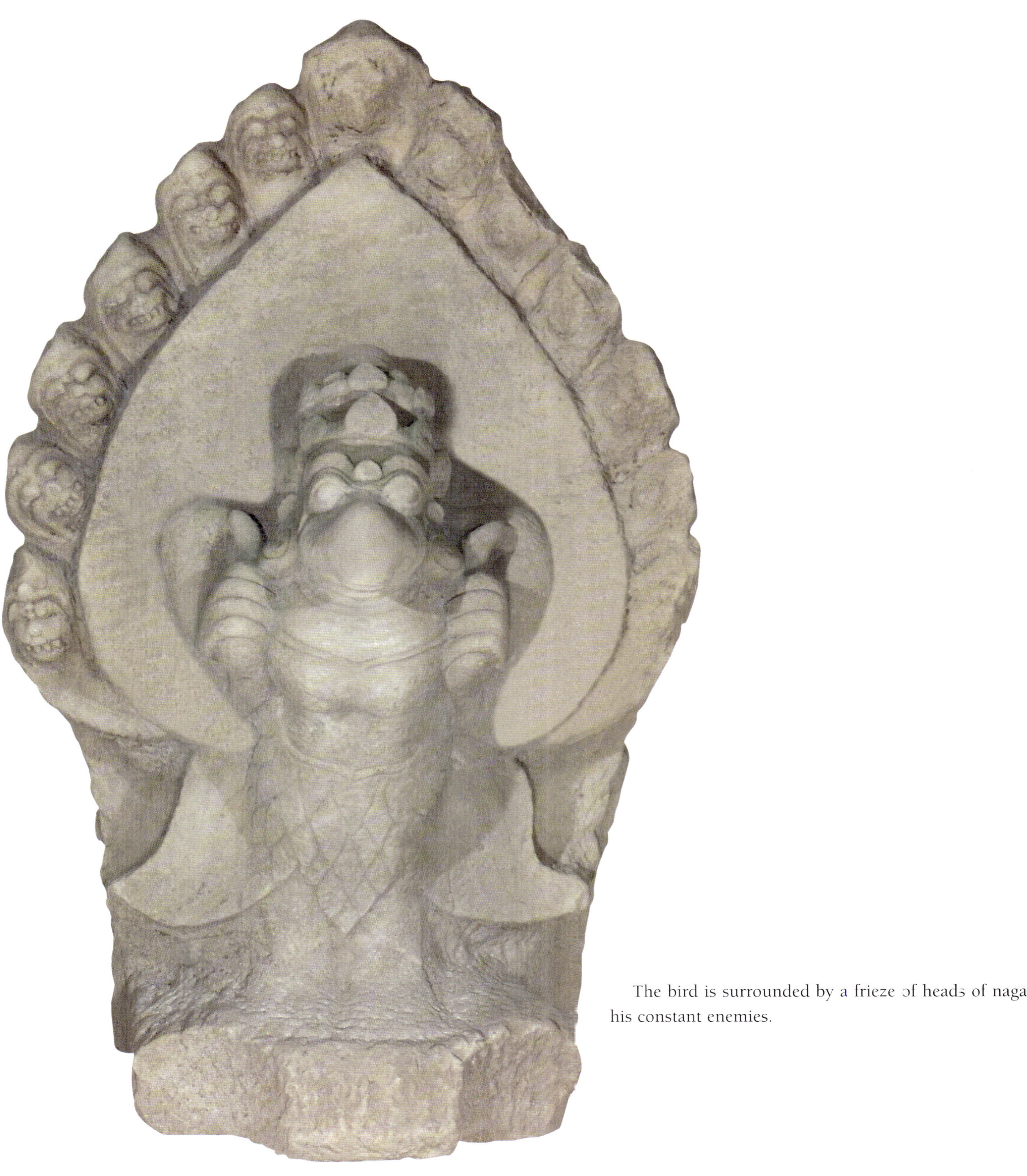

The bird is surrounded by a frieze of heads of naga, his constant enemies.

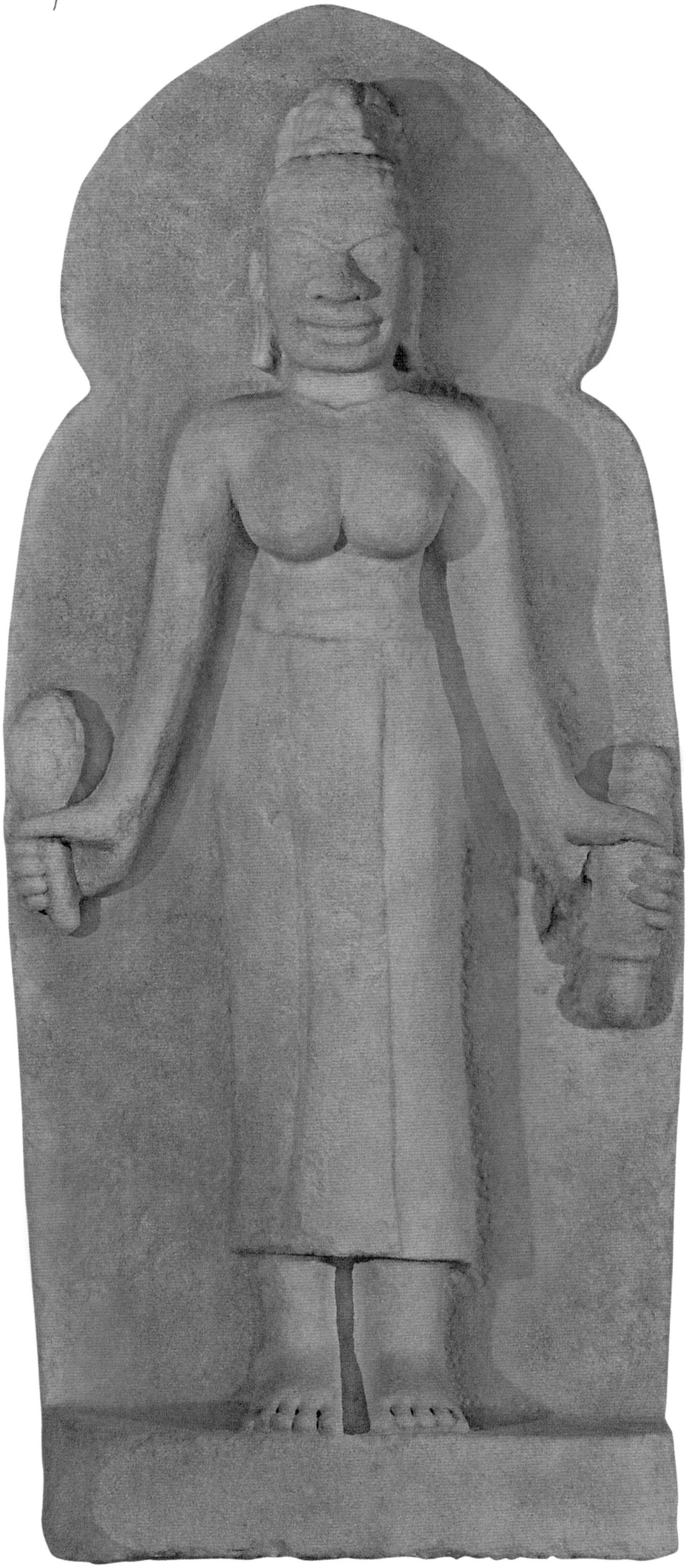

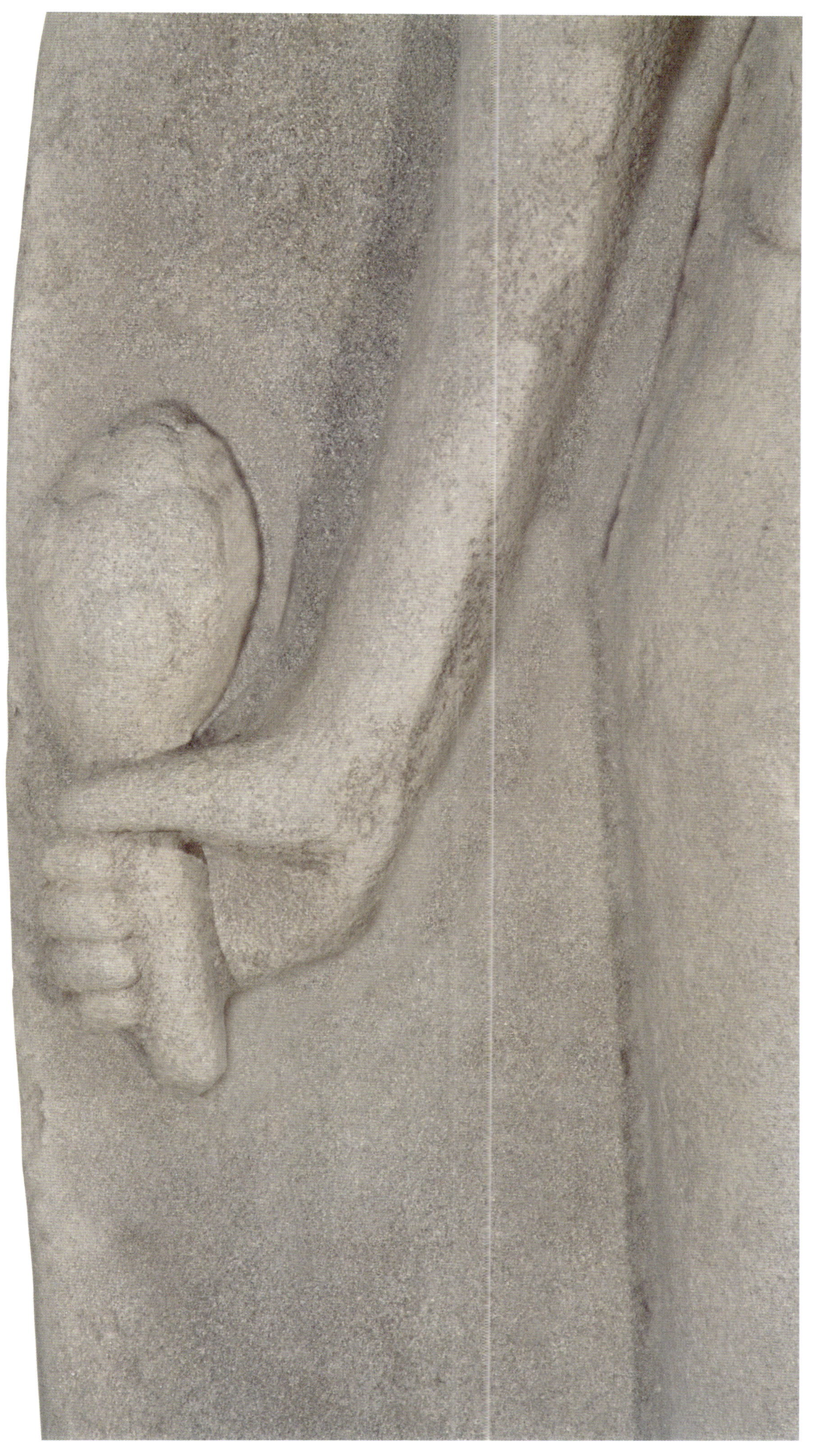

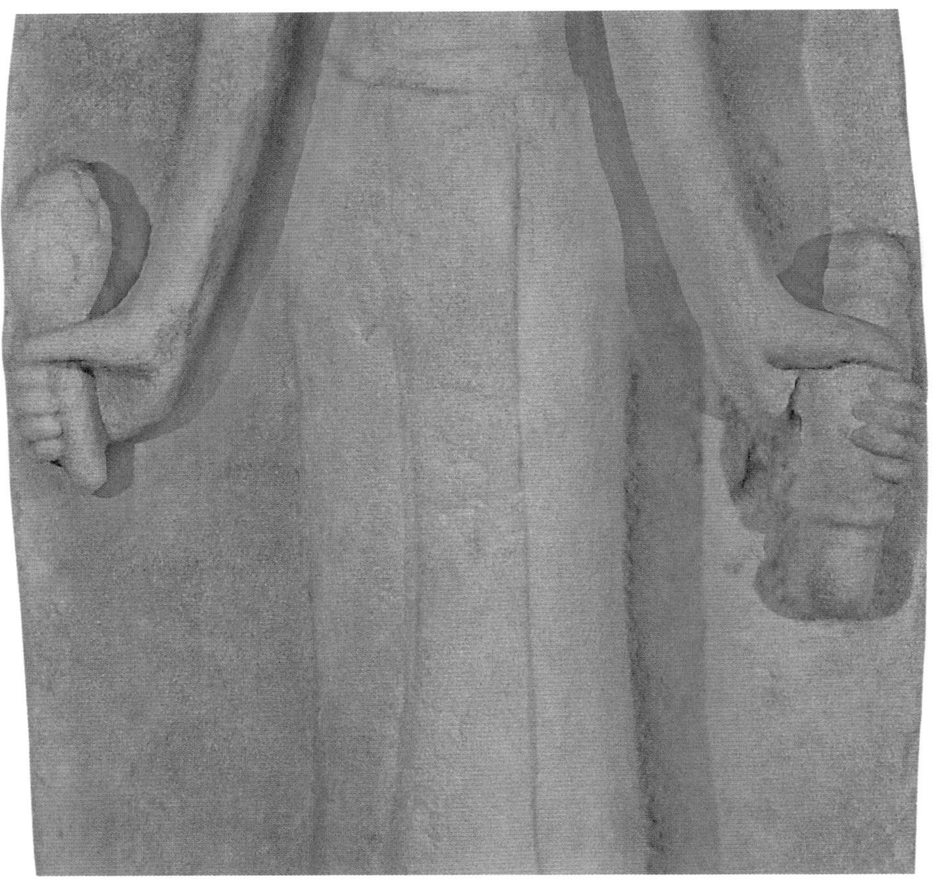

Vajrapani or Prajnaparamita ("perfection of divine wisdom"), Lokesvara's consort (who is a bodhisattva) wears the Amitabha Buddha in the front of her hair. A tuft of hair, the urna, can be noticed on her forehead; this is sometimes confused with the eye of Shiva. The divinity is holding a lotus flower in her right hand and a Vajra ("diamond-lightning") or long flask in her left. The torso bears three discreet rolls of fat. The god's back is against a support; his arms are flattened against an ogival recess. The sarong is undecorated. The large smile and very elongated eyes with an indication of the pupil are worthy of note.

Page 60

51. *Vajrapani or Prajnaparamita*, High relief, Sandstone, Height 88.5 cm (without the tenon), Dong Duong style, 9th - 10th Century.

52. *Vajrapani or Prajnaparamita*, High relief, Sandstone, Height 88.5 cm (without the tenon), Dong Duong style, 9th - 10th Century, (detail of the Lotus Flower).

53. *Vajrapani or Prajnaparamita*, High relief, Sandstone, Height 88.5 cm (without the tenon), Dong Duong style, 9th - 10th Century (detail).

Following Page

54. *Vajrapani or Prajnaparamita*, High relief, Sandstone, Height 88.5 cm (without the tenon), Dong Duong style, 9th - 10th Century (detail of Face).

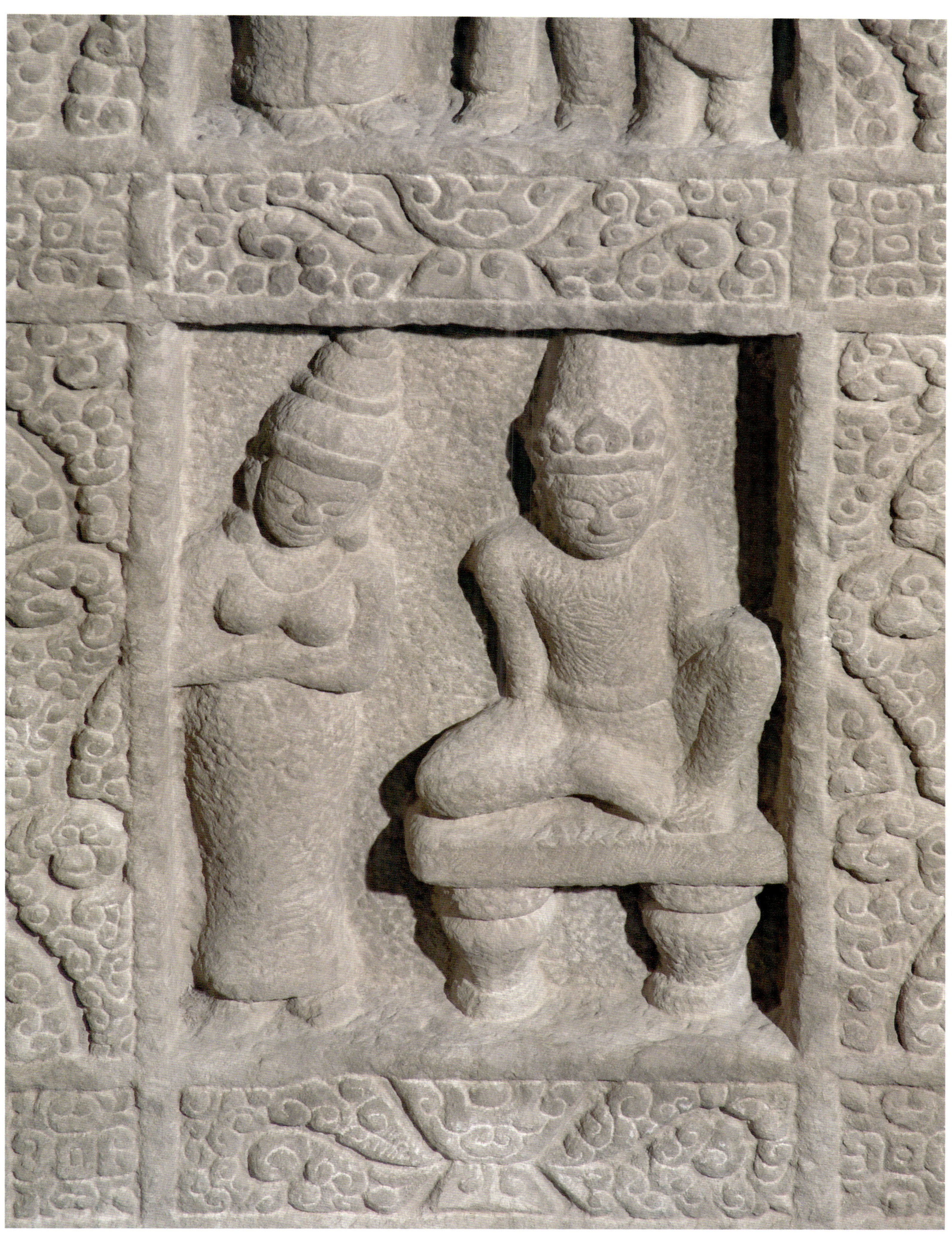

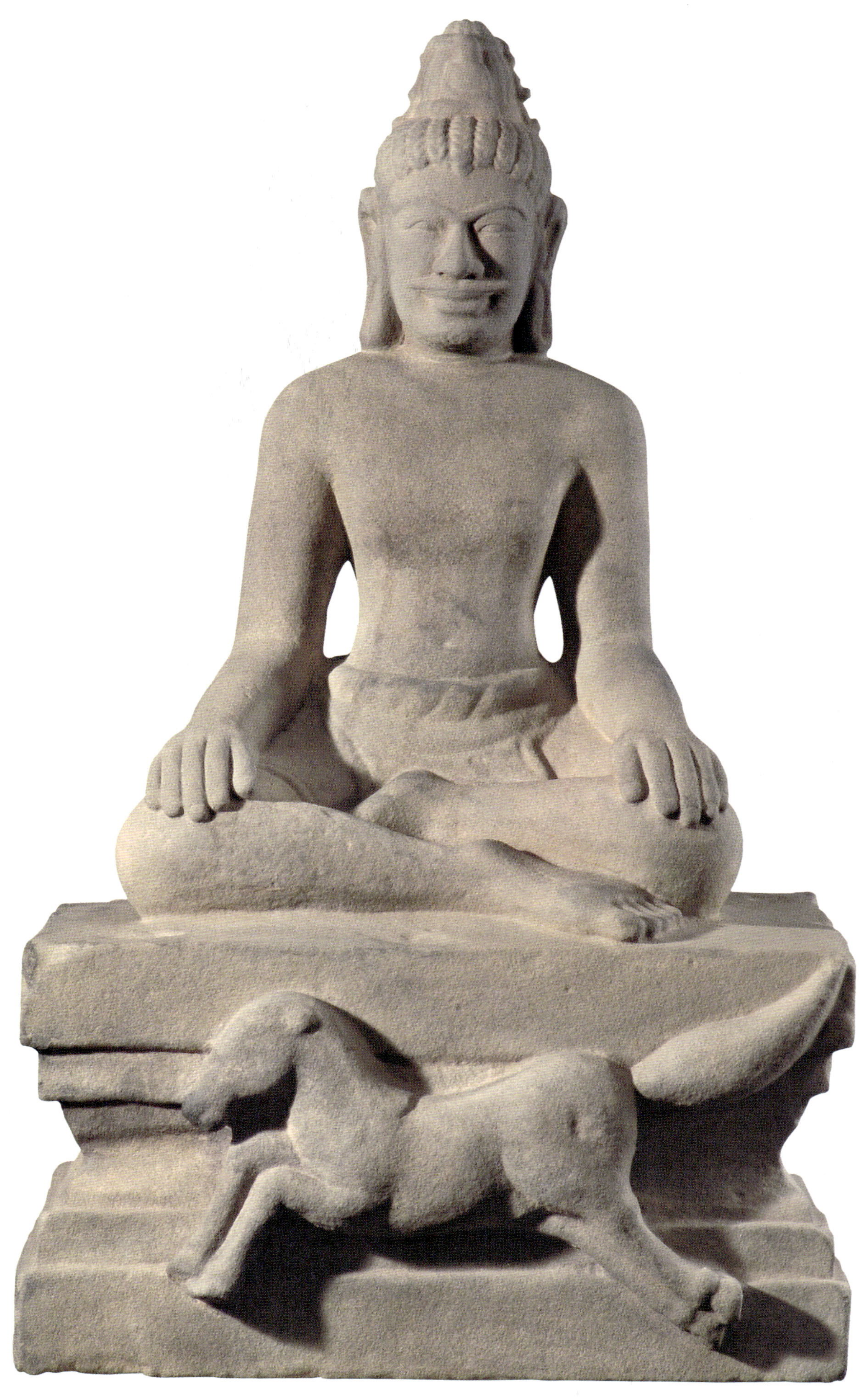

A bas-relief of a horse, a god's mount, on the front of a tiered base. The sculpture is monolithic.

Previous Page
69. *Vayu*, Free-standing, Sandstone, Height 100 cm, Dong Duong style, 9th - 10th Century.

70. *Vayu*, Free-standing, Sandstone, Height 100 cm, Dong Duong style, 9th - 10th Century (profile).

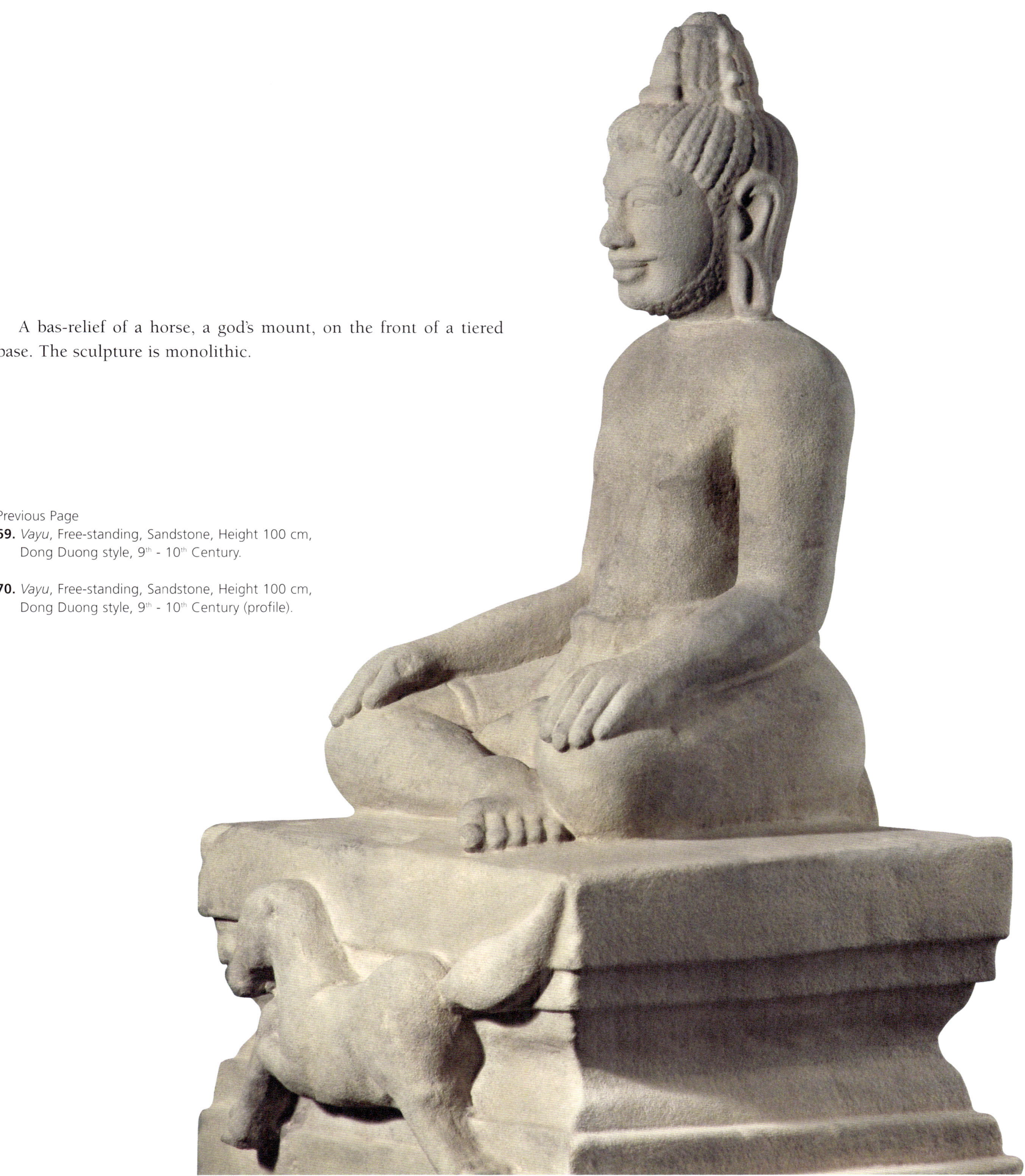

A monolithic piece as the previous one. Bayu is sitting in sattvaparyanka, with the left leg over the right. The top of the sampot and its belt can be seen.

The god's mount, a horse, is sculpted in high-relief on the front of a tiered base.

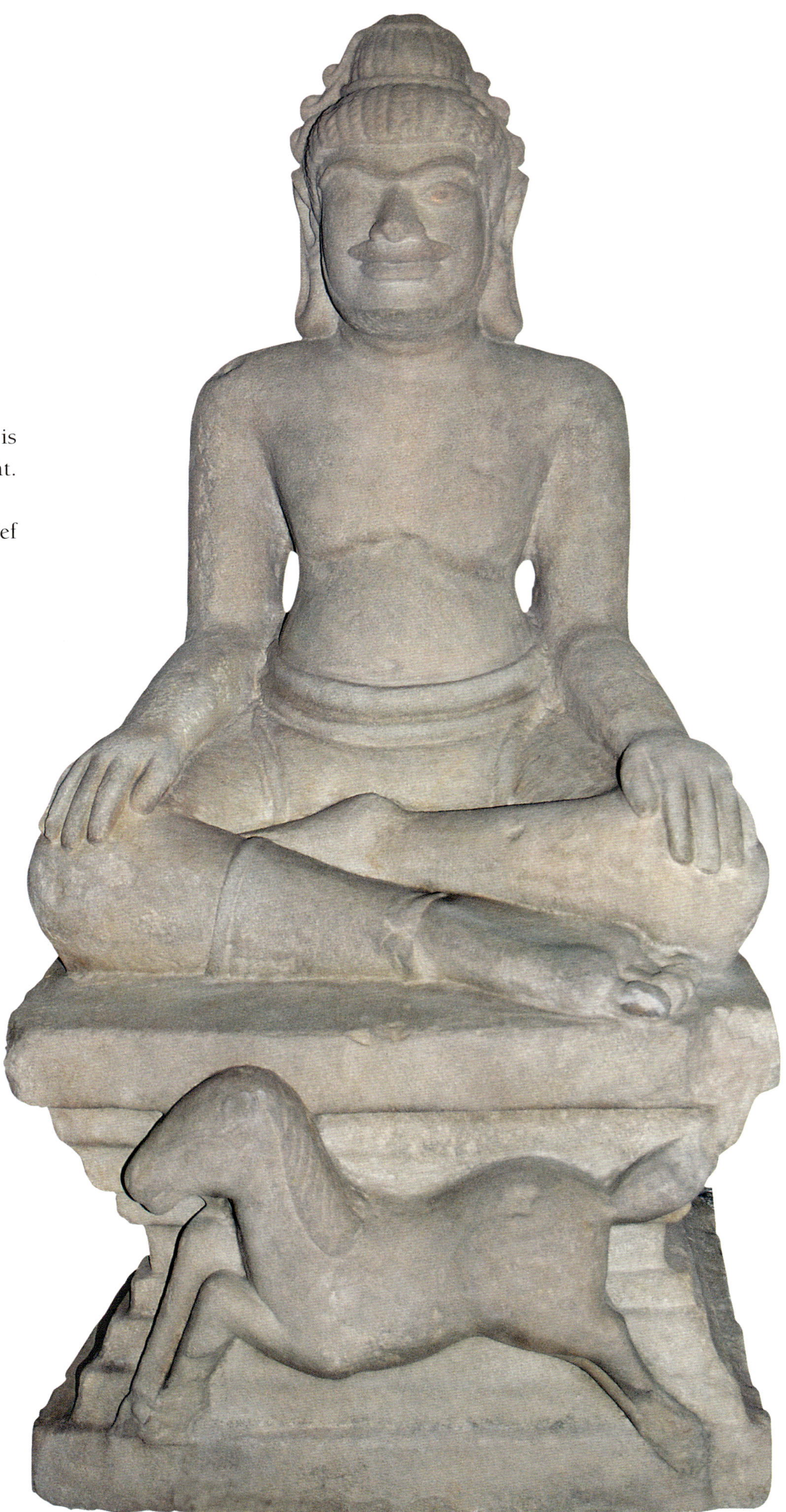

71. *Vayu*, Free-standing, Sandstone, Height 100 cm, Dong Duong style, 9th - 10th Century.

Following Page
72. *Donor*, High-relief, Sandstone, Height 53 cm, Dong Duong style, 9th - 10th Century

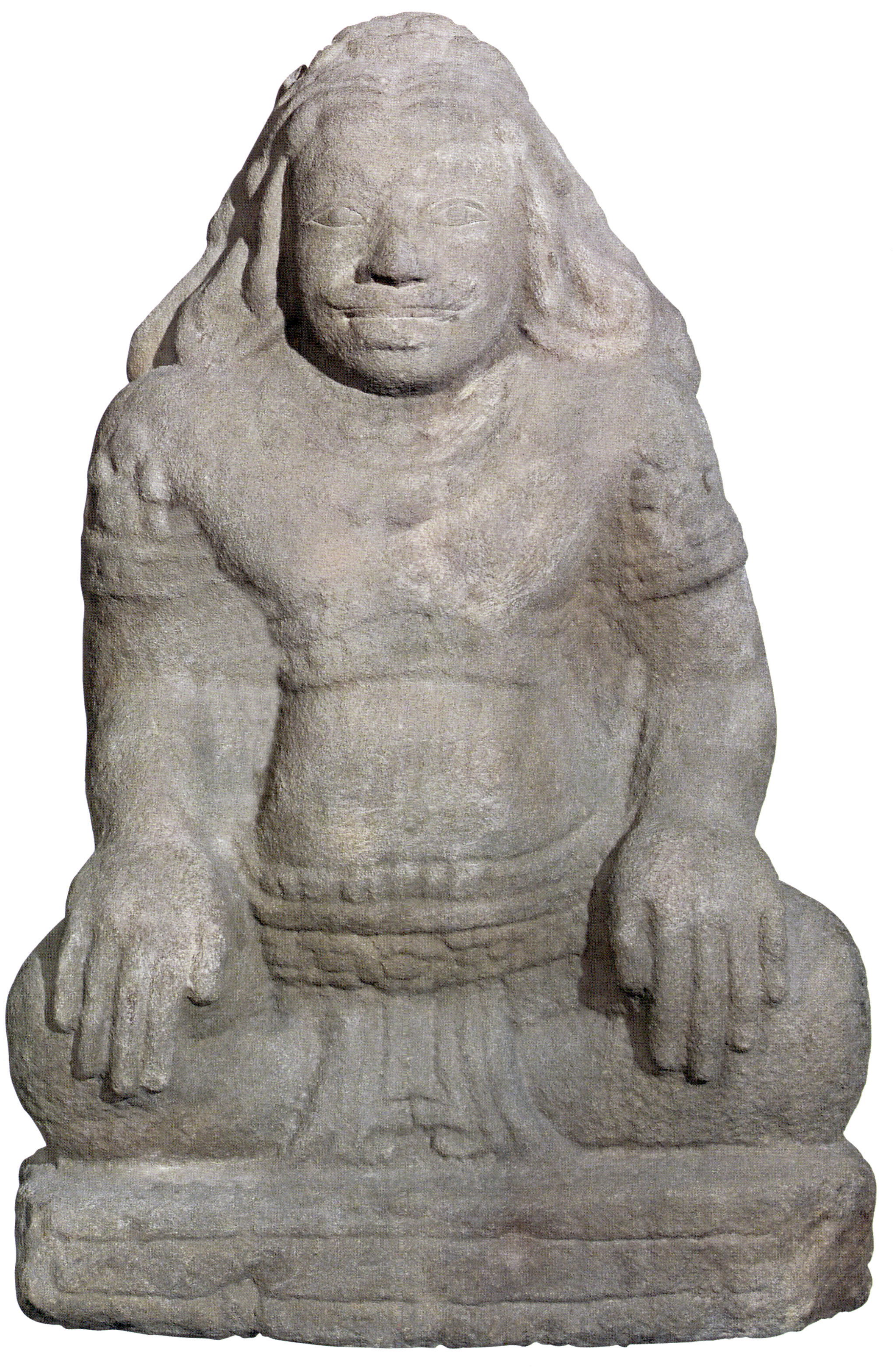

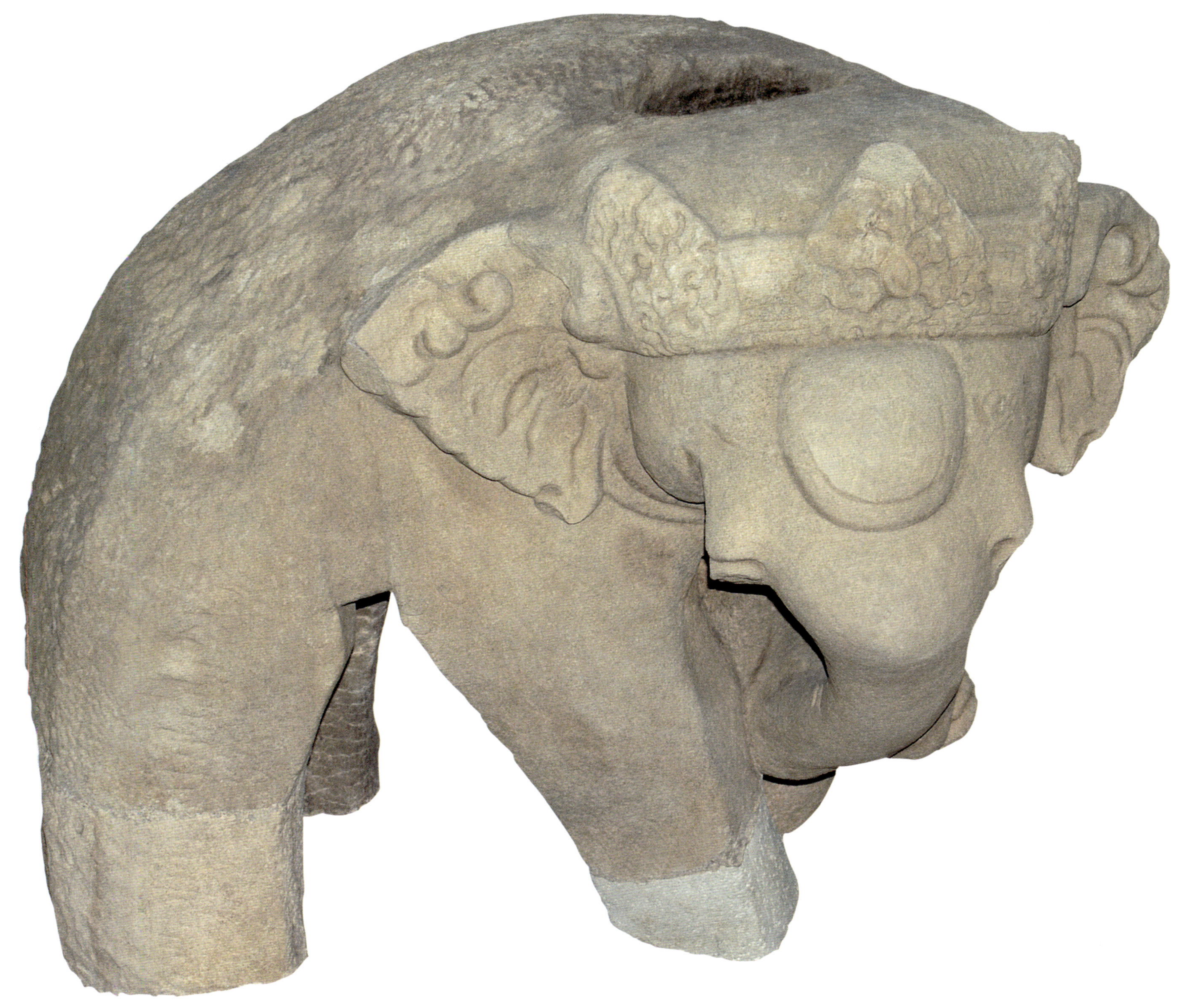

73. *Elephant*, Free-standing, Sandstone, Height 100 cm, Dong Duong style, 9th - 10th Century.

Following Page
74. *Dancer*, Bas-relief, Sandstone, Height 89 cm, Dong Duong style, 9th - 10th Century.

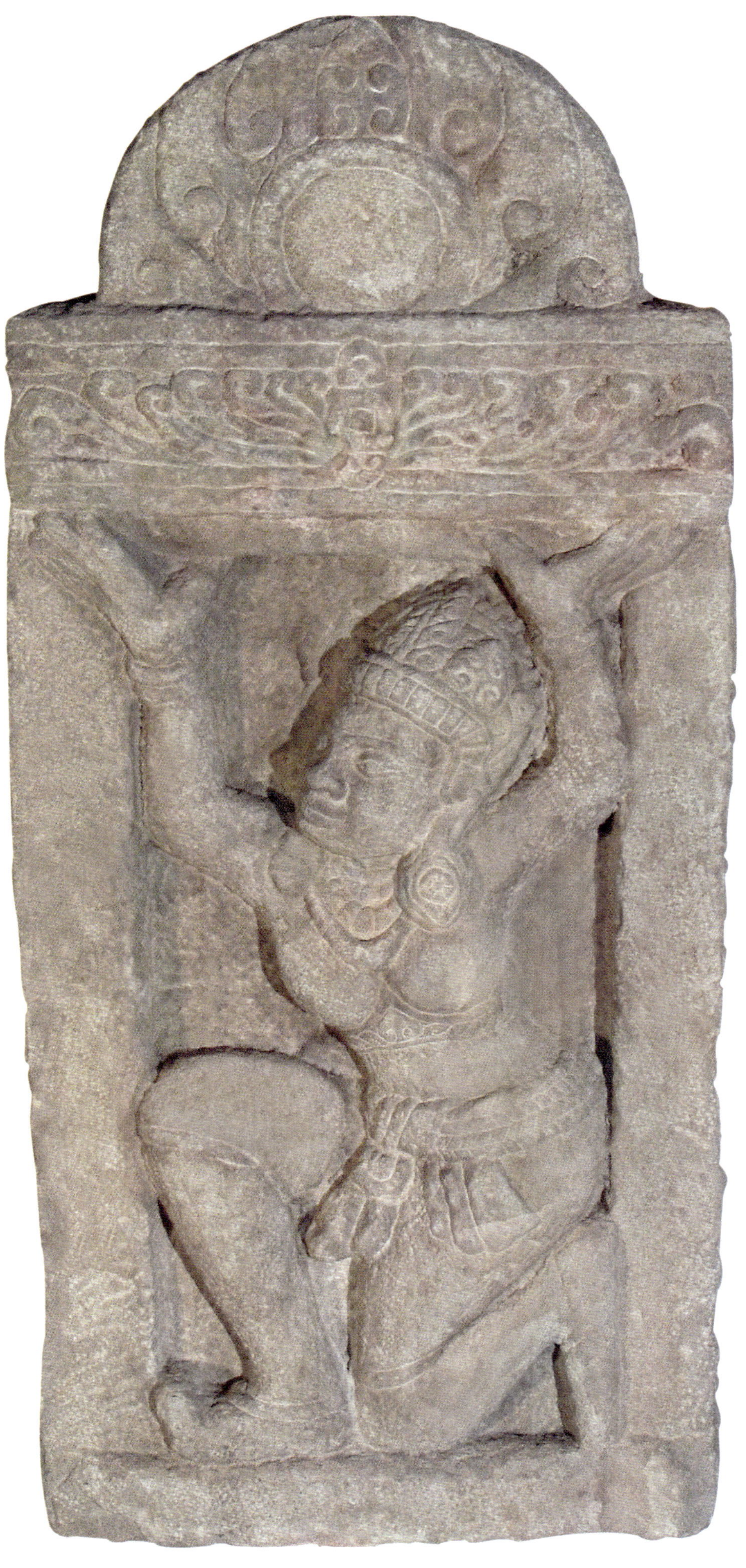

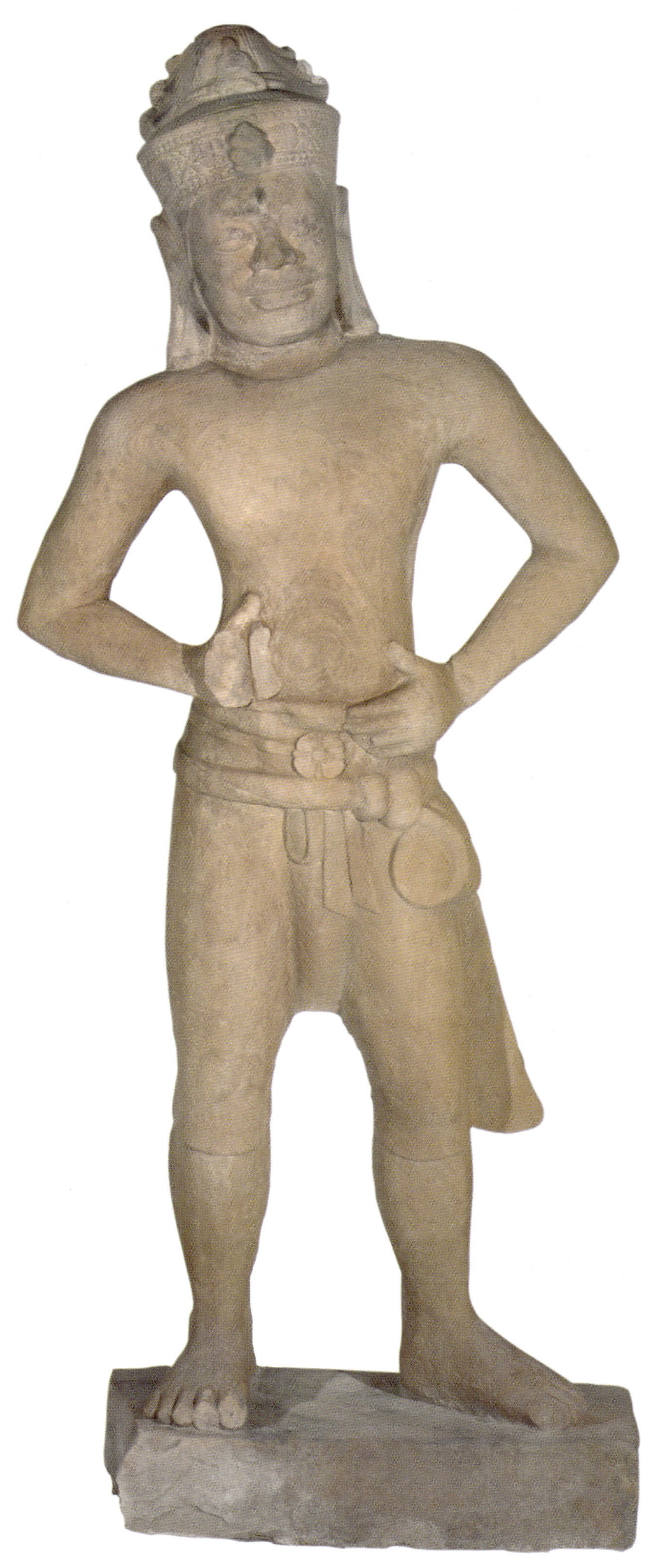

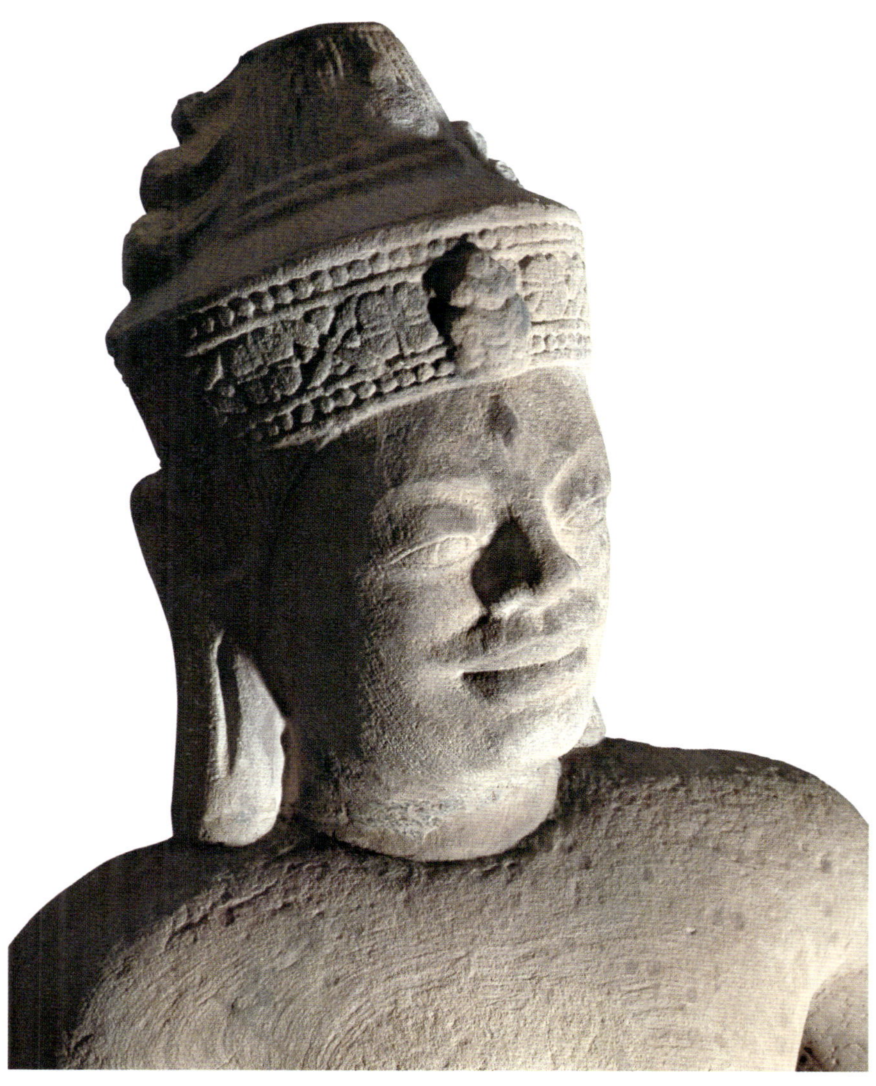

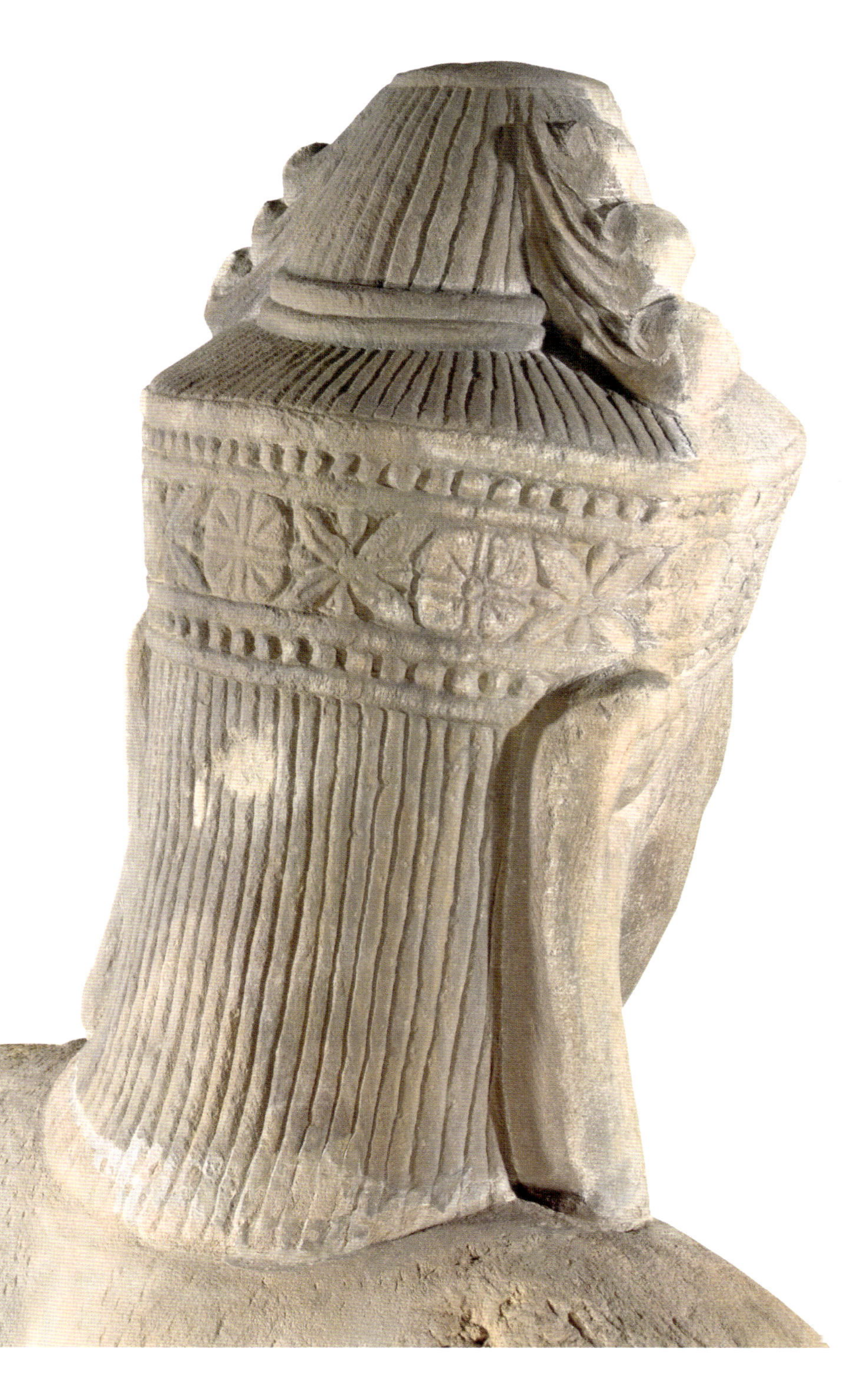

Previous Page

75. *Dvarapala*, Free-standing, Sandstone, Height 175 cm, Dong Duong style, 9th - 10th Century.

76. *Dvarapala*, Free-standing, Sandstone, Height 175 cm, Dong Duong style, 9th - 10th Century (detail).

77. *Dvarapala*, Free-standing, Sandstone, Height 175 cm, Dong Duong style, 9th - 10th Century (detail).

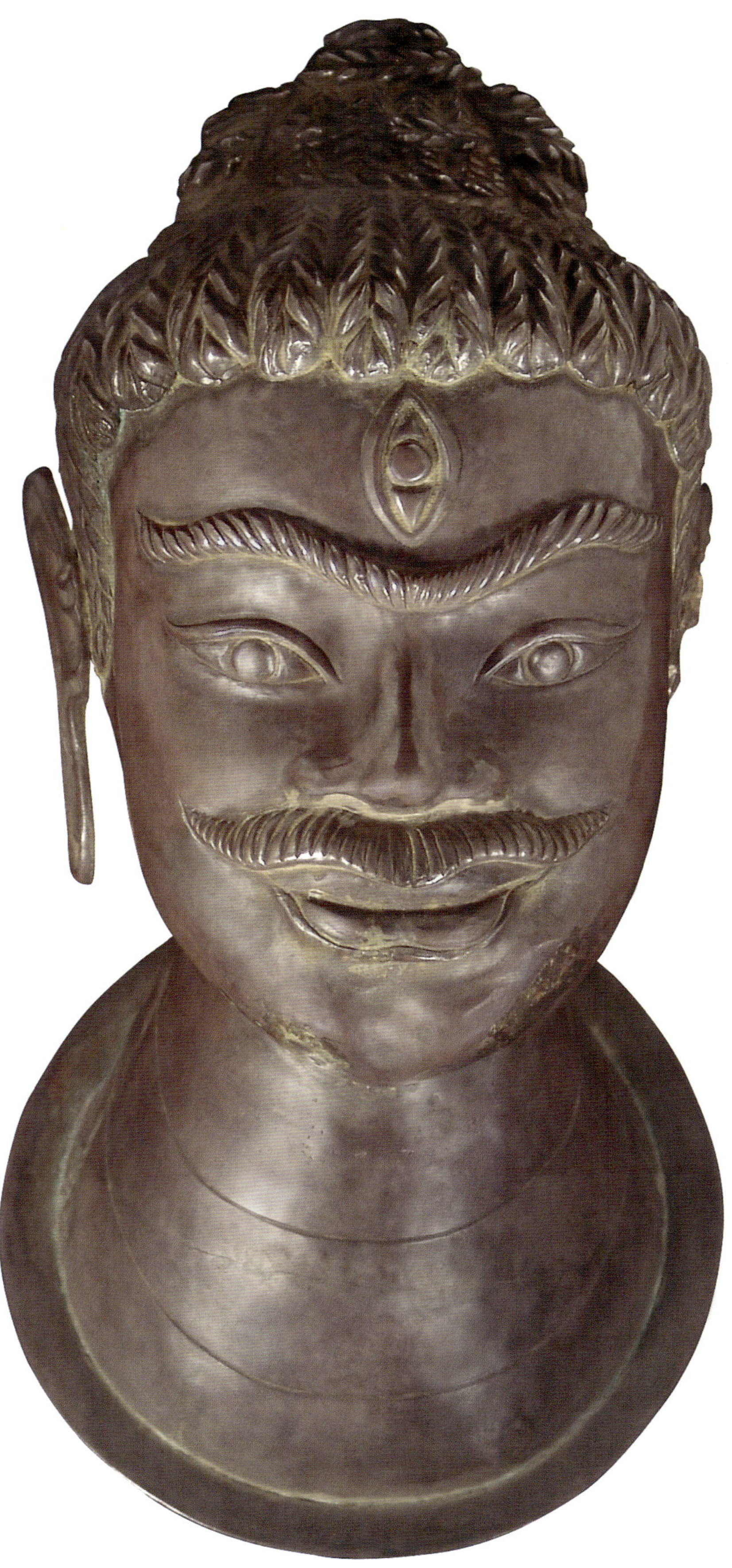

78. *Head of Shiva*, Free-standing, Silver, Height 27.4 cm, Dong Duong style, 9th - 10th Century.

This is probably a shiva-linga that could either be placed in kosa on a stone linga, as it has a twenty-four centimetre diameter, or be carried in procession.

Following Page
79. *Head of Shiva*, Free-standing, Silver and bronze, Height 38 cm, Dong Duong style, 9th - 10th Century.

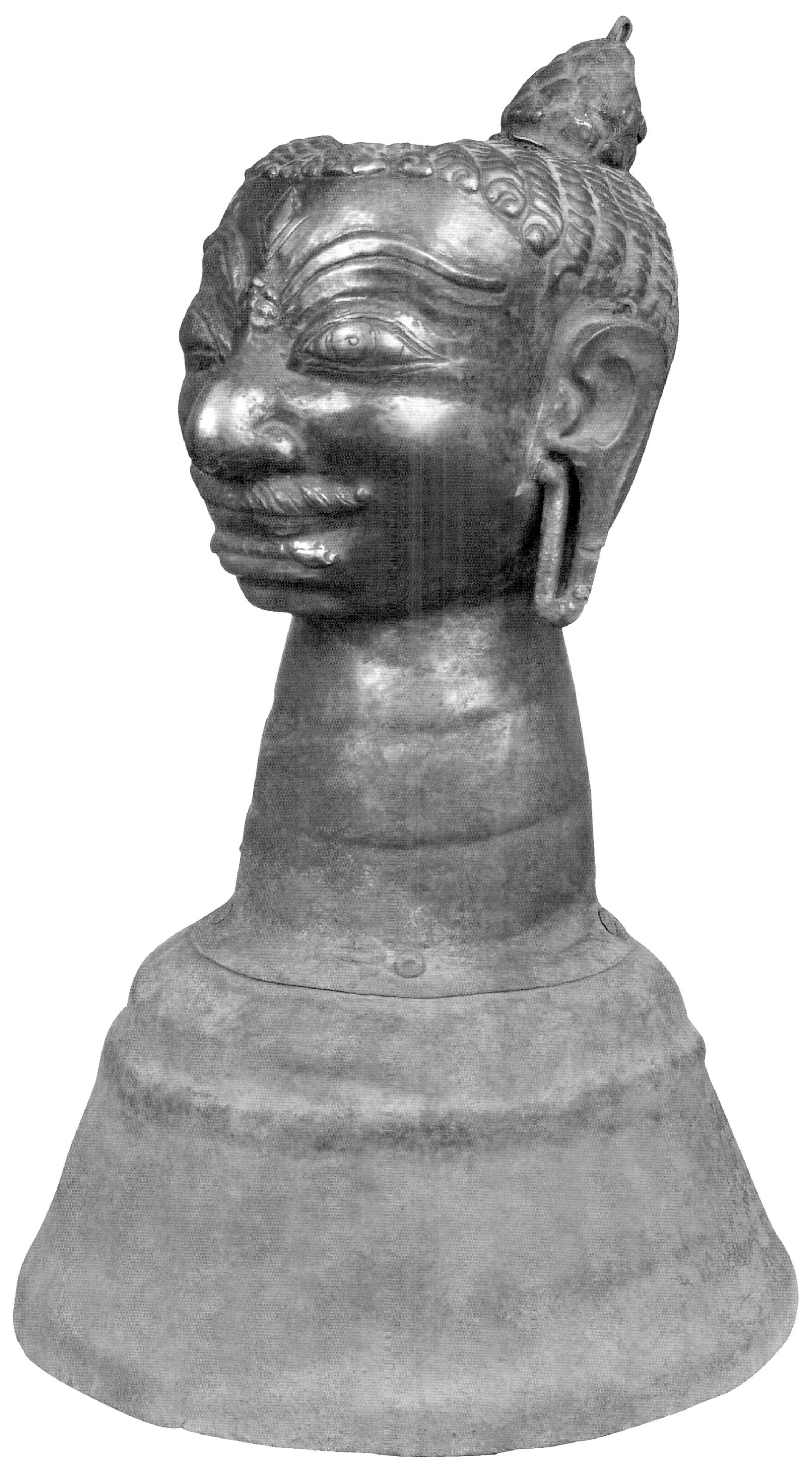

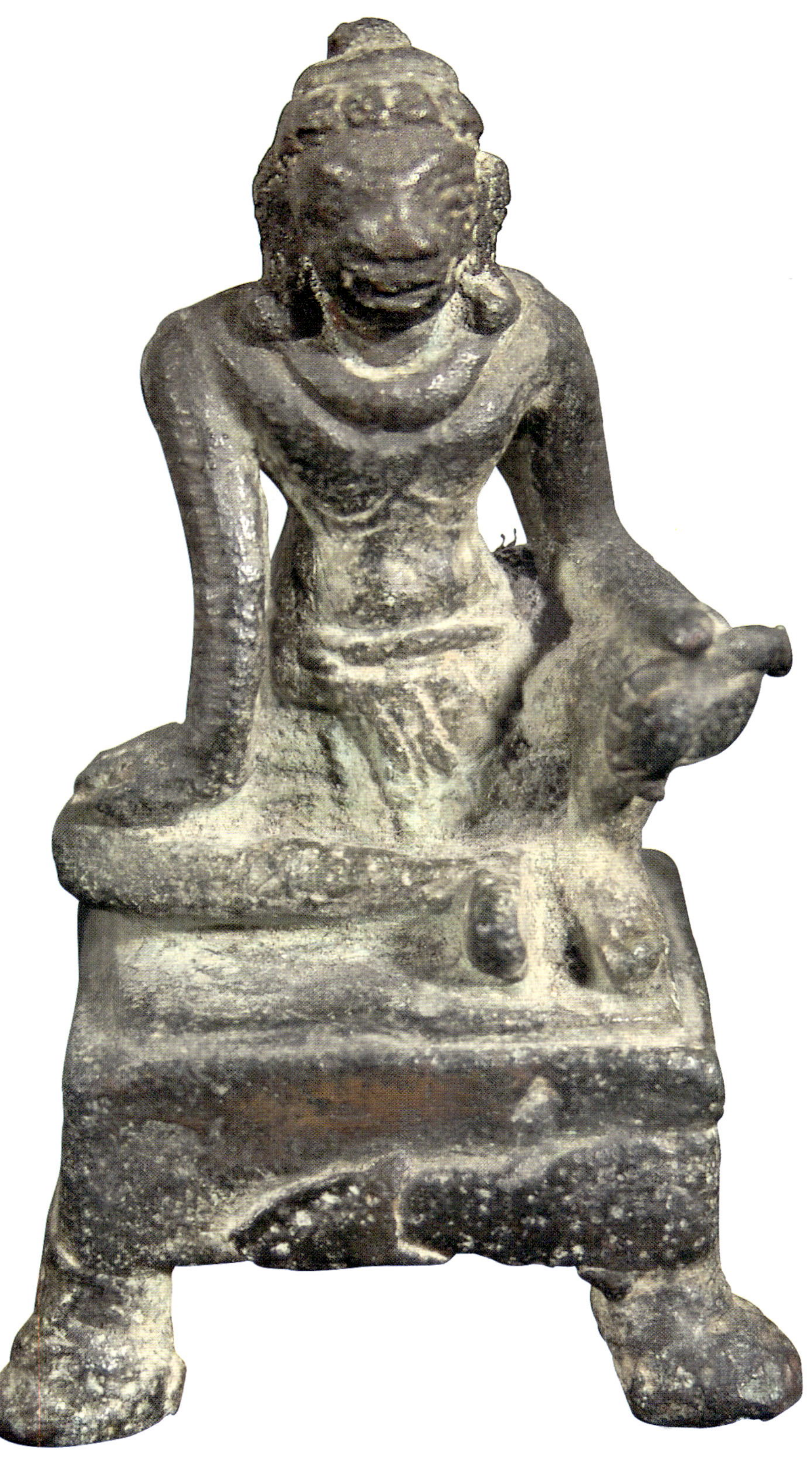

This is a lost-wax sculpture. The bronze is an alloy of copper (Cu: 82.8%) and pewter (Sn: 12.6%), with a small amount of lead (Pb: 4.1%). The lead acts as a liquifier that allows the alloy to infuse and line the mould, thereby minimises touch ups. The alloy contains no zinc. In its composition, this bronze corresponds to the typical production of India before the fifteenth century. The presence of lead is a characteristic of bronzes produced in southern India. The technical analysis thus allows us to confirm Indian influence.

80. *Divinity (Rishi)*, Free-standing, Bronze, Height 12cm,
Dong Duong style, 9th - 10th Century.

Following Page
81. *Head of Vishnu*, Nearly free-standing, Sandstone, Height 35 cm,
Dong Duong style, 9th - 10th Century.

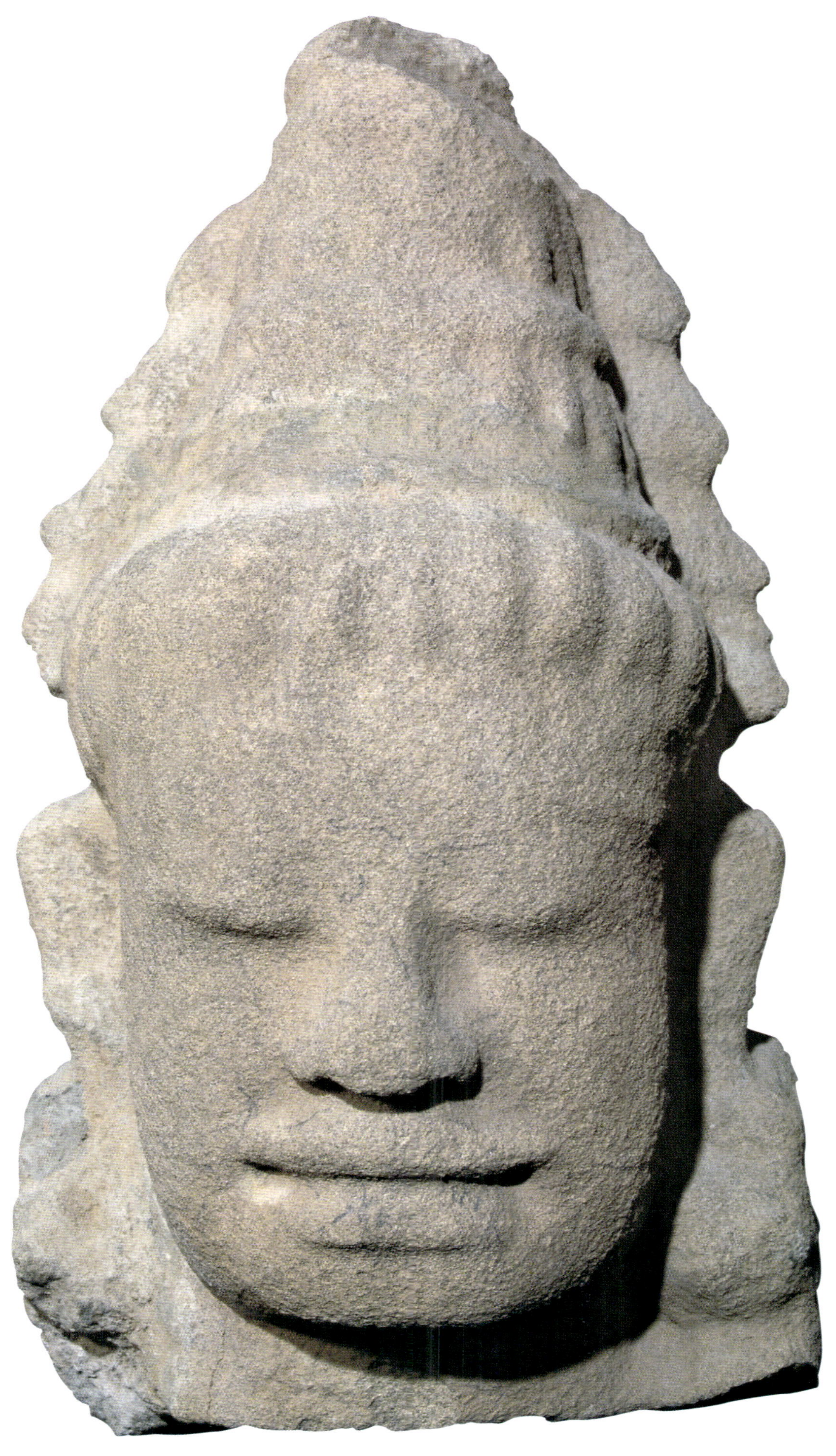

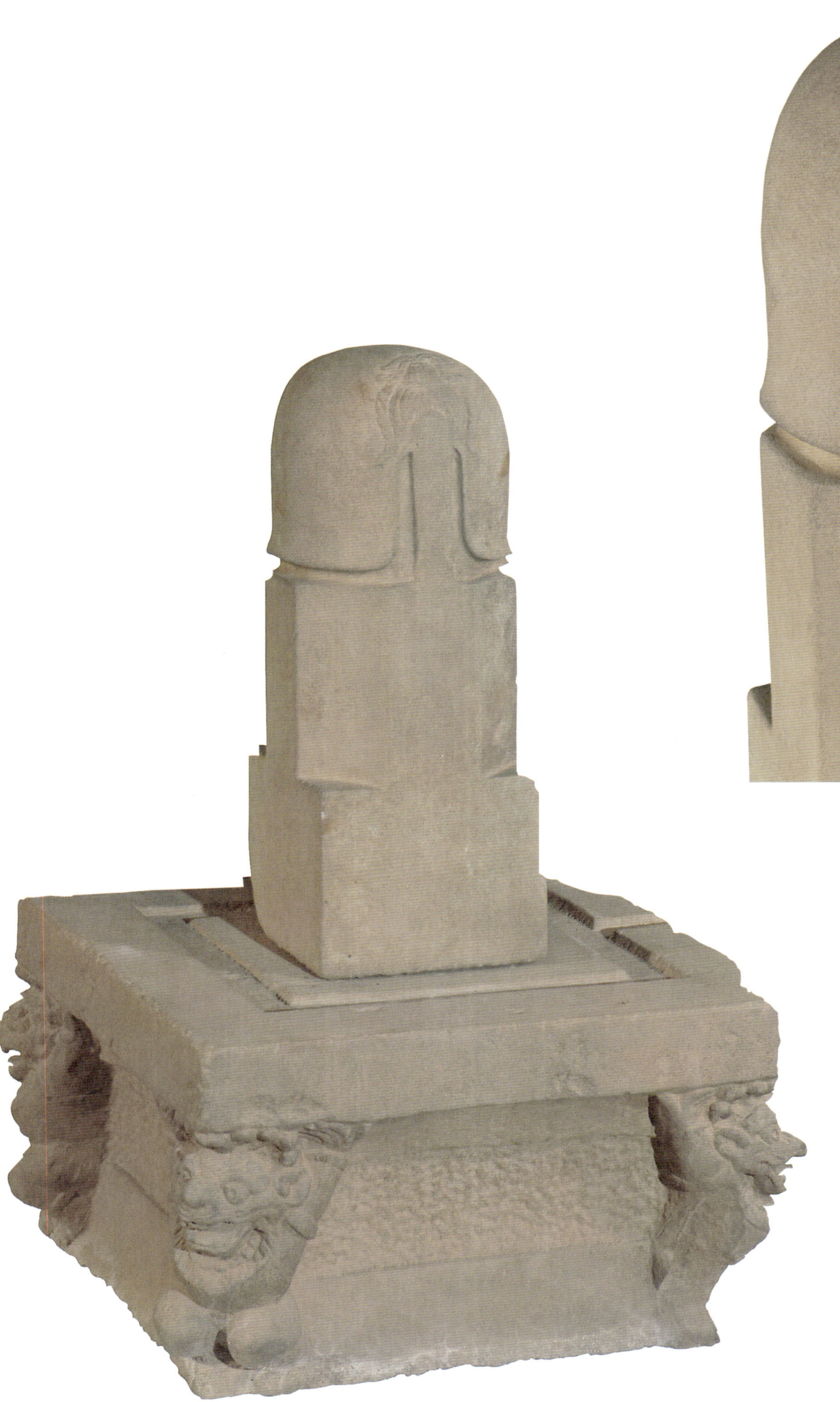

The linga is removable.

82. *Jatalinga and a pedestal with four bearing lions,*
Free-standing, Sandstone, Height 68 cm,
Dong Duong style, 9th - 10th Century or earlier.

83. *Jatalinga and a pedestal with four bearing lions,*
Free-standing, Sandstone, Height 68 cm,
Dong Duong style, 9th - 10th Century or earlier (detail).

Following Page
84. *Jatalinga and a pedestal with four bearing lions,*
Free-standing, Sandstone, Height 68 cm,
Dong Duong style, 9th - 10th Century or earlier (detail).

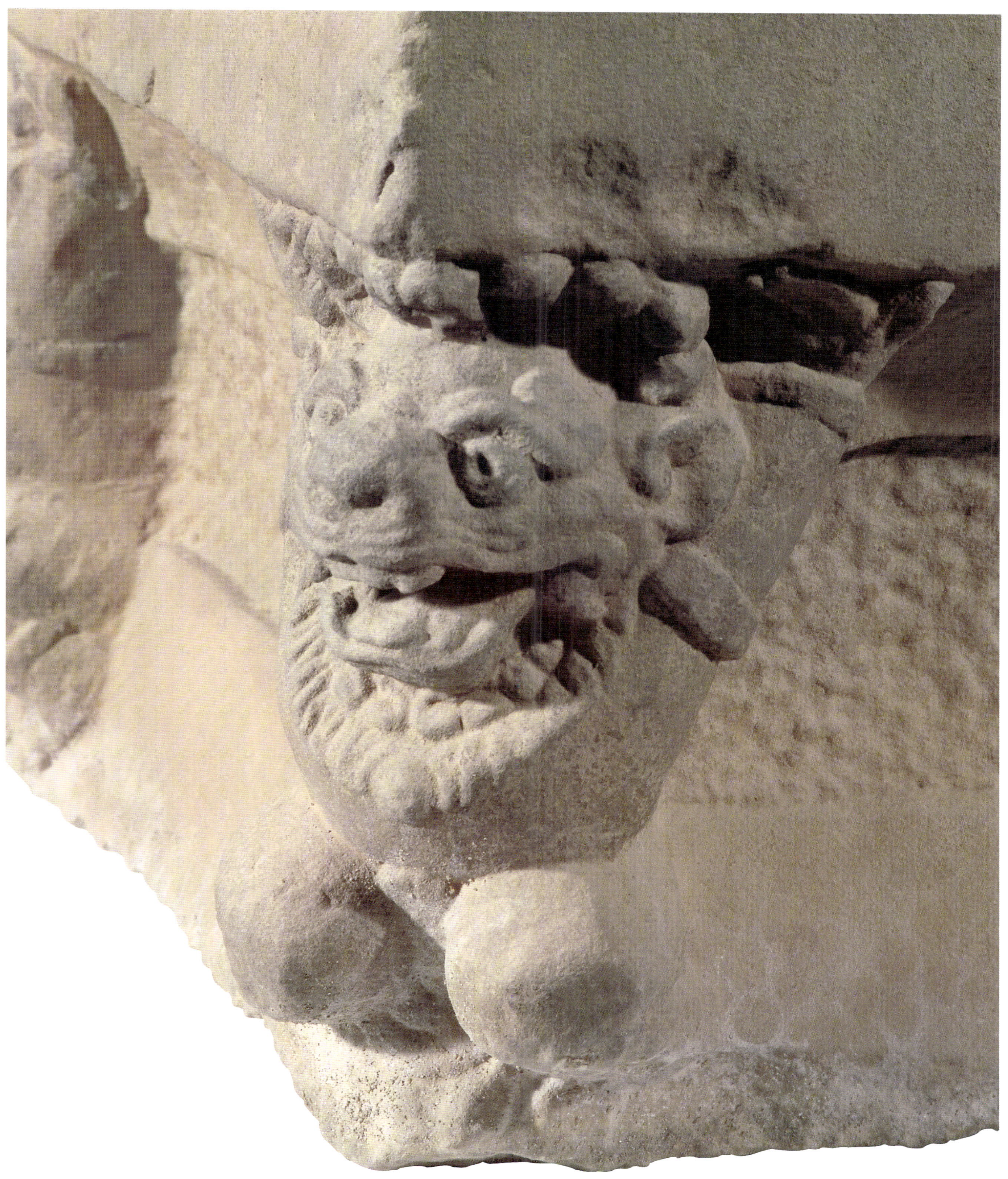

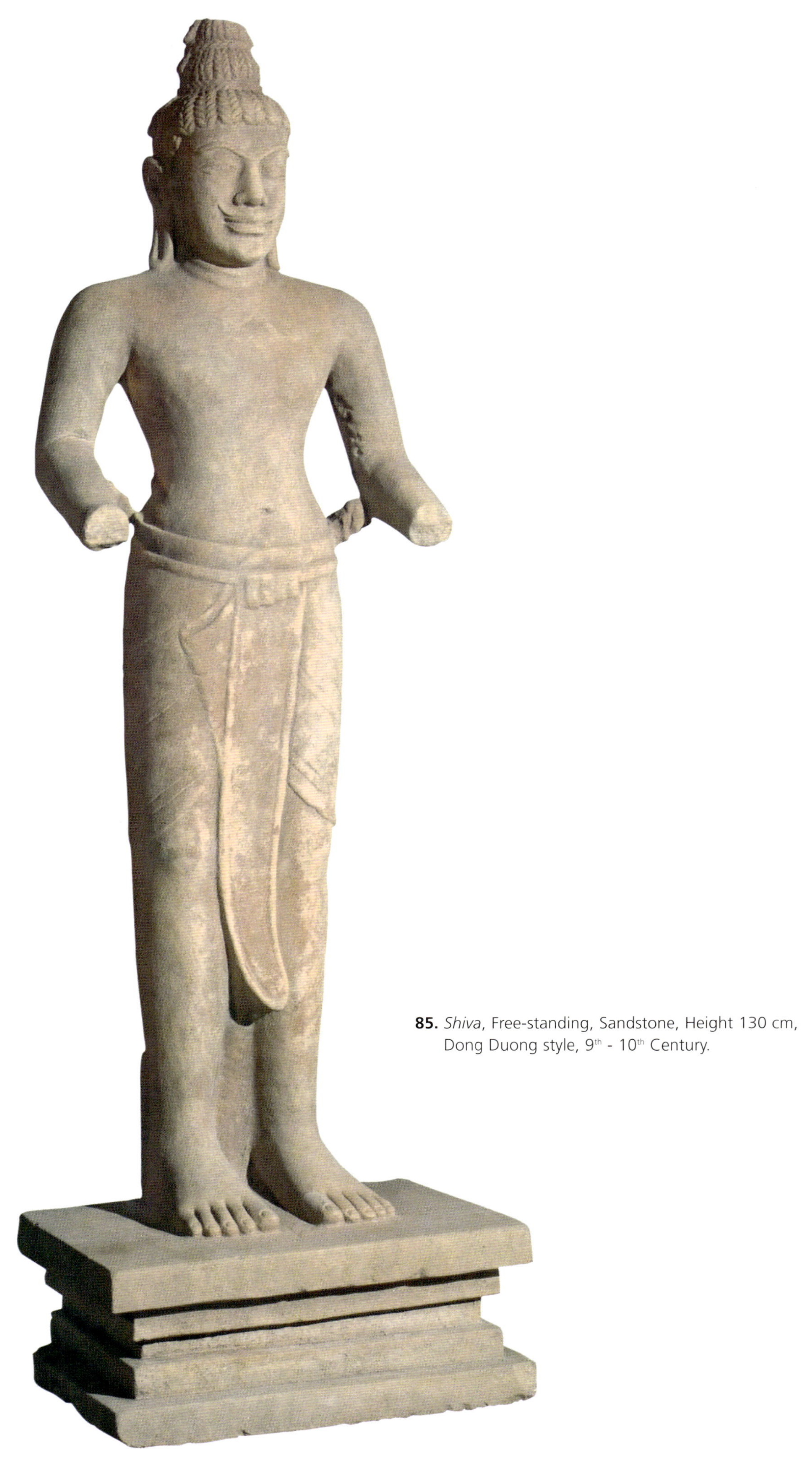

85. *Shiva*, Free-standing, Sandstone, Height 130 cm, Dong Duong style, 9th - 10th Century.

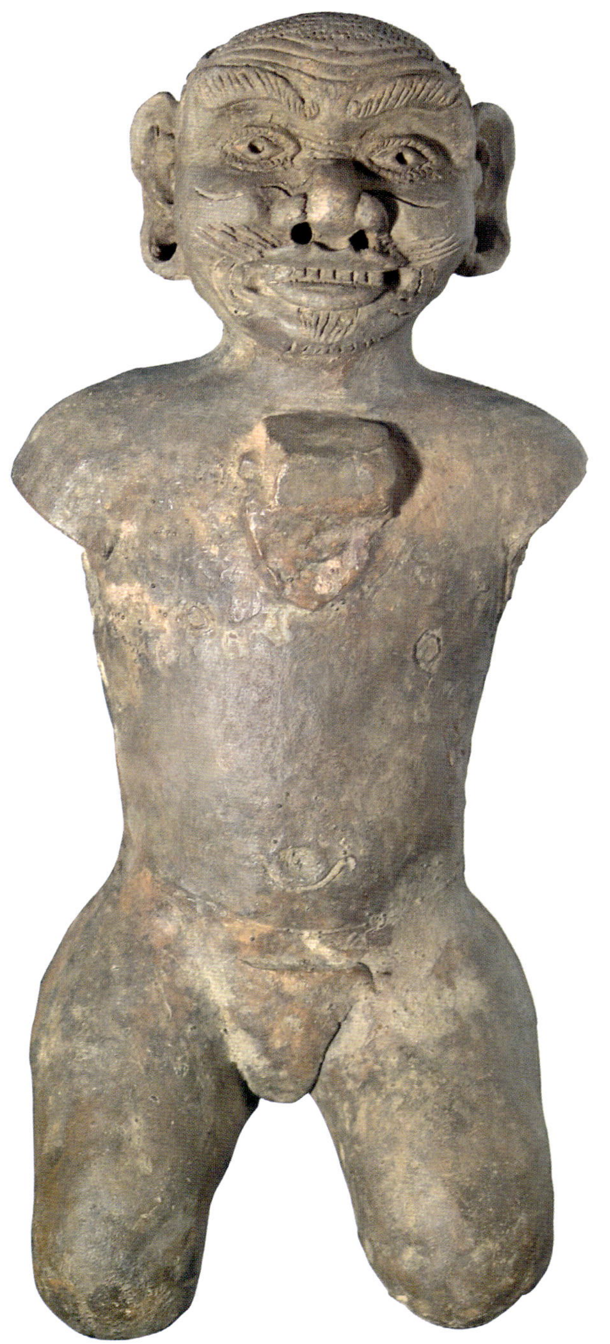

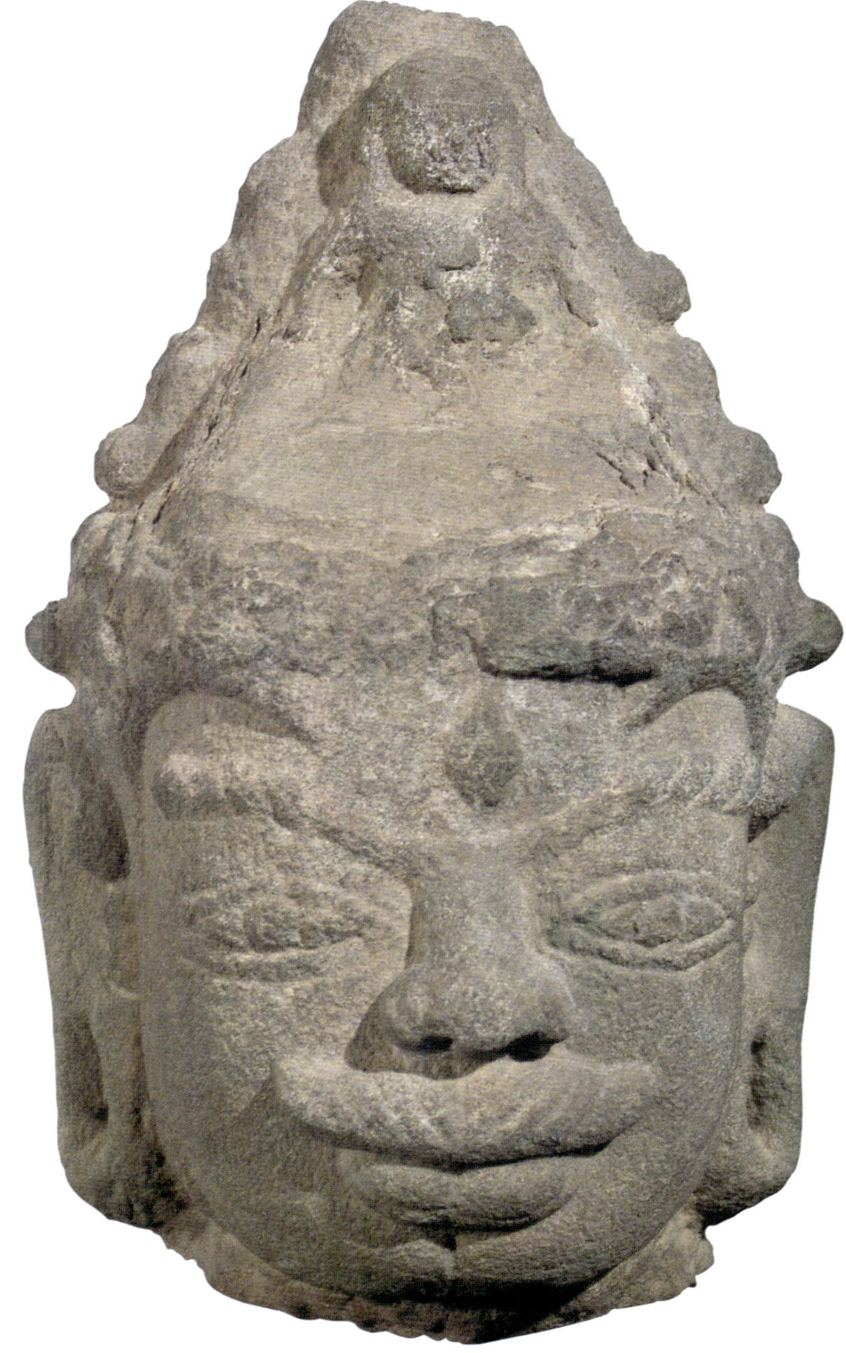

86. *Kneeling person*, Free-standing, Clay,
Height 24 cm, 10th Century.

87. *Head of Shiva*, Free-standing, Sandstone,
Height 19 cm, Dong Duong style, 9th - 10th Century.

This very compact piece was fired at extremely high temperatures. Clay pieces are usually in more porous and crumbly material, which indicates firing at lower temperatures.

The Dong Duong temple was built toward the end of the ninth century, during the reign of Indravarman (II).

An inscription discovered near the temple records that the king had a Buddhist monastery (Vihara in Sanskrit) built in 875 CE as well as a temple dedicated to the worship of Laksmindra-Lokesvara, the monarch's protective god. This name, which combines two Hindu names (Lakshmi and Indra) and a Buddhist one (Lokesvara), proves that a mixture of Hinduism and Buddhism reigned at the time.

Although fairly rare in Buddhist sculpture, dominant at the time, Shivaist sculptures can be found that regroup all the characteristics of the Dong Duong style.

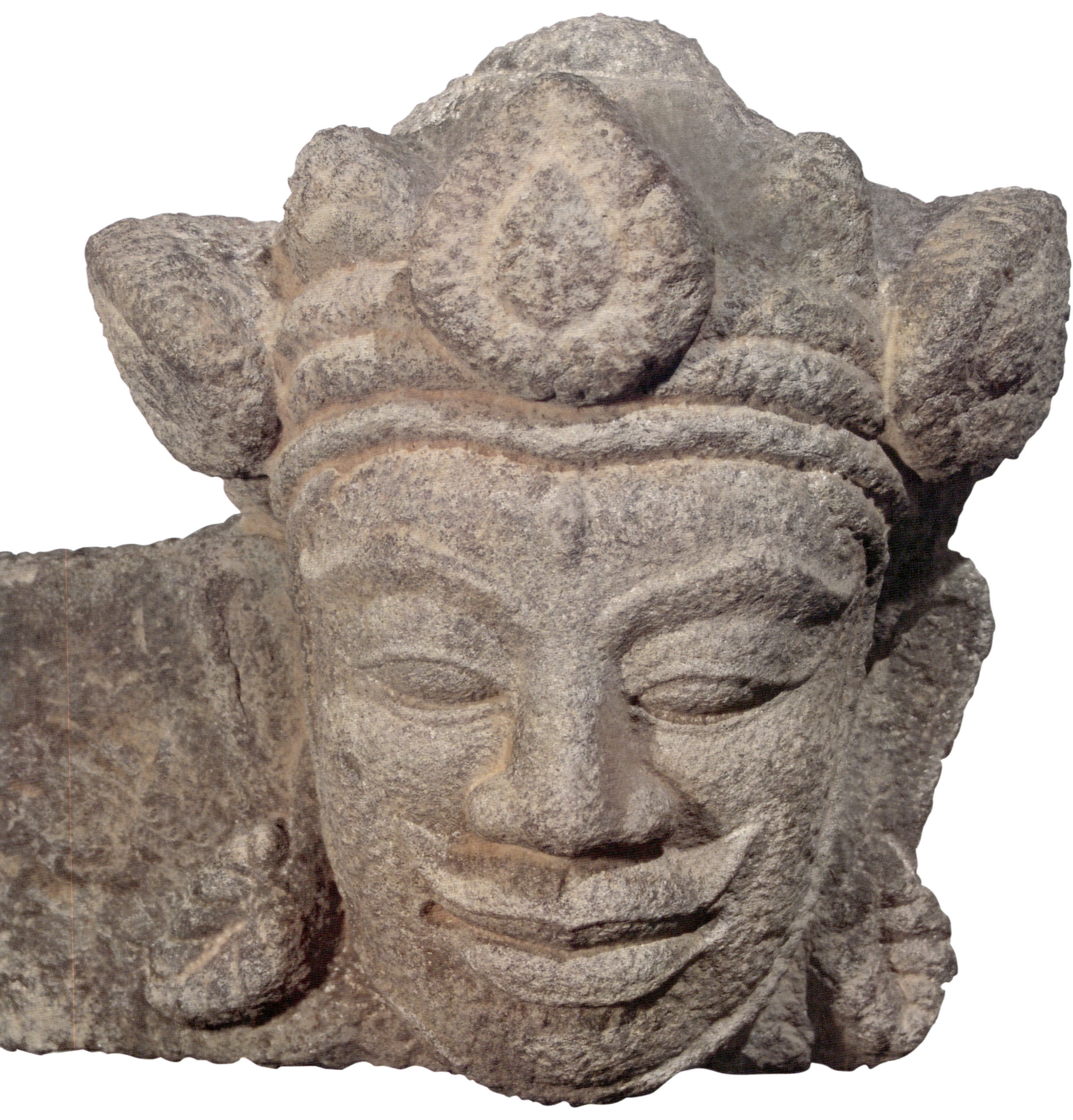

The head is equipped with a quadrangular tenon (25 cm long) that allows it to be placed in the bricks of a temple wall.

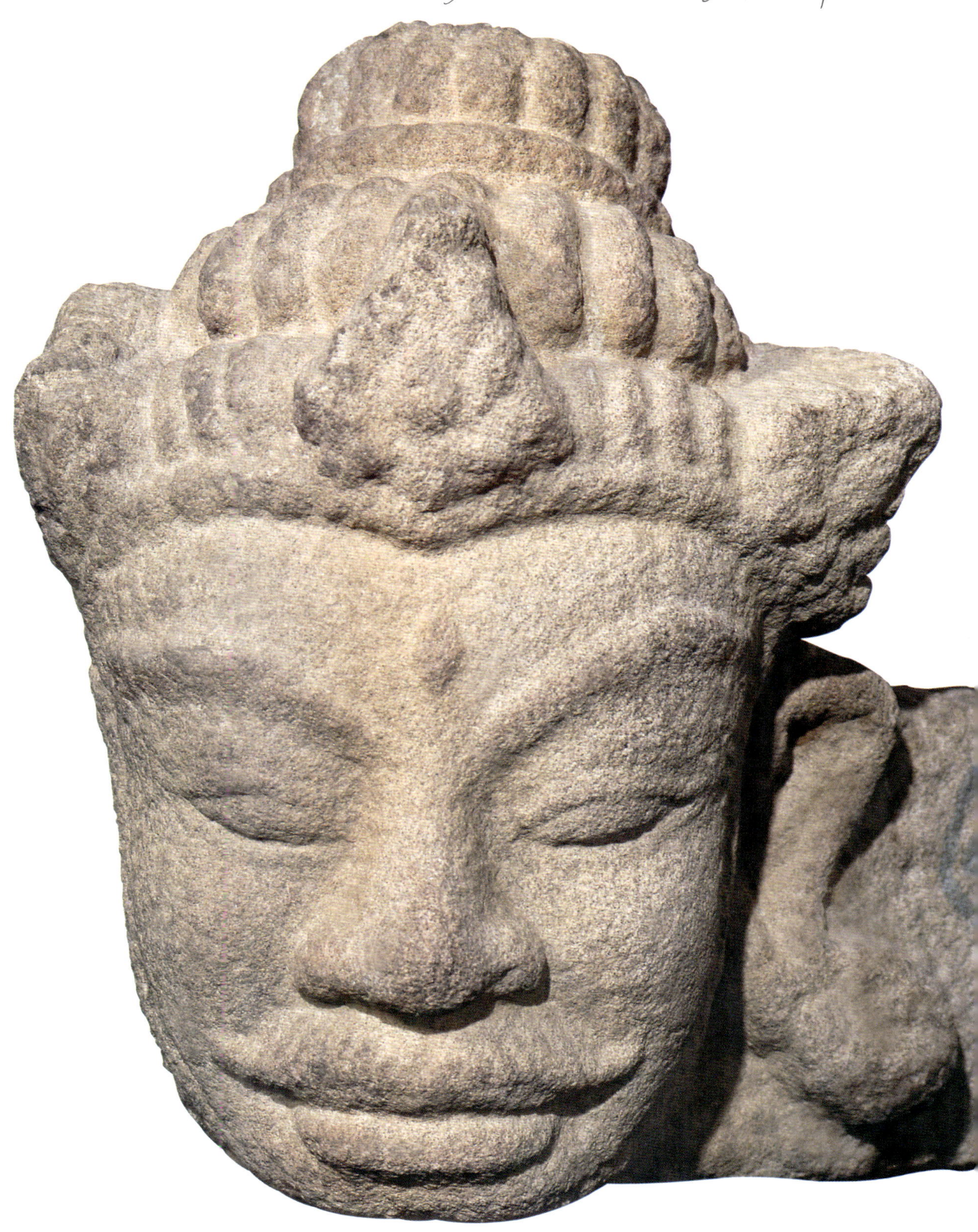

The head is equipped with a transversal quadrangular tenon that is 20 cm long, and allowed the head to be inserted in the bricks of a temple. It can be identified as Shiva's head by the eye and the hairstyle. The head has all the distinctive characteristics of the Dong Duong style: slanted eyes without pupils, bushy eyebrows, a large nose, a combed moustache that turns up at each end, and thick lips with clearly defined outlines. The earlobes are decorated by earrings. The divinity is wearing a tiara.

Previous Page
88. *Head of Shiva*, Nearly free-standing, Sandstone, Height 25 cm, Dong Duong style, 9th - 10th Century.

89. *Head of Shiva*, High-relief, Sandstone, Height 20 cm, Dong Duong style, 9th - 10th Century.

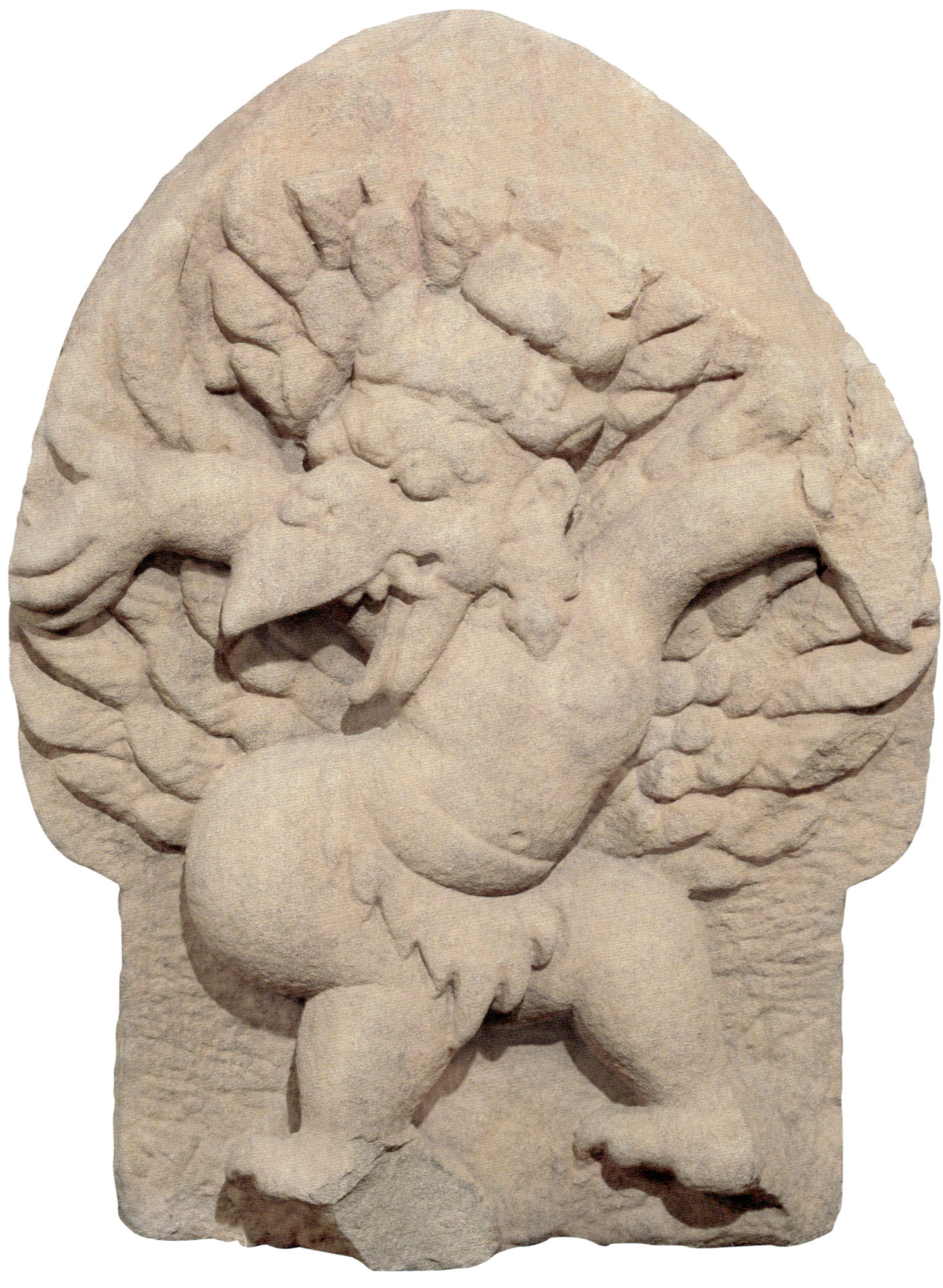

This mythical bird (Garuda), Vishnu's mount, and the sworn enemy of snakes is standing and in motion. It has the body of a man, dressed in a loincloth, with feathery wings. Its long beak of a bird of prey is open. Crowned with a tiara, it is also wearing earrings.

90. *Garuda*, High-relief, Sandstone, Height 60 cm, Dong Duong style, 9th - 10th Century.

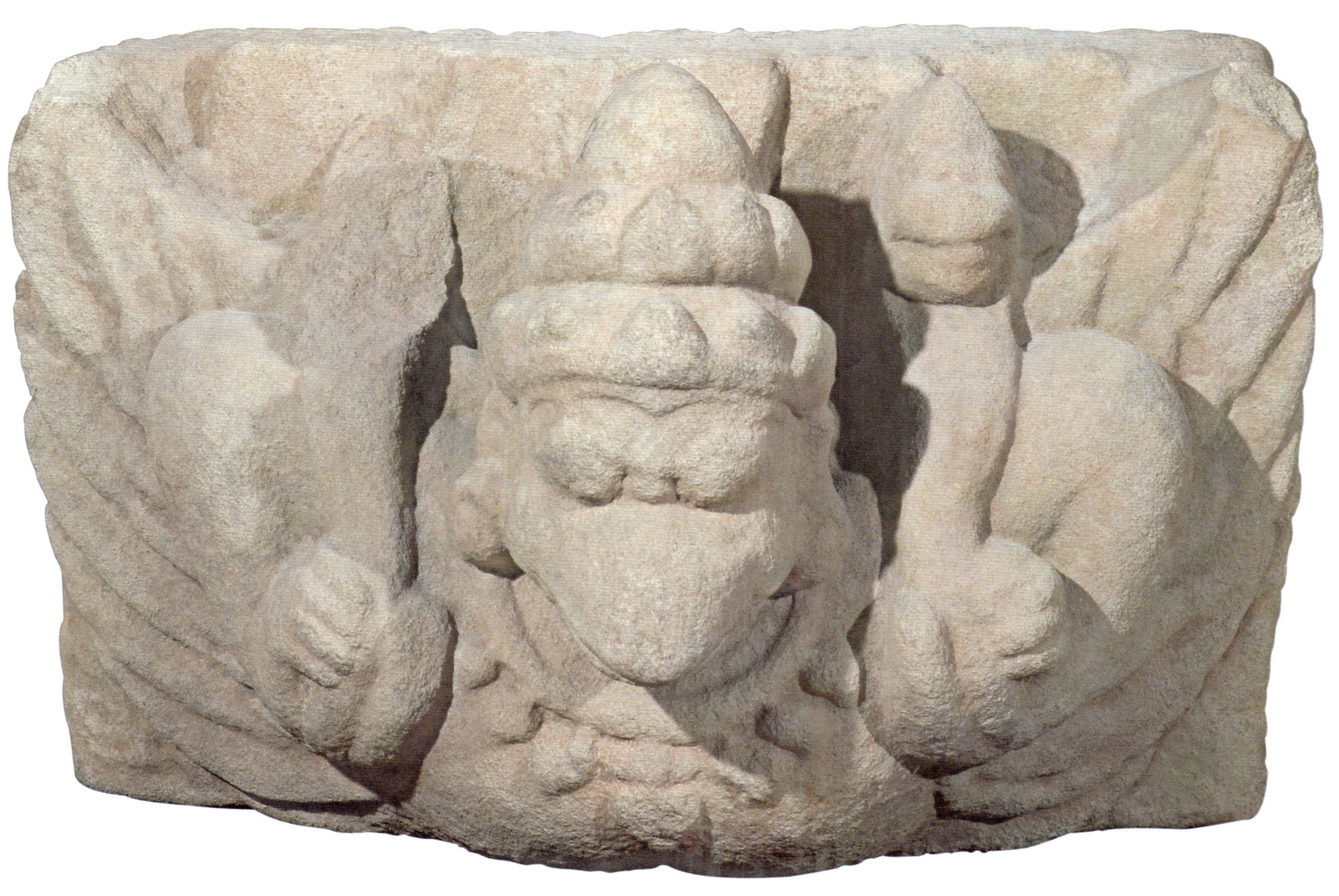

91. *Garuda*, High-relief, Sandstone, Height 33 cm, Tra Kiêu style, 10th Century or Before.

Here, the animal's beak is closed

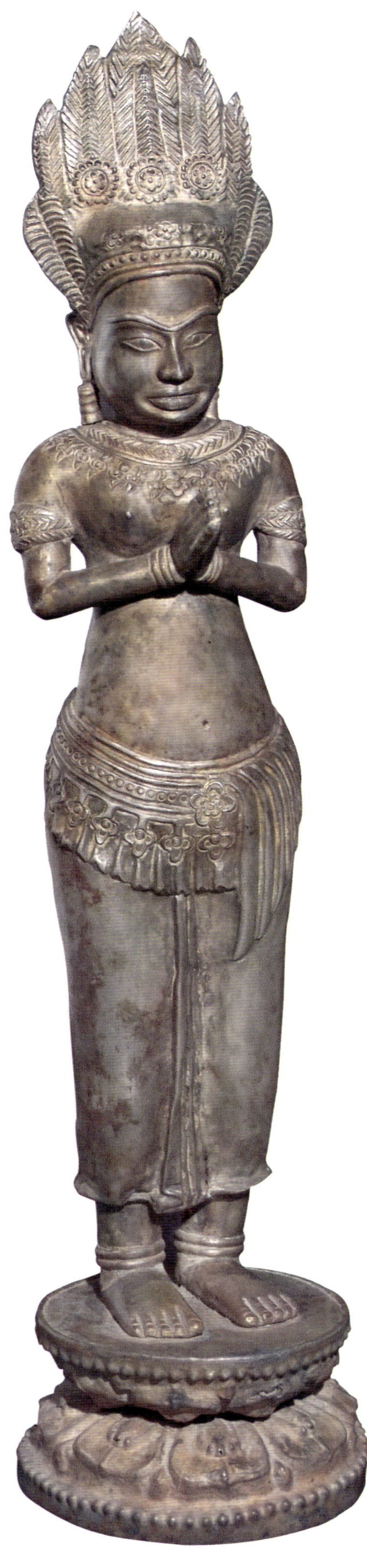

Cyclotron analysis of Champa metals and jewellery

The objects themselves, and not samples, were analysed using the PIXE/PIGE method. This method is based on localised irradiation of the pieces by a beam of charged particles, protons or cores of hydrogen atoms. The beam of particles was produced by the AVF40 cyclotron at the Institute of Nuclear, Atomic Physics and Spectroscopy at the University of Liège in Belgium.

The beam was extracted in the open air and then focused on the zone under study; the diameter of the point of impact is about a millimetre. As a result of the interaction of the beam of particles and the material, X and gamma rays are emitted. These emissions explain the name of the method: Proton Induced X-ray Emission or PIXE and Proton Induced Gamma-ray Emission or PIGE. The detecting, identifying and counting of the rays provide analyses that are qualitative and quantitative.

Measurements were made for about ten minutes at each point of impact. The zones to study were designated by the art historian who heads the programme. Before the measurement of any piece of art, each material – glass, bronze, silver, etc. – was gauged. Objects made of silver were cleaned, at the points of impact, with a dentist's drill, to the depth of ten to twenty micrometers. The objective of this procedure is to eliminate the naturally corroded outer layer that may have been enriched or of a different composition from that of the mass. Precious stones and glass are simply rubbed with cotton soaked in isopropyl alcohol. The results of the tests are given in the information on each piece studied.

The feminine divinity represented standing on a base of lotus petals, hands joined in anjali, the sign of respect and adoration, has a camphor wood frame. Two points of impact, one chosen on the statuette's back and the other on the base yield the same results: this is silver (Ag) for 960 thousandths alloyed with 2.4% copper (Cu). The absence of mercury in the metallic mass seems to exclude the preparation of the metal by amalgamation. In tiny quantities, lead (Pb: 0.08%) and zinc (Zn: 0.8%) were identified, which differentiates the original silver ore from that used for the older head of Shiva (see p.84). In the case of the latter, there are no impurities although traces of nickel (Ni) were found (0.02%). A difference in age between the two pieces could explain the divergence as far as impurities are concerned, which confirms the a priori dating of the stylistic analysis, this divinity being at least one hundred years younger than the head of the Dong Duong style.

Originally set on a linga, directly or – most likely – via a kosa, the head of the god Shiva can be recognised by the central eye and by the crescent moon in the high ancestral chignon (jatamukuta). It was made using several sheets of silver, embossed and later assembled: two for the head, four for the ears and two for the chignon.

The ears, created separately, are pinned on. Above them is a ring that is attached to the head in the same way. These elements may have been intended as support for a diadem (kirita-mukuta) placed on the chignon.

The piece was fixed to a metal sheath or, more probably, directly to the stone by rivets, some of which still exist. Boisselier mentions an inscription from the reign of Prakasadharma that refers to a perforation (of silver) (ruphabeda) and the term "injury" (ksata) is used several times; this might indicate that putting the kosa into place necessitated the placement of several mortises on the linga. The elaborate treatment of the chignon, made of three rows of braids, a characteristic frequently found in the tenth century, induces dating to the tenth century. But the natural treatment of the face, the prominent cheekbones, the large almond-shaped eyes tilted toward the temples, the cleft chin, the full lips with their fine outline and the moustache that looks like a braid are all characteristic elements that allow this facial anatomy to be considered comparable to the stone images of the second half of the seventh century or the first half of the eighth century (see p.53).

The head looks to be made of gold, but around the nose, a small flaw in the layer of gold-leaf is noticeable. A pinpoint analysis shows a substratum of silver. The head, once removed from the mould, was covered with an amalgamate of gold (Au: 52.1%) and silver (Ag: 22.1%) that gives it its final appearance. The outside layer is rich in mercury (Hg: 24.8%). The difficulty encountered in a visual analysis of such pieces is illustrated by the terms "electrum" or "chrysargyre" often used in the descriptions. As for the head, it was poured in silver (935 thousandths) alloyed with 6.4% copper, making it the single example of this type published to date.

The Chams were familiar with gold. The Chinese Annals recount that they knew how to reroute rivers and wash the sand of the dry riverbed to extract gold nuggets. Inscriptions mention offerings to the gods and specify their material: gold, silver or copper. The Chinese Annals also refer to the tributes sent to the Chinese court (the "Middle Empire" being, at the time, Champa's overlord) and list the quantities of gold ore that were worked with. Gold was abundant in Champa. The Chinese Annals, once again, speak of a "mountain of gold" where all the "red-coloured" stones contain a bar of gold. Gold was a known entity in the region, sometimes in abundance, as at the Bone Mieu mine, famous at the time of French colonisation, located "in the mountains in the Quang Nam province about 100 km south-south-east of Tourane" (Teston and Percheron). Legends say mines at Kim Son (Binh Dinh) were exploited for the court of Annam "for hundreds of years" and also refer to mines in Kontum and gold-rich alluvium. Gold is precisely measured, in drams (3.09g) or thils (theis) (12g). The Chams were excellent goldsmiths: they knew how to smelt and shape it. They poured "metal statues ten empans high and made, in addition to the statues, various boxes, vases for betel and whitewash, funerary vases, pitchers, kosa, jewellery, weapon hilts". (Maspero)

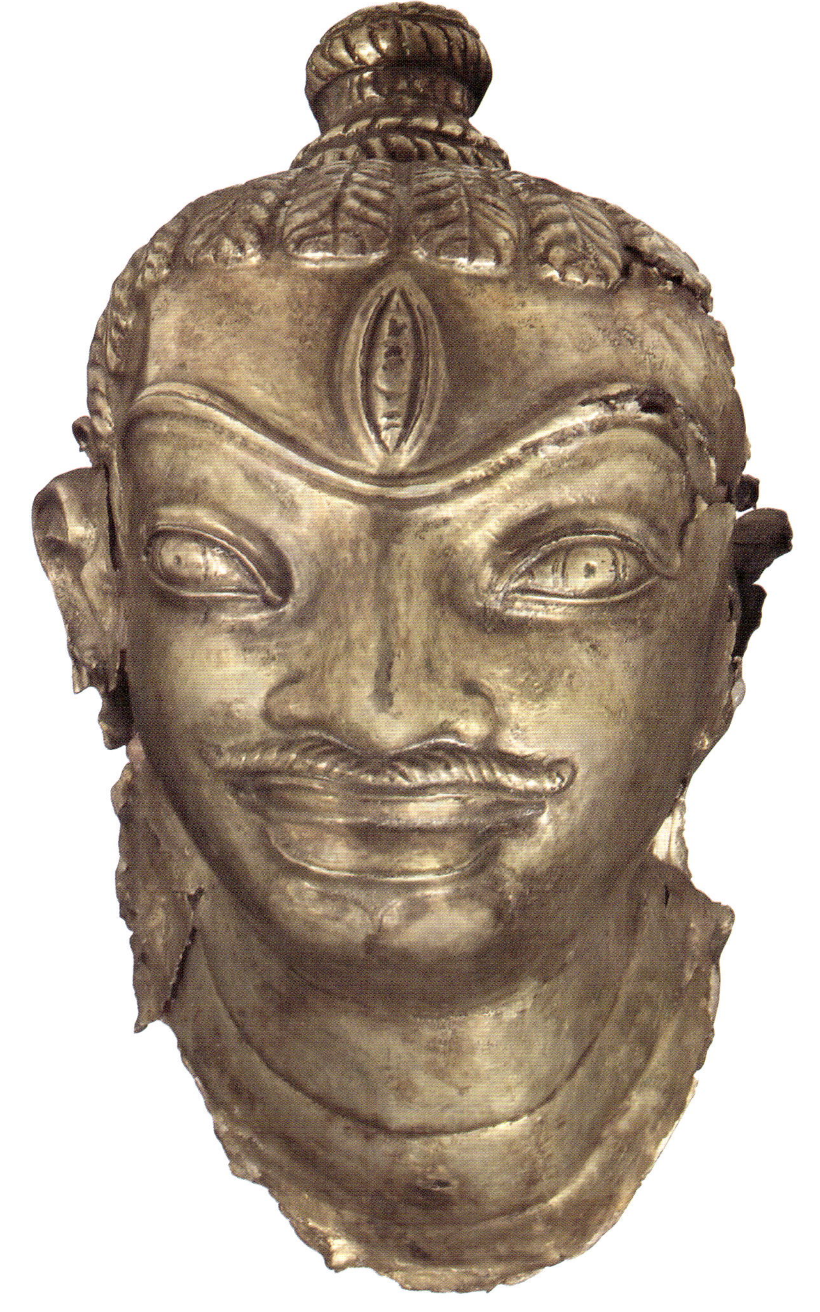

Previous Page
92. *Feminine divinity*, Free-standing, Silver on camphor wood frame, Height 50 cm, 11th Century.

93. *Head of Shiva*, Free-standing, Gilded silver, Height 15.3 cm, Dong Duong style, 9th - 10th Century.

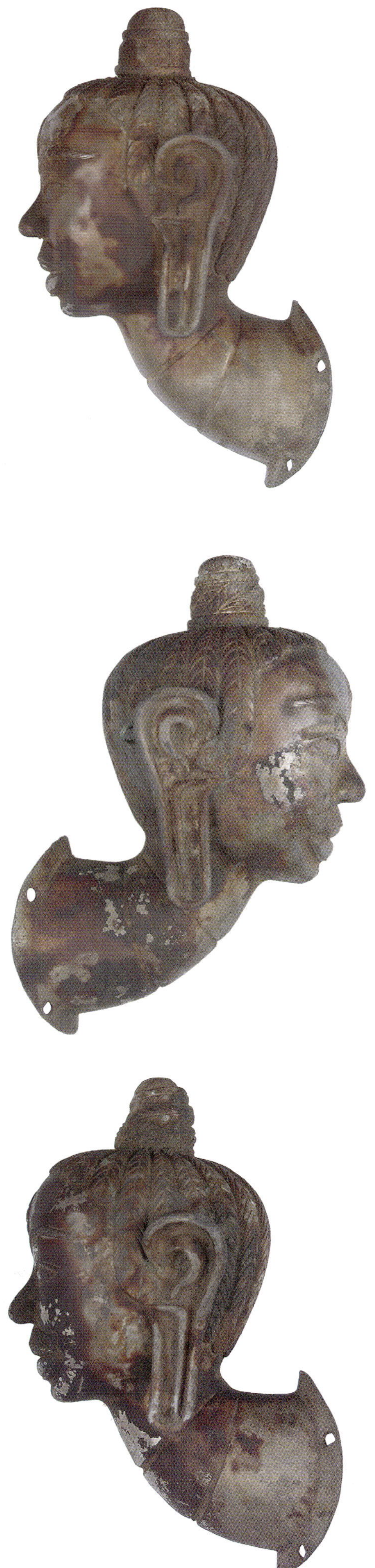

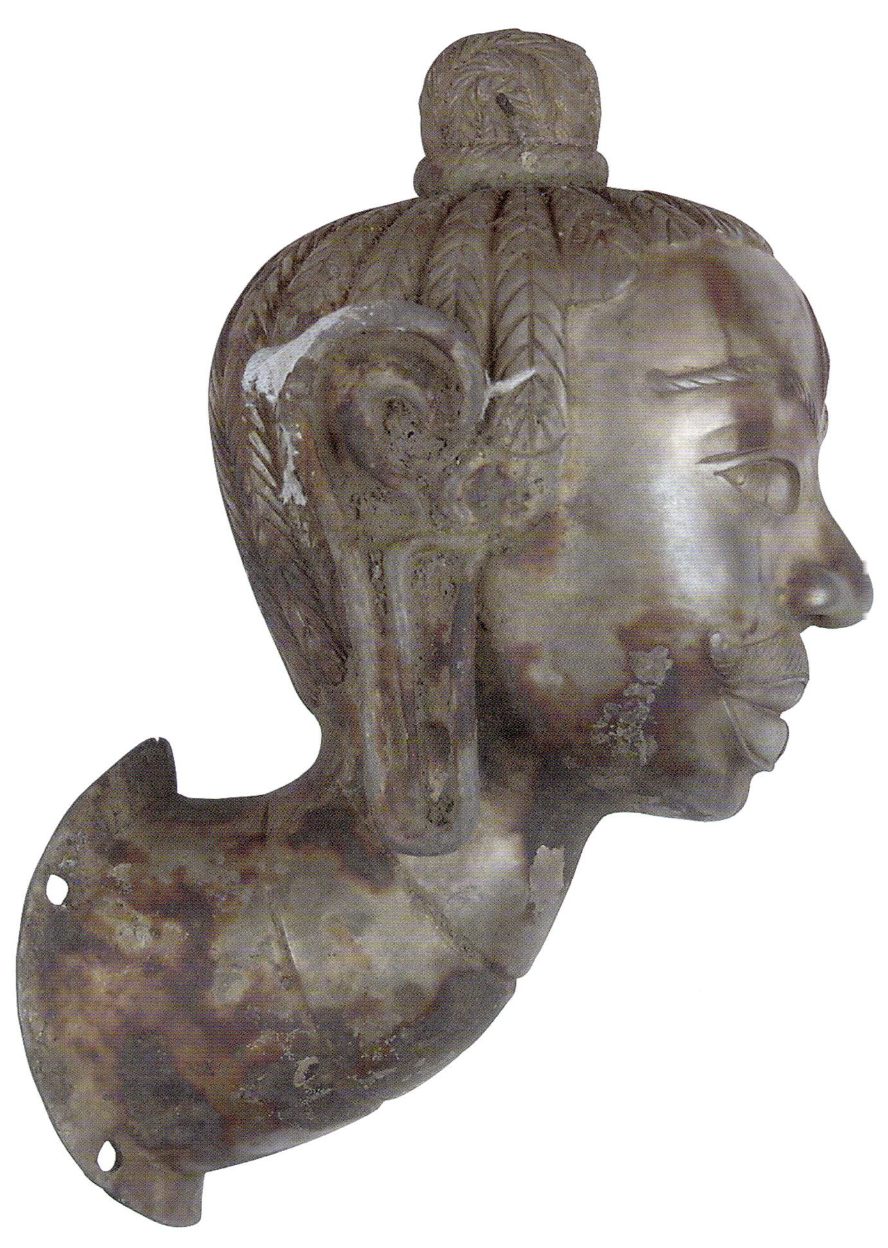

These four heads were originally riveted to one linga of the same metal. Attention can be drawn to the different hairstyles of each.

94. *Head of Shiva*, Free-standing, Silver, Height 13 cm each, 10th Century.

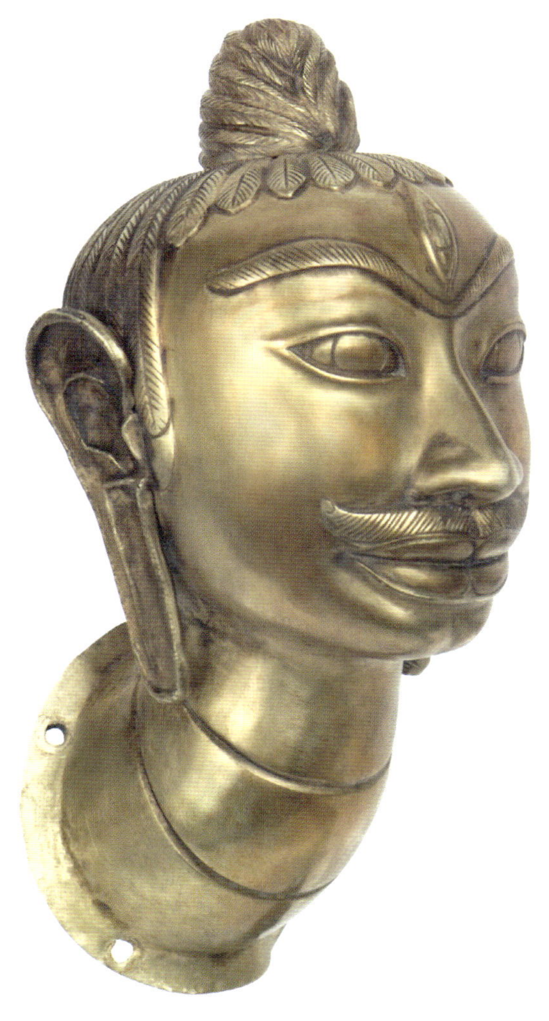

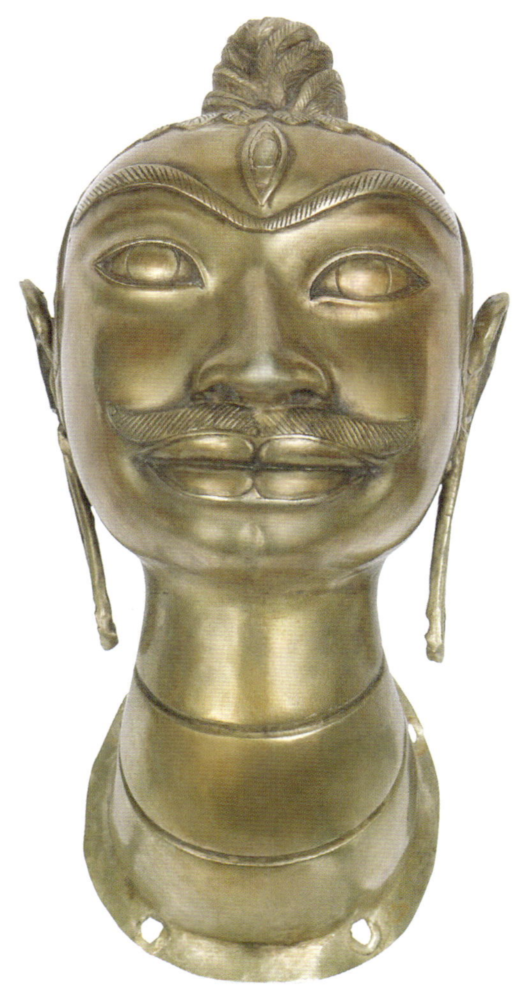

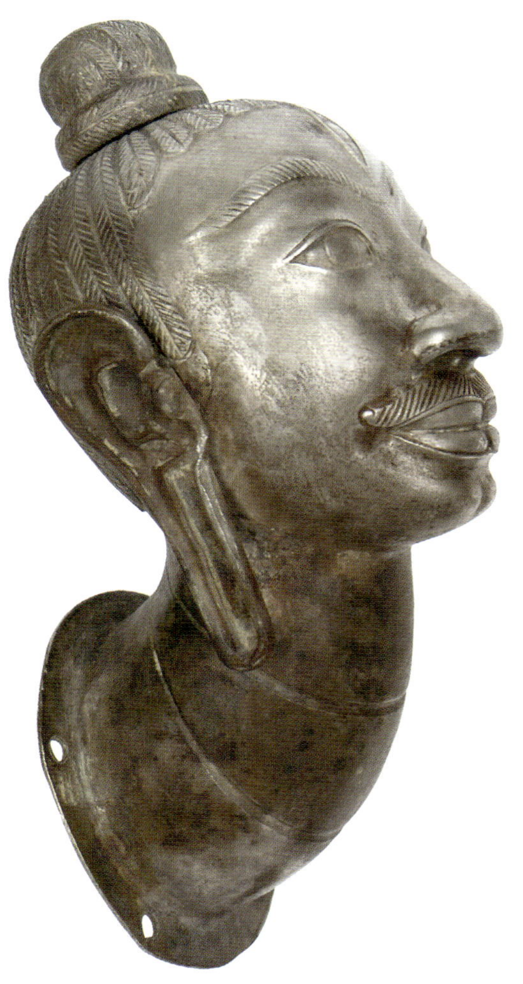

Top Left
95. *Head of Shiva*, Free-standing, Gold, Height 13 cm, Tra Kiêu Style, 10th Century.

Top Right
96. *Head of Shiva*, Free-standing, Gold, Height 12 cm, Tra Kiêu Style, 10th Century.

Bottom Left
97. *Head of Shiva*, Free-Standing, Silver, Height 13 cm, Tra Kiêu style, 10th Century.

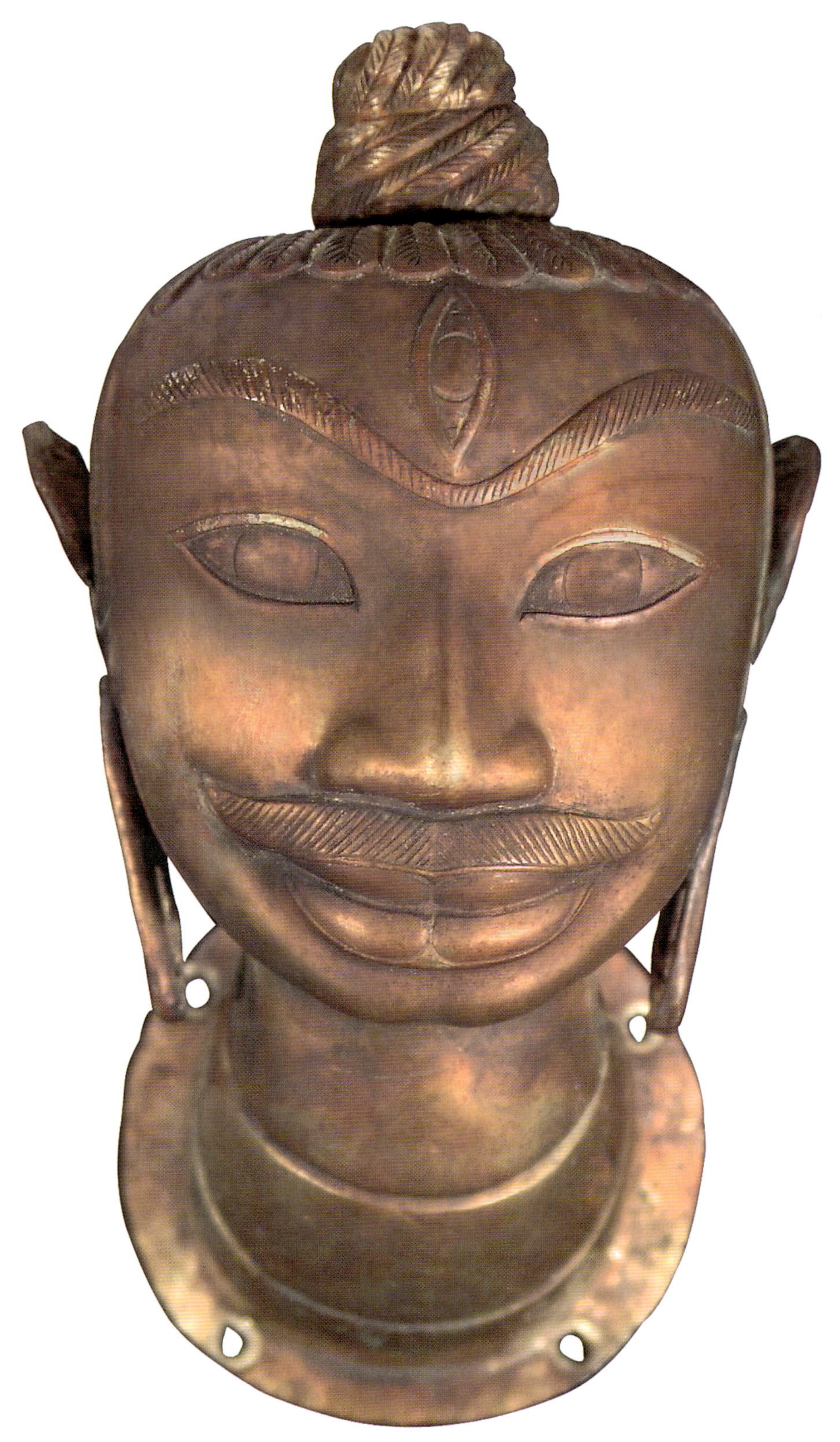

98. *Head of Shiva*, Free-standing, Gold, Height 13 cm, Tra Kiêu style, 10th Century.

Following Page
99. *Panchamukhalinga*, Free-standing, Bronze and Silver, Tra Kiêu style, Height 15.5 cm, 10th Century.

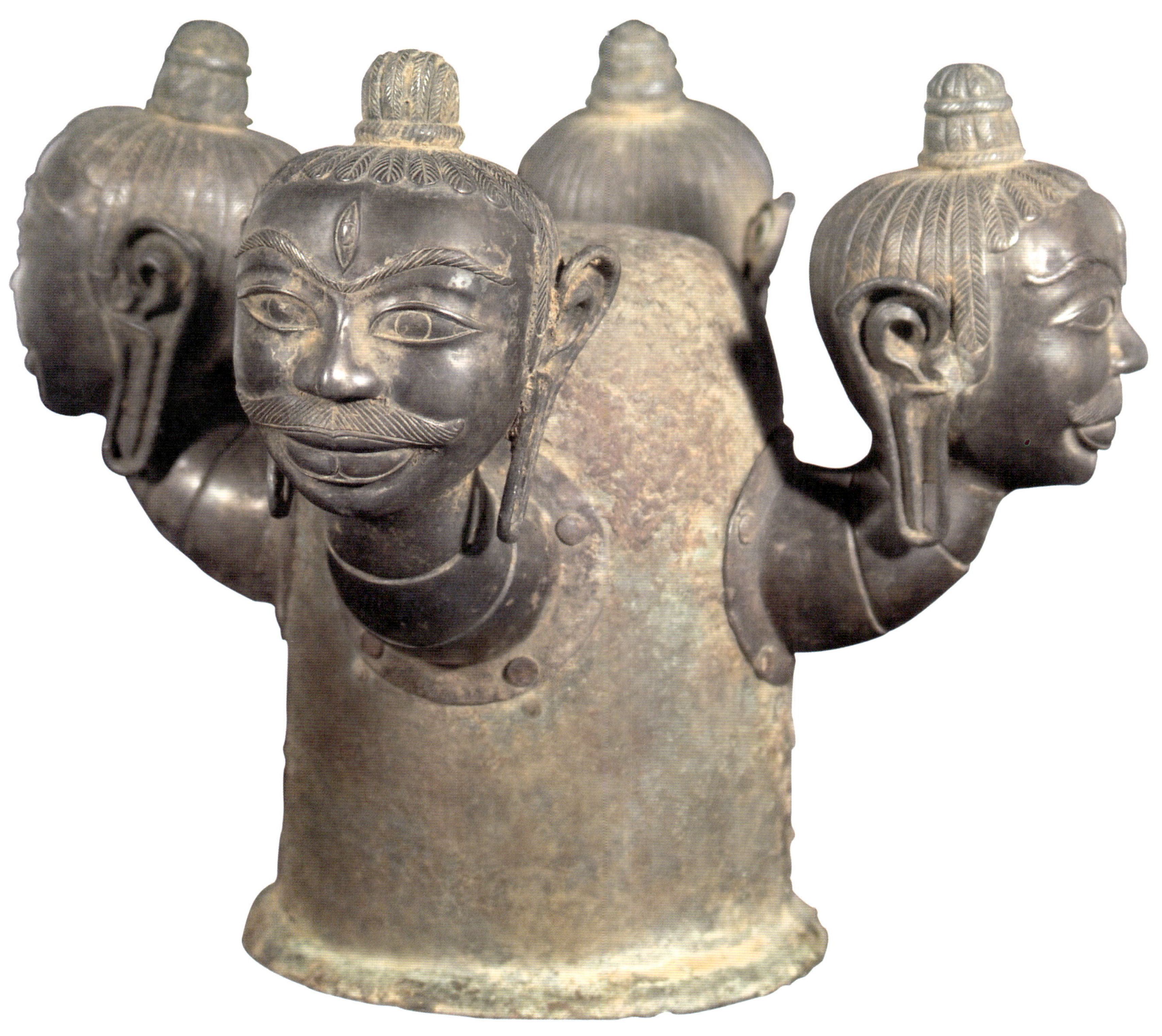

From the Sanskrit "pancha", "mukha" and "linga": "five-headed monkey".

Four of Shiva's five heads, attached to the linga itself, express the four cardinal directions.

A Shivite entity is also connected to each one: Bhairava ("terrible" in Sanskrit) for the south, Nandin for the west, Tamreshvara for the north, Mahadeva for the east. The fifth head is virtual and not represented because it stands for the absolute, unrepresentable by definition. Sometimes a rock crystal at the top of the linga is, symbolically, this absolute. The five faces of the god also symbolise the five elements: earth, wind, fire, ether and water. Each of the faces has a name: Sadyojata ("new born"), Aghora ("inspiring fear"), Vamadeva ("god of the left"), Tatpurusha ("this being so"), and Sadasiva ("always beneficial").

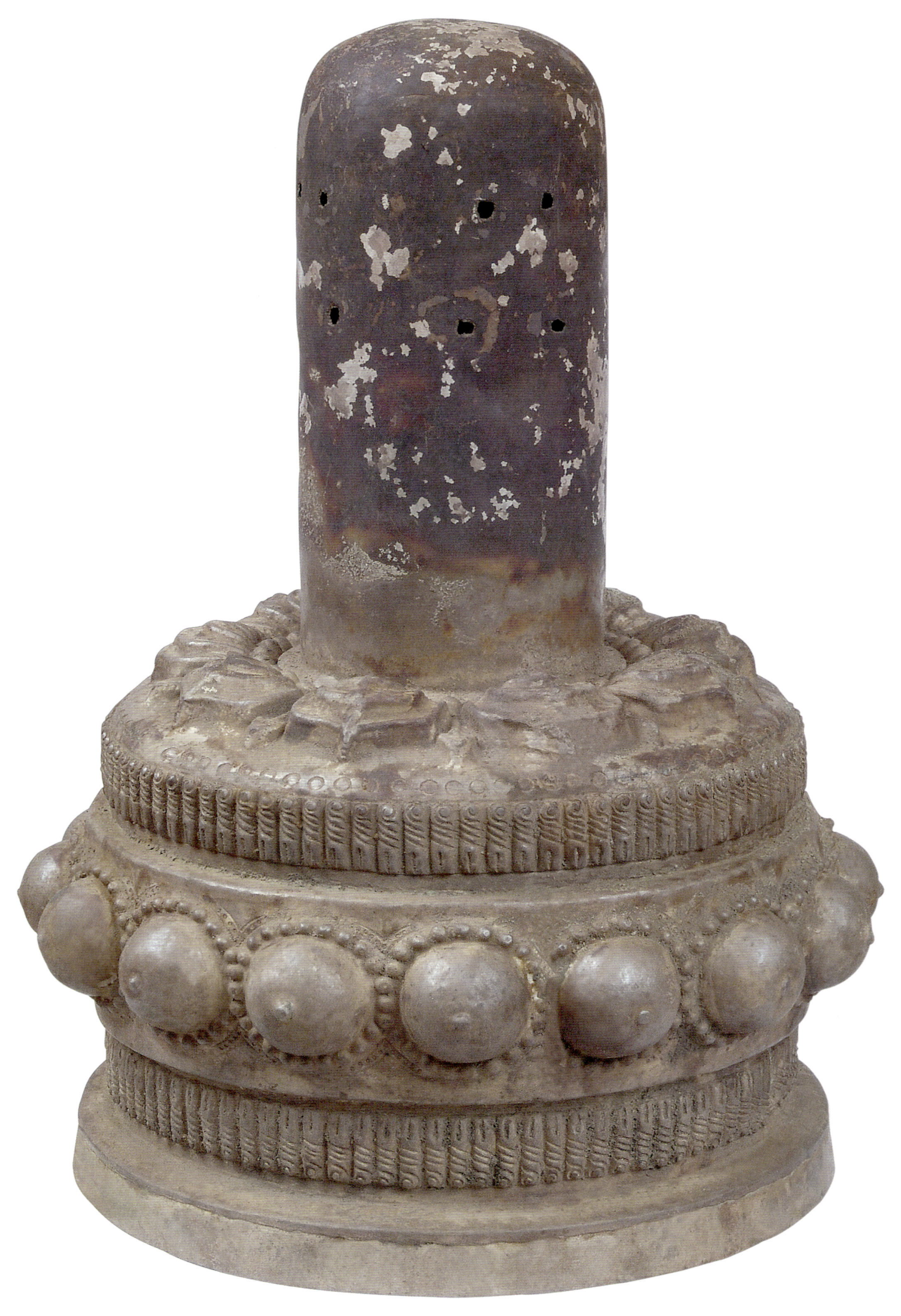

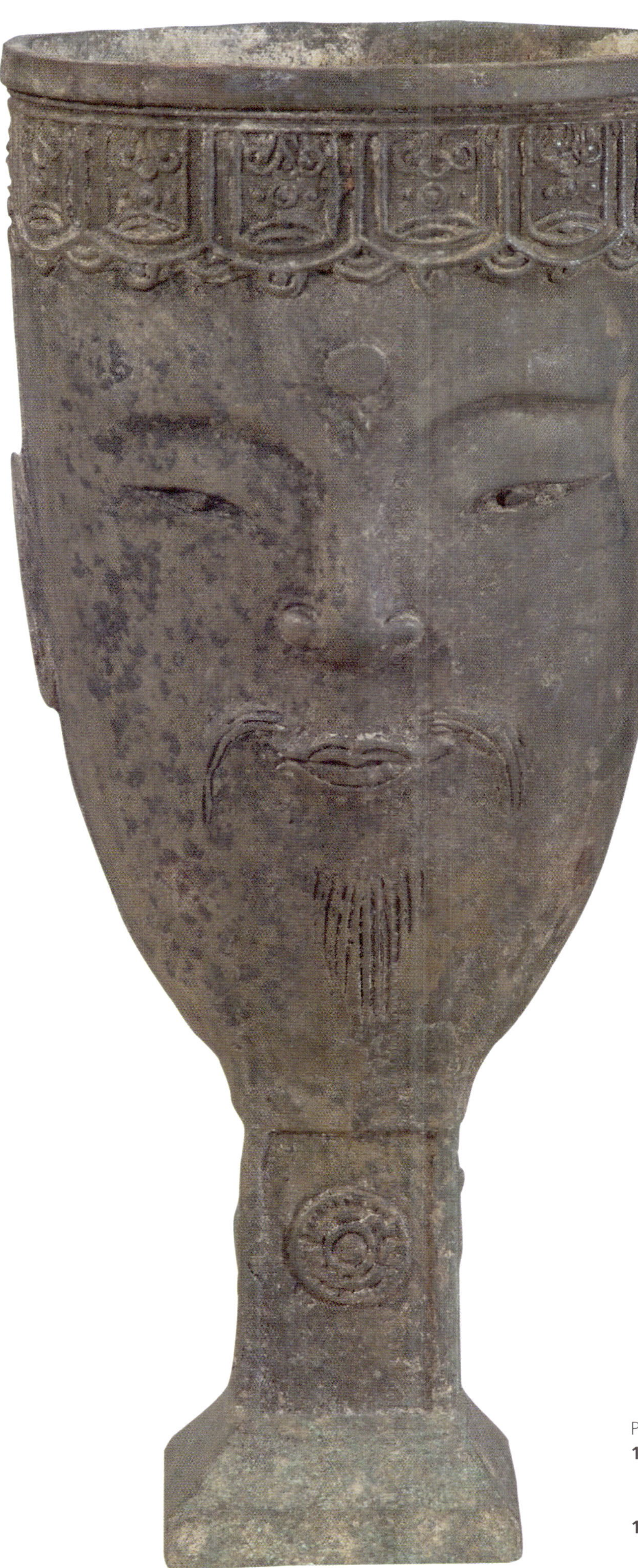

Previous Page
100. *Linga within a ring*, Silver, Height 27.5 cm, 11th Century.

101. *Cup with sage's face*, Bronze, Height 15.7 cm, 10th - 12th Century.

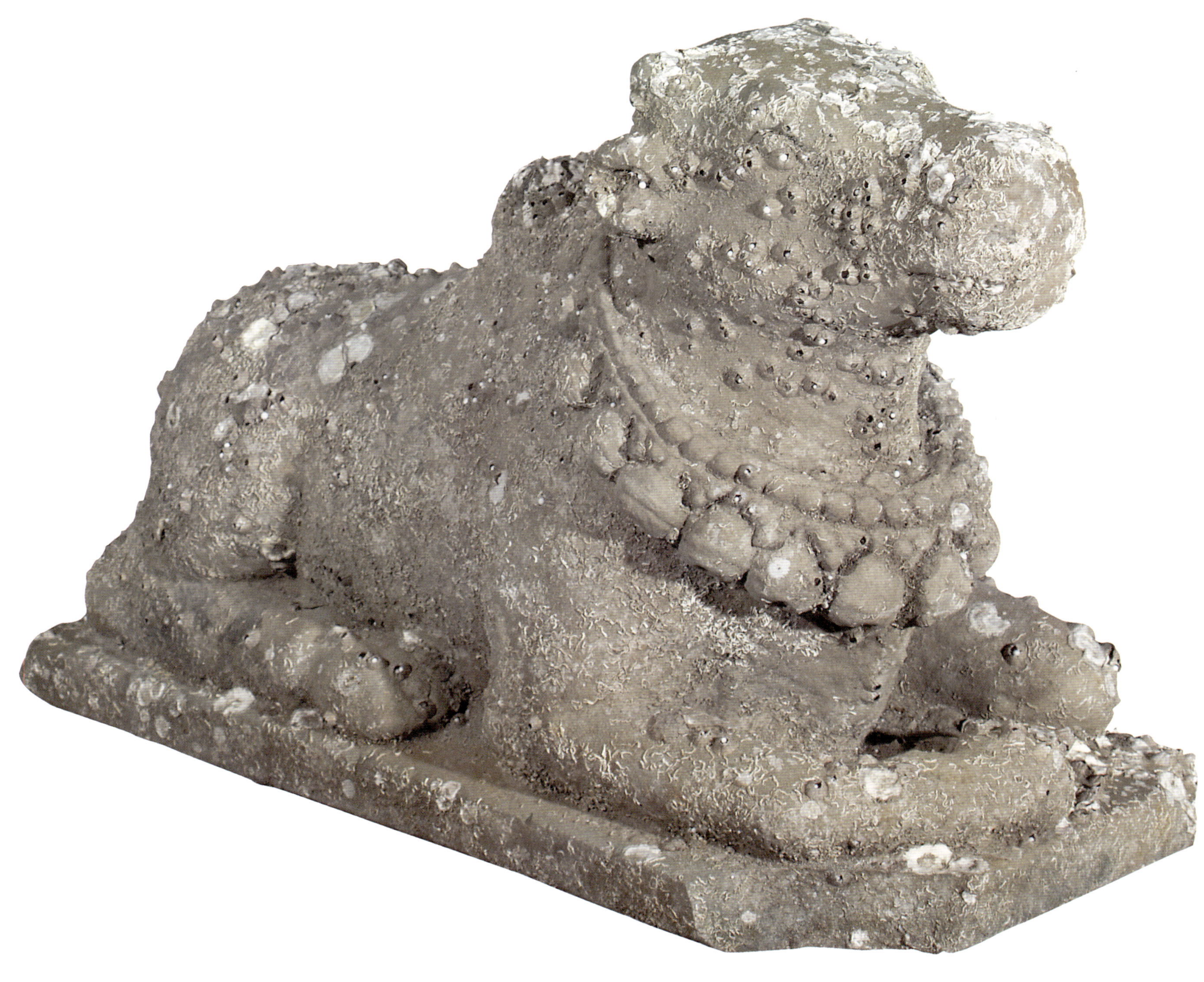

102. *Nandin bull*, Free-standing, Sandstone, Length 80 cm, Pre-Angkorian Khmer art, 7th Century.

Following Page
103. *Bull Nandin*, Free-standing, Sandstone, Length 68 cm, Tra Kiêu style, 10th Century.

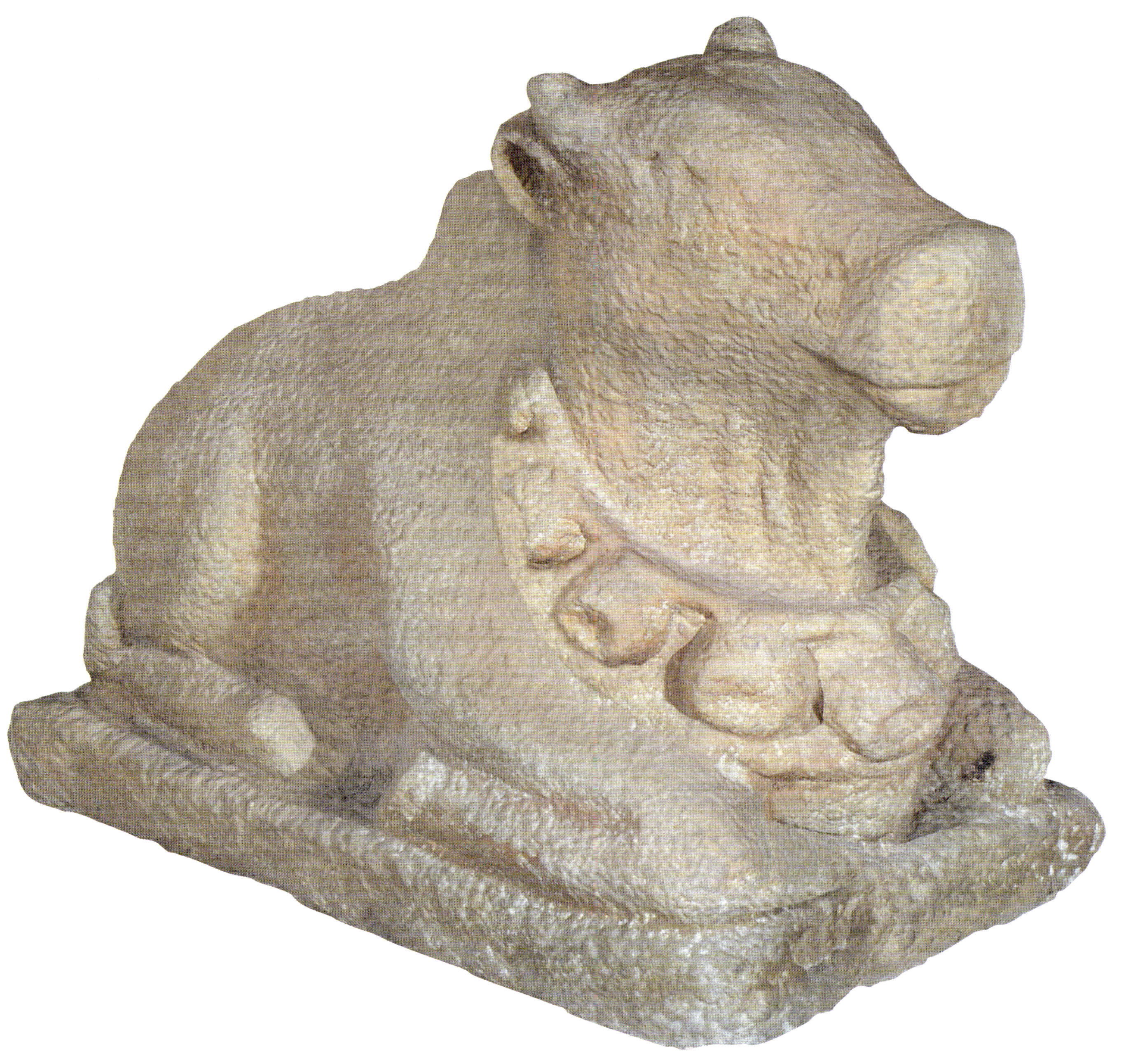

Nandin is Shiva's mount ("vahana" in Sanskrit). He is generally painted white. He is almost always found lying down, in a pavilion built in front of the entrance to temples dedicated to Shiva. And here again, after three centuries, the influence of pre angkhorien art on Cham art is particularly striking.

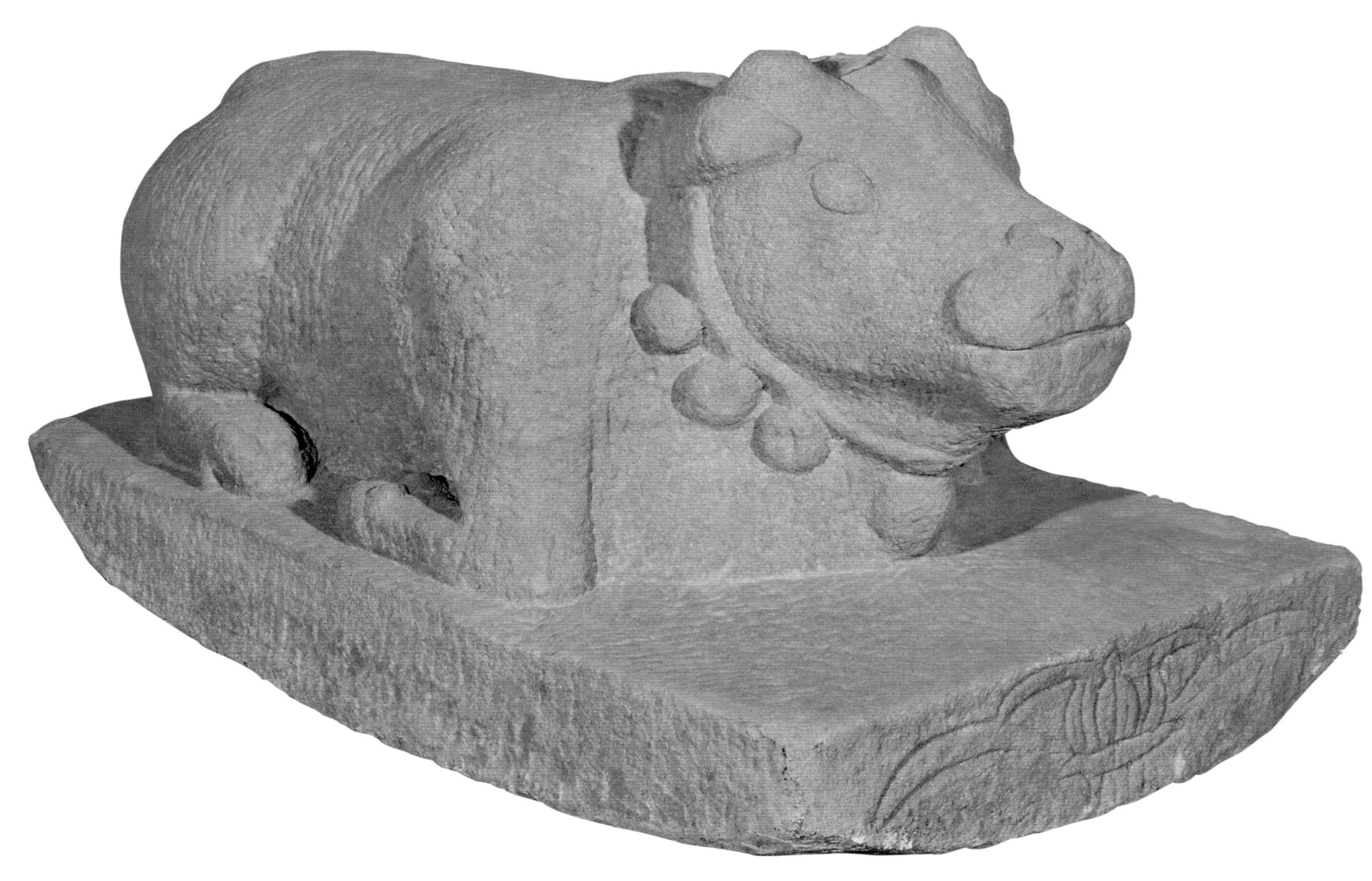

104. *Bull Nandin*, Free-standing, Sandstone, Length 83 cm, Tra Kiêu style, 10th Century.

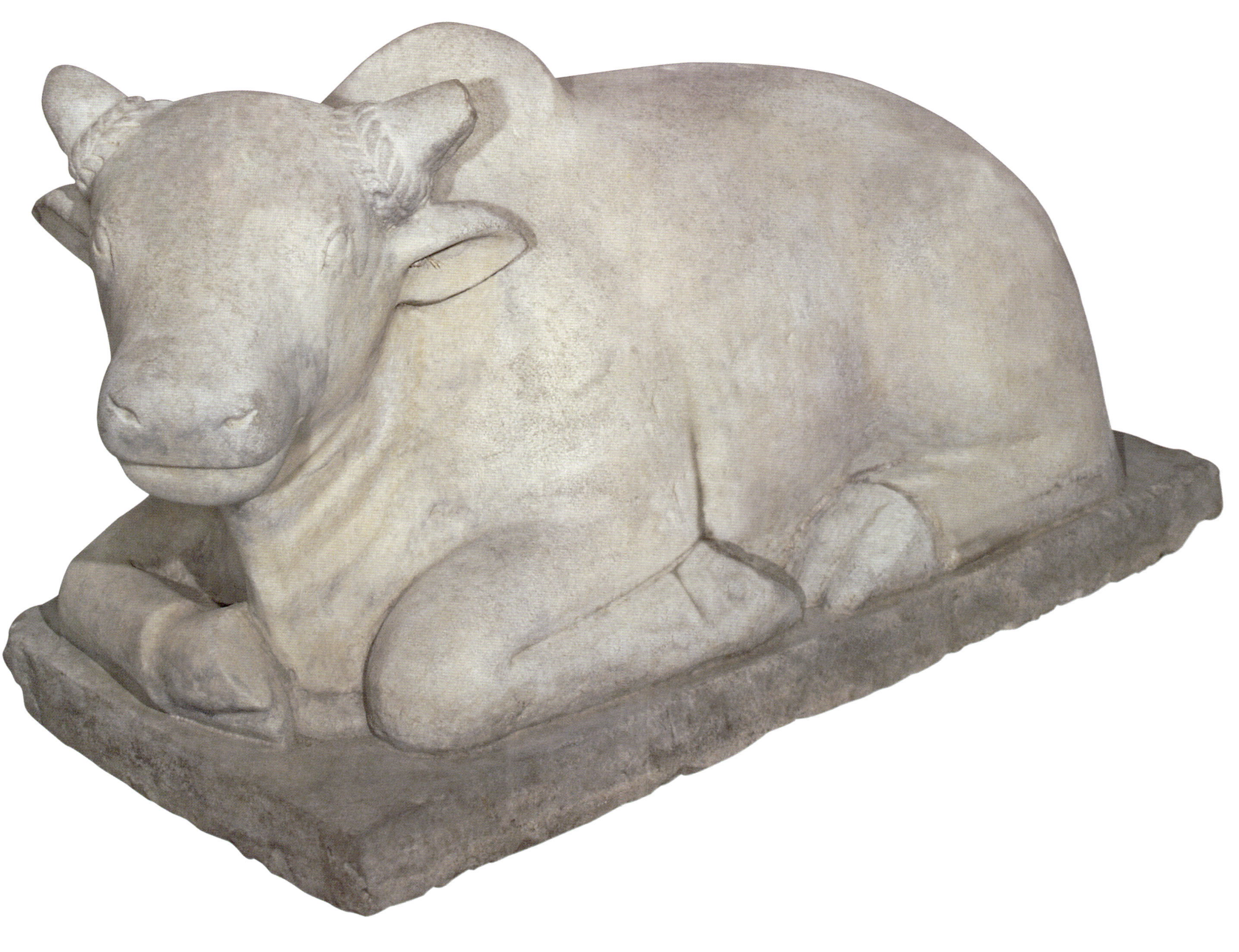

105. *Nandin bull*, Free-standing, Sandstone, Length 70 cm, Khmer art from the delta, 10th - 11th Century.

The white stone is characteristic of the Chau Doc region.

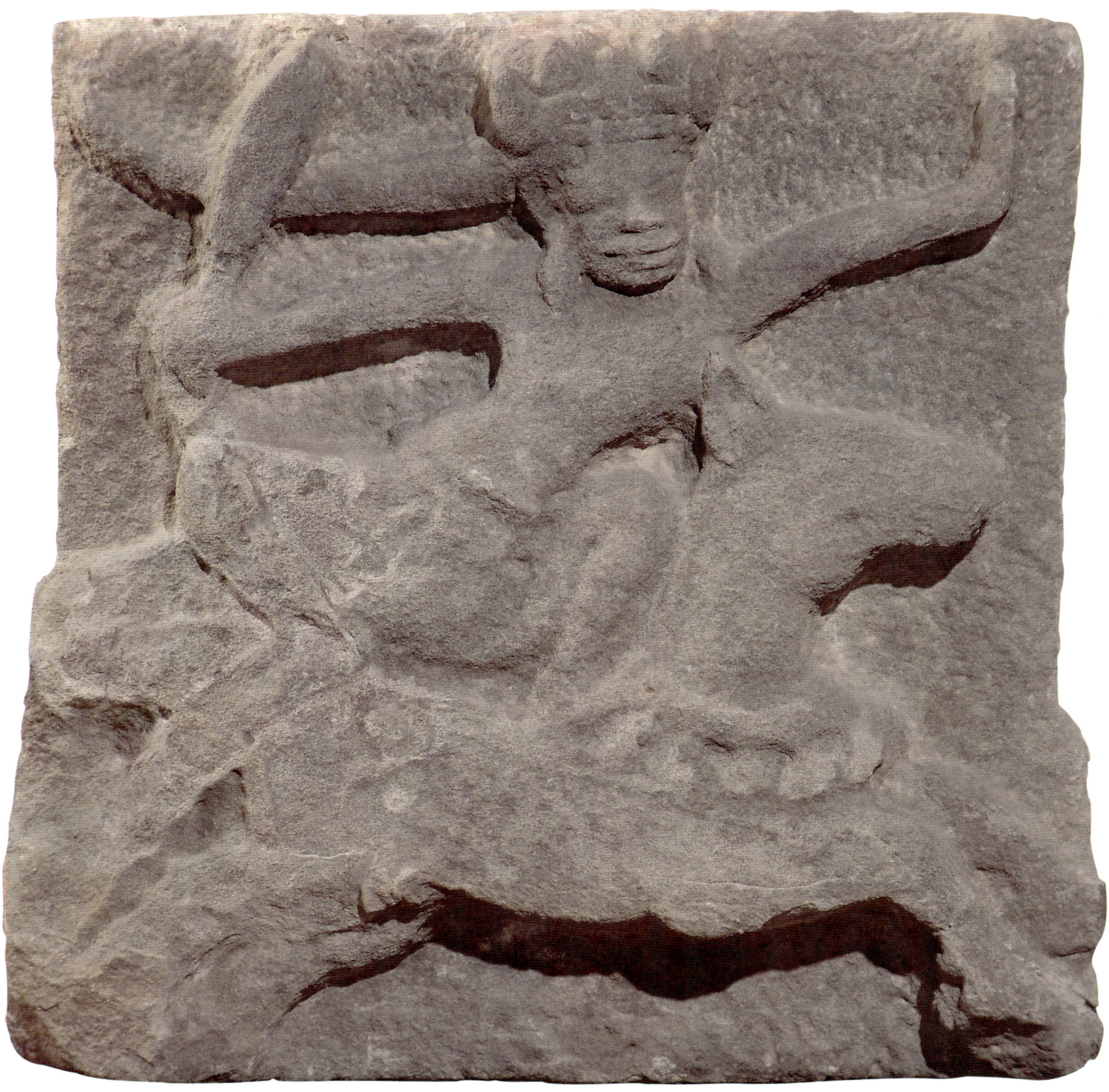

The figure carries a sabre, but his position on the animal, crouching, with outstretched arms, suggests a dance. The facial traits repeat, in a softer way, the characteristics of the Dong Duong style.

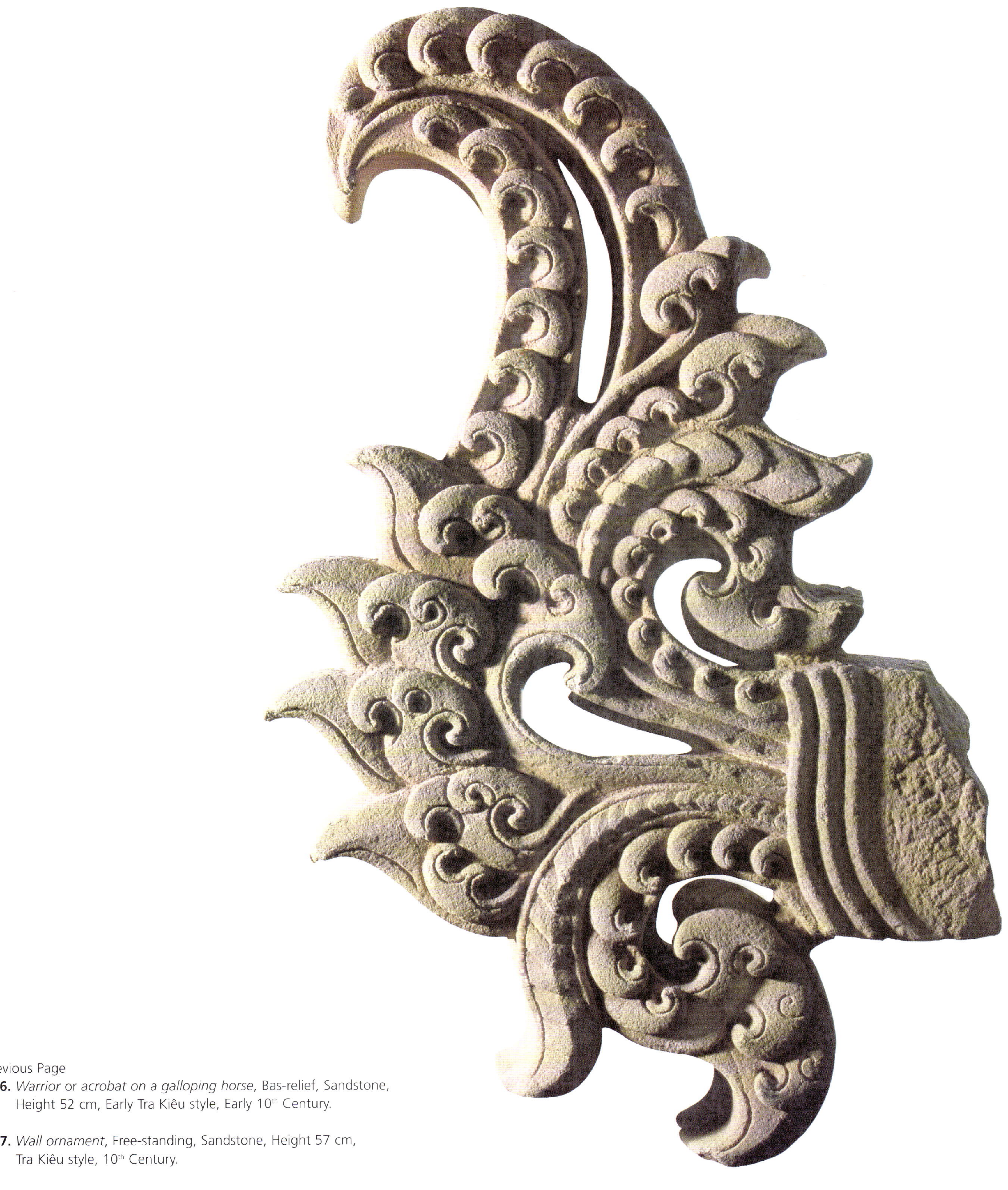

Previous Page
106. *Warrior* or *acrobat on a galloping horse*, Bas-relief, Sandstone, Height 52 cm, Early Tra Kiêu style, Early 10th Century.

107. *Wall ornament*, Free-standing, Sandstone, Height 57 cm, Tra Kiêu style, 10th Century.

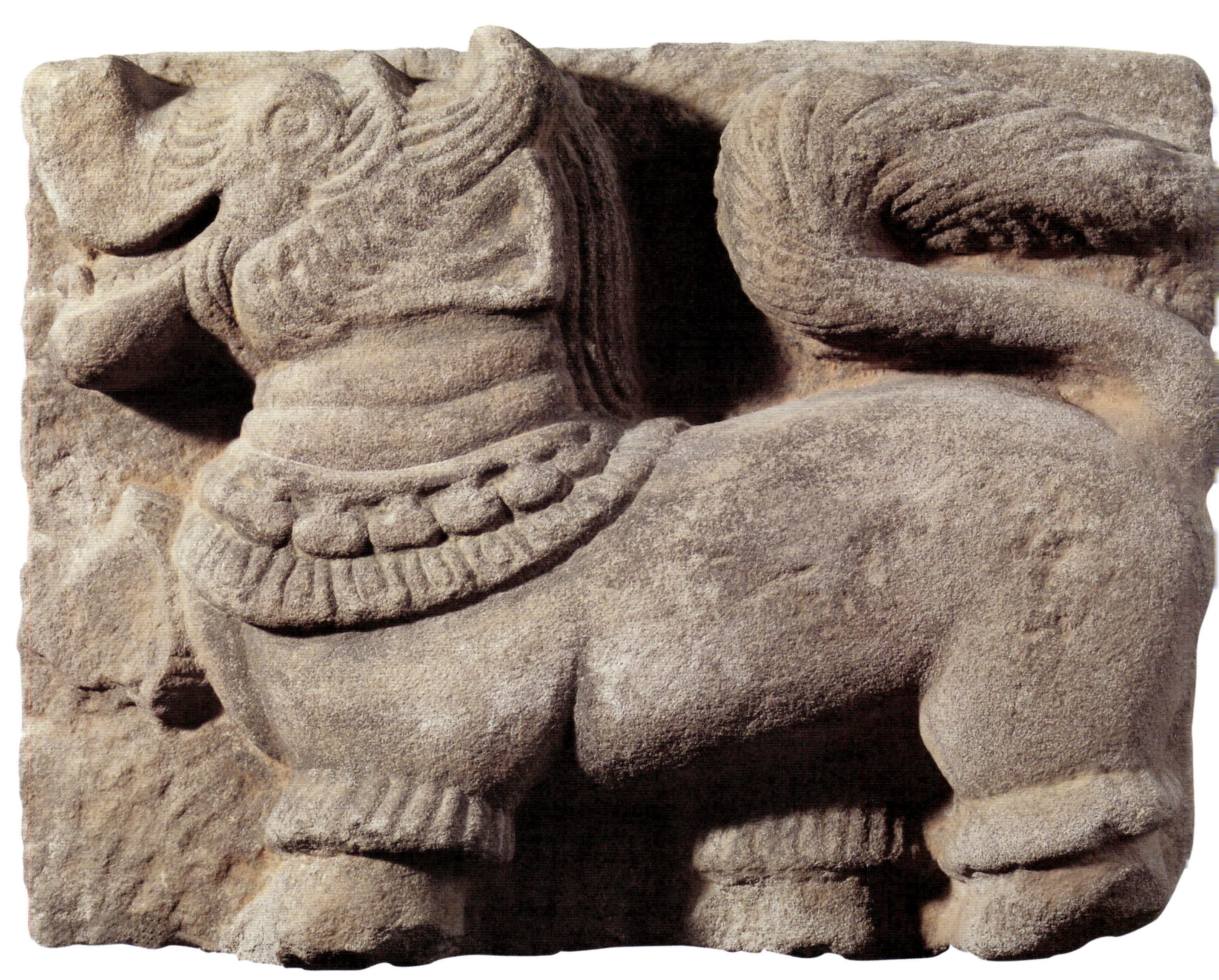

108. *Gajasimha*, Bas-relief, Sandstone, Height 31 cm, Tra Kiêu style, 10th Century.

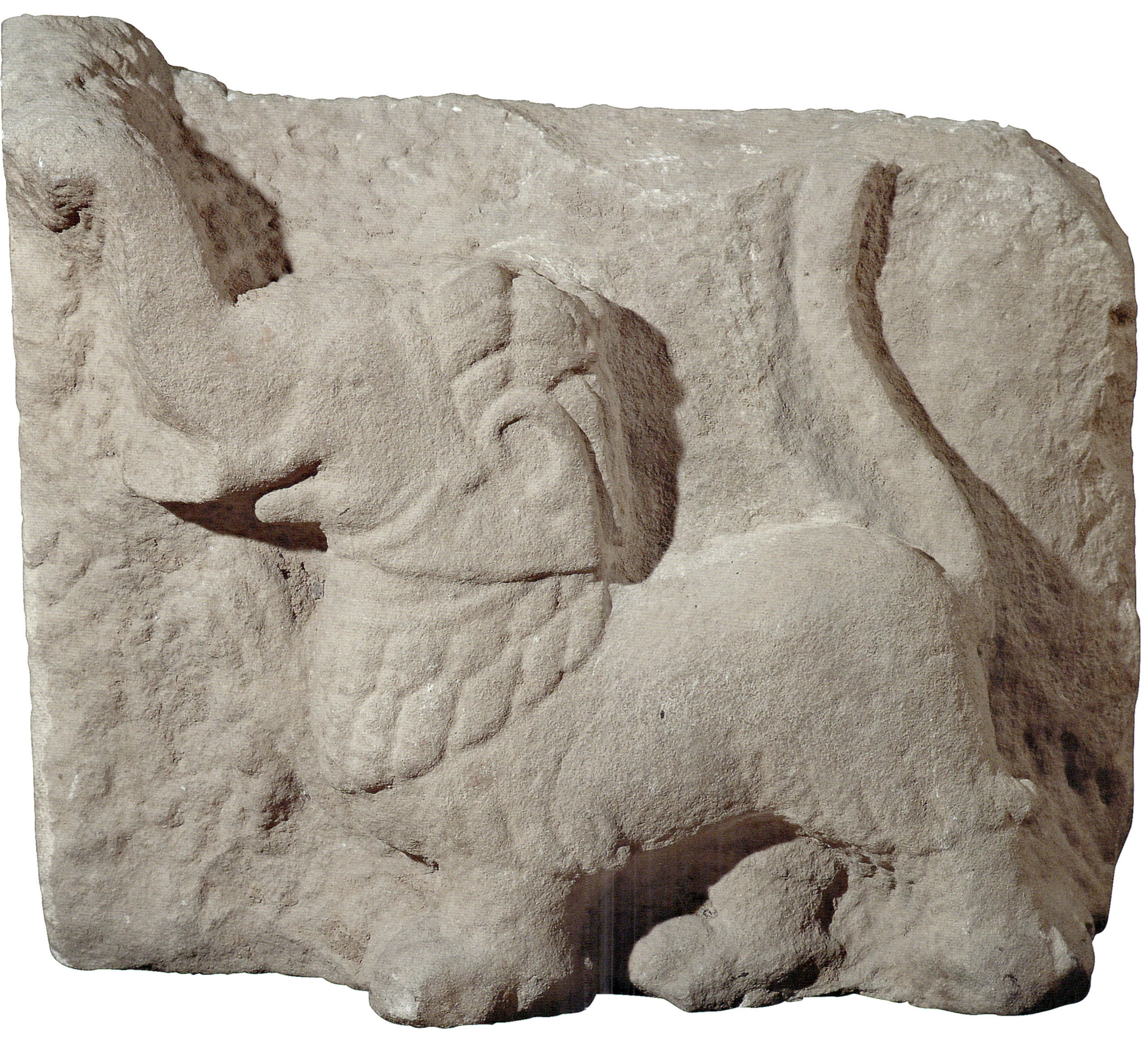

109. *Gajasimha*, High-relief, Sandstone, Height 50 cm, Tra Kiêu style, 10th Century.

One could propose an older dating for this type of representation.

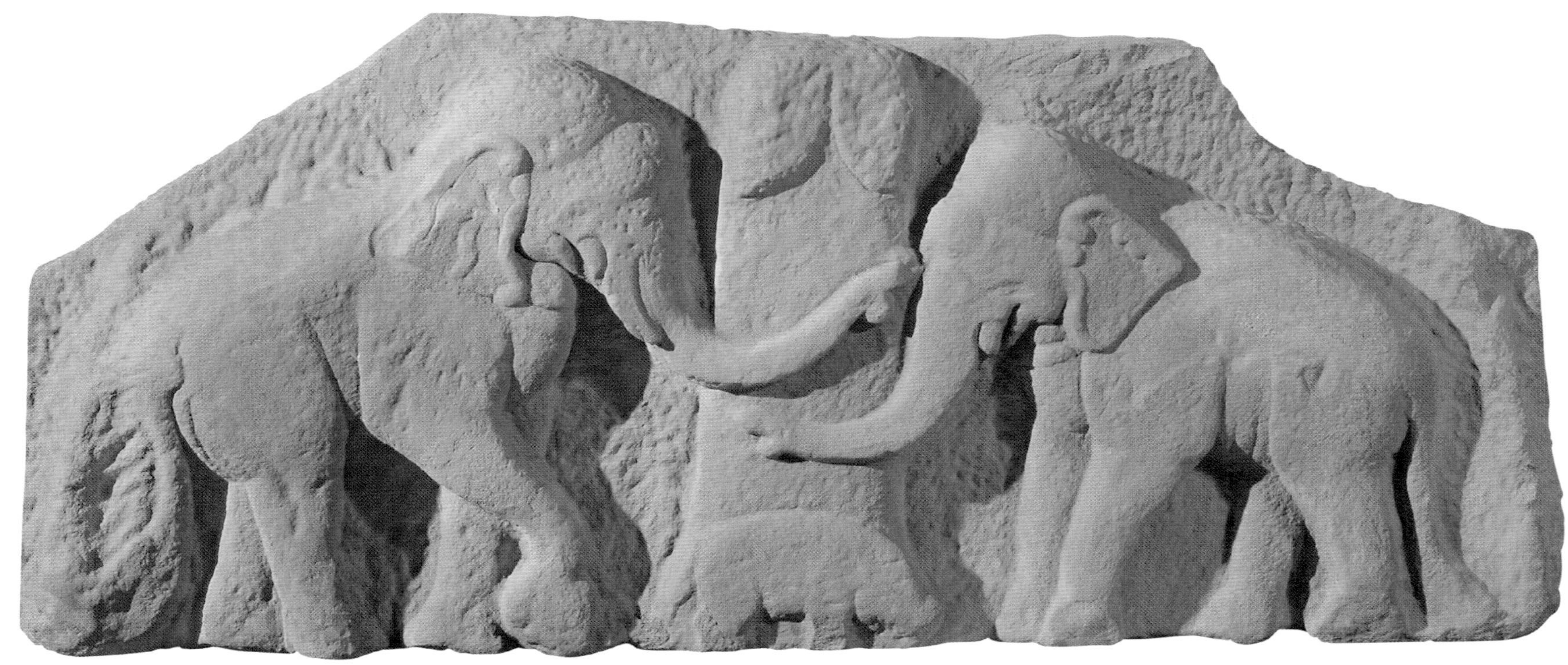

Despite all our research, we have been unable to discover a religious explanation for the boar sculpted in bas-relief. Nevertheless, in the interest of research, it can be remembered that very old Indian texts such as the Shatapatha Bramhana report that Brahma himself may have become a boar to lift the Earth out of the mud during the great flood. The Ramayana picks up a similar theme in referring to the boar Emusha. Finally, let us keep in mind that the boar Varaha is an avatar of Vishnu.

110. *Elephants adoring a linga*, Bas-relief, Sandstone, Length 95 cm, Tra Kiêu style, 10th Century.

Following Page
111. *Crowned elephant*, High-relief, Sandstone, Height 70 cm, Tra Kiêu style, 10th Century.

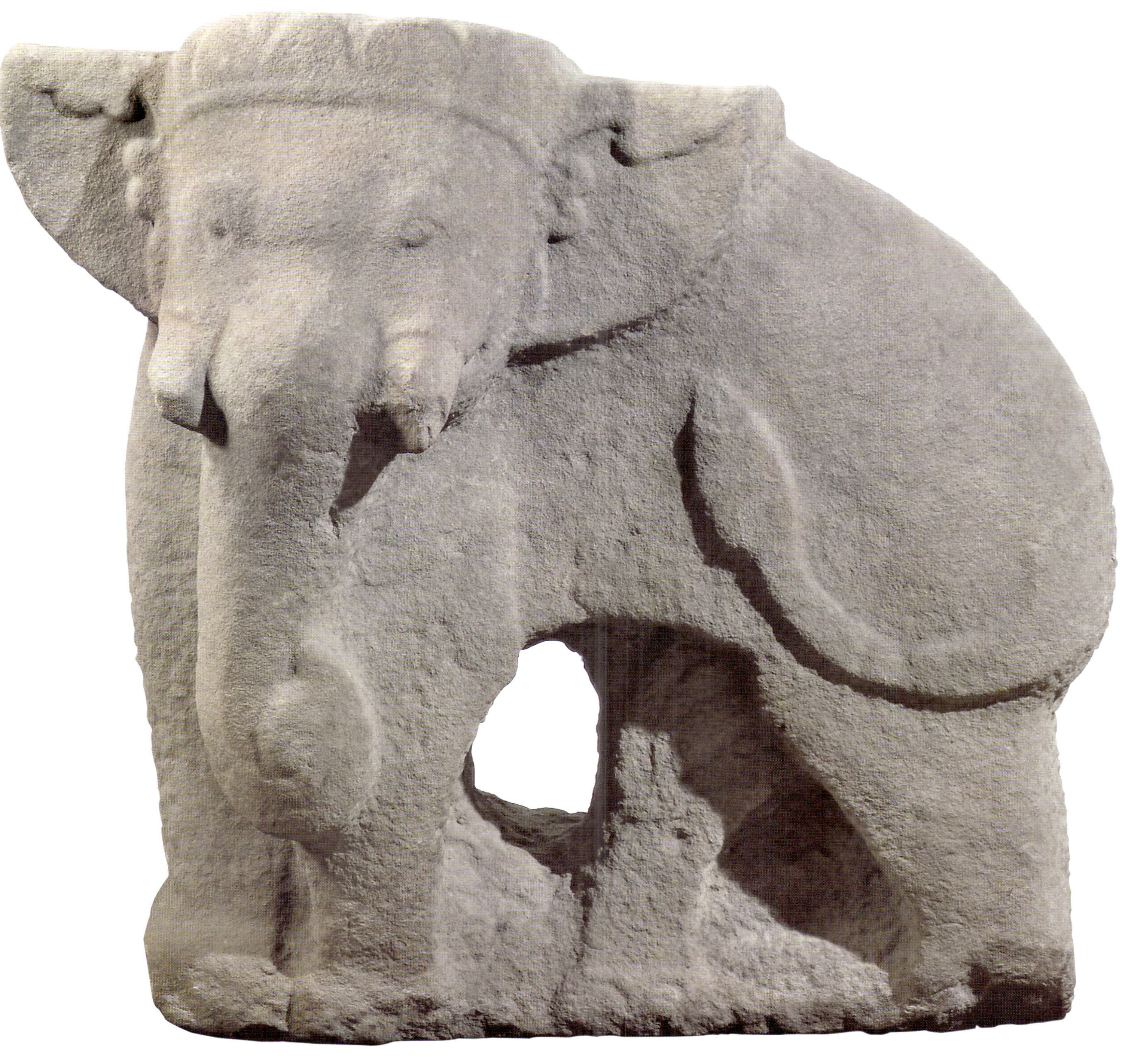

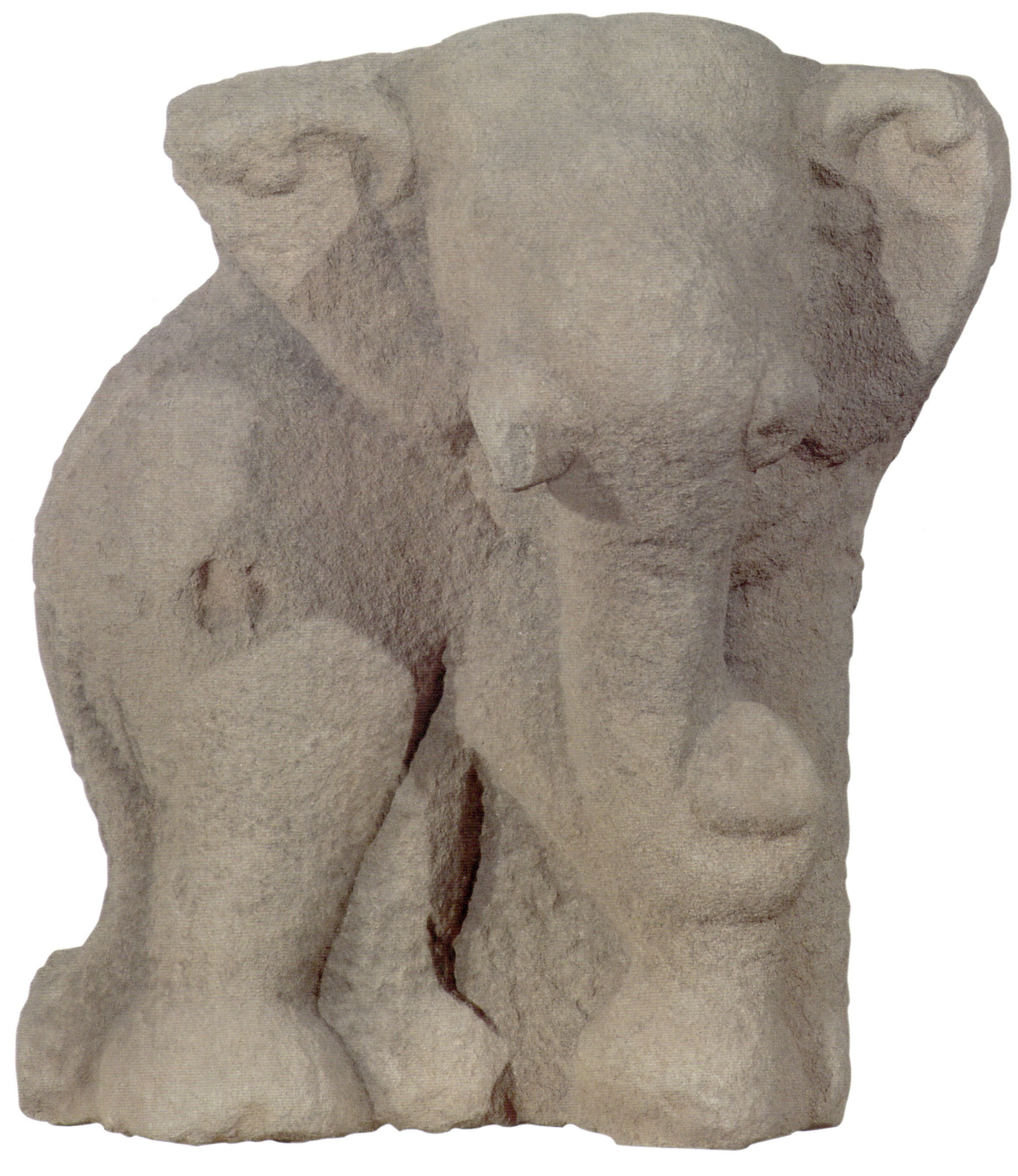

112. *Elephant*, High-relief, Sandstone, Height 33 cm, Tra Kiêu style, 10th Century.

Following Page
113. *Elephant*, High-relief, Sandstone, Height 44.5 cm, Tra Kiêu style, 10th Century.

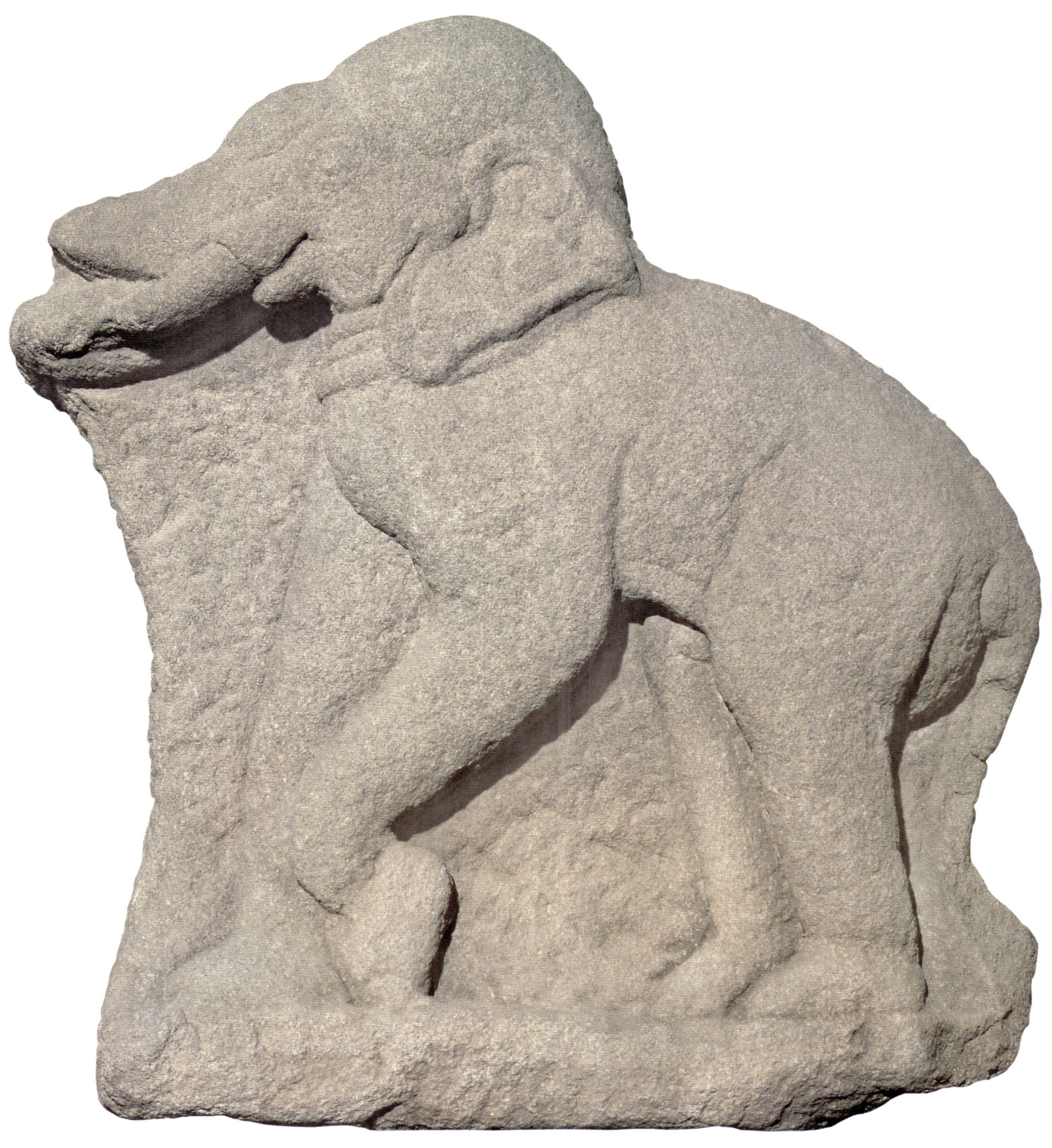

The animal is shown here in profile, which is rarer than a frontal view.

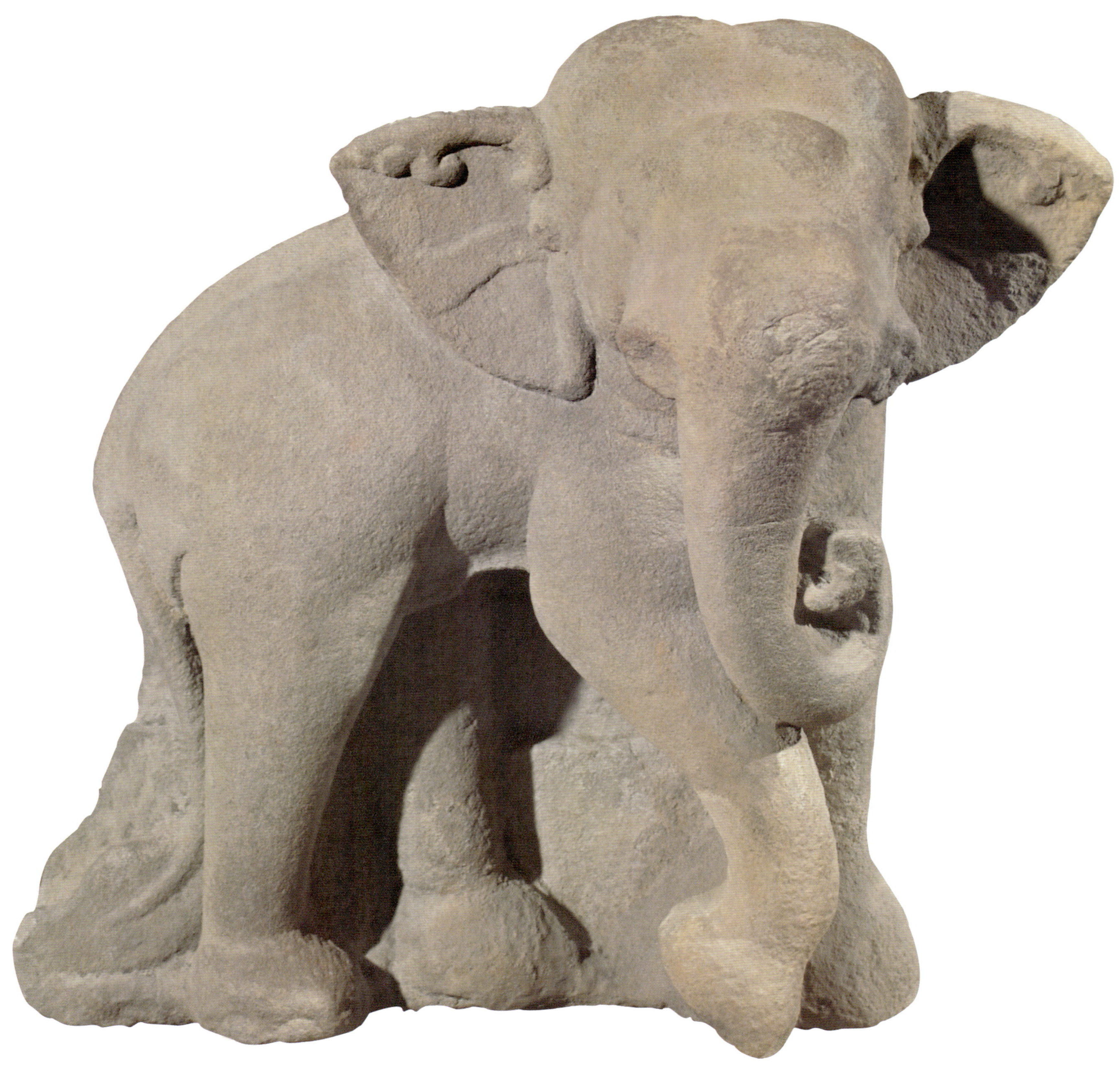

114. *Elephant*, High-relief, Sandstone, Height 51 cm, Tra Kiêu style, 10th Century.

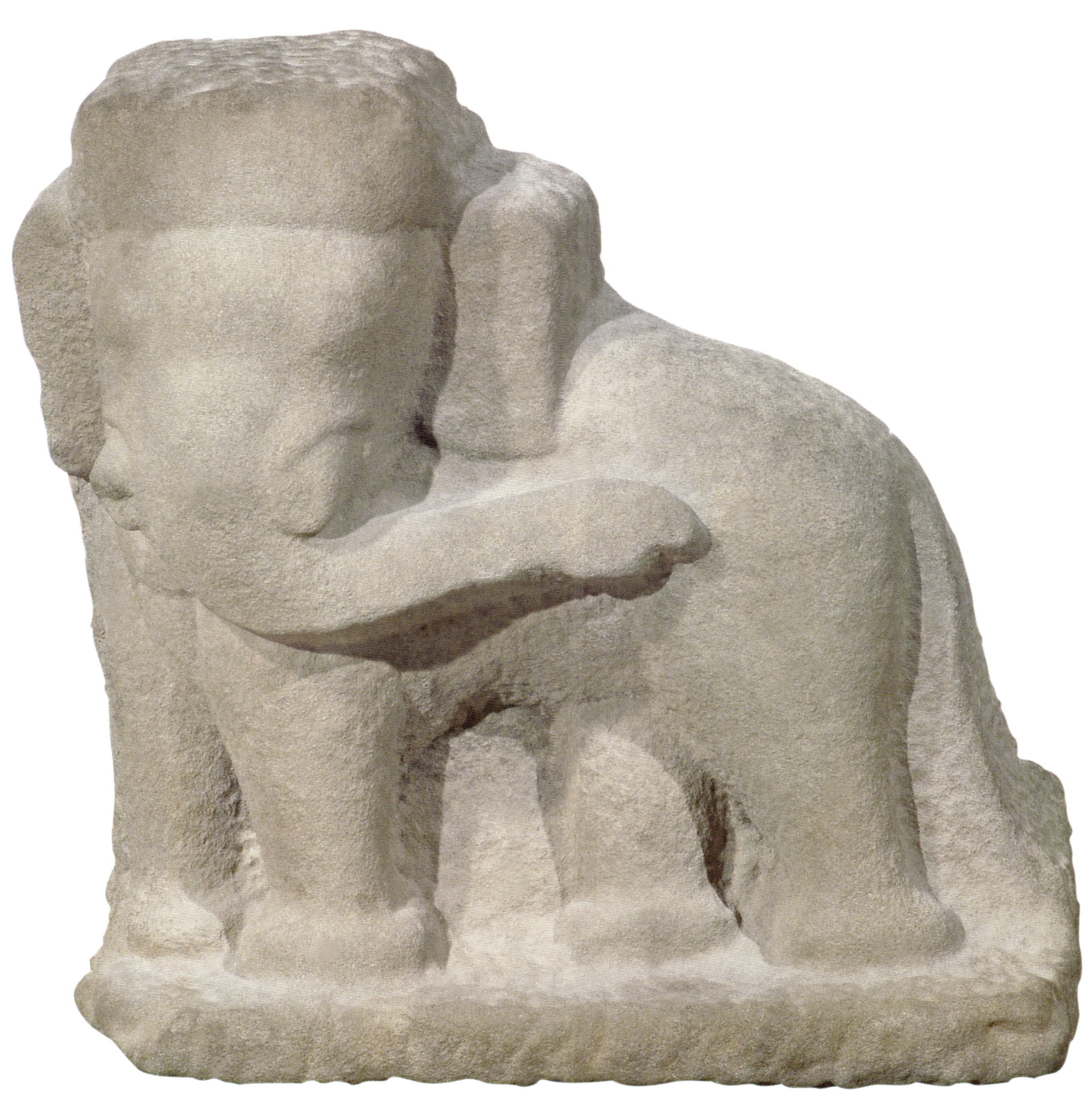

115. *Elephant*, High-relief, Sandstone, Height 38 cm, Tra K êu style, 10th Century.

A scarcely traced crown sits on the animal's head.

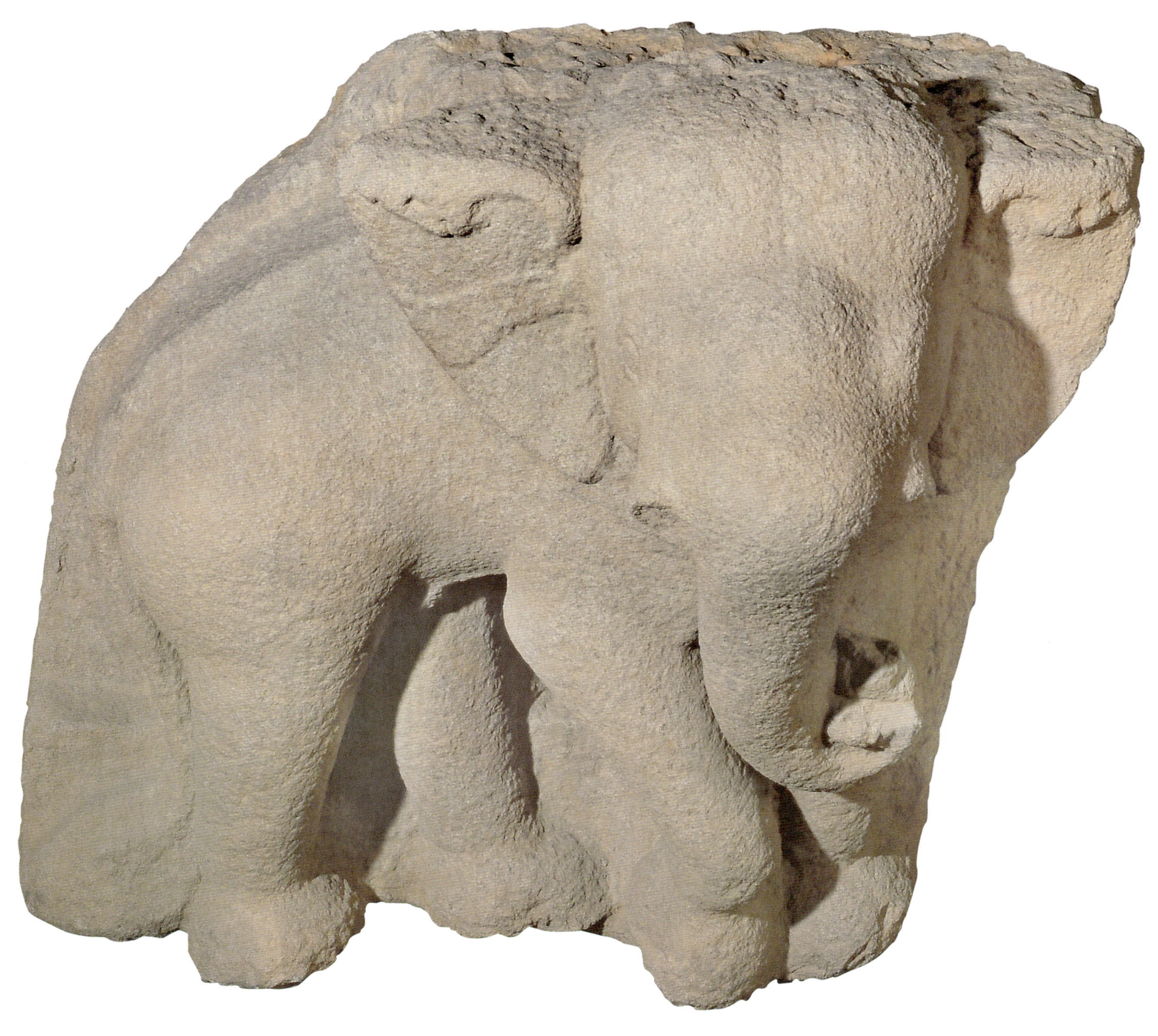

116. *Elephant,* High-relief, Sandstone, Height 50 cm, Tra Kiêu style, 10th Century.

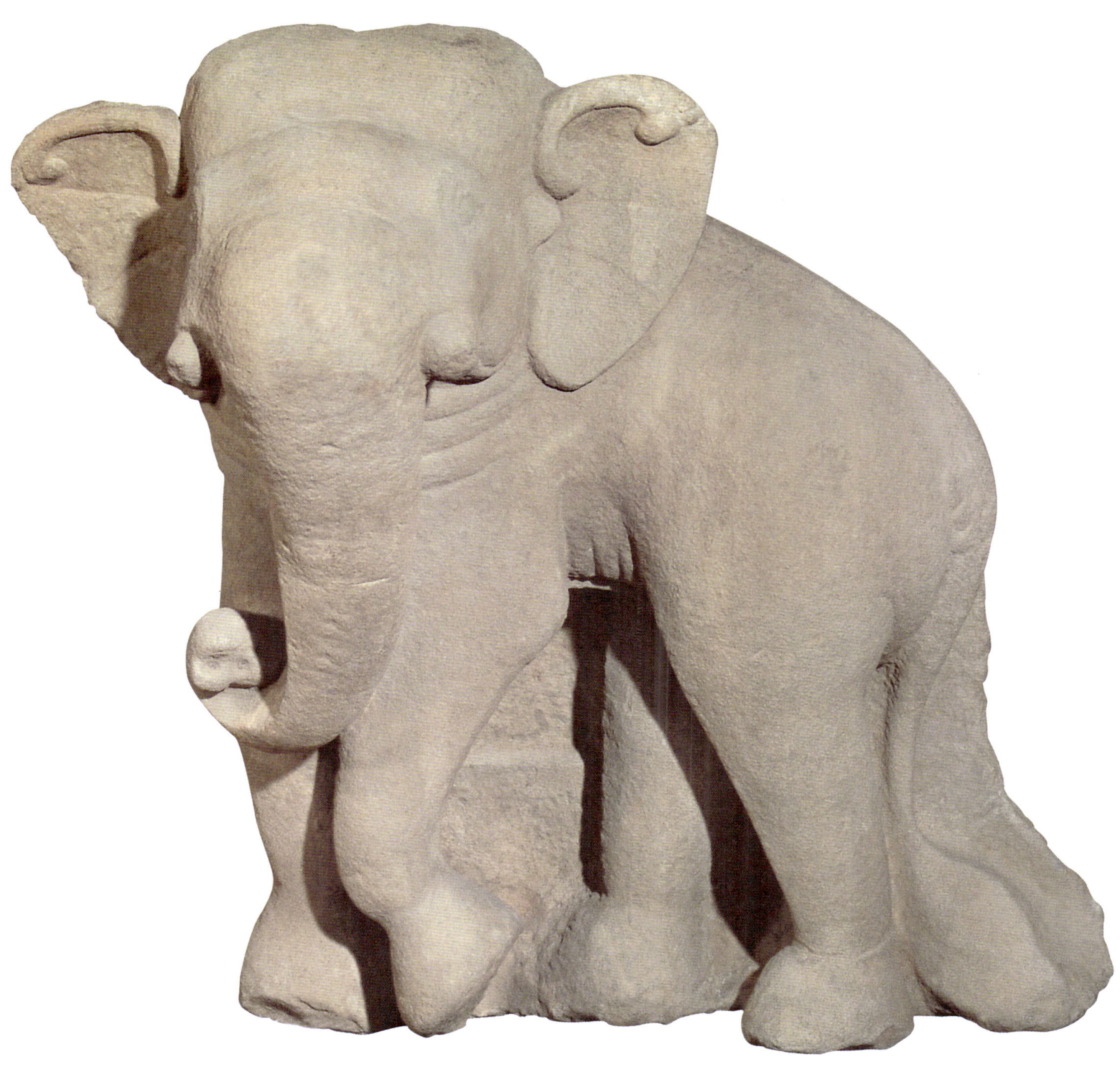

117. *Elephant*, High-relief, Sandstone, Height 50 cm,
Tra Kiêu style, 10th Century.

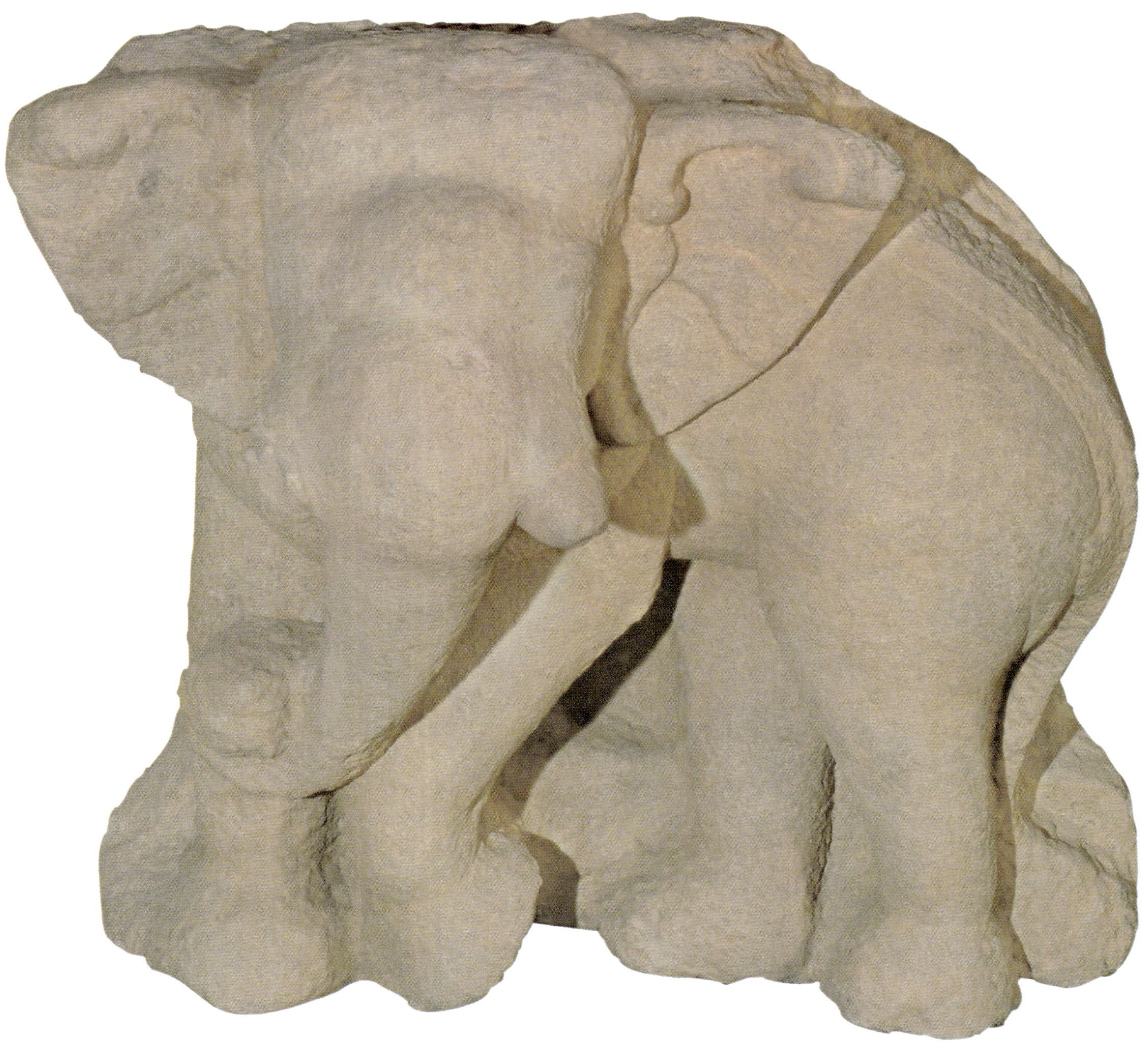

Elephants decorated bases and pedestals in honour of this animal's strength. In the tenth century, elements that characterised the preceding Dong Duong style (a somewhat stiff attitude, a bump on the forehead, stylised "hooves") disappeared. The animal was sculpted in a more natural way. It can be noted that it seems to be dancing, its front leg raised, its trunk swinging slightly to the left and very partially curled up. The animal is shown very realistically, if we get past its exaggeratedly squat appearance; the stylised ears and discreet rolls of fat in the neck. The elephant was at the heart of Cham civilisation. Weapon of combat, an elephant could be part of a herd of 1000 for a battle. A skilled porter, it accomplished household chores and could, if necessary, become an executioner in the case of punishment for murderers: the condemned was crushed under the feet of a pachyderm specially trained for this purpose. Such training was required because, by nature, an elephant kills a victim by lifting and then throwing him to the ground. Finally, the elephant was a member of parades. Usually, the animal is shown with short tusks as in Champa, following Indian custom, elephants' tusks were trimmed every three years in order to sell the ivory.

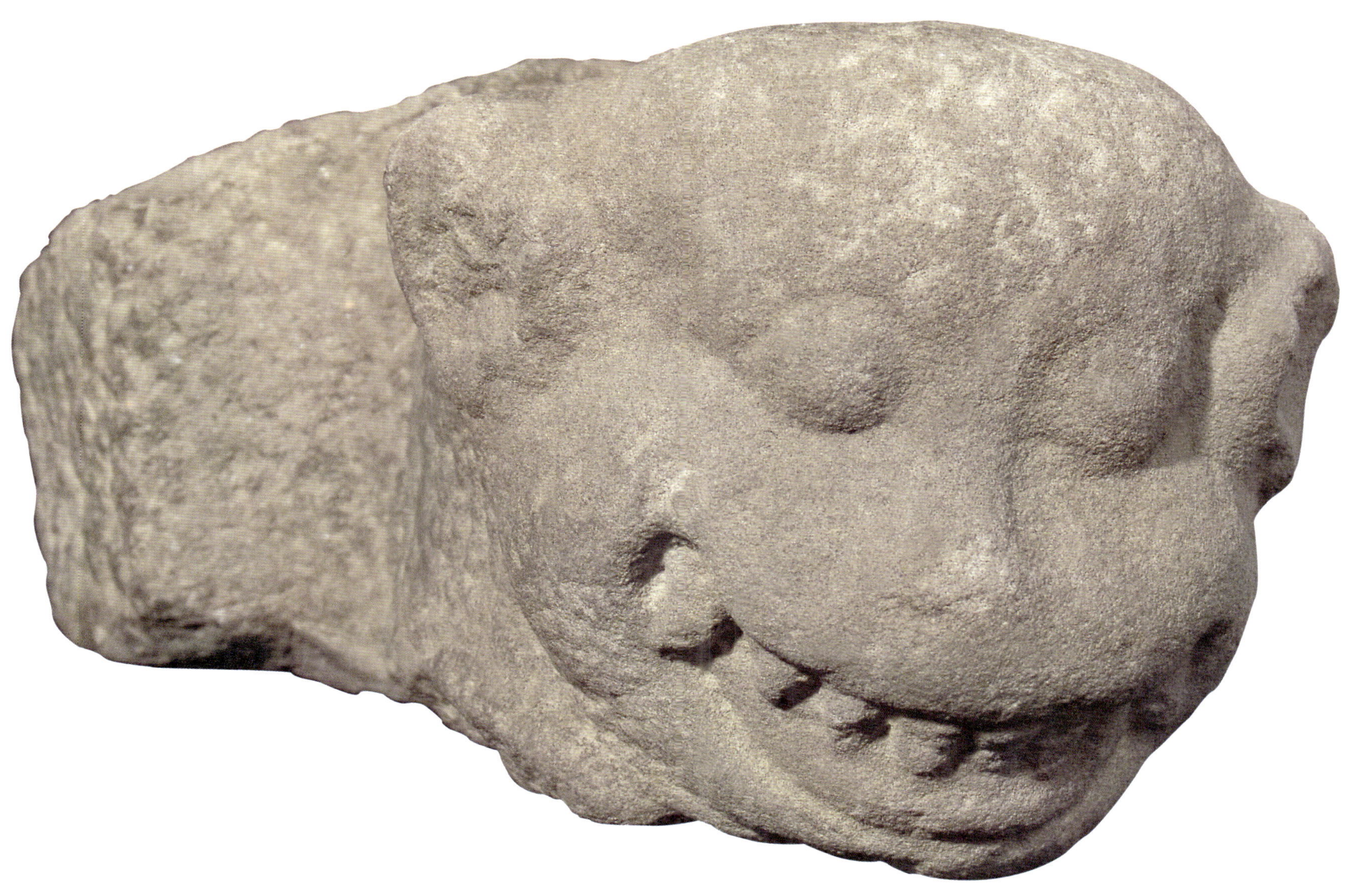

Previous Page
118. *Elephant*, High-relief, Sandstone, Height 50 cm, Tra Kiêu style, 10th Century.

119. *Monkey's head*, Nearly free-standing, Sandstone, Height 18 cm, Tra Kiêu style, 10th Century.

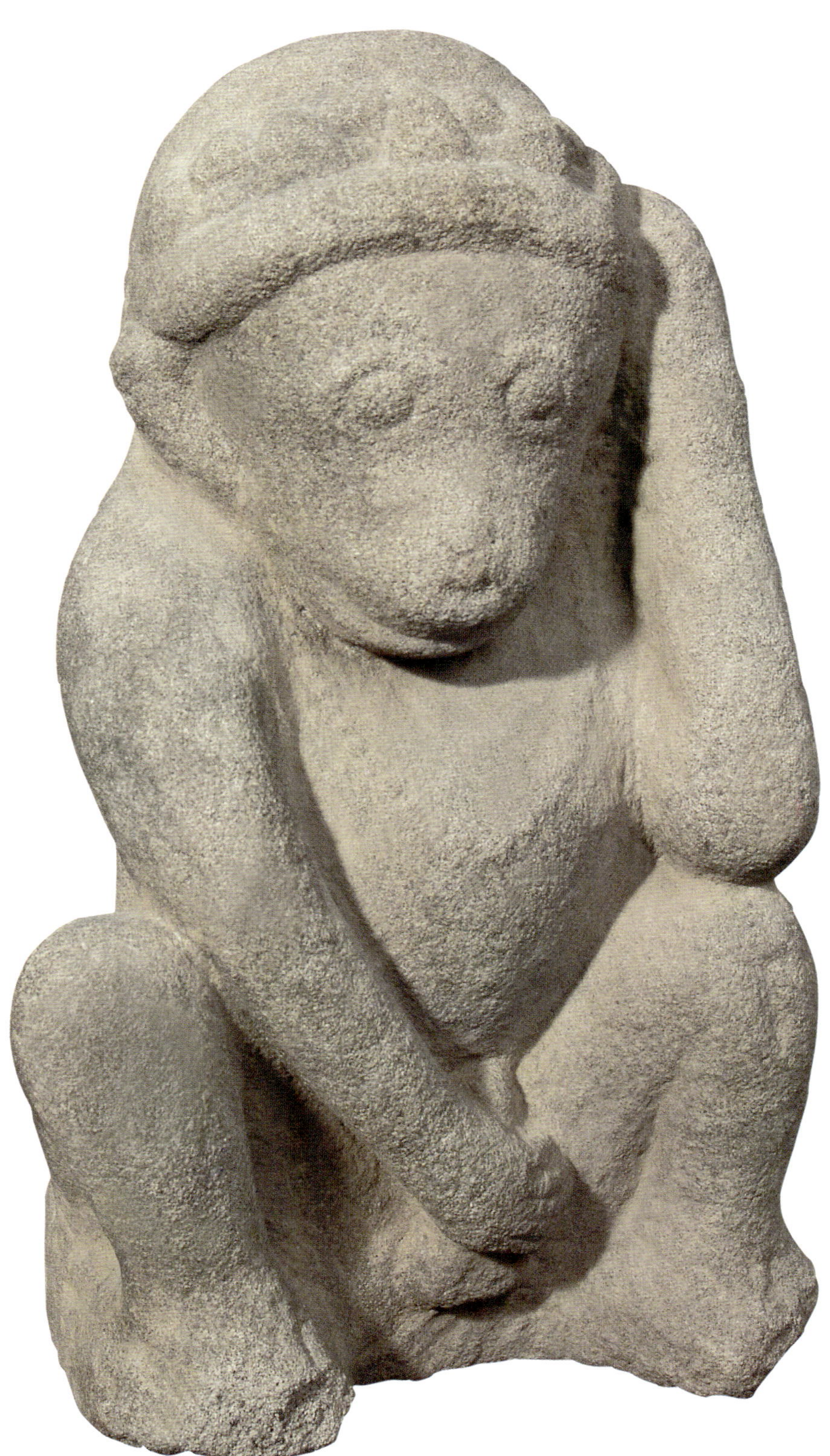

The monkey, wearing a crown, mischievously holds his hand over his sex. Sugriva is the king of the monkeys, Rama having made it possible for him to become ruler of the simian kingdom called Kiskindha by killing his rival and brother, the monkey Valin. Hanuman, the great white monkey, is commander-in-chief of the army. He also is described in the Ramayana, the great epic poem in Sanskrit that is (attributed to the monkey Valmiki) where Hanuman is Rama's main ally in his quest to find his wife Sita who was kidnapped by Ravana, king of the demons. Gifted with phenomenal powers (he is immortal and flies) he jumped in the course of his victorious journey directly from the Himalaya to Lanka (Sri Lanka). He is generally found in temples dedicated more to Vishnu. For a very long time, all monkeys were considered to represent Hanuman. Nevertheless, the crown clearly speaks of the animal's royalty and must lead us to identify him as Sugriva.

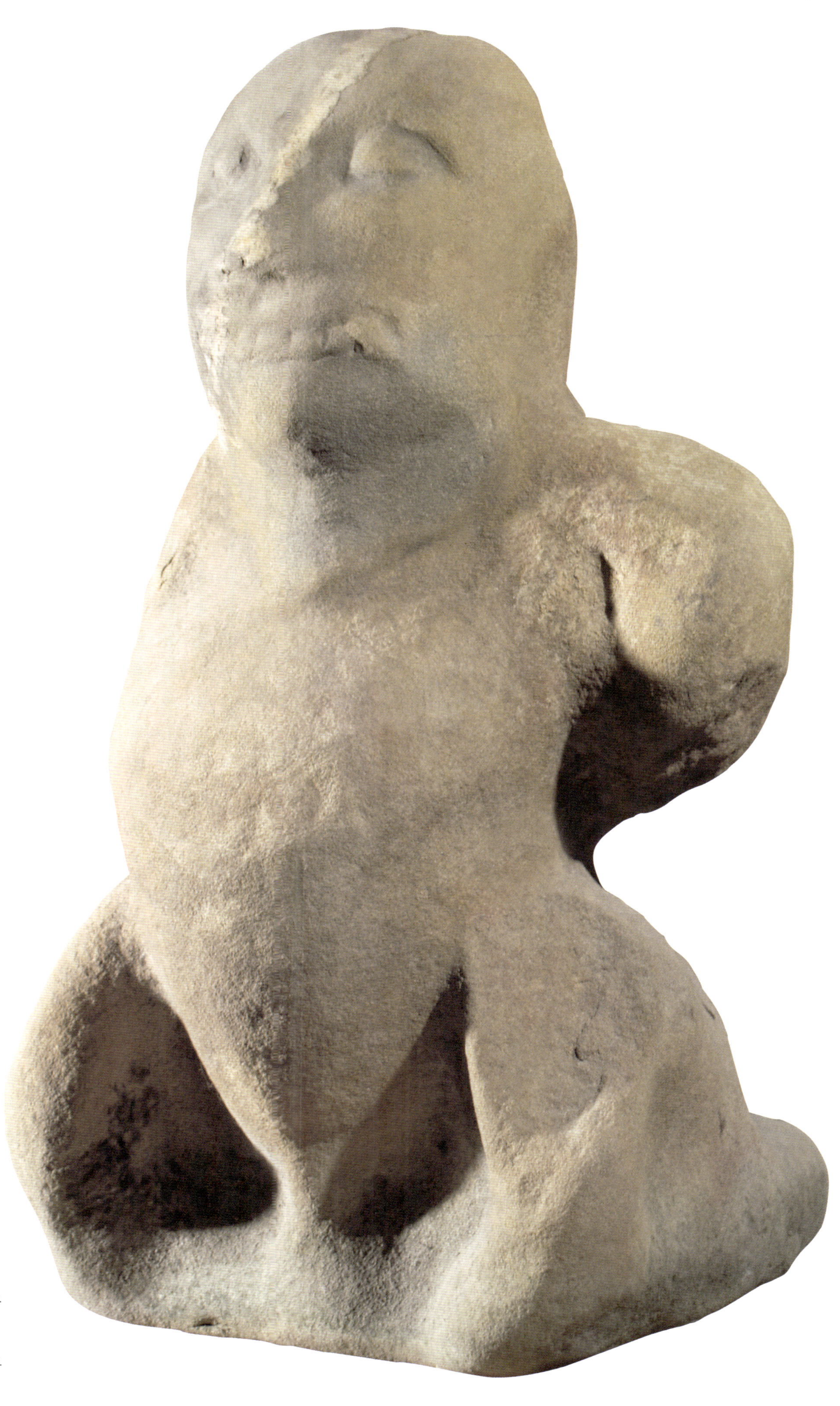

Previous Page
120. *Sugriva,* Free-standing, Sandstone, Height 35 cm, Tra Kiêu style, 10th Century.

121. *Monkey*, Free-standing, Sandstone, Height 50 cm, Tra Kiêu style, 10th Century.

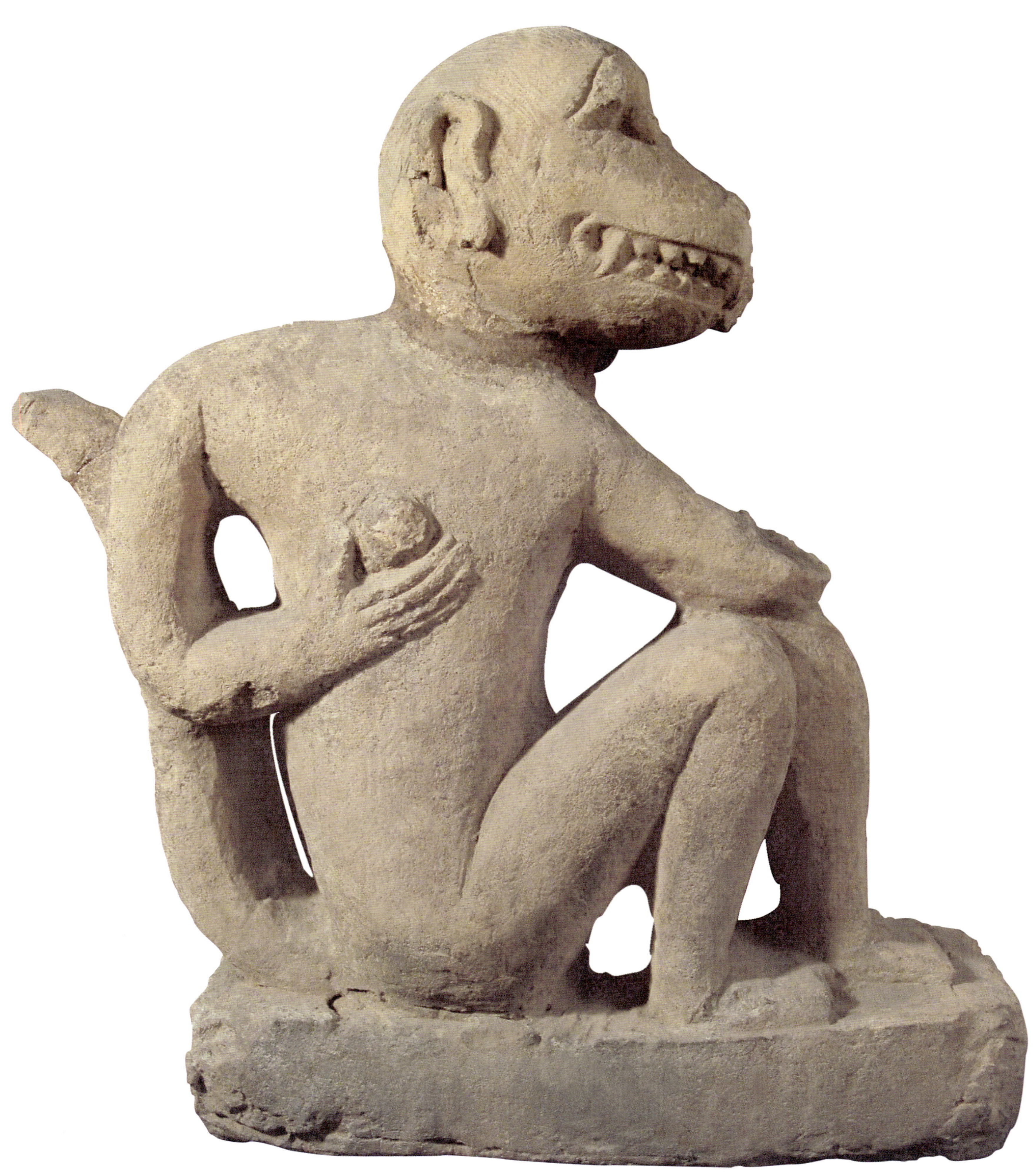

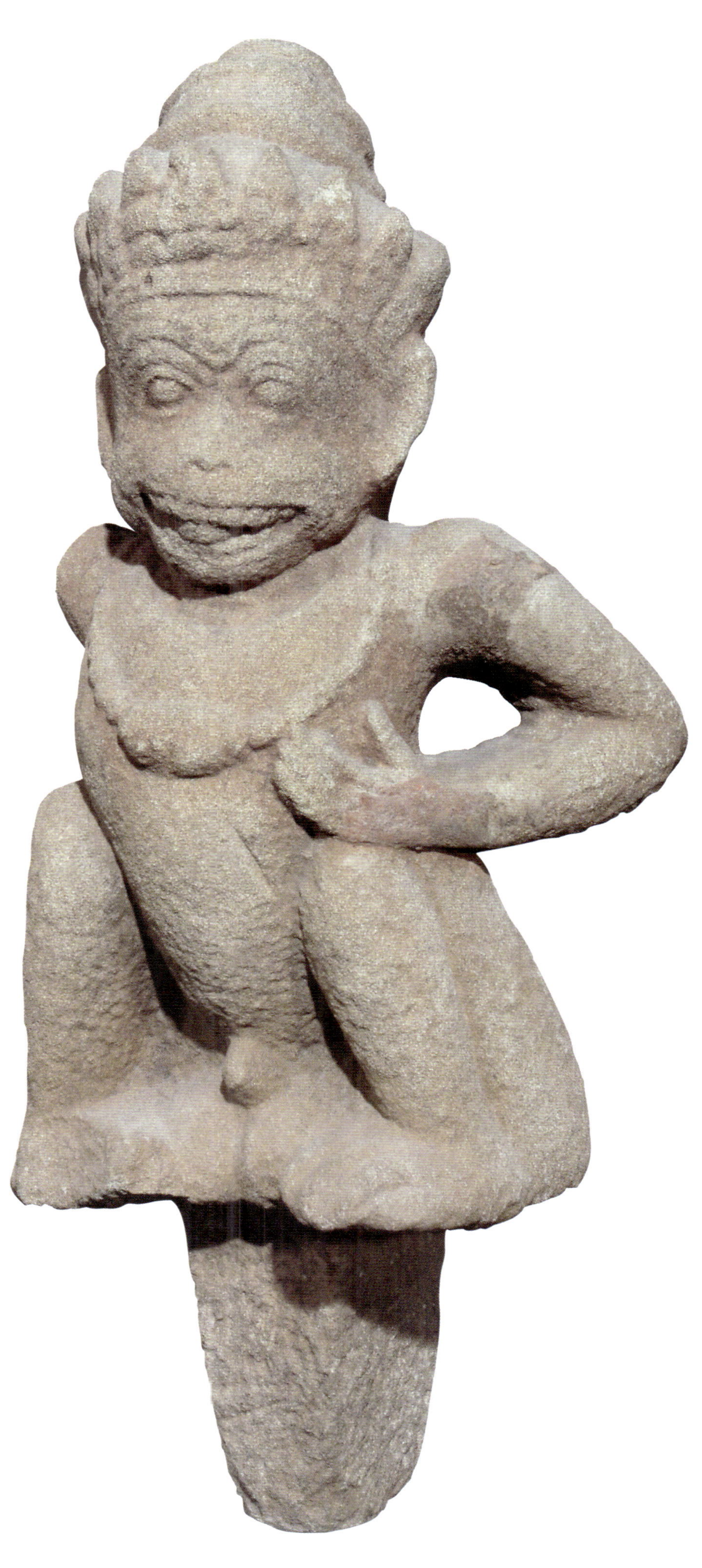

Previous Page
122. *Hanuman*, Free-standing, Clay, Height 40 cm, Tra Kiêu style, 10th Century.

123. *Sugriva,* Free-standing, Sandstone, Height 47 cm, Tra Kiêu style, 10th Century.

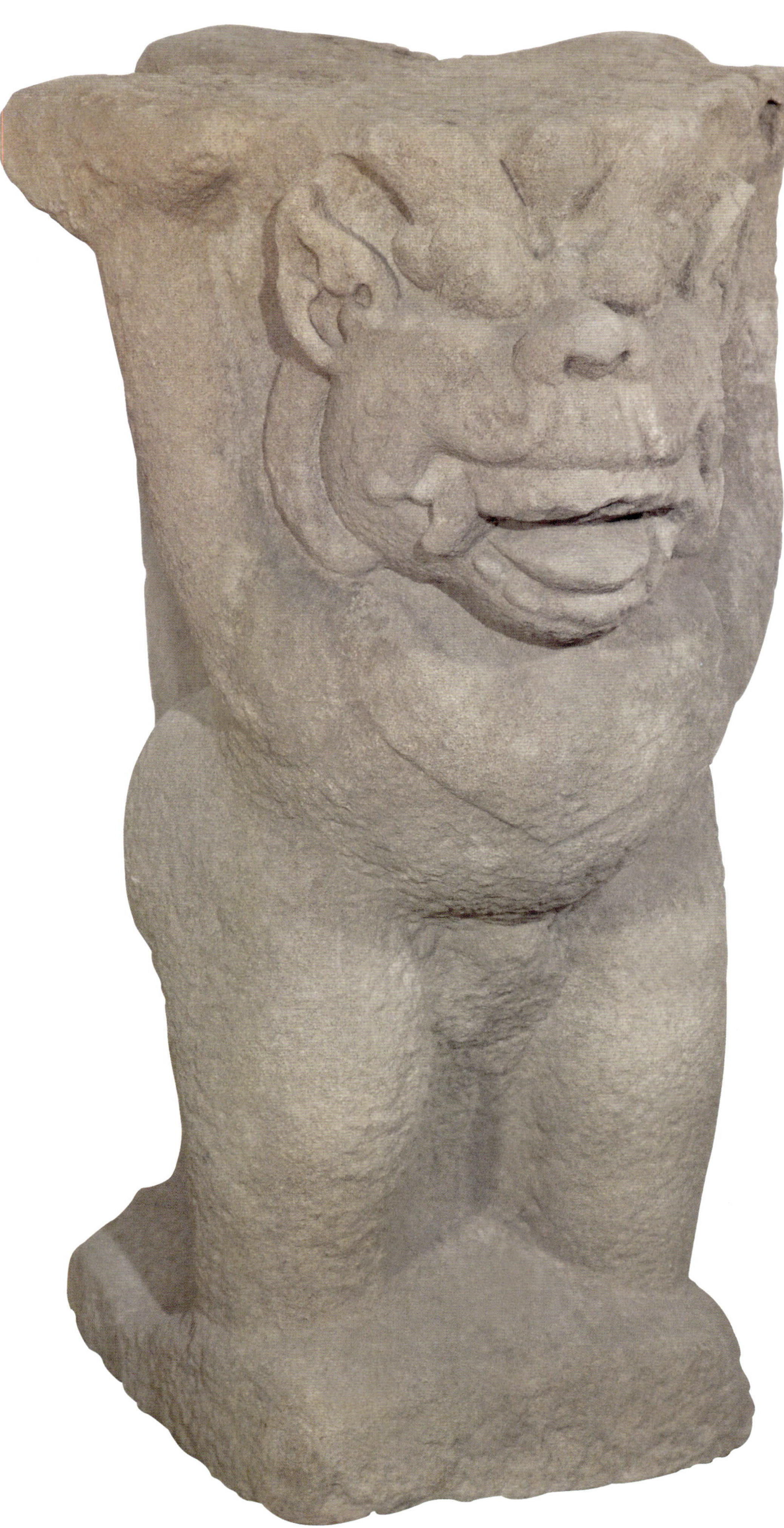

Here, the lion is an architectural support. It can also be shown walking by, or with only the bust visible. Always highly interpreted (Chams had never seen lions, as they were not present in Champa), the lion, nearly fantasised, here has horns that continue the eyebrow ridges. The eyes are protruding, the upper lip is curled up and the fangs are bared. His fur is apparent on the head a breastplate covers his chest, his sexual organ is visible.

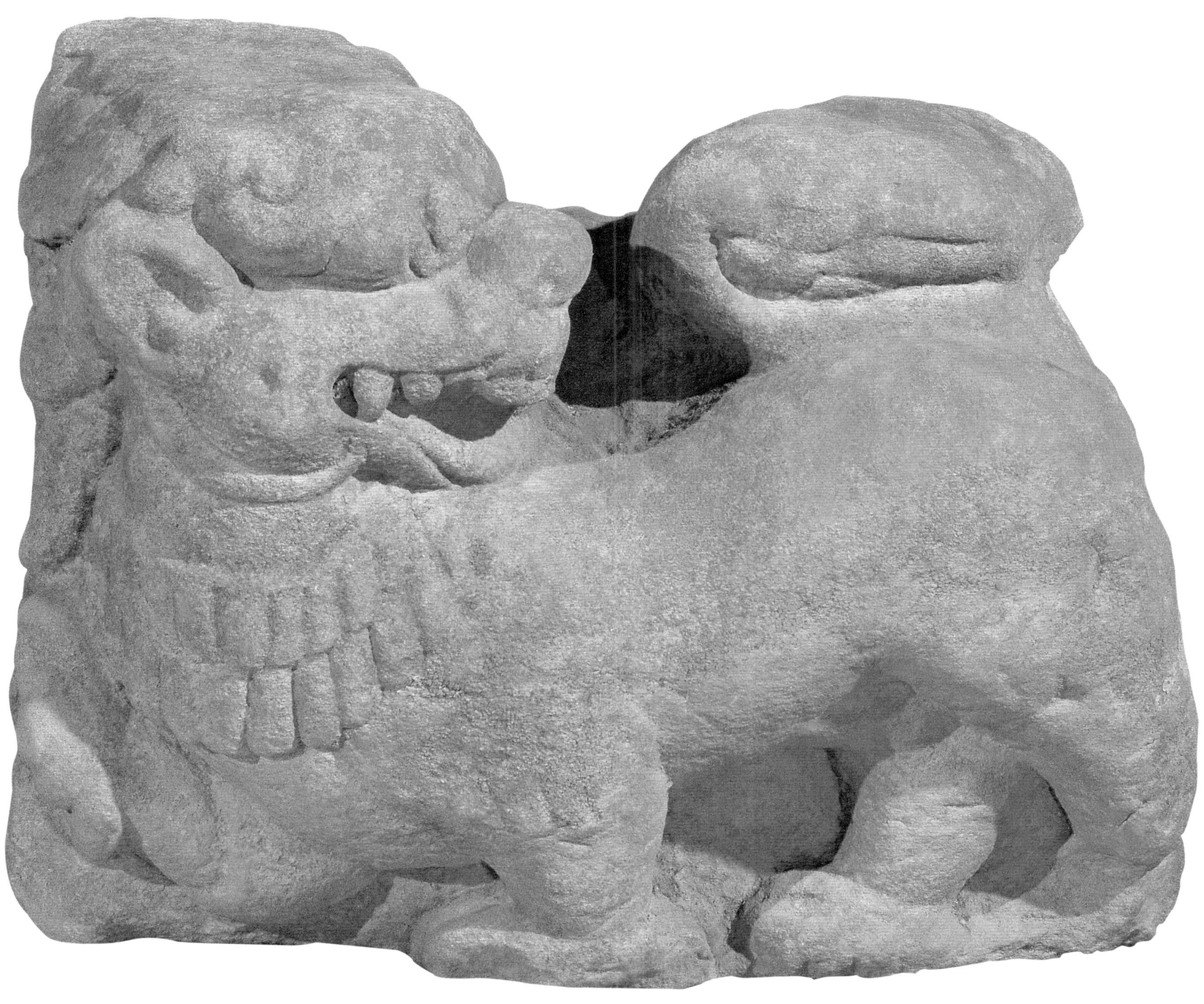

Previous Page
124. *Bearing lion*, High-relief (nearly free-standing), Sandstone, Height 73 cm, Tra Kiêu style, 10th Century.

125. *Walking lion*, High relief, Sandstone, Height 36 cm, Tra Kiêu style, 10th Century.

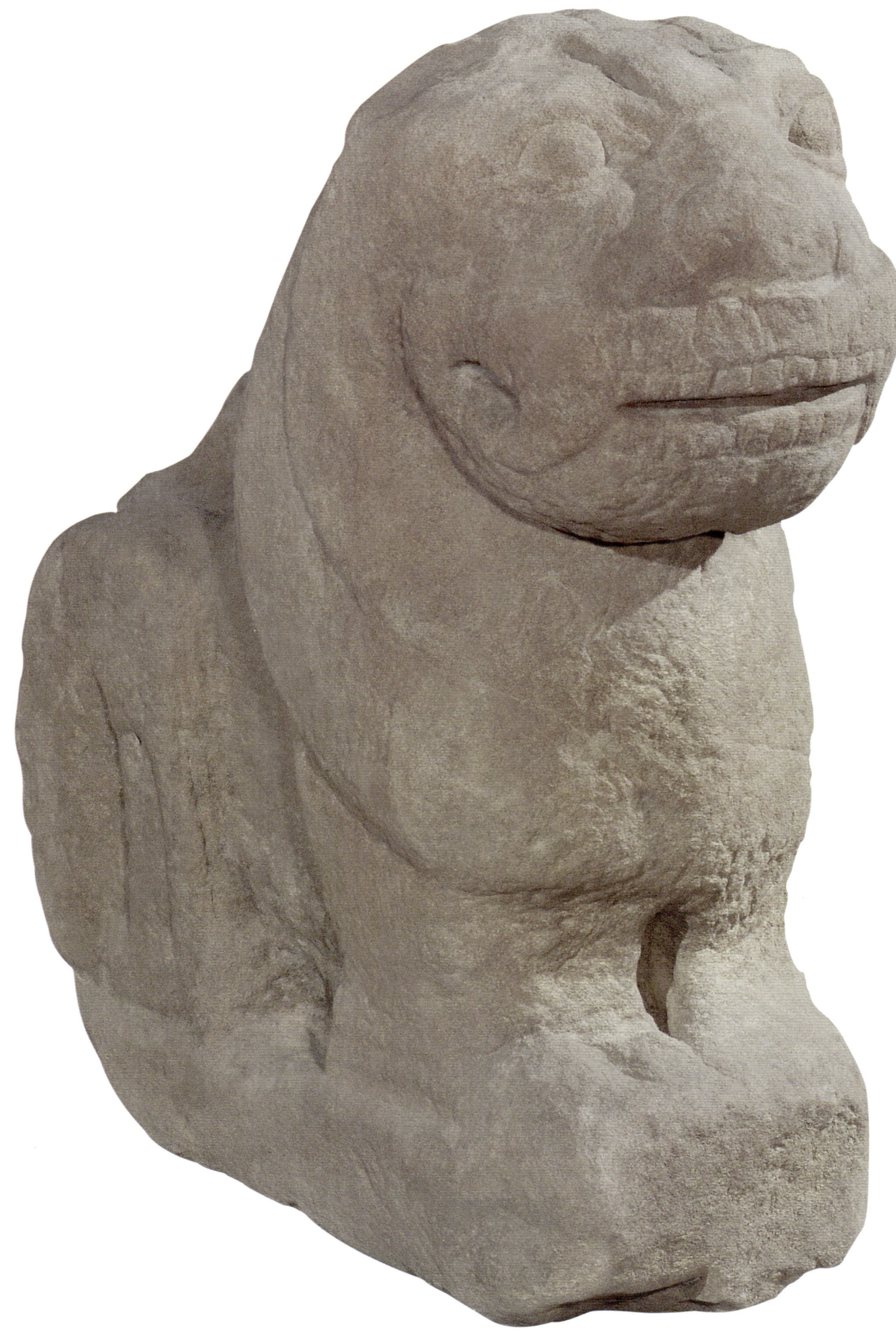

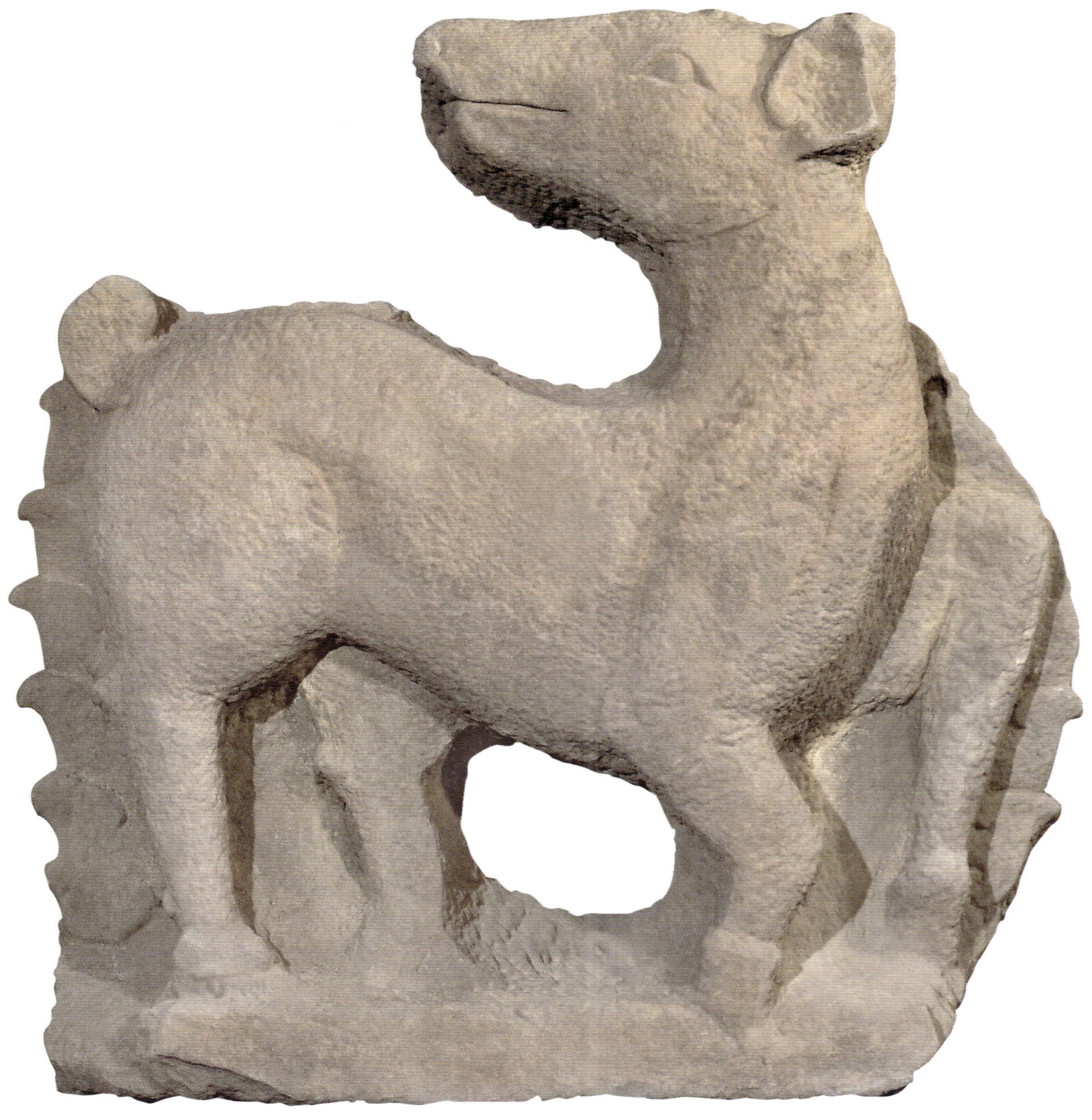

Previous Page
126. *Seated dog*, Free-standing, Sandstone, Height 40 cm, Tra Kiêu style, 10th Century.

127. *Deer* or *gazelle*, High-relief, Sandstone, Height 80 cm, Tra Kiêu style, 10th Century.

The sculpture of an animal in Cham art can have a double meaning:

- Either the animal is a god's mount ("vahana"), such as Garuda for Vishnu, or it constitutes a precise reference to a god, such as Nandin installed in a Shivaist temple. In both of these cases it is part of a religious expression.

- Or it is secular, simply an element of the temple's decoration. Very often, these two meanings are cannot be clearly separated.

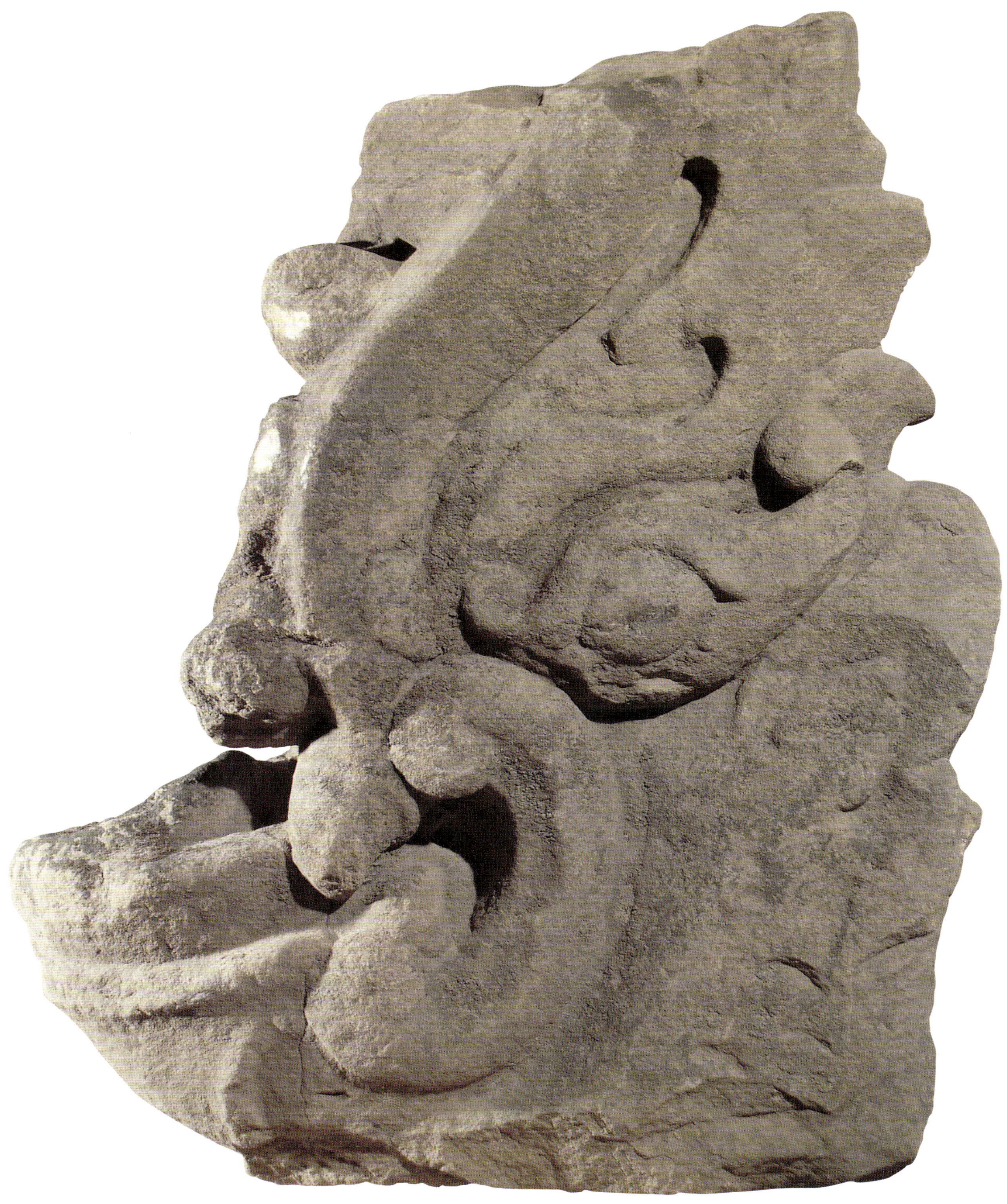

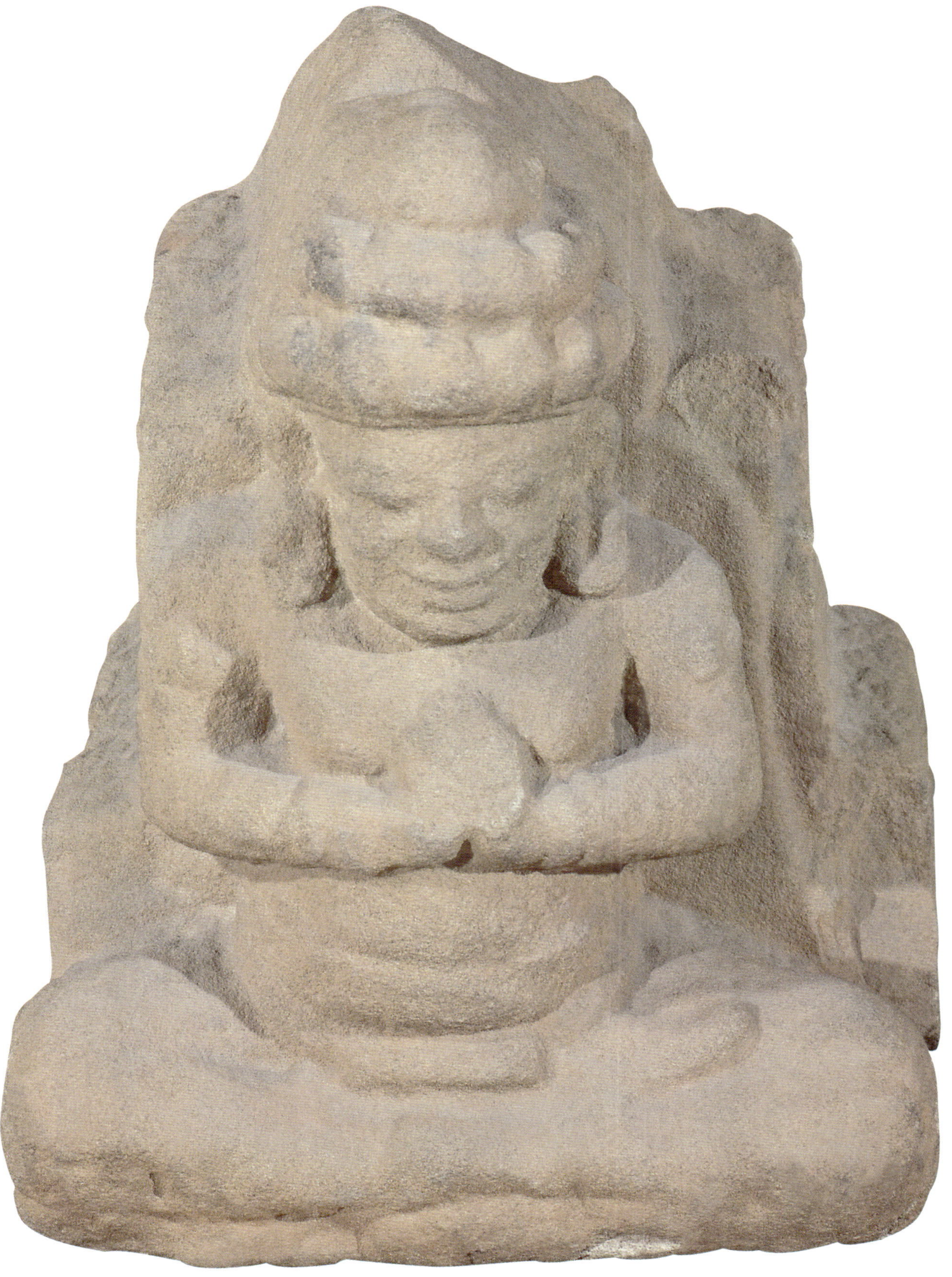

Previous Page
128. *Makara*, Free-standing, Sandstone, Height 54 cm, Tra Kiêu style, 10th Century.

129. *Figure*, High-relief, Sandstone, Height 35 cm, Tra Kiêu style, 10th Century.

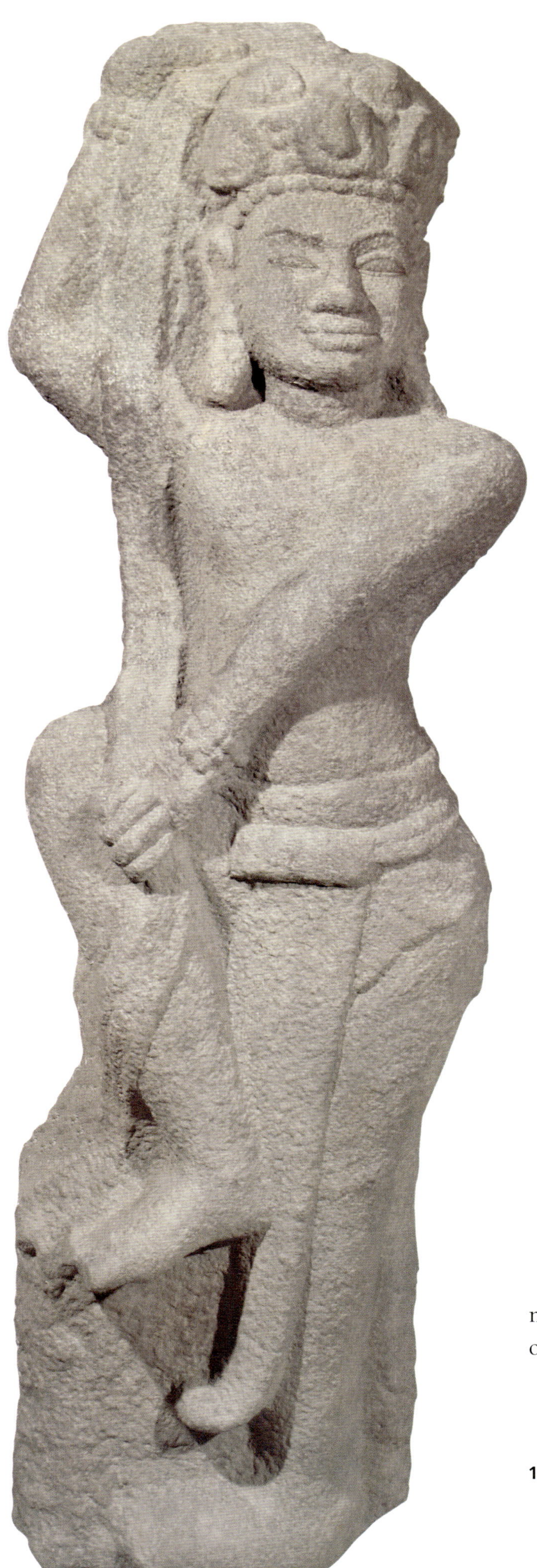

In Cham sculpture, male dancers are much more rarely represented than female ones.

130. *Dancer*, High relief, Sandstone, Height 113 cm, Tra Kiêu style, 10th Century.

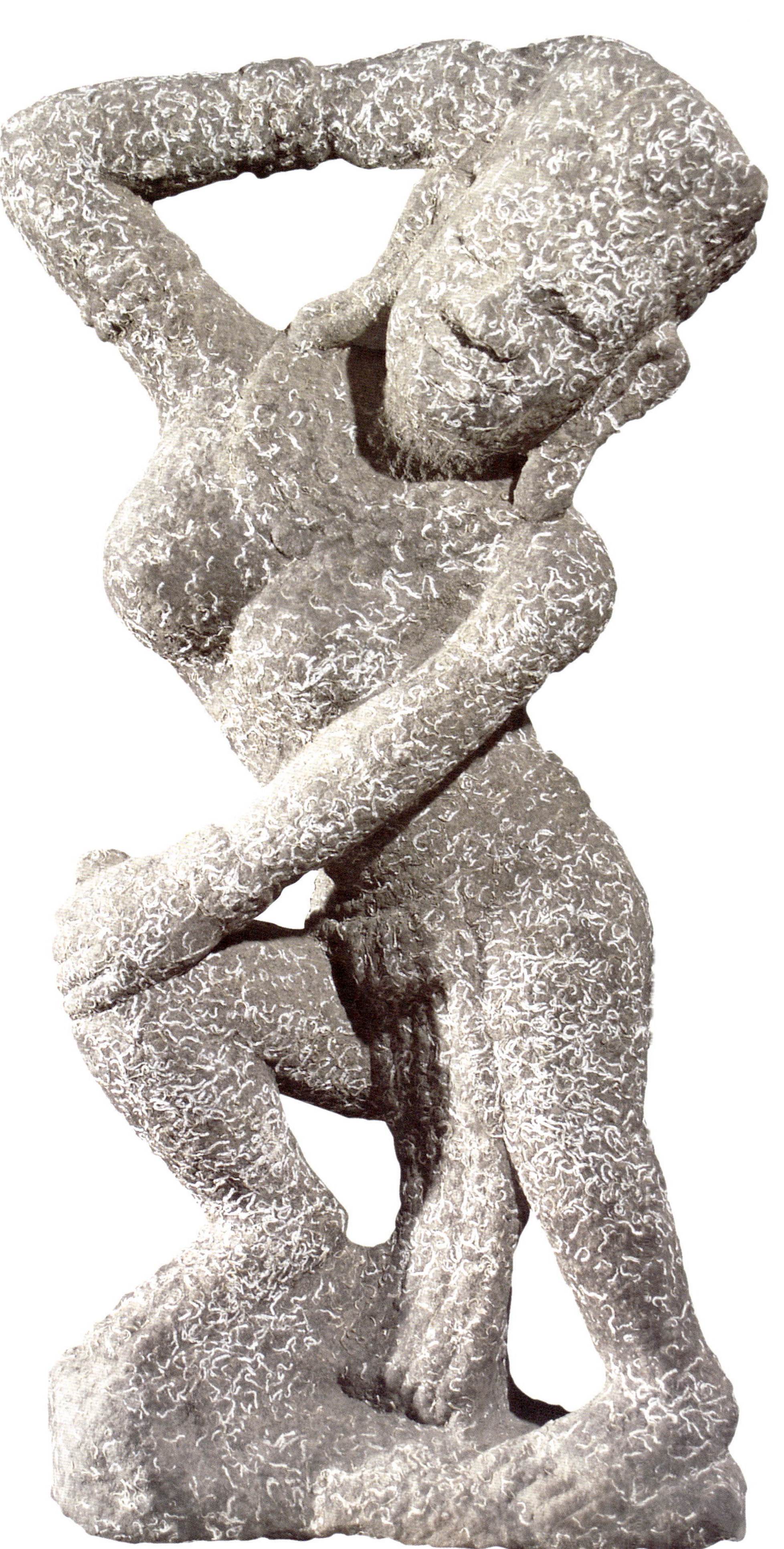

To the best of our knowledge, this is the only free-standing sculpture of a female dancer recorded, the others being high-reliefs. Marine concretions cover this piece of work, like the previous. The reason for this, is because both of them were found during marine explorations.

131. *Female dancer*, Free-standing, Sandstone, Height 63 cm, Tra Kiêu style, 10th Century.

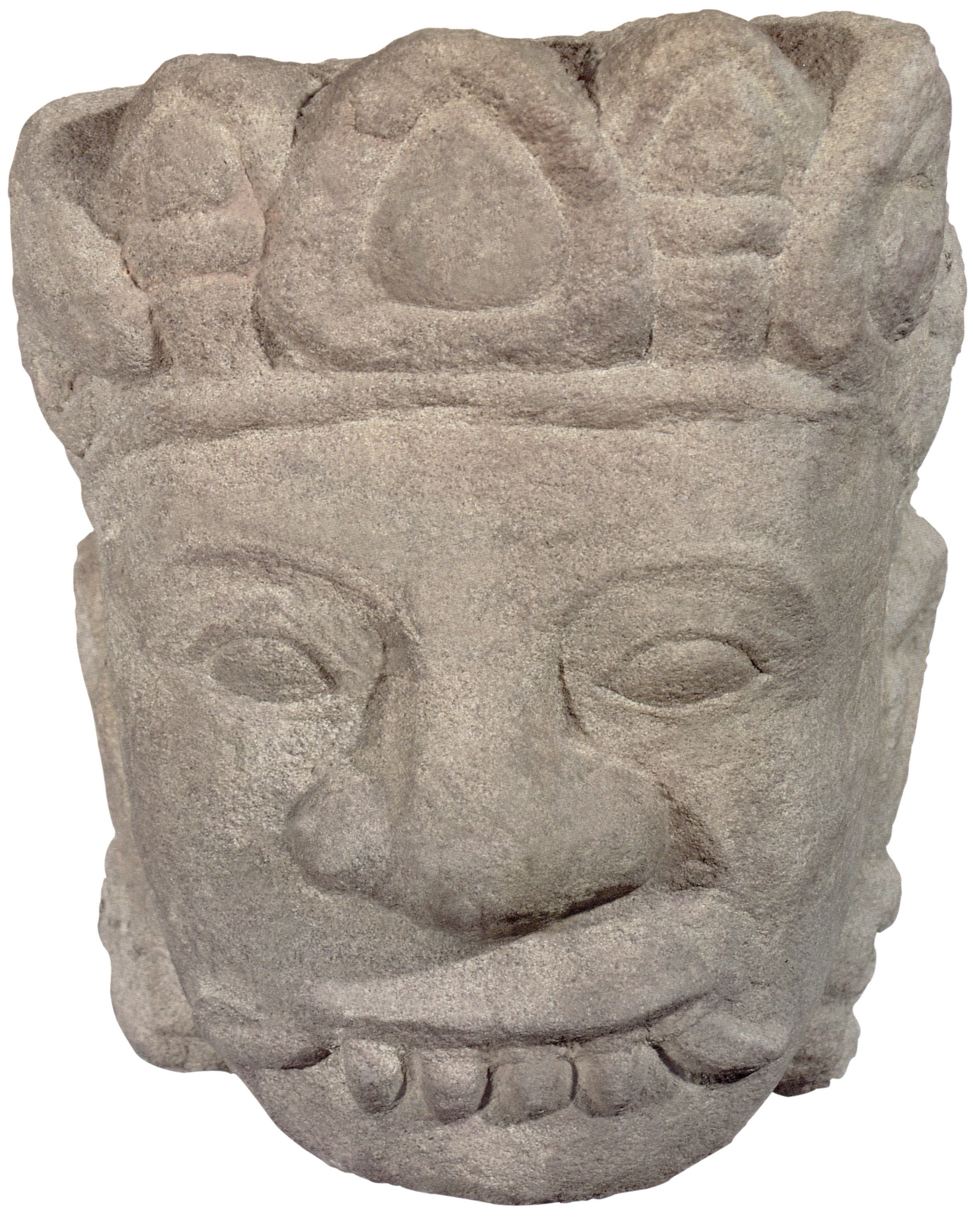

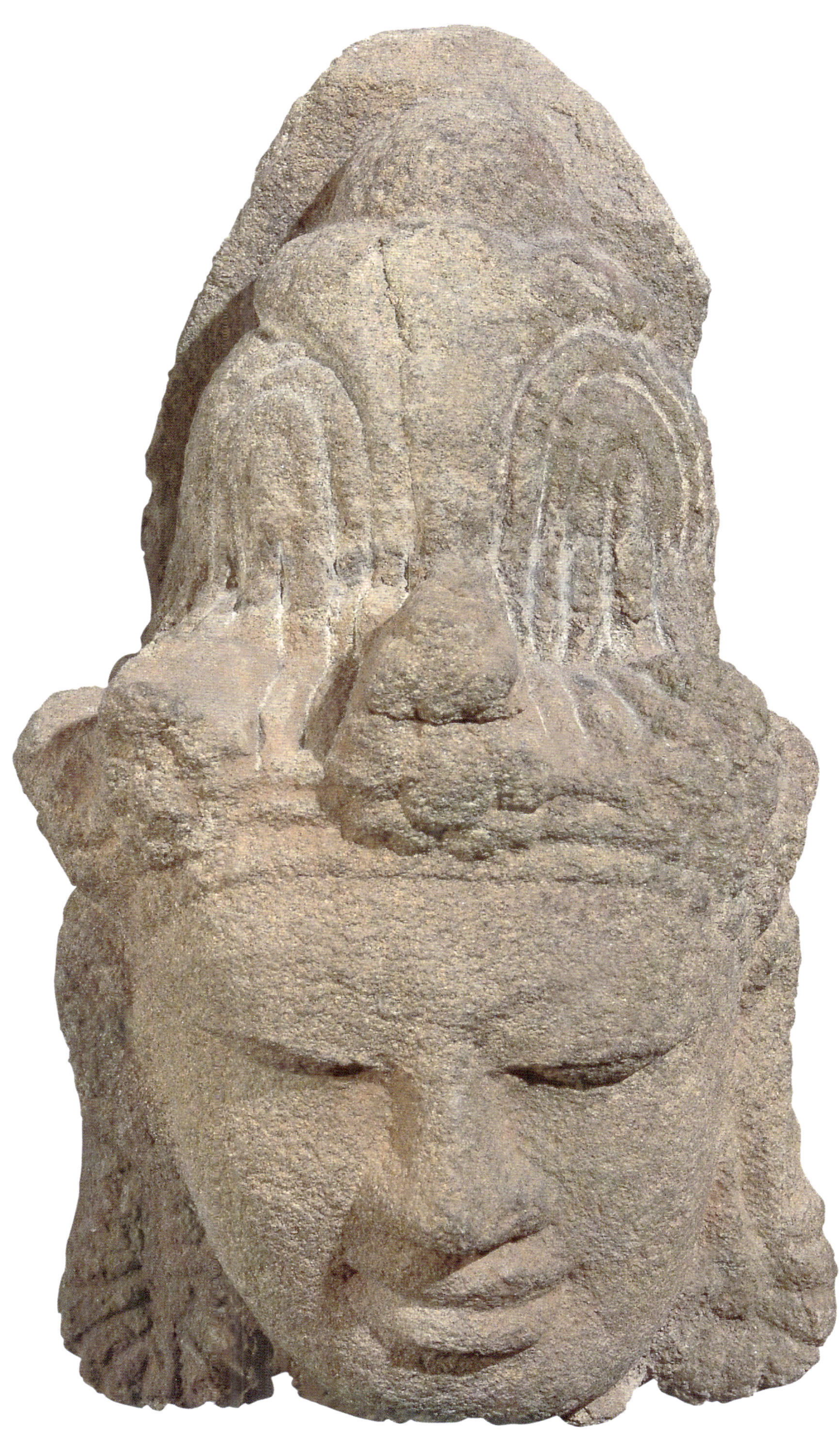

Previous Page
132. *Yaksha*, Nearly free-standing, Sandstone, Height 23 cm (with a quadrangular back tenon 39 cm long), Tra Kiêu style, 10th Century.

133. *Head of divinity*, Nearly free-standing, Sandstone, Height 16 cm, Tra Kiêu style, 10th Century.

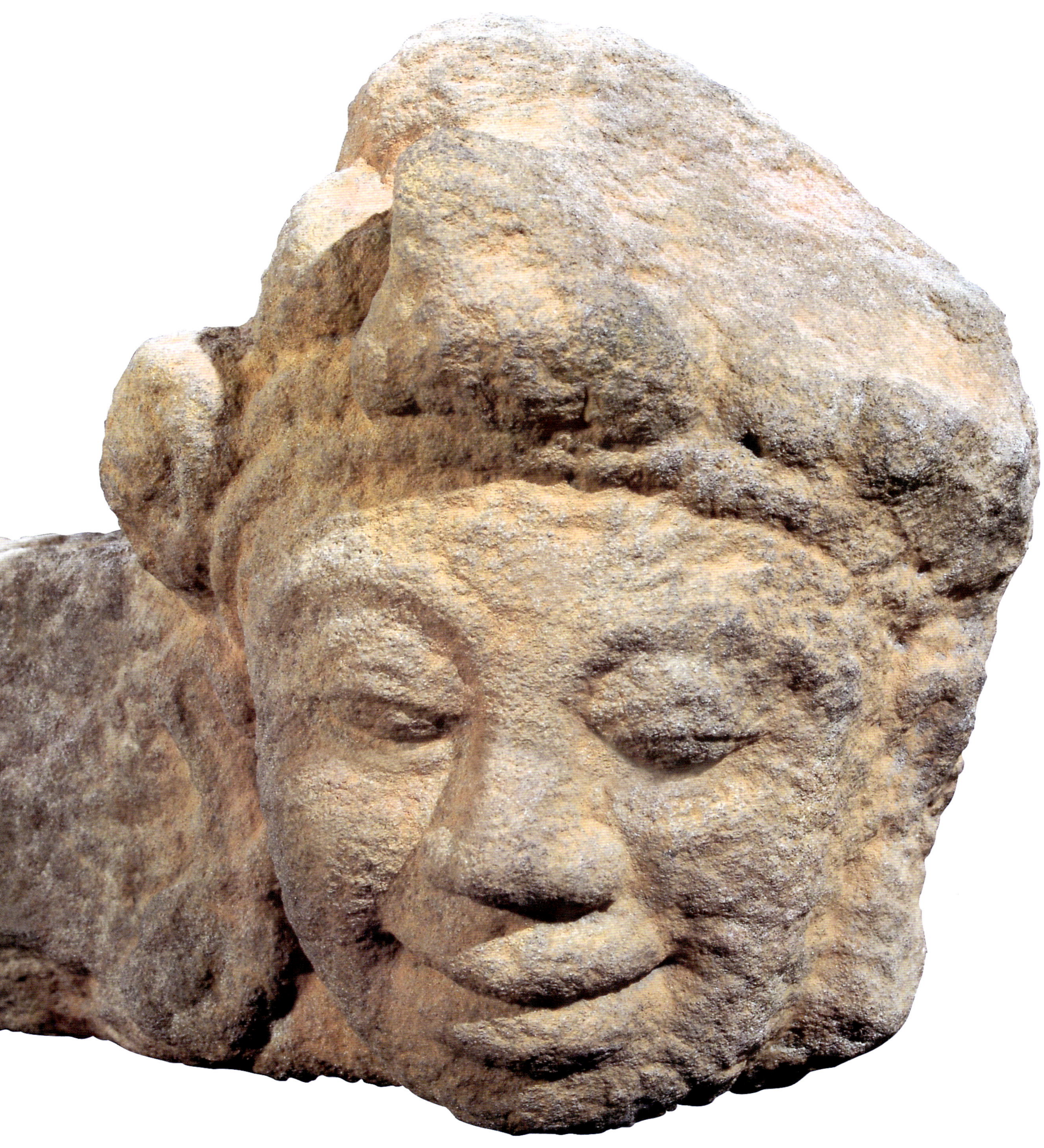

The piece is equipped with a quadrangular tenon that allows its insertion into the bricks of a temple.

His garment is organised as one long vertical sheet with a draped top panel and a hemmed edge. The figure is holding a lotus flower in his hands.

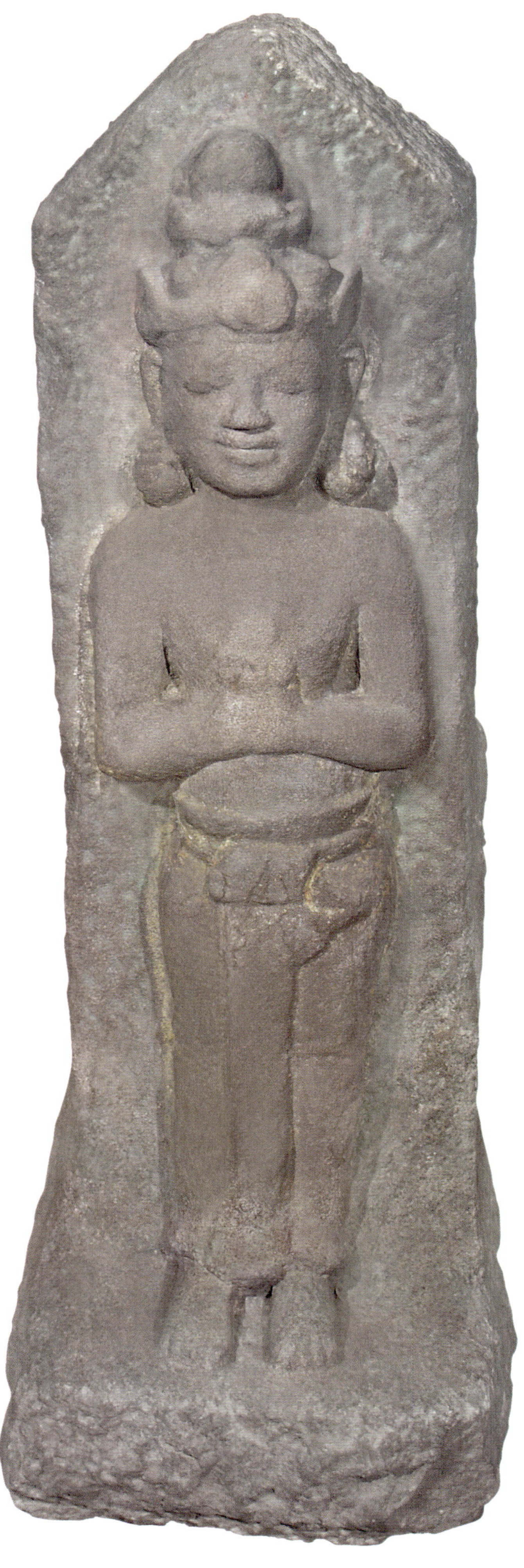

Previous Page
134. *Head of divinity*, Nearly free-standing, Sandstone, Height 18.5 cm, Tra Kiêu style, 10th Century.

135. *Worshipper*, High-relief, Sandstone, height 75 cm. Tra Kiêu style, 10th Century.

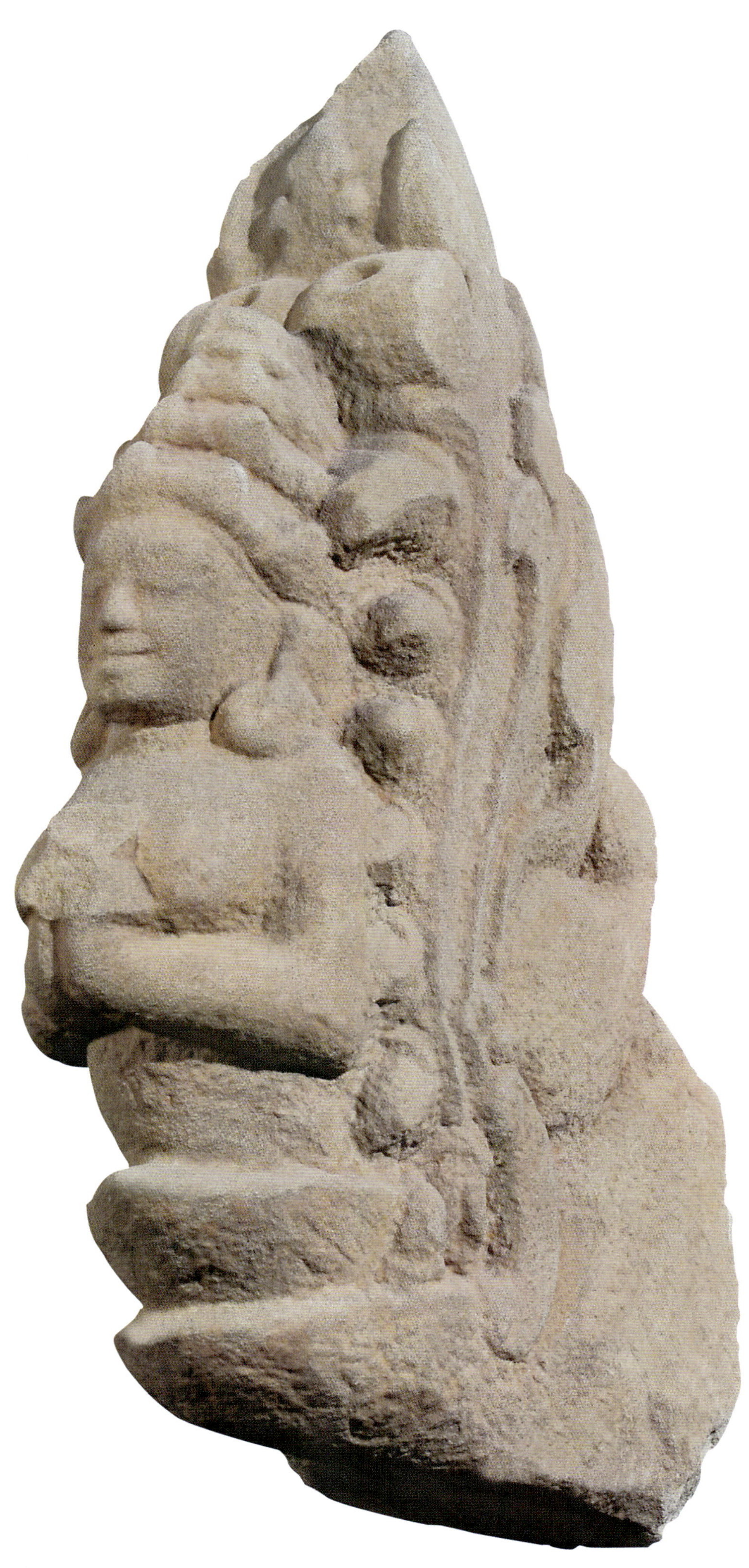

136. *Figure coming out of the maw of a Makara,*
Nearly free-standing, Sandstone, Height 55 cm,
Tra Kiêu style, 10th Century.

Following Page
137. *Figure coming out of the maw of a Makara,*
Nearly free-standing, Sandstone, Height 55 cm,
Tra Kiêu style, 10th Century (detail).

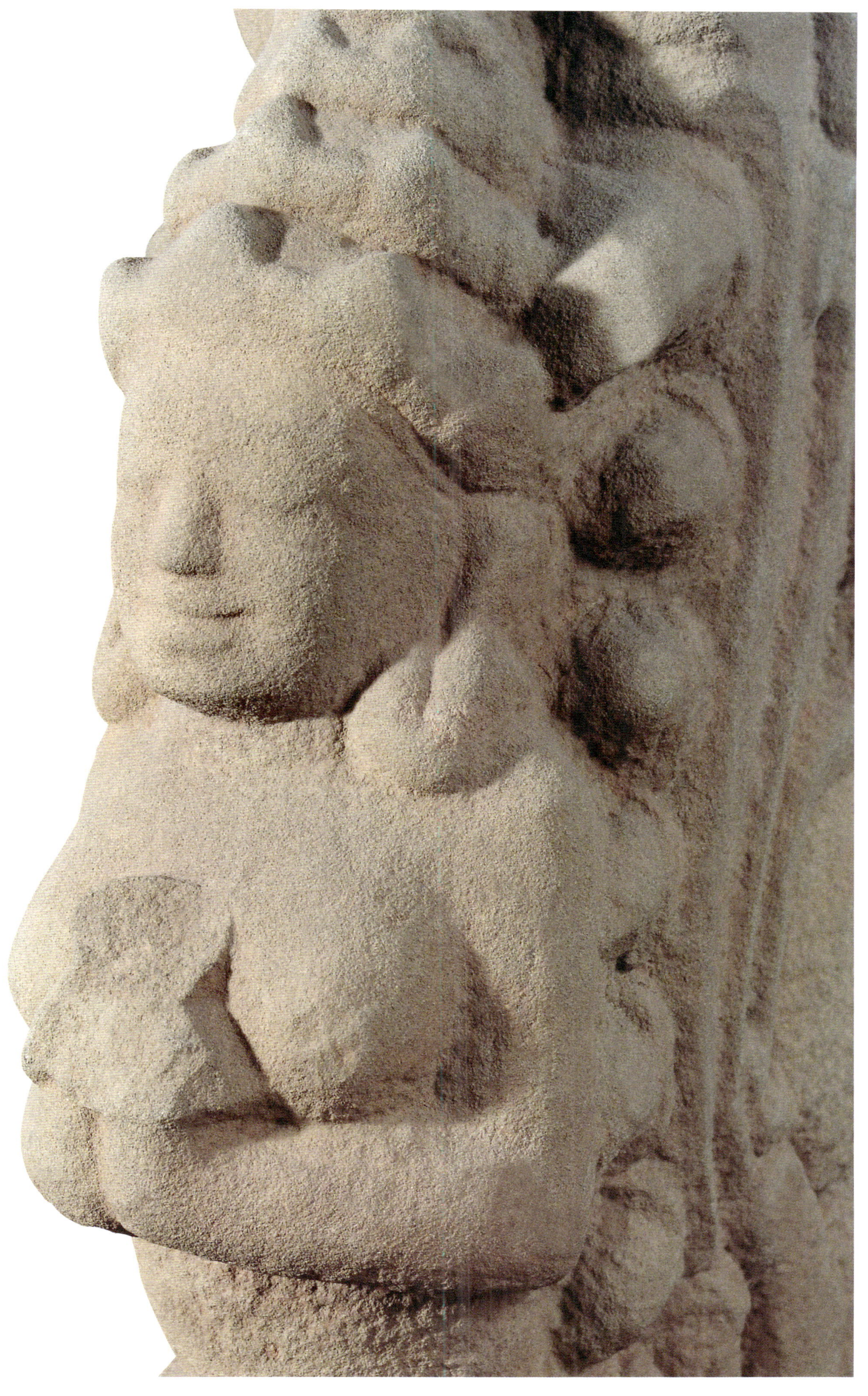

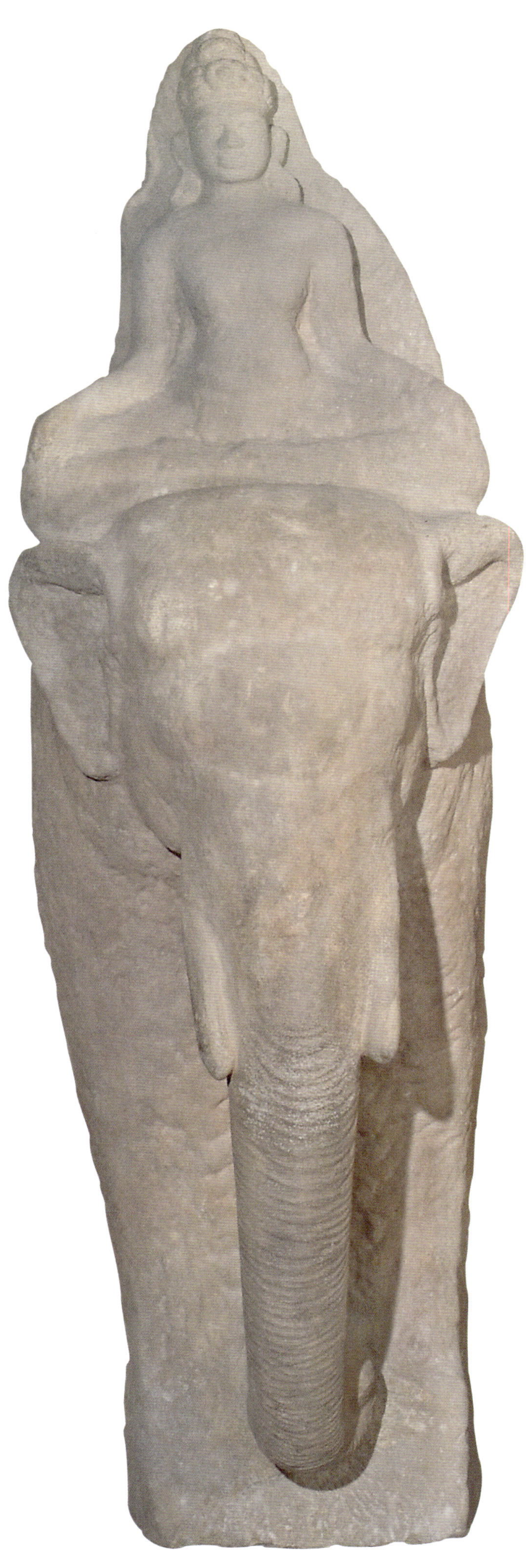

Indra (in Sanskrit "strength, power") is the god of war, atmosphere and lightning. Very important in the Vedic pantheon, he becomes secondary in Hinduism and in Buddhist art. He is rarely sculpted. His supporting animal is the elephant Airavata, on which he sits Indian style. He is usually armed with a chakra ("wheel, disk") and a vajra ("diamond").

In ancient India, the chakra was a disk made of gold, copper or iron, symbol of the sovereign's power, witness to the fact that the monarch turns the wheel of fortune for men. The vajra is a throwing weapon, originally made for Indra out of bronze, by Tvashtri, who is described in the Rig-veda as a divine artist.

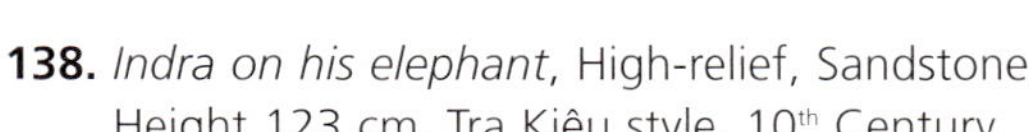

138. *Indra on his elephant*, High-relief, Sandstone, Height 123 cm, Tra Kiêu style, 10th Century.

Following Page
139. *Indra on his elephant*, High-relief, Sandstone, Height 123 cm, Tra Kiêu style, 10th Century (detail).

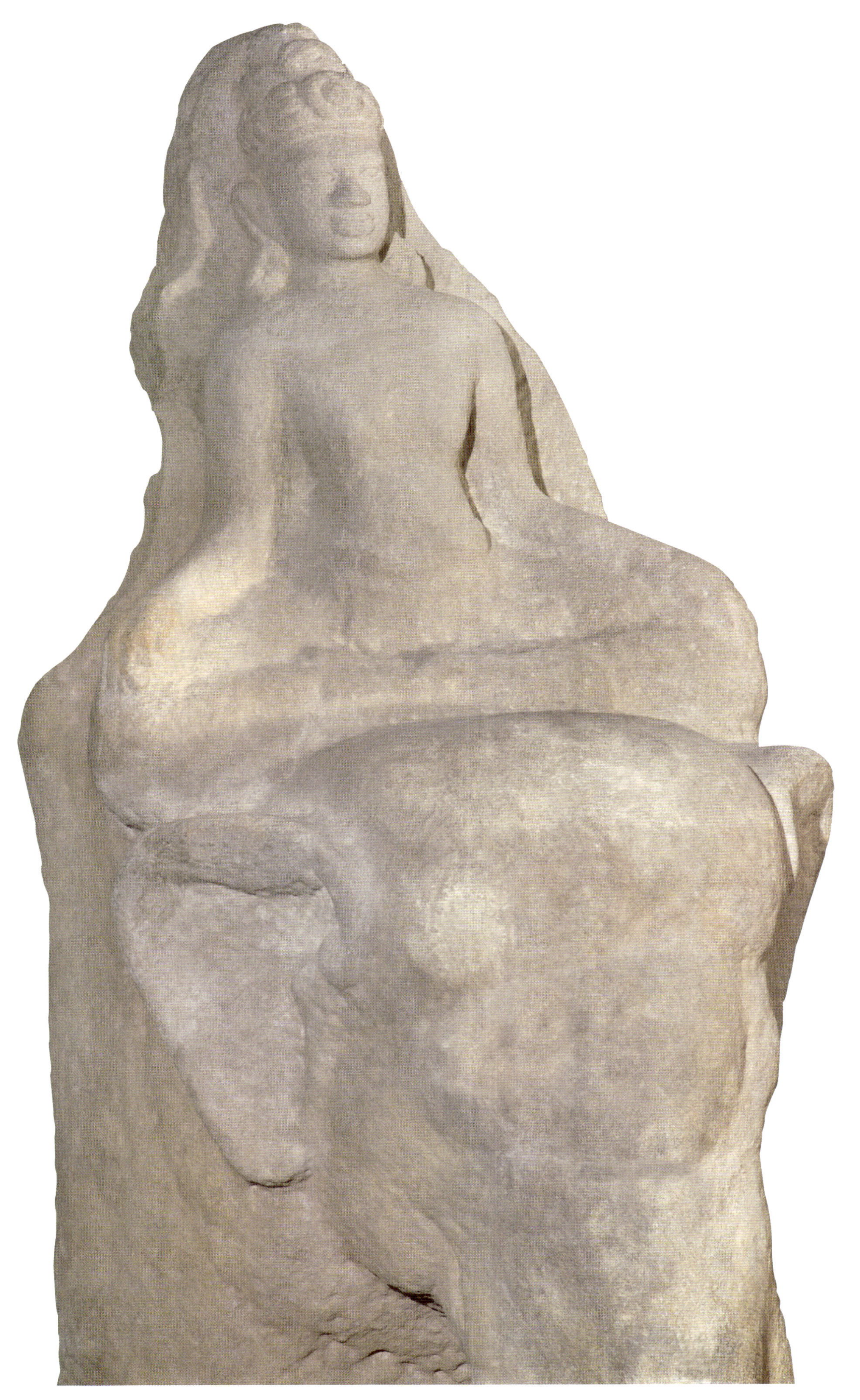

The goddess of the multiplicity of happiness and of good fortune, is the daughter of Shiva and Parvati, and Vishnu's wife ("sakti"). She is holding a lotus and a piece of fruit in her hands. Without attributes that are visible, it is sometimes difficult to be sure of the statue's true identity. (Is this in fact Lakshmi, or Sarasvati, or Uma?)

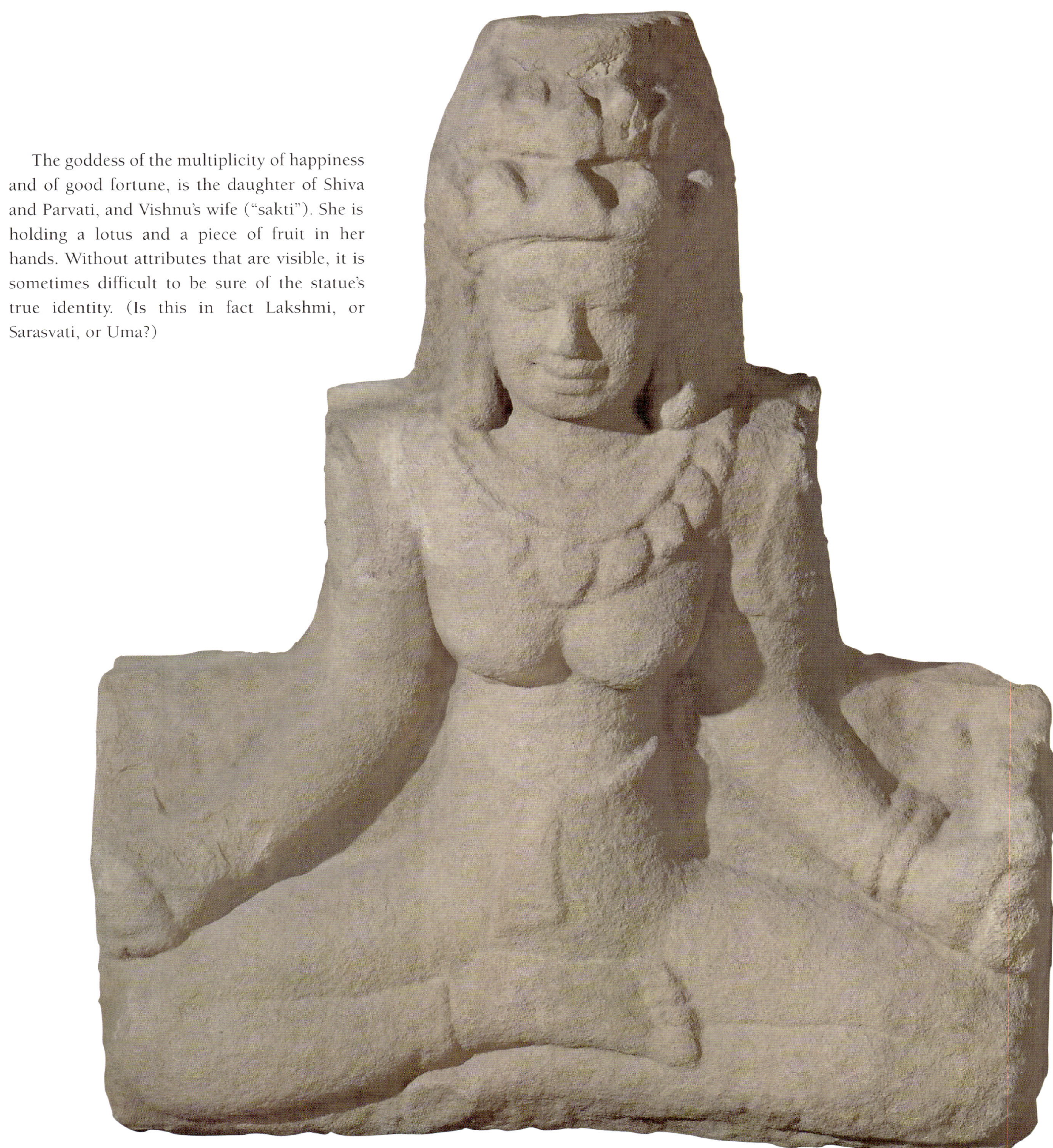

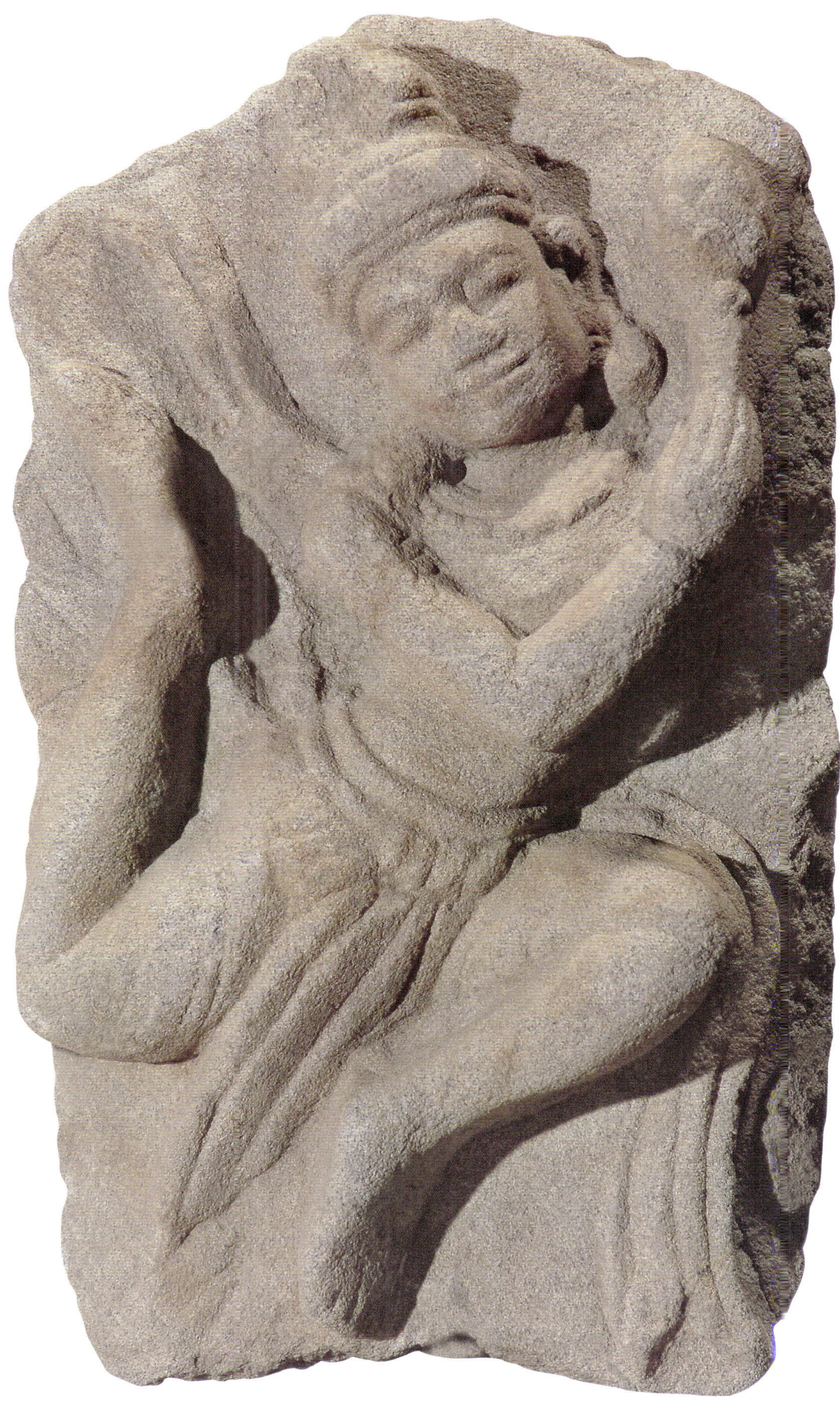

Previous Page
140. *Lakshmi,* High-relief, Sandstone, Height 66 cm, Tra Kiêu style, 10th Century.

141. *Apsara*, Bas-relief, Sandstone, Height 22 cm, Tra Kiêu style, 10th Century.

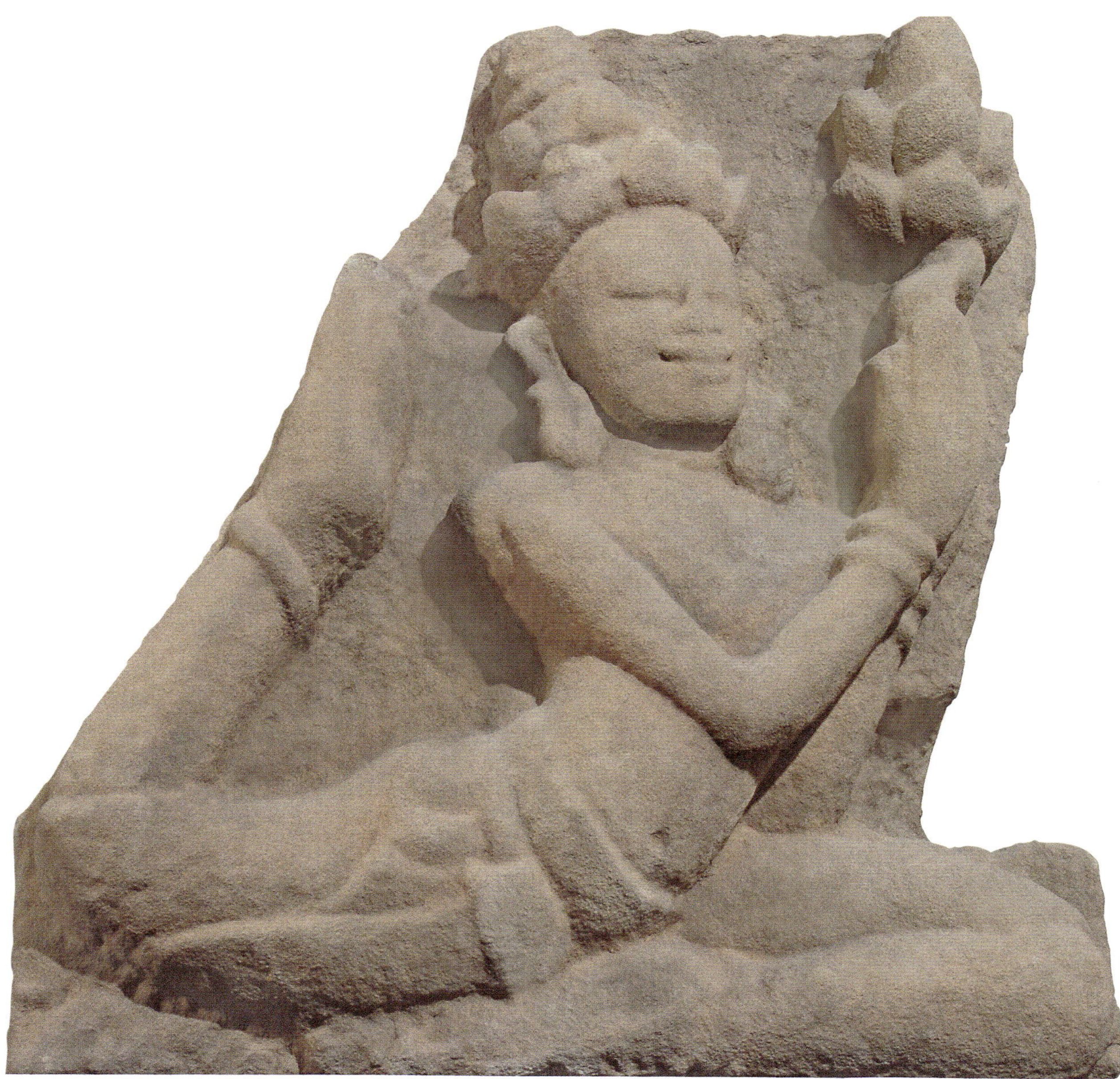

An Apsara ("from the water" in Sanskrit) is a gracious and charming nymph born of the churning of the sea of milk. The gods ("Deva") beaten in a battle by the anti-gods ("Asuras") asked Vishnu for his help. The god had an idea. "Join with your enemies, gather all together magic herbs and then throw them into the sea of milk. Then, use Mount Mandara as a pivot, place it on the back of the turtle Akupara (in fact, an avatar of Vishnu) and thanks to Vasuki, the mythical snake, used as a rope, make Mount Mandara spin very fast, thereby churning the sea of milk." The Deva and Asura did what Vishnu had ordered and took hold, one group after the other, of the serpent Vasuki rolled around Mount Mandara placed on Akupara and pulled alternately. From this churning came true marvels: Shurabhi, the sacred cox; Varuni, the goddess of wine; Parijata, the tree of heaven that perfumes the world, the moon (that Shiva wears in his hair); a poison (that Shiva drank to keep the world from being poisoned); Uchaisshrava, the wonderful white horse that Indra claimed; Shrï, the goddess of beauty and good fortune; Airavata, the elephant, Indra's mount; Dhanvantari, the doctor of the gods Indra's student; and our Apsaras.

But from the churning also came the amrita ("immortal"), the nectar of eternal life collected in a cup, stolen by the Asuras but recovered by Vishnu (in his Mohini form) who returned it to the Deva. The latter, thanks to the strength furnished by the nectar, were able to vanquish the Asura and send them to Hell.

This legend is in the Vishnu-Purana, the Mahabharata and the Ramayana.

Asparas thus have a magical and divine origin. They are the companions of pleasure for the Deva and for the Asura as well. Extremely beautiful women, temptresses of ancestors, they can be celestial (Daivika) or terrestrial (Laukika).

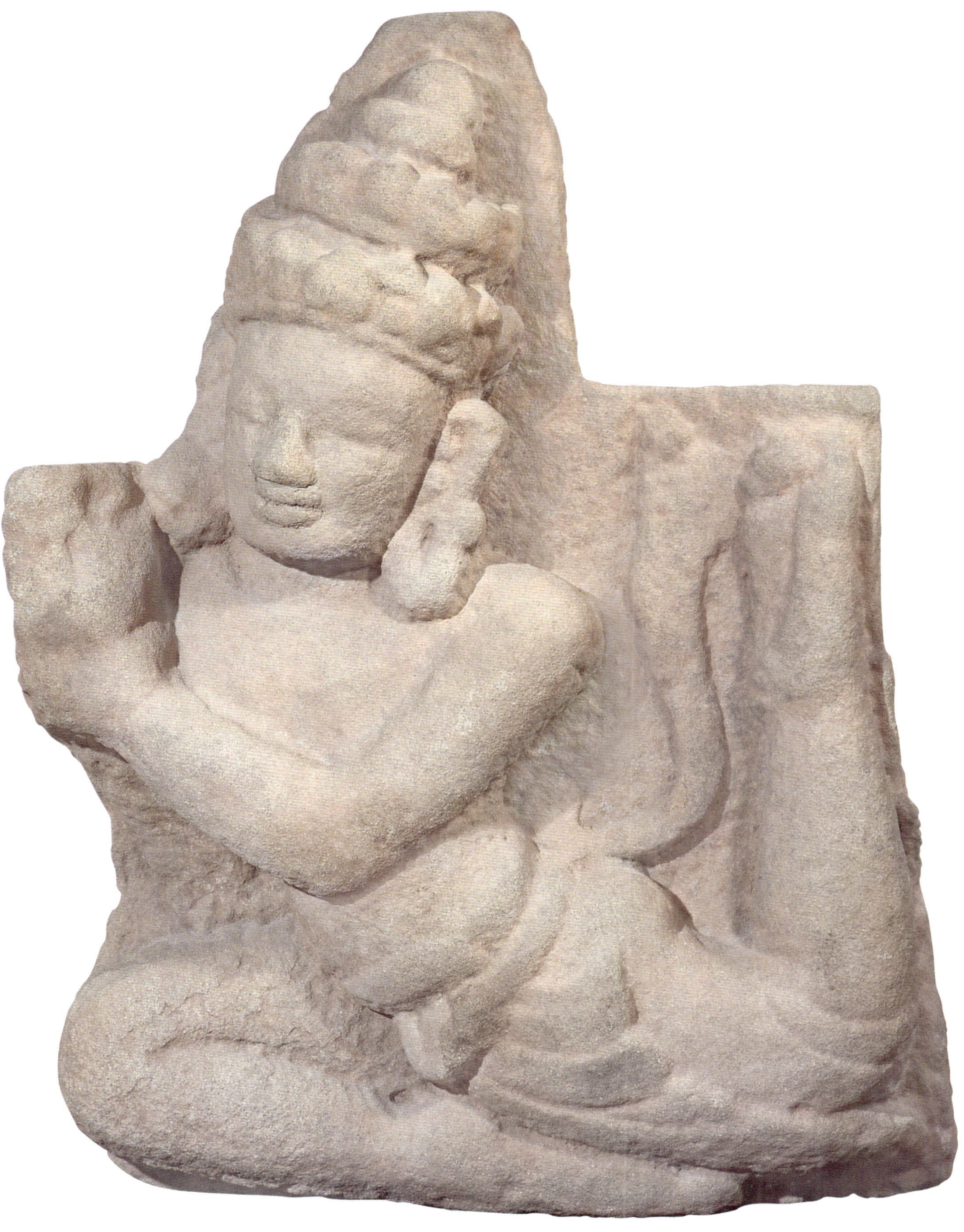

The nymph holds a lotus flower in her hands.

Previous Page
142. *Apsara,* High-relief, Sandstone, Height 50 cm, Tra Kiêu style, 10th Century.

143. *Apsara*, High-relief, Sandstone, Height 50 cm, Tra Kiêu style, 10th Century.

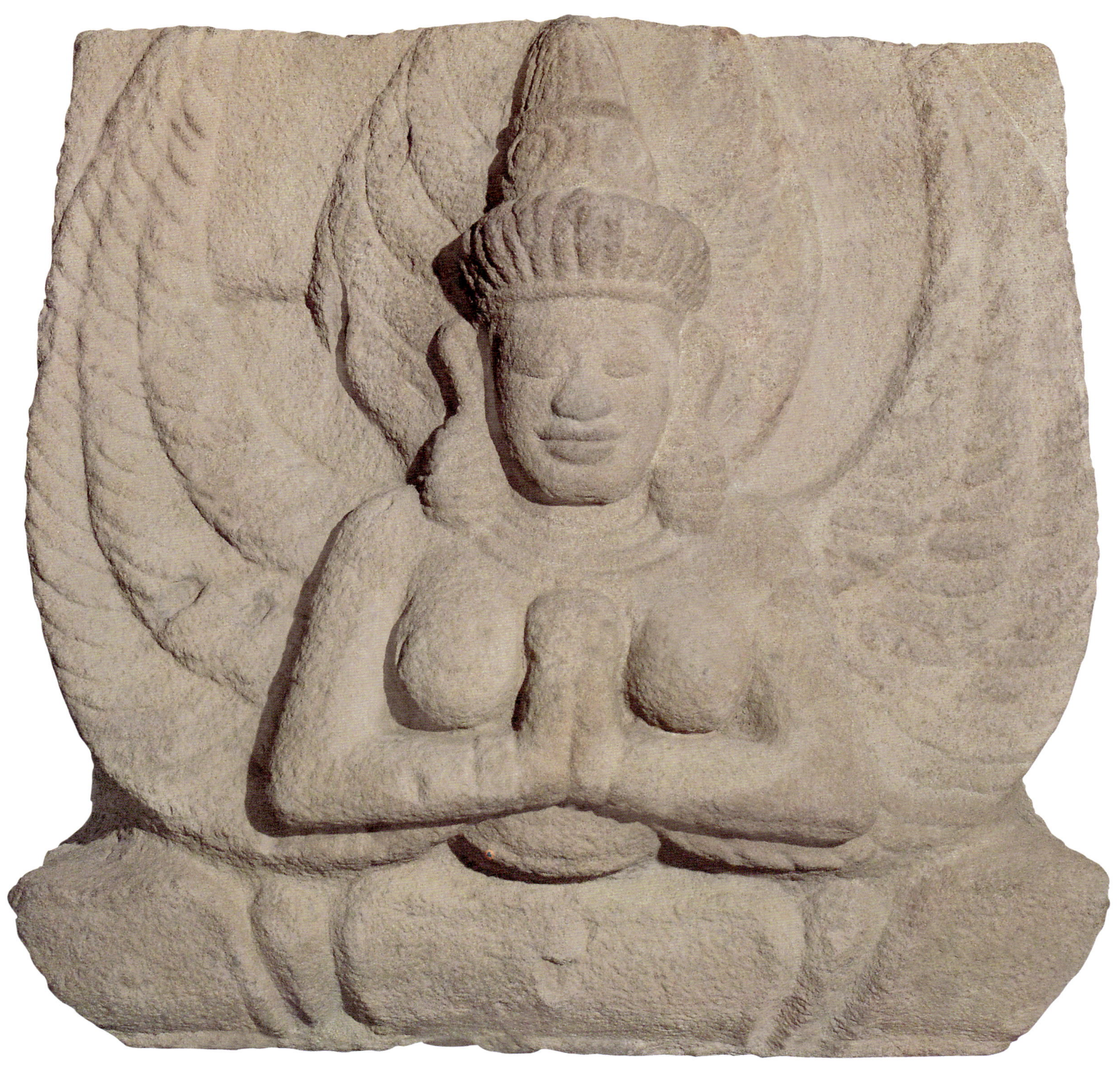

144. *Kinnari*, High-relief, Sandstone, Height 36.5 cm, Tra Kiêu style, 10th Century.

The kirita-mukuta is, in this case, a high conical diadem with clearly drawn wings. The mythical being is in anjali and rests on a base of lotus leaves. It is ornamented with rich jewels and its eyebrows are slightly outlined.

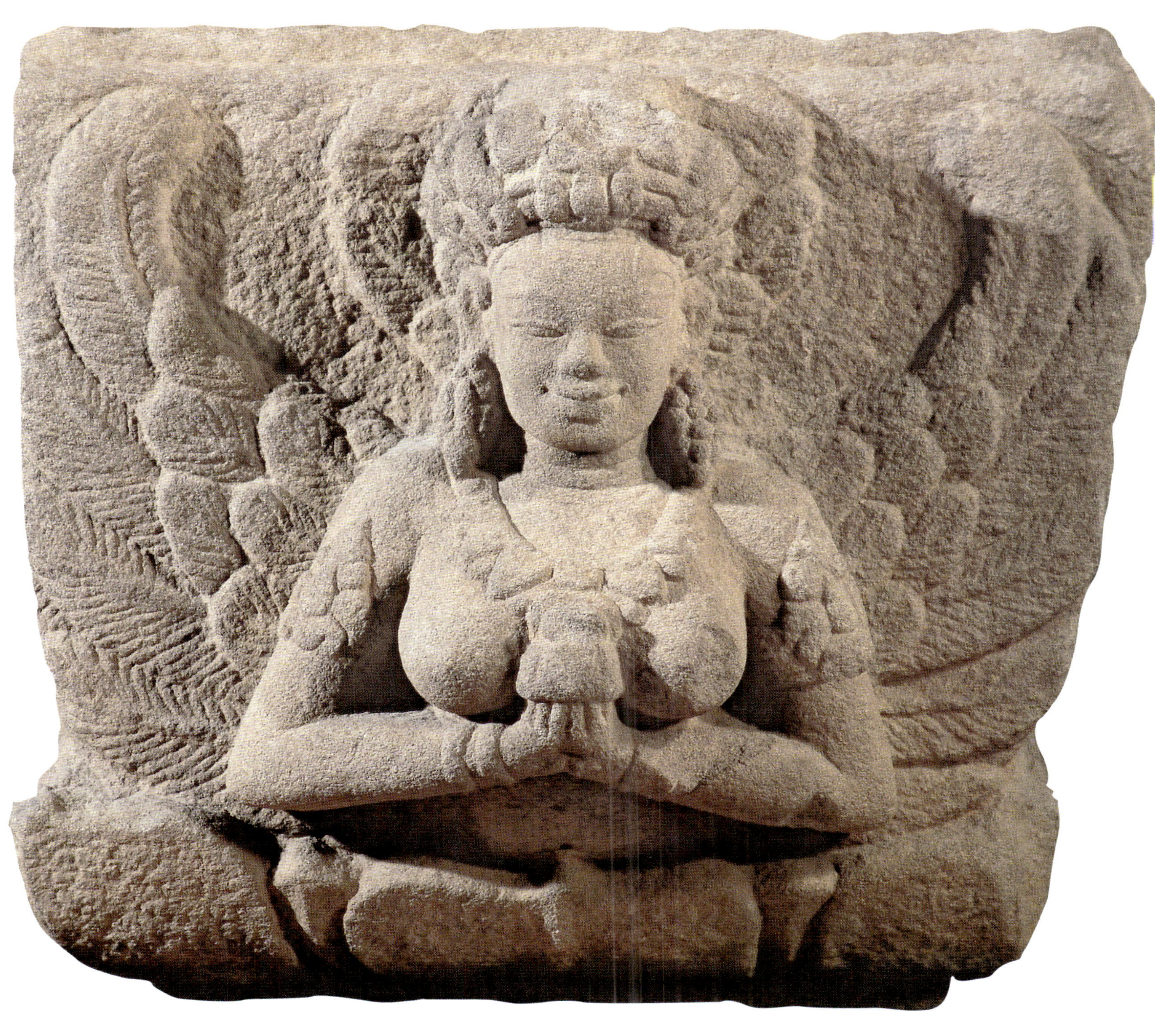

145. *Kinnari*, High-relief, Sandstone, Height 31 cm, Tra Kiêu style, 10th Century.

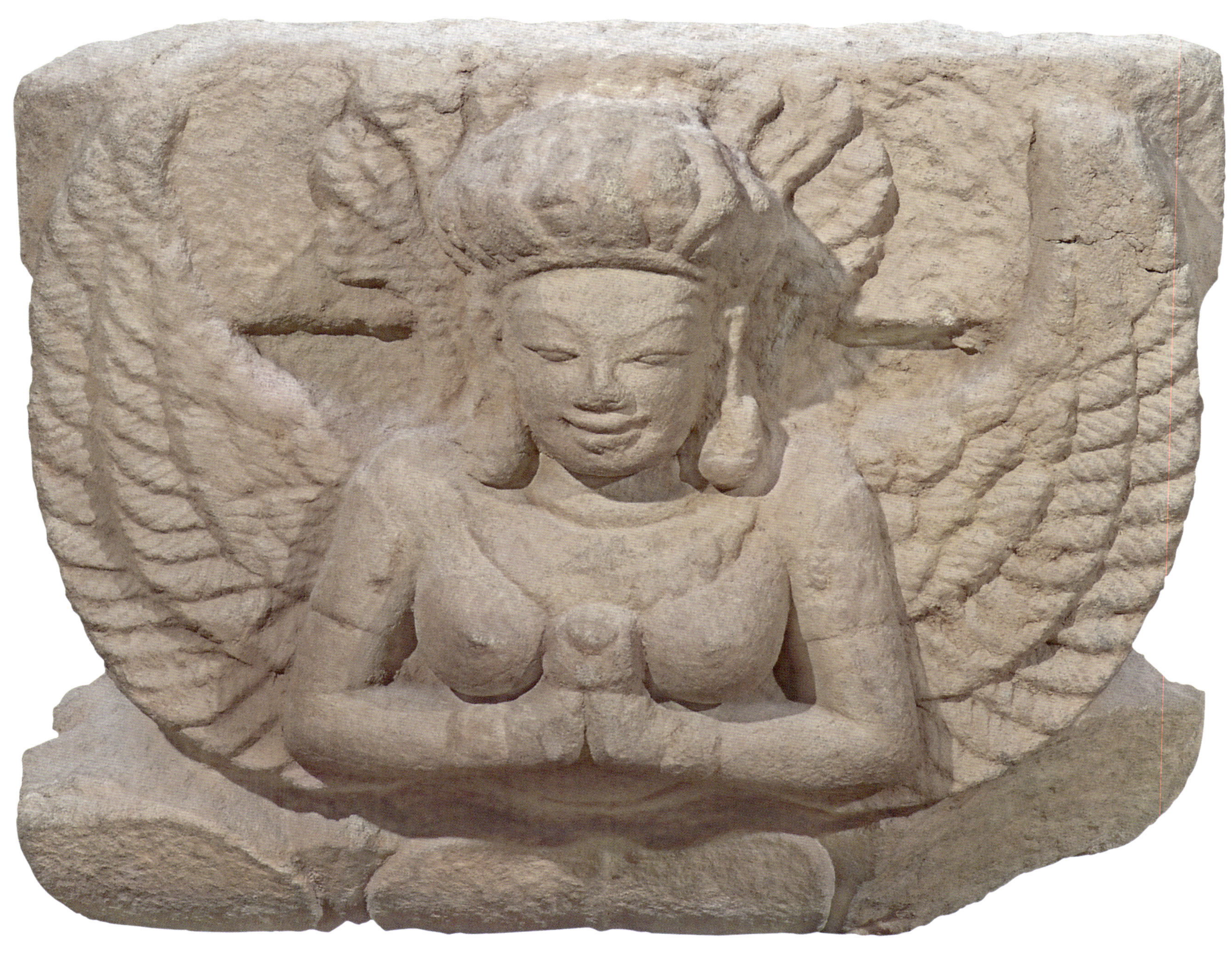

146. *Kinnari*, High-relief, Sandstone, Height 31 cm, Tra Kiêu style, 10th Century.

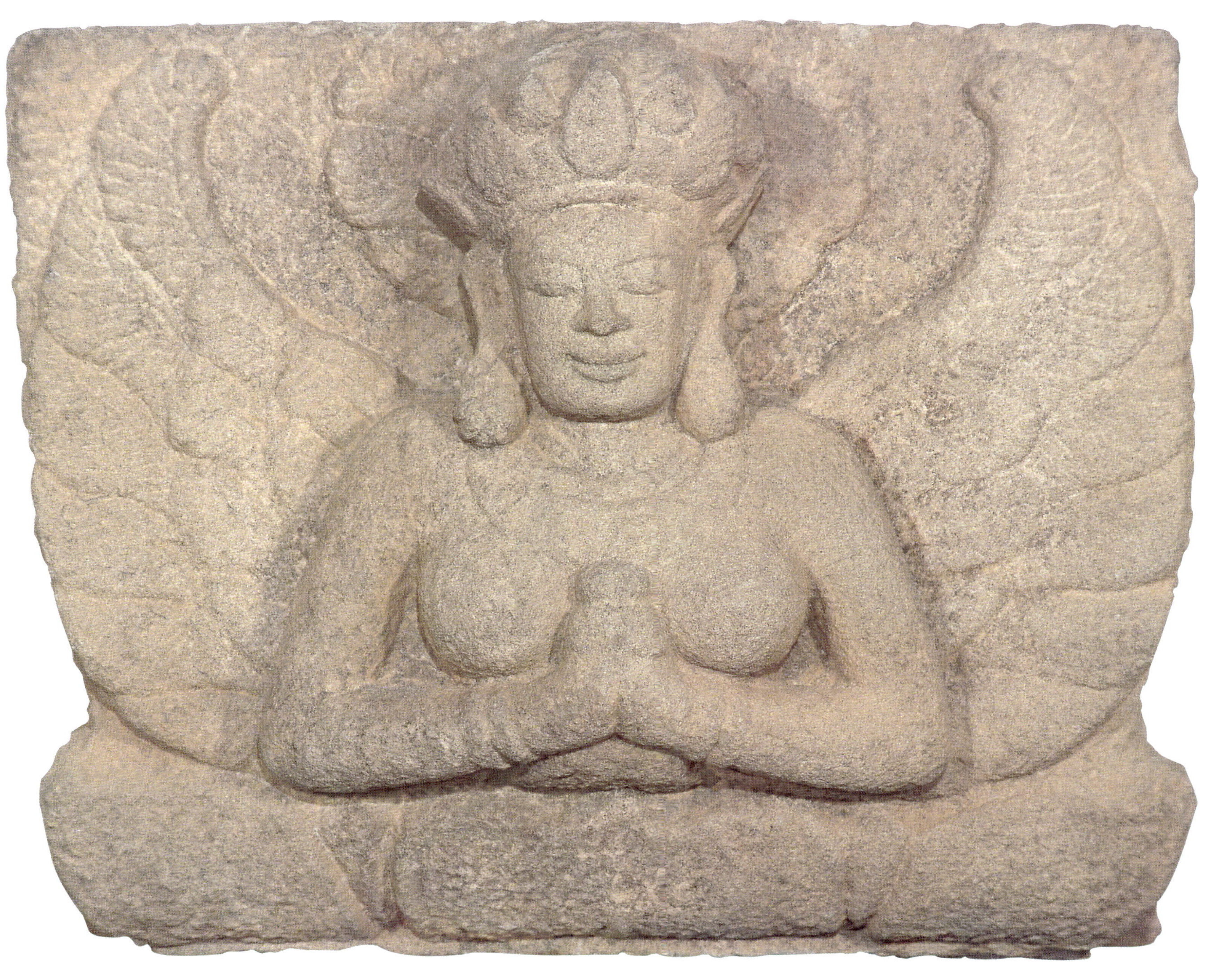

147. *Kinnari*, High-relief, Sandstone, Height 30 cm, Tra Kiêu style, 10th Century.

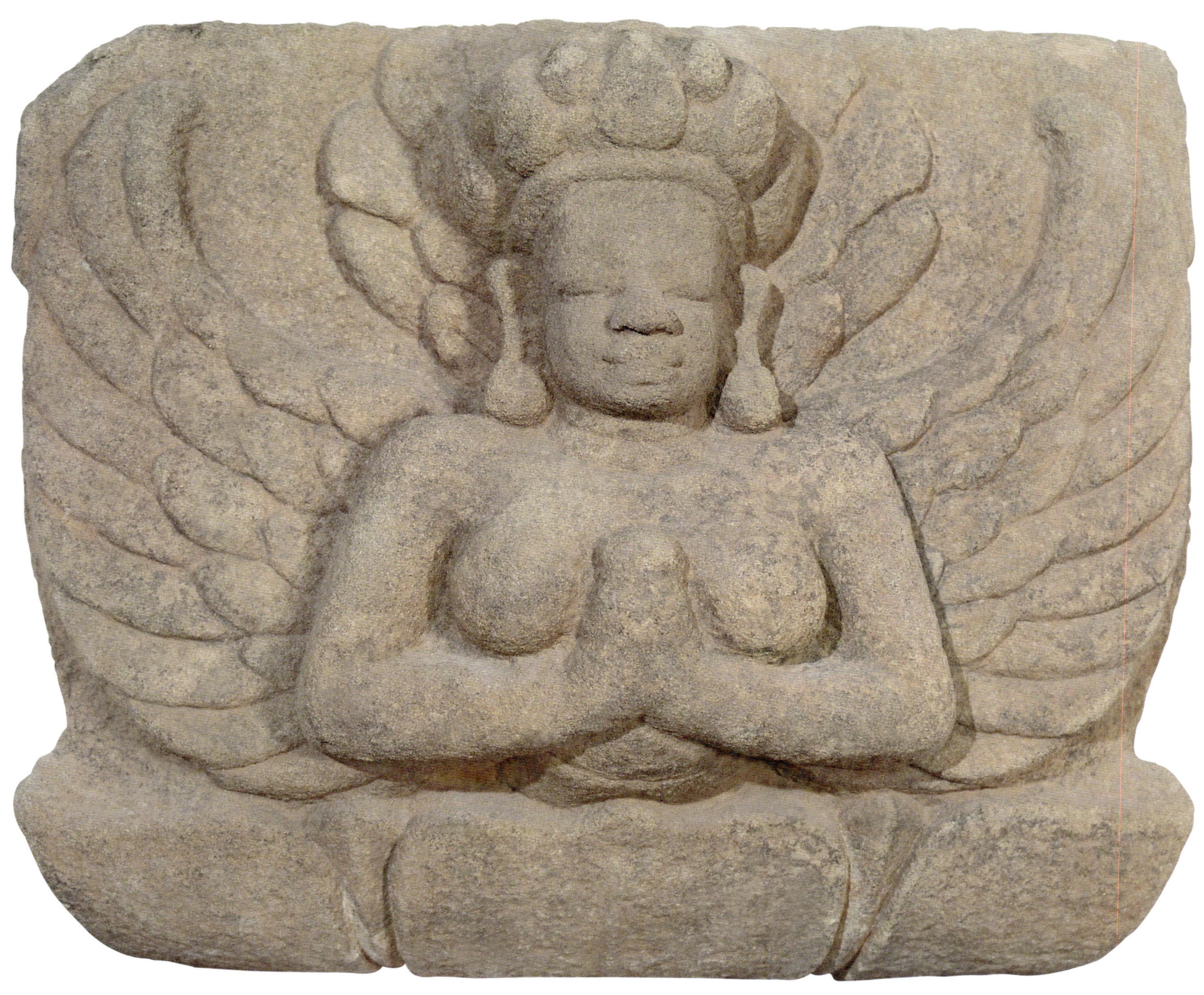

The mythical being holds a lotus in its hands. A quadrangular tenon in its back allows it to be inserted into the brick frame of a temple.

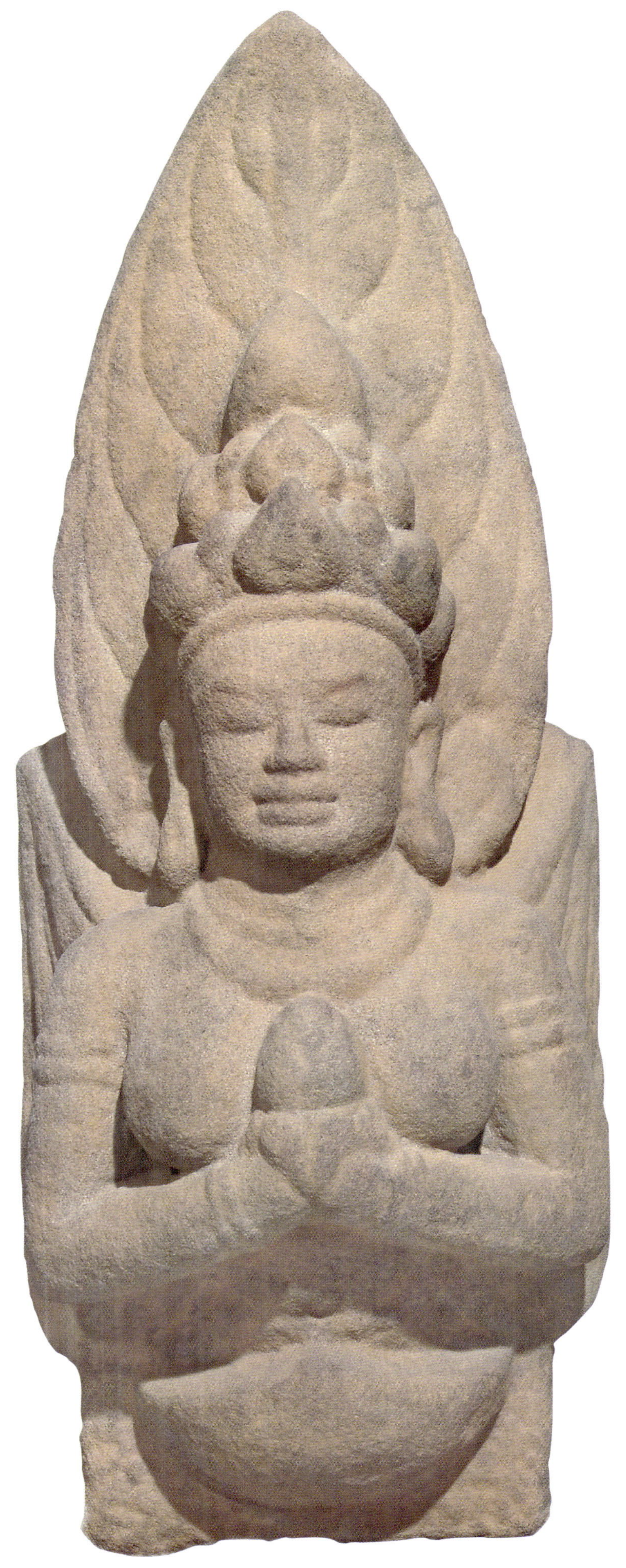

Previous Page

148. *Kinnari*, High-relief, Sandstone, Height 32 cm, Tra Kiêu style, 10th Century.

149. *Kinnari*, High-relief, Sandstone, Height 42 cm, Tra Kiêu style, 10th Century.

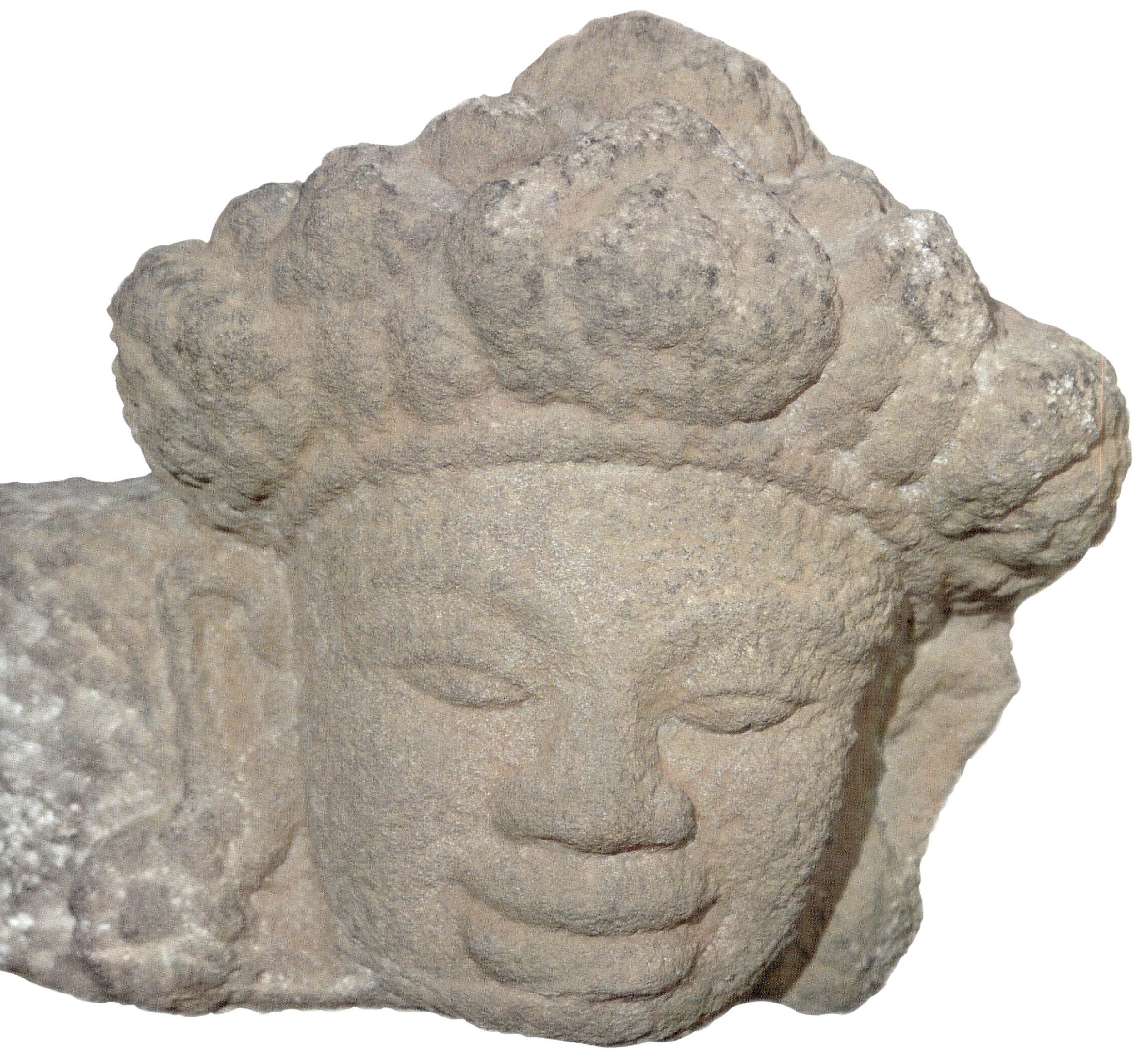

150. *Head of feminine divinity,* High-relief, Sandstone, Height 20 cm, Tra Kiêu style, 10th Century.

Following Page
151. *Garuda*, High-relief, Sandstone, Height 60 cm, Dong Duong style, 9th - 10th Century.

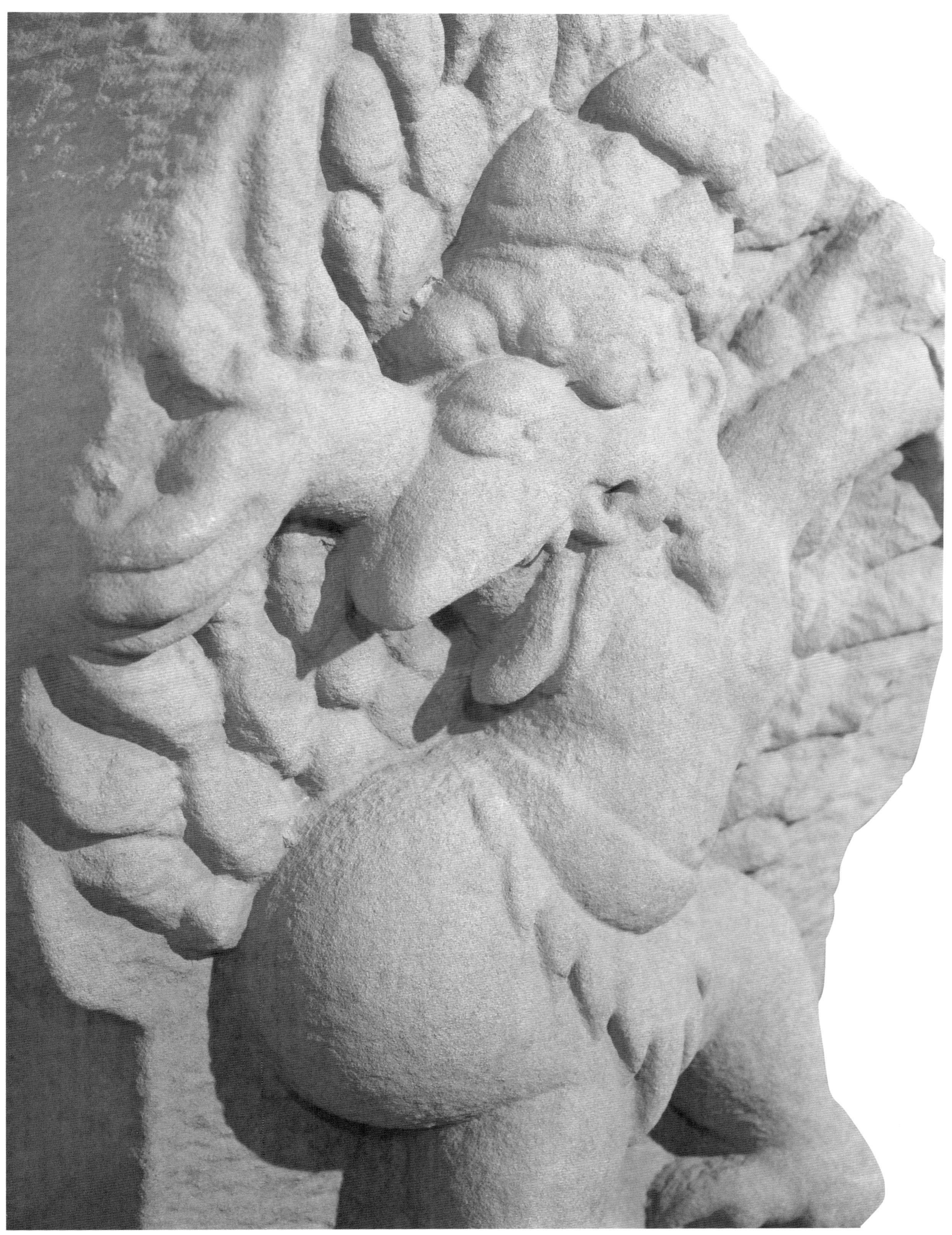

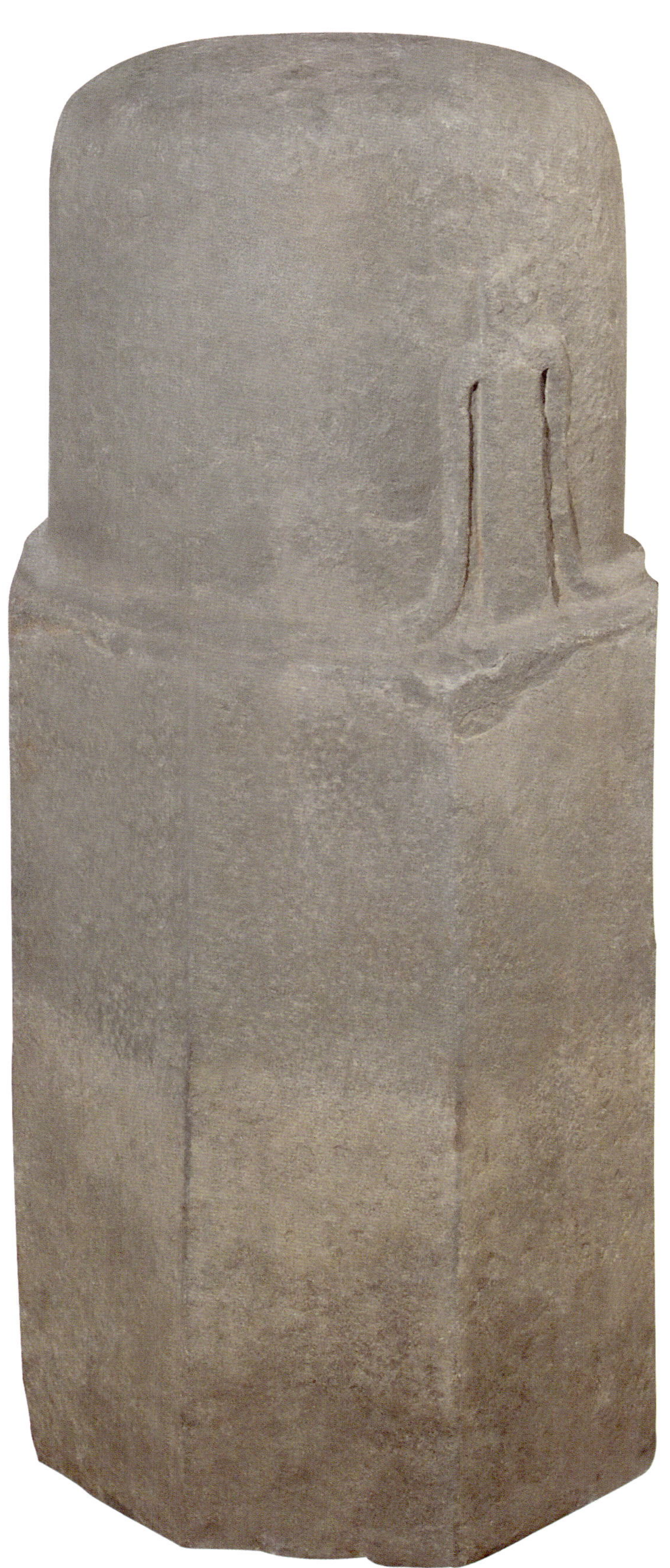

From "jata" ("chignon" in Sanskrit) and "linga" ("sign") the jatalinga is a linga with a chignon – Shiva's hairstyle and therefore symbol but also that of Vayu, the god of wind – sculpted or carved into it. Only the two top sections of the linga are present here: the highest one (Rudrabhaga) and the middle one (Vishnubhaga).

In styles that predate the tenth century, the chignon was realistic. Later, it became stylised to finally reach the representation seen here.

152. *Jatalinga,* Free-standing, Sandstone, Height 71 cm, Tra Kiêu style, 10th Century.

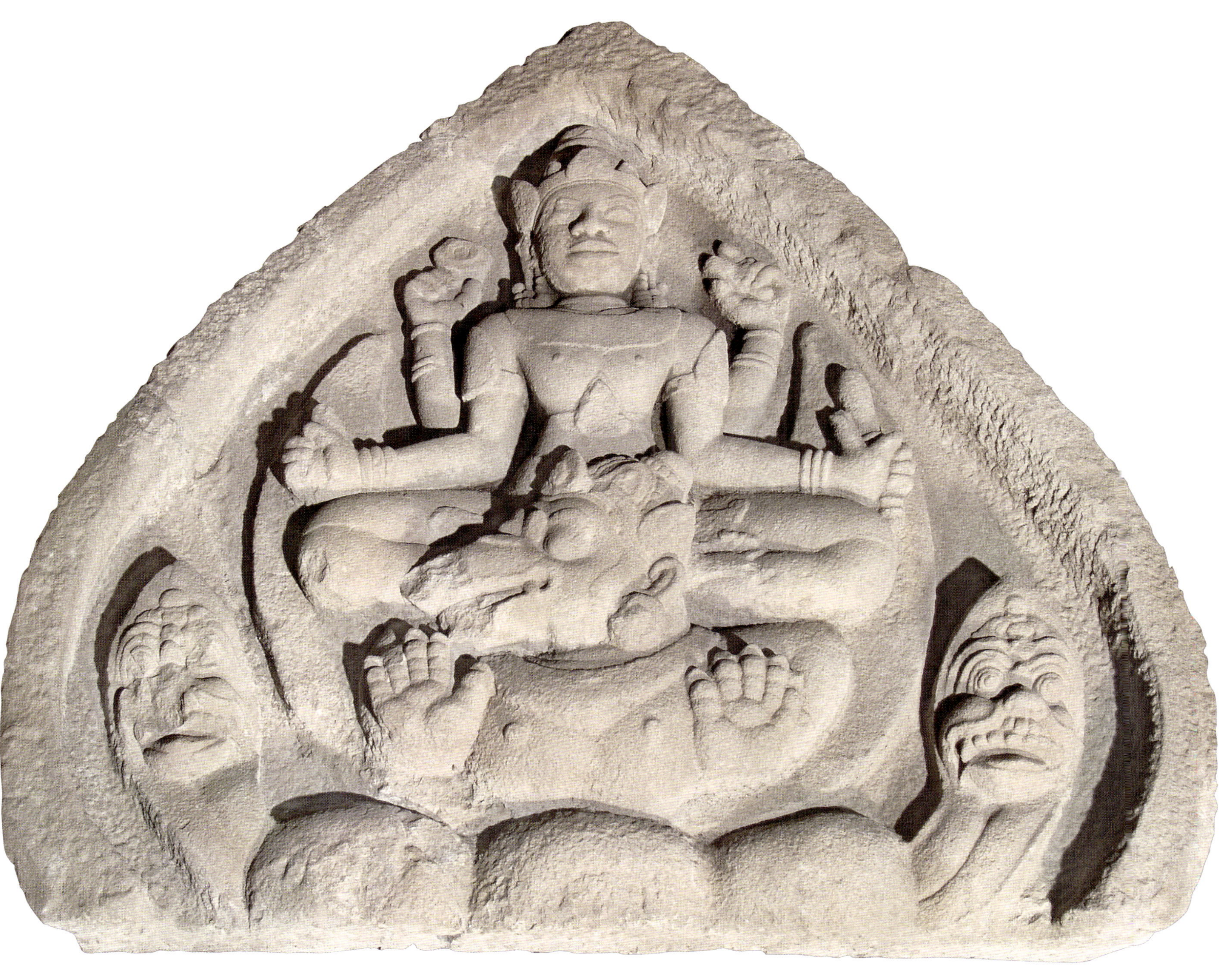

153. *Vishnu on Garuda*, High-relief, Sandstone, Height 106 cm, Chien Dan style, 10th - 11th Century.

Following Page
154. *Vishnu on Garuda*, High-relief, Sandstone, Height 106 cm, Chien Dan style, 10th - 11th Century (detail).

155. *Vishnu on Garuda*, High-relief, Sandstone, Height 06 cm, Chien Dan style, 10th - 11th Century (detail of a naga head).

The god is seated, Indian style, on Garuda. He can also ride it (see ill. 163). We can see the heads of nagas, Garuda's hereditary enemies.

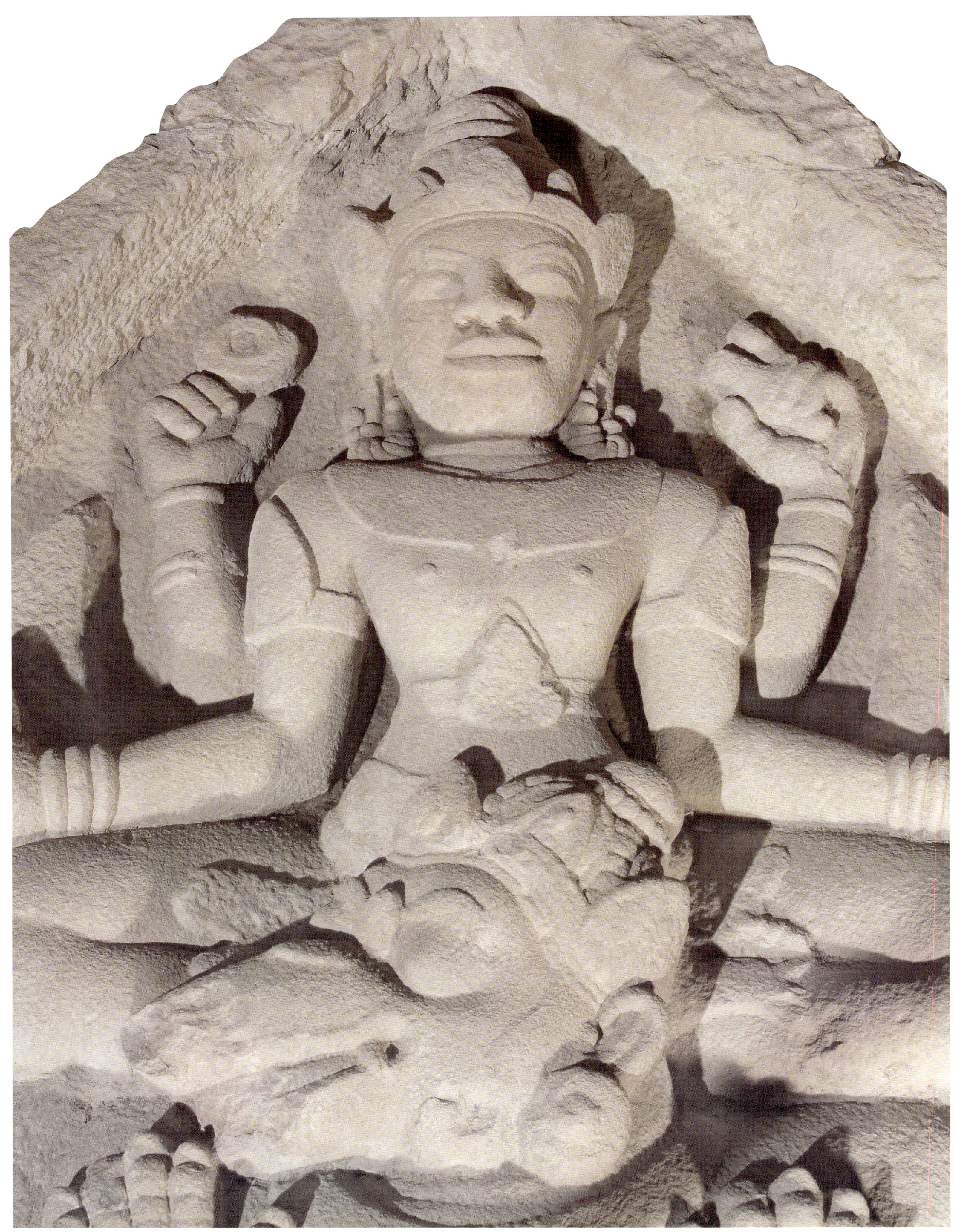

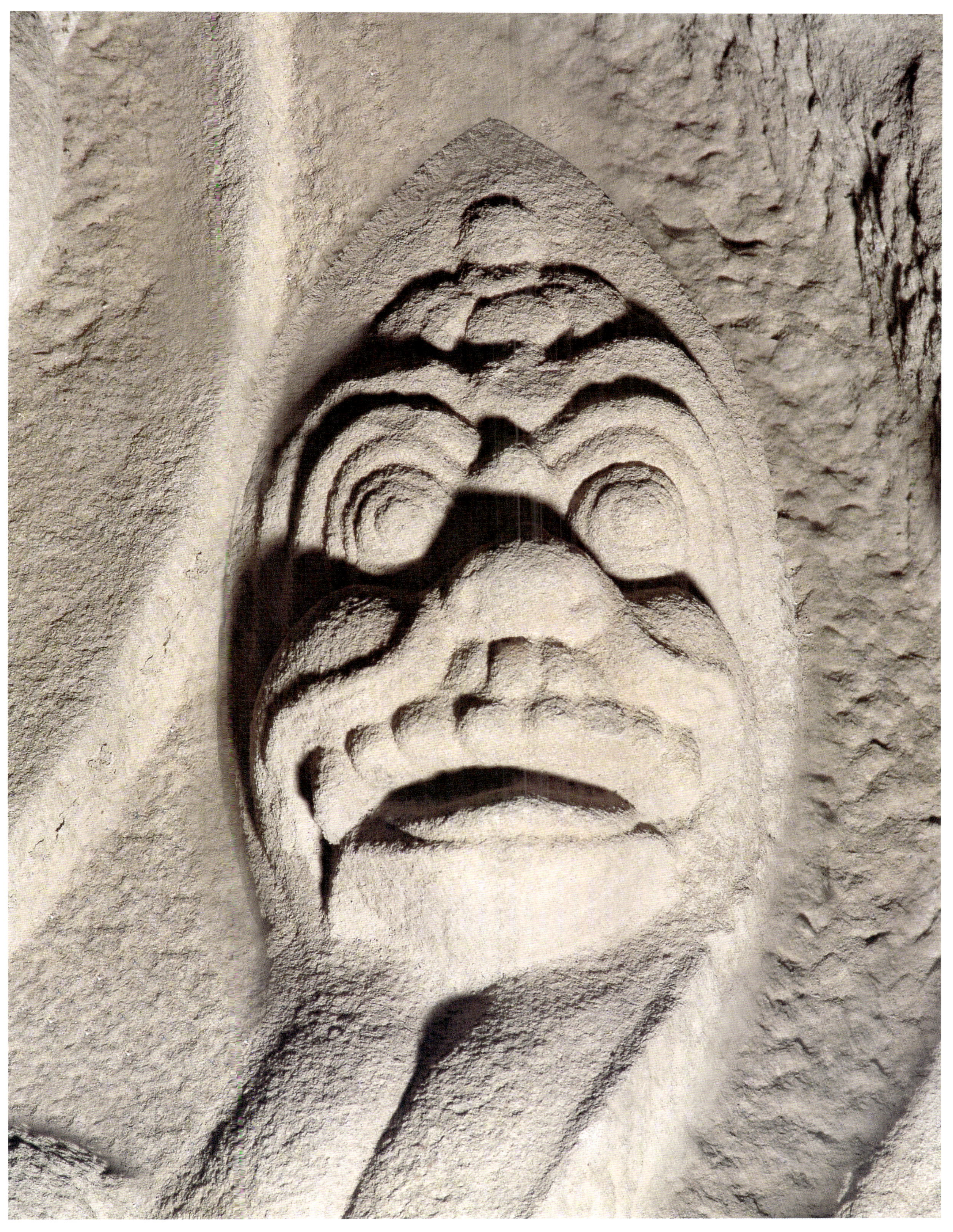

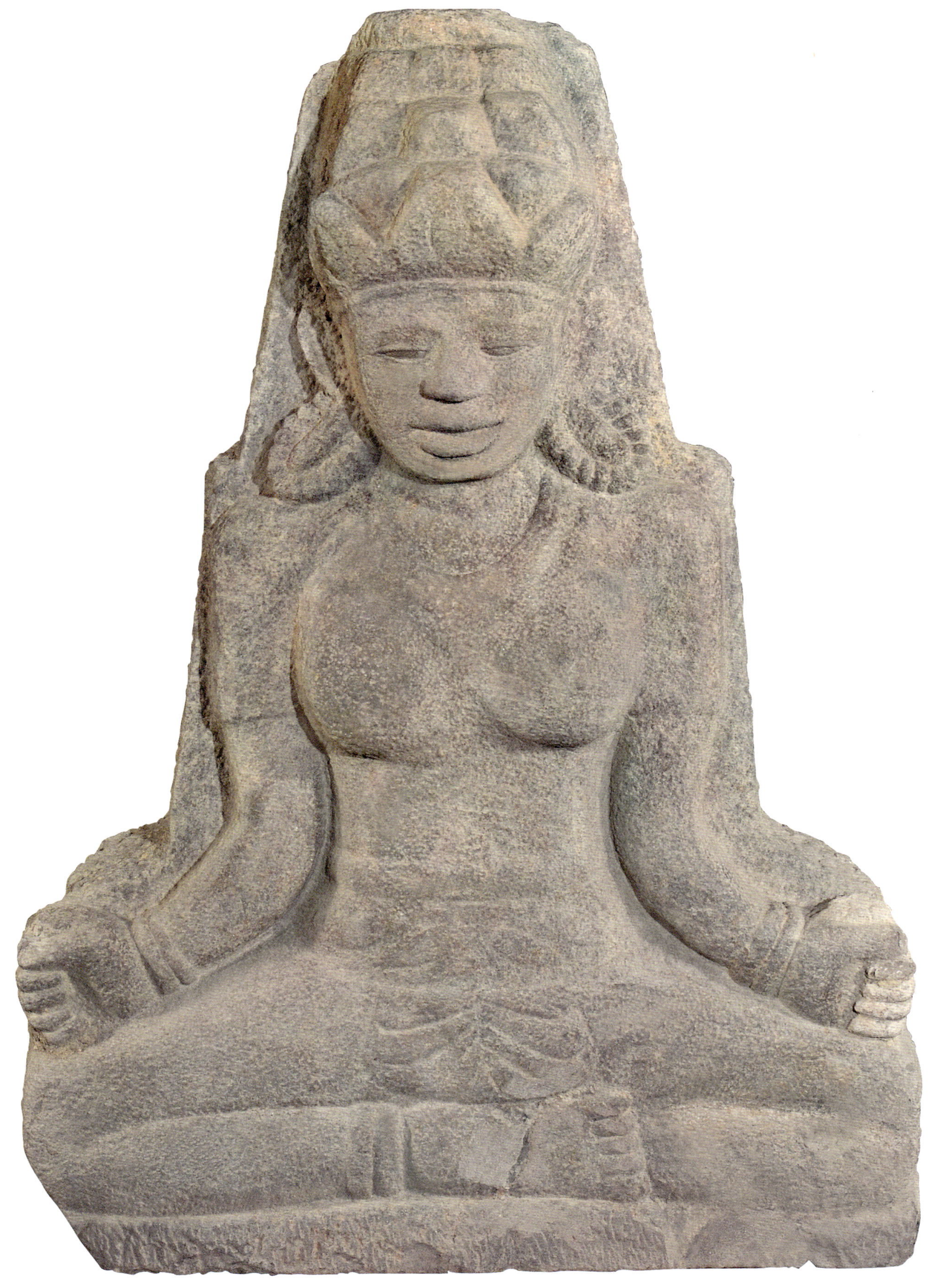

156. *Lakshmi,* High relief, Sandstone, Height 63 cm, Chien Dan style, 11th Century.

Following Page
157. *Lakshmi,* High relief, Sandstone, Height 63 cm, Chien Dan style, 11th Century (detail).

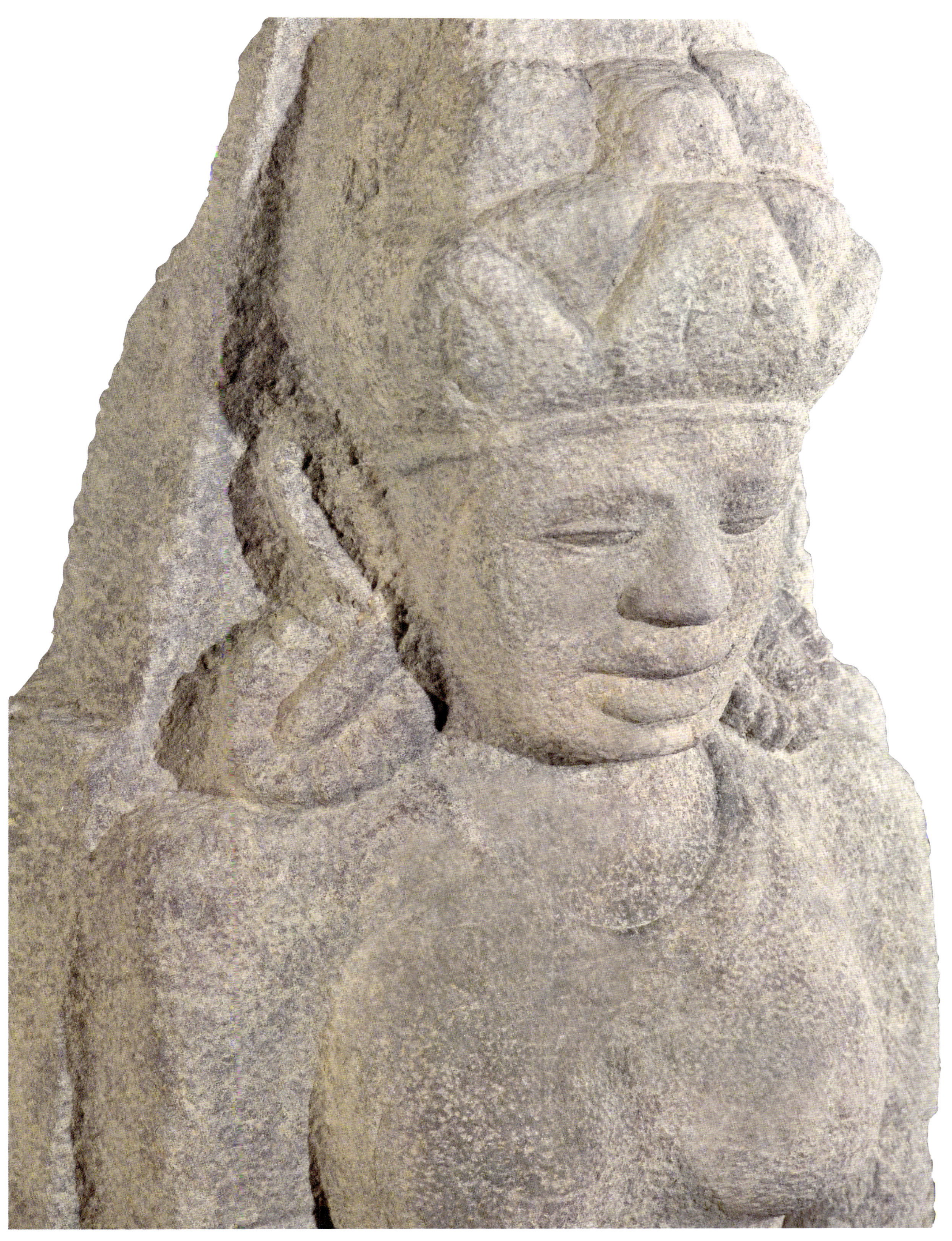

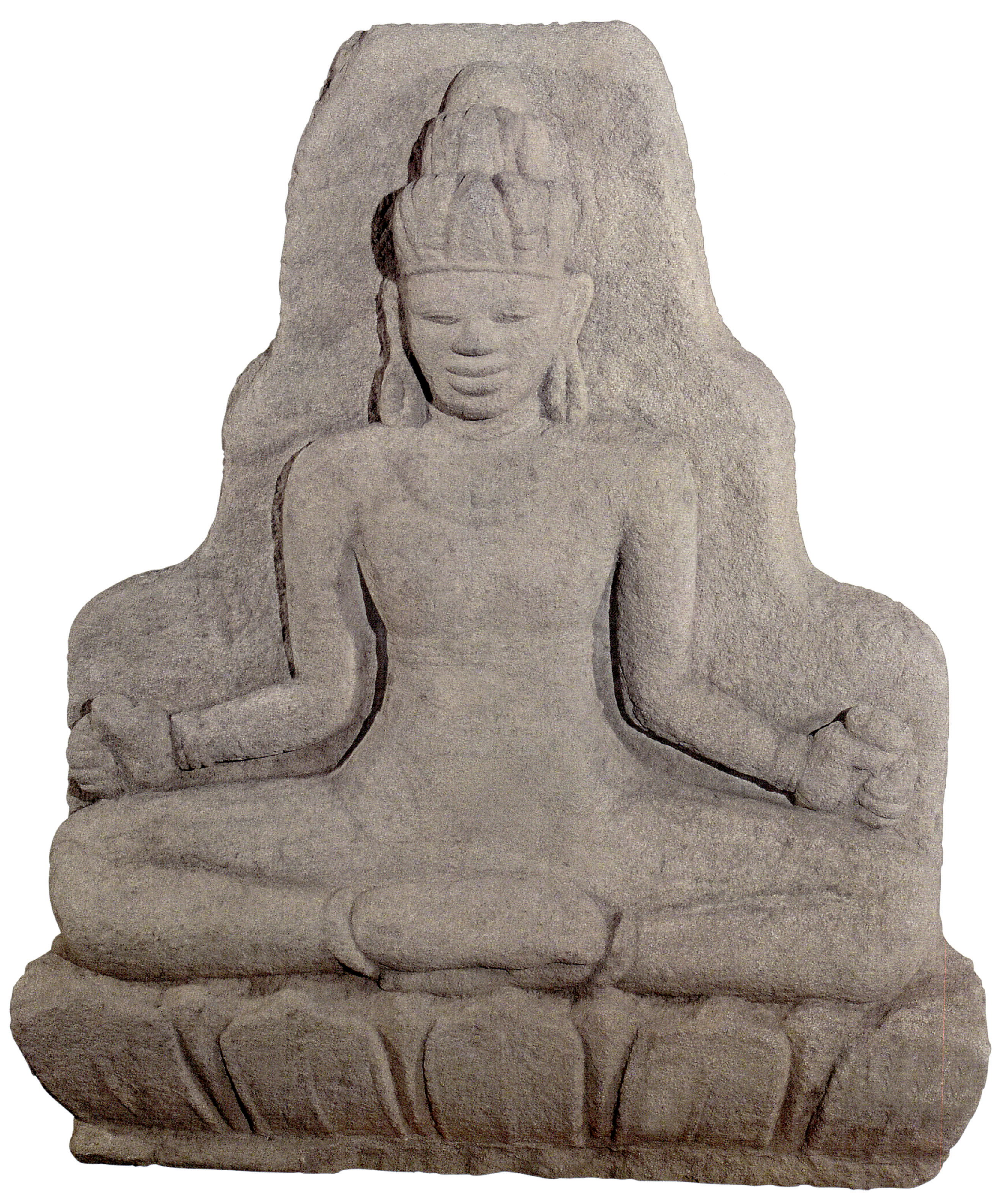

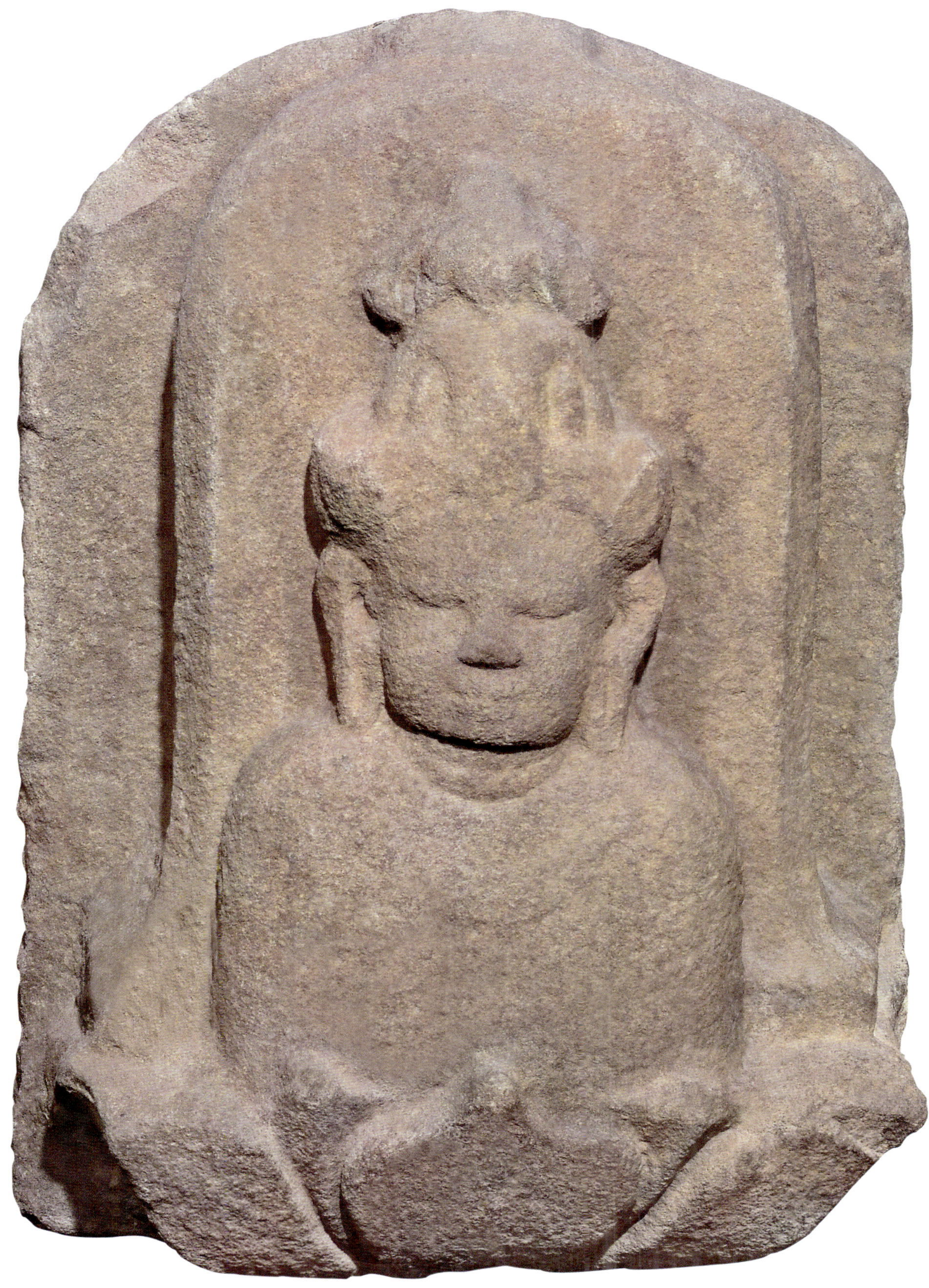

Previous Page
158. *Lakshmi,* High-relief, Sandstone, Height 66 cm, Chien Dan style, 11th Century.

159. *Figure*, Bas-relief, Sandstone, Height 42 cm, Chien Dan style, 11th Century.

A very unusual hairstyle.

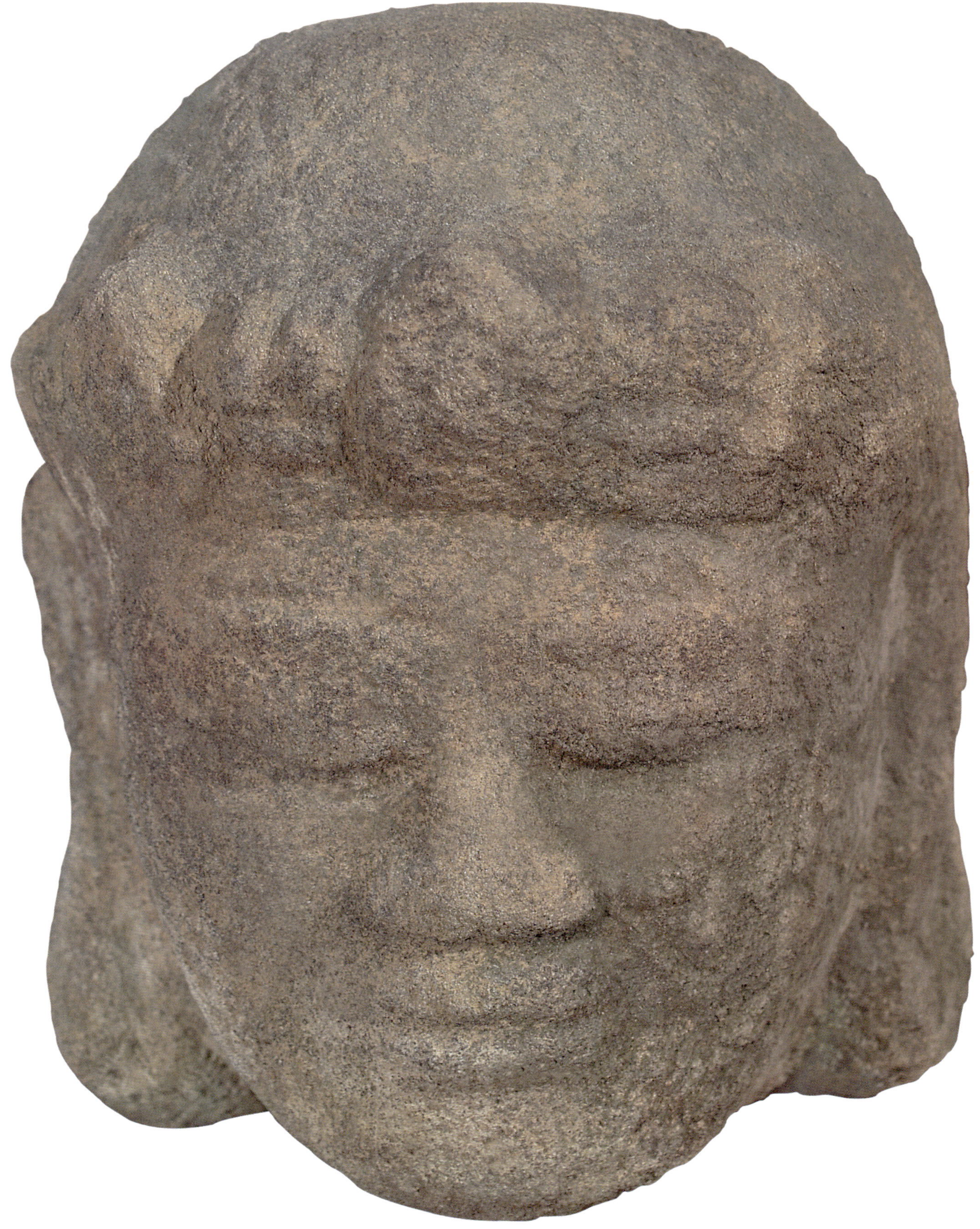

160. *Head,* Nearly free-standing, Sandstone, Height 19 cm, Chien Dan style, 10th Century.

Following Page
161. *Head of Vishnu*, High-relief, Sandstone, Height 25 cm, Chien Dan style, 11th Century.

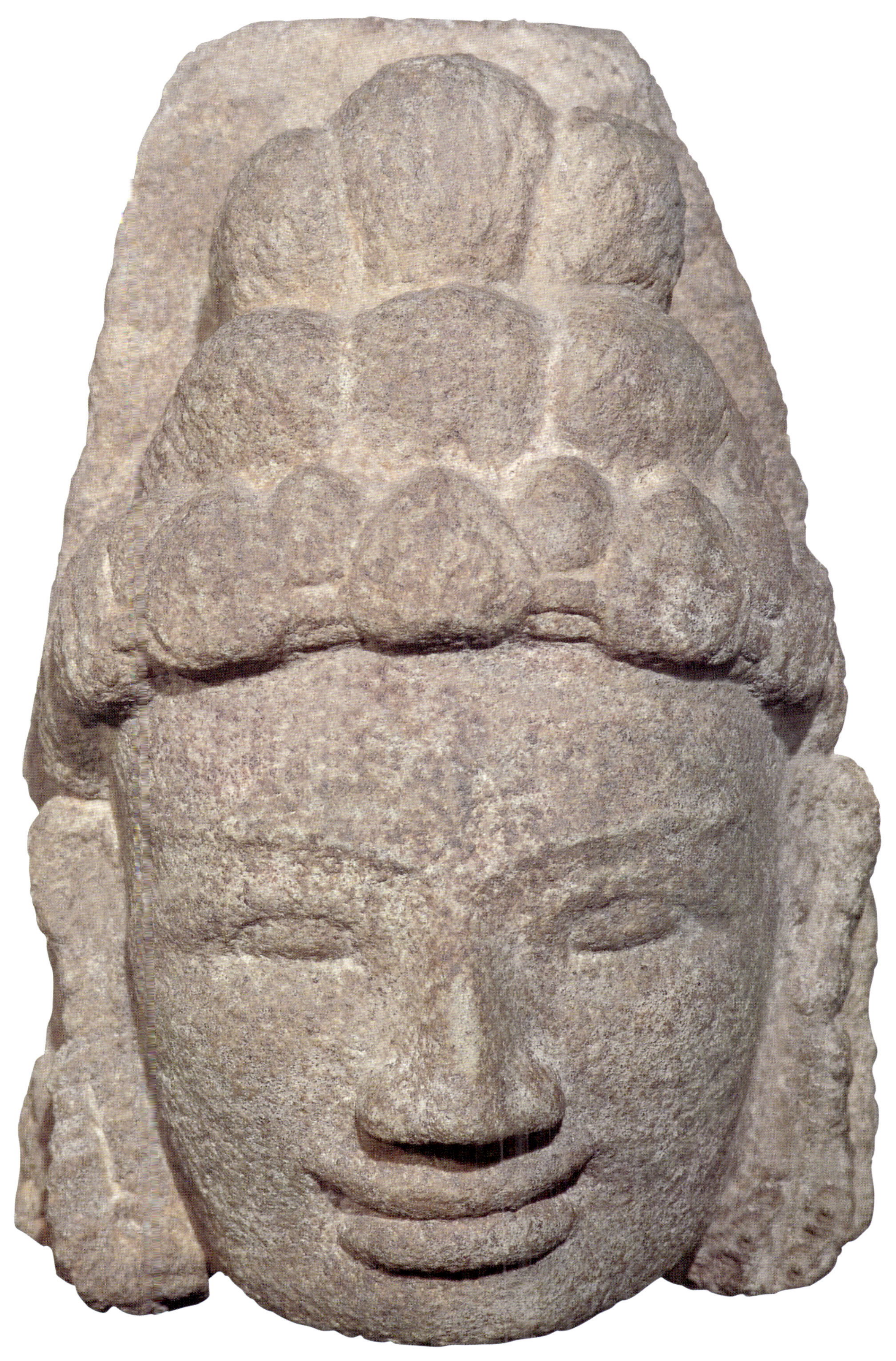

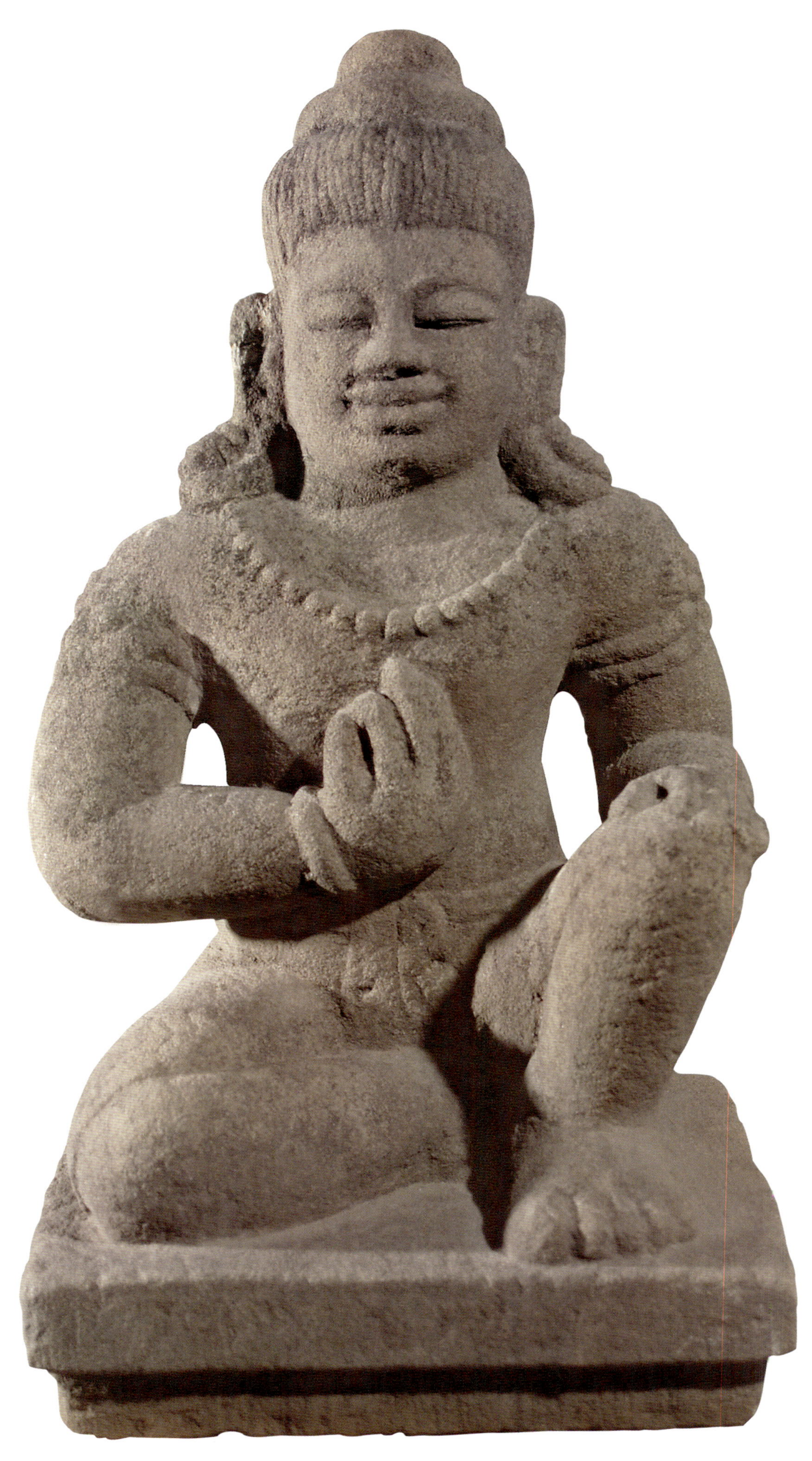

162. *Seated figure*, Free-standing, Sandstone, Height 44 cm, Chien Dan style, 10th-11th Century.

Following Page

163. *Vishnu on Garuda*, High-relief, Sandstone, Height 91 cm, Chien Dan style, 10th-11th Century.

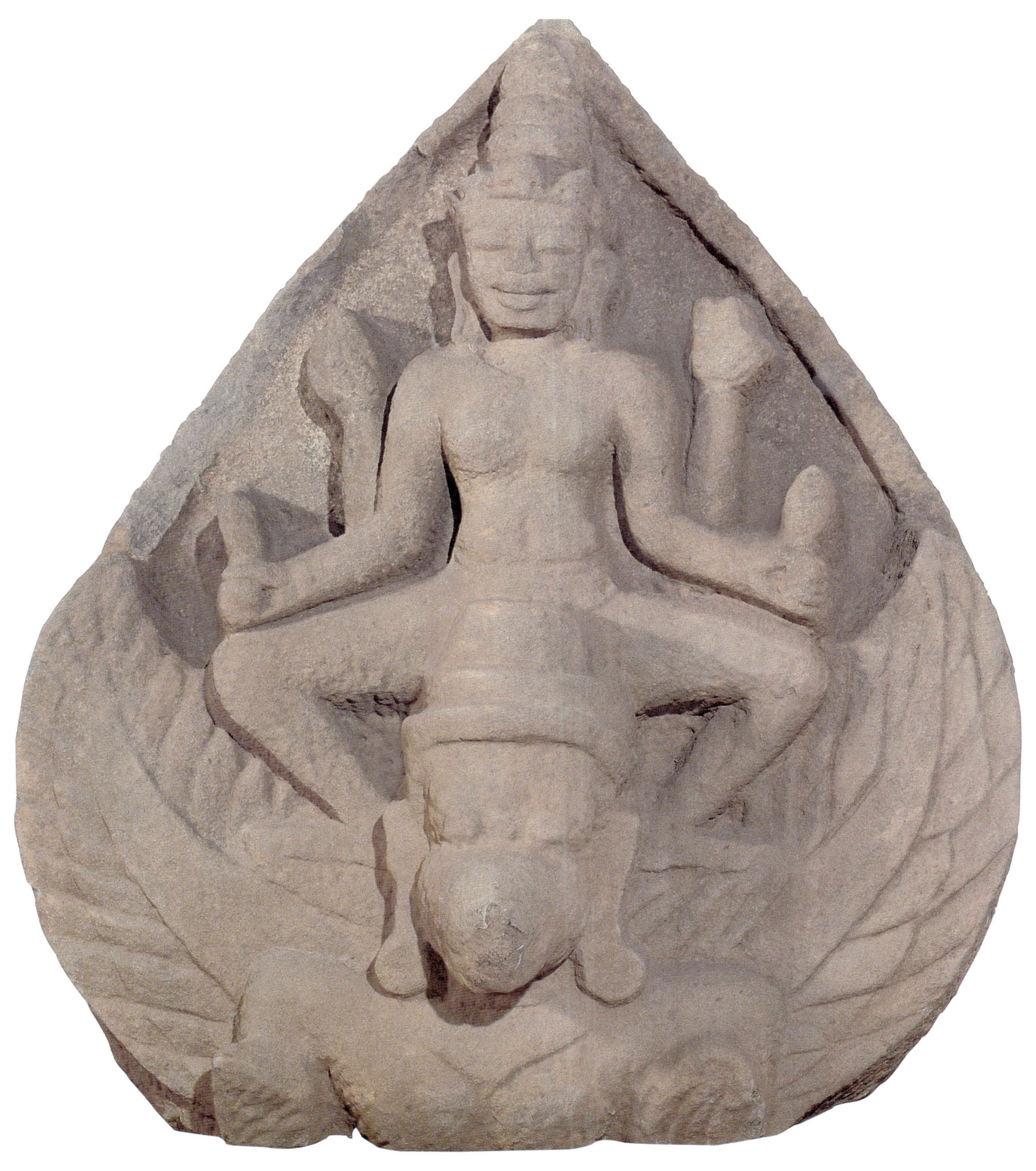

Vishnu, the Vedic god, Indra's younger brother and assistant, is one of the two most important Hindu gods with Shiva. Here, he is riding Garuda ("wings of speech" in Sanskrit) the divine eagle, his mount. In another posture, he can be seated on the bird Indian style. (See ill. 153.) The god holds his four attributes in his hands: the sphere (upper left hand), the chakra as a ring gripped the lower left hand, the sledgehammer (lower right hand), the conch shell (upper right hand). Garuda is wearing a high, ringed, tiered kirita-mukuta, has a wide beak and – contrary to Vishnu – ears decorated with pendants. The bird's feathers are stylised.

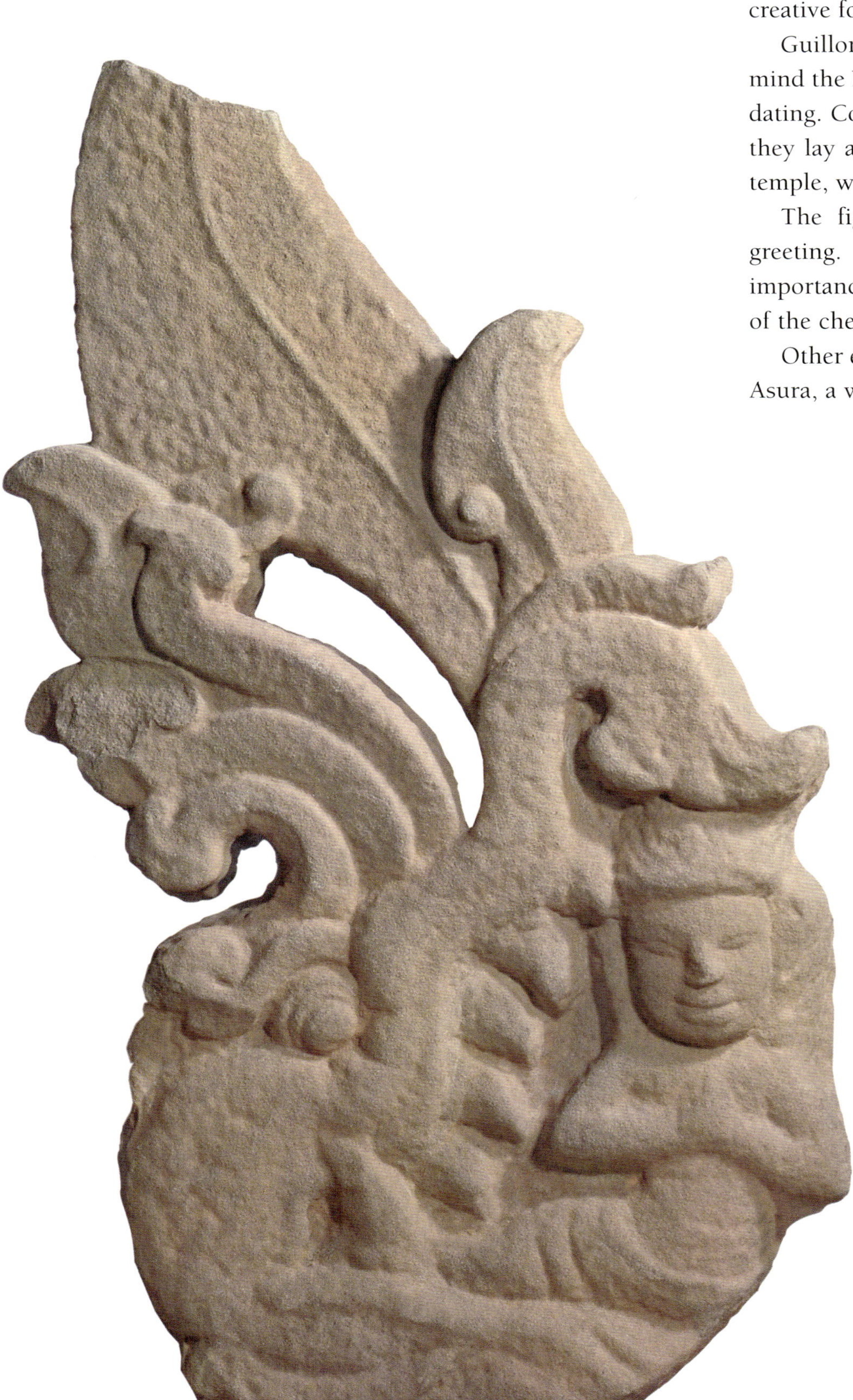

The Makara is a mythical sea monster that here resembles a crocodile. (Elsewhere, he can have the appearance of a fish or a tapir.) His maw, wide open, spits out flowers or plants, pearls or, as is the case here, beings. His eye is round, the eyebrow ridge is an ornamental shepherd's crook. Sinuous lines or decorative flames and "pig" ears complete the ornamentation. The Makara symbolises the creative force of the liquid element.

Guillon remarks that its profile with double inverse slits calls to mind the My Son E4 style accent pieces and therefore allows precise dating. Comparable elements were found buried in the earth where they lay after falling from the temple's structure at the Chien Dan temple, where new digs were carried out in 1989.

The figure is in anjali mudra, a gesture of veneration and greeting. The gesture must not, however, be given over-much importance. In India as in all of South-east Asia, made at the height of the chest or the forehead, it is an habitual salutation.

Other elements coming out of Makara's maw have been recorded: Asura, a warrior with a shield (or a dancer), a deer, naga.

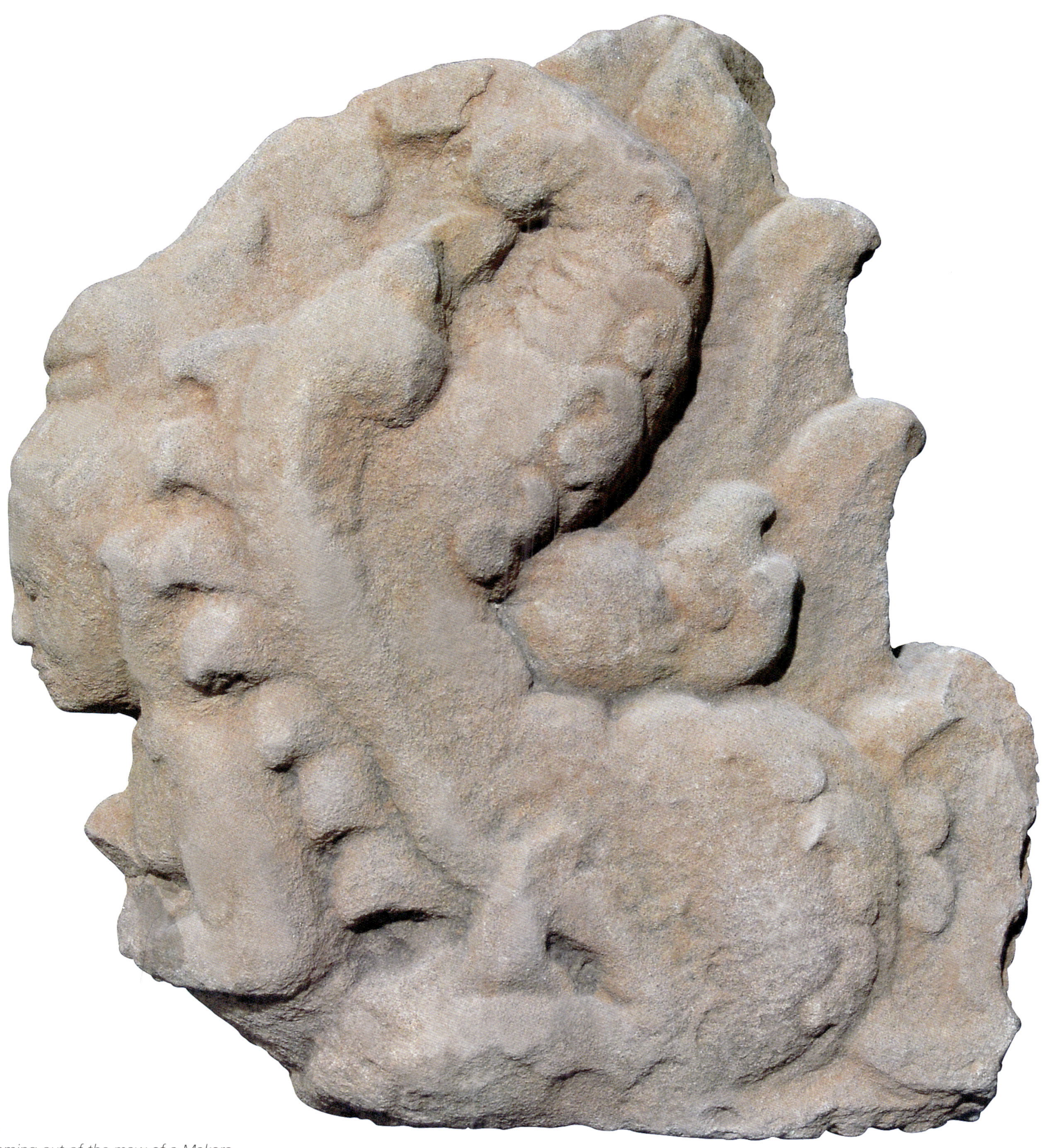

Previous Page

164. *Figure coming out of the maw of a Makara,*
Free-standing,Sandstone, Height 65 cm,
Chien Dan style, 10th - 11th Century.

165. *Figure coming out of the maw of a Makara,*
Free-standing, Sandstone, Height 40 cm,
Chien Dan style, 10th - 11th Century.

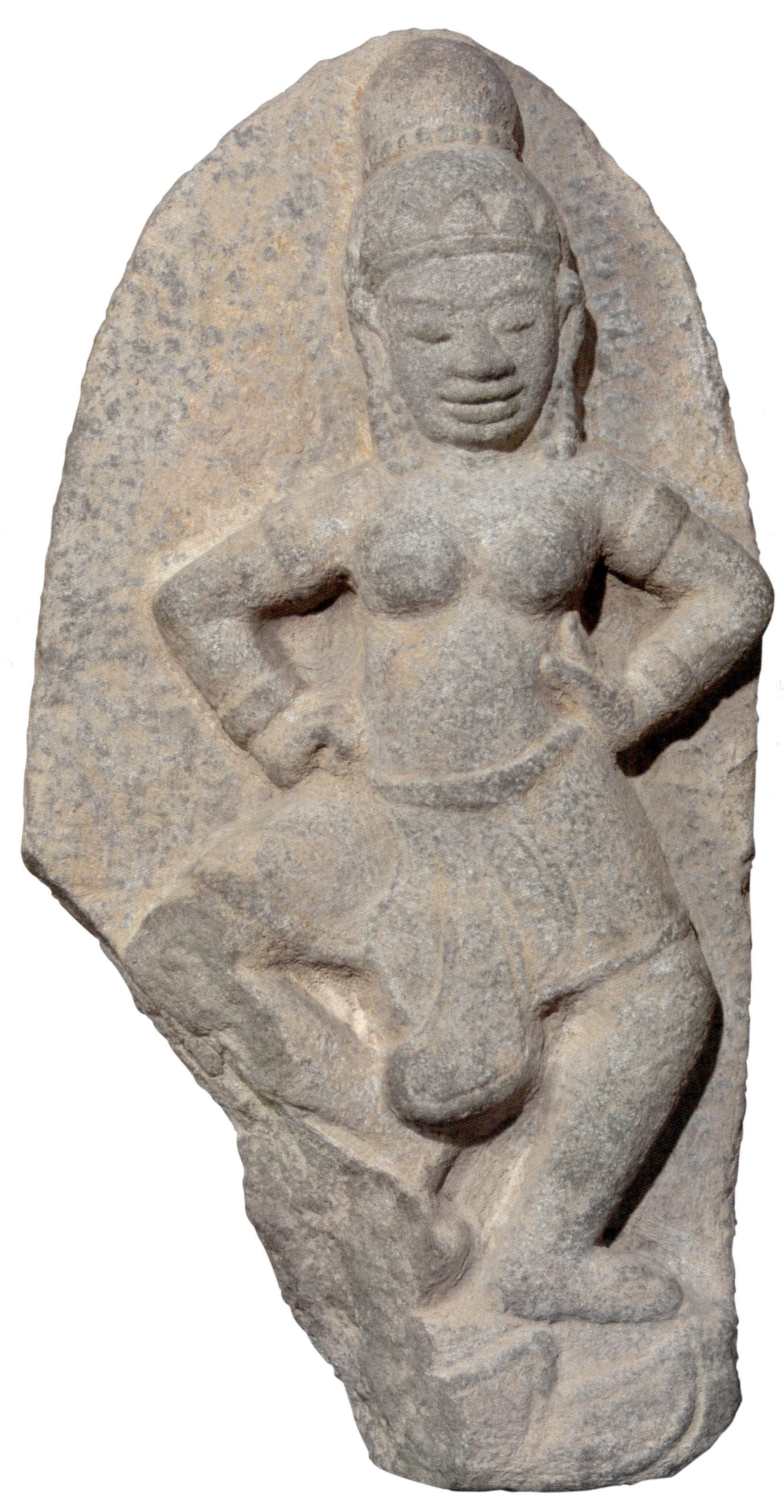

166. *Female dancer,* Sandstone, Height 35 cm, Chien Dan style, 11th Century.

Following Page
167. *Female dancer,* Sandstone, Height 35 cm, Chien Dan style, 11th Century (detail).

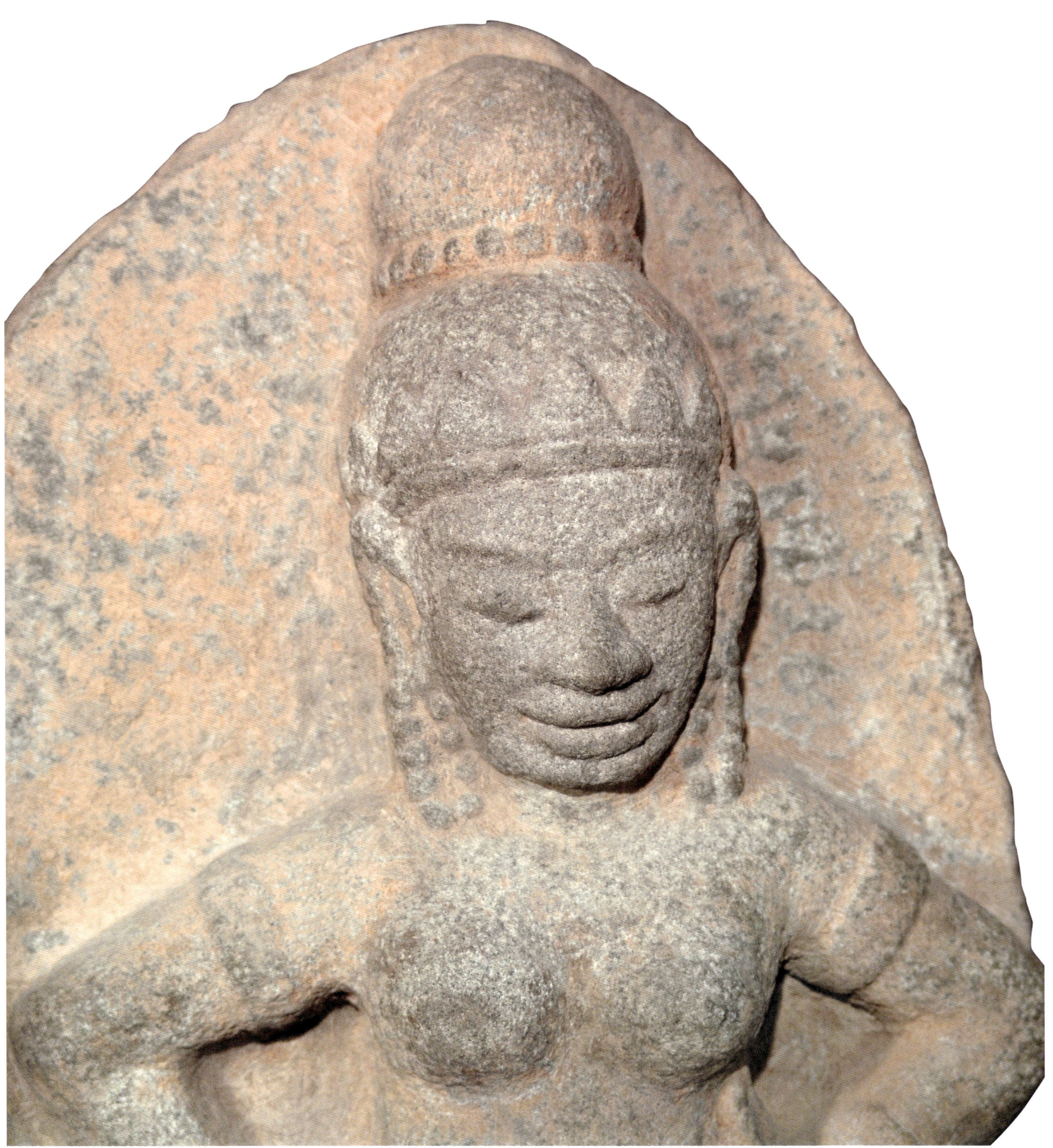

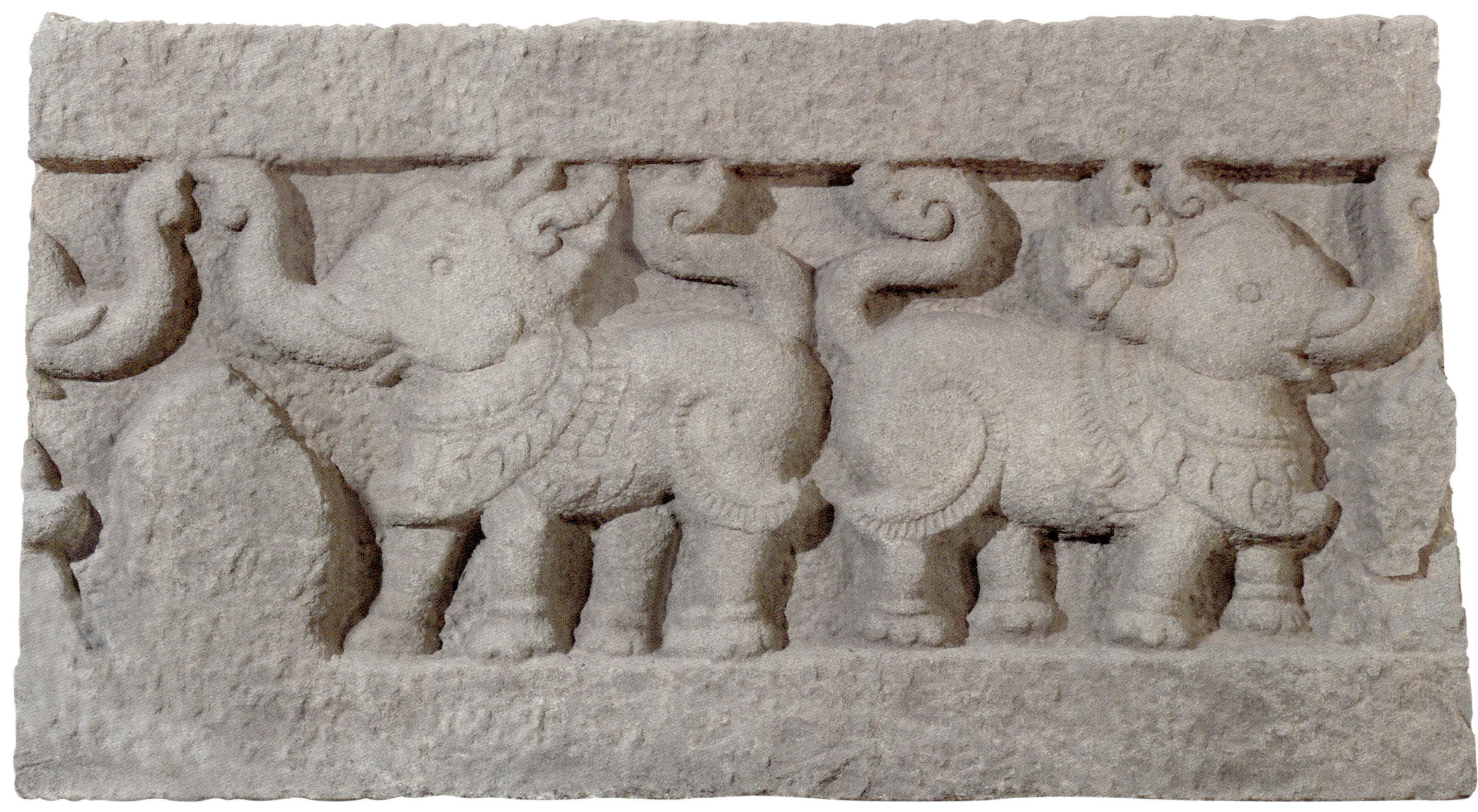

The Gajasimha is a mythical animal often encountered in Cham art. It has an elephant's head (elephant is "gaja" in Sanskrit) and the body of a lion ("simha"). He is the guardian of the temple.

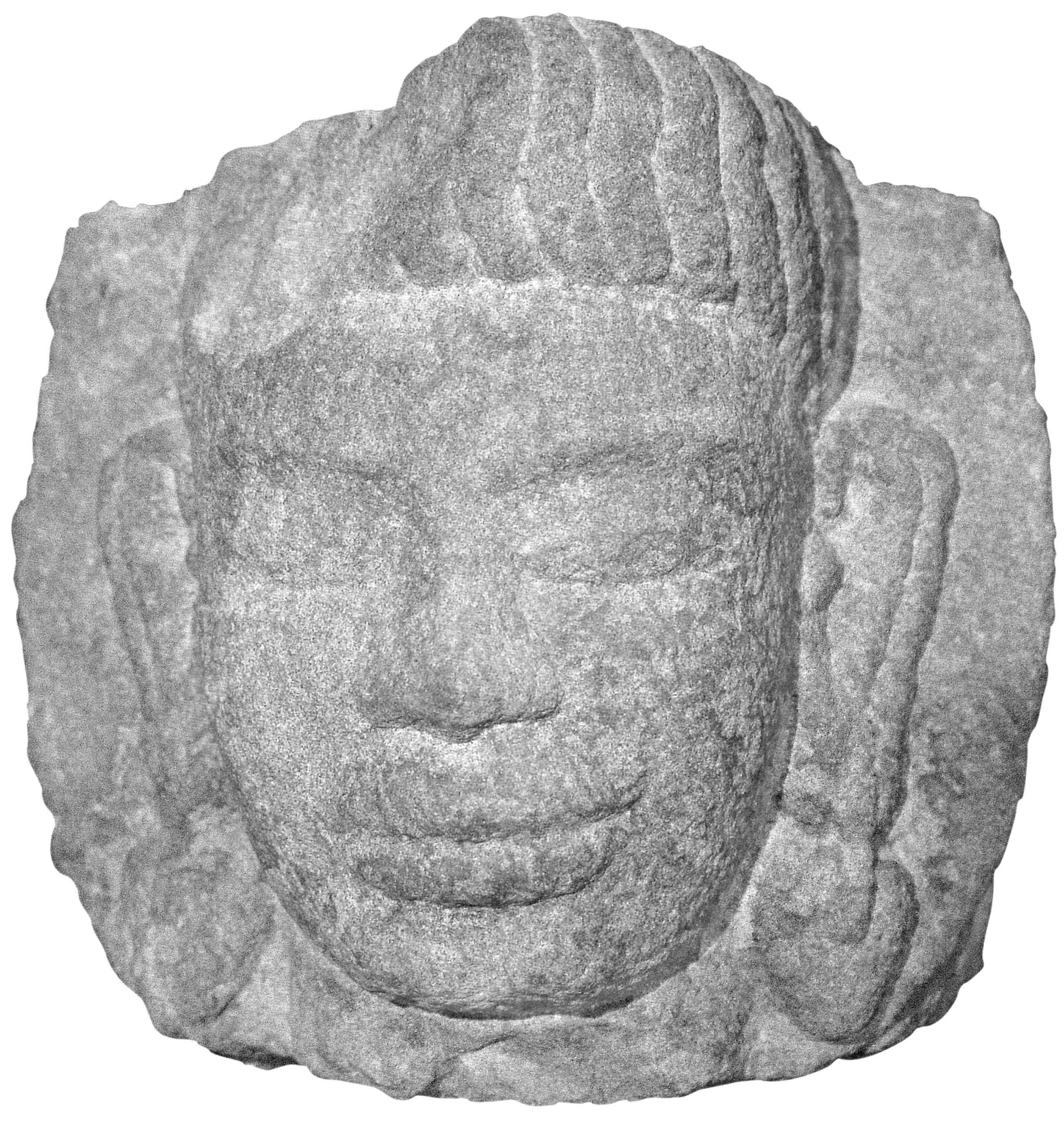

Previous Page
168. *Frieze of Gajasimha,* Bas-relief, Sandstone, Length 75 cm, Chien Dan style, 10th - 11th Century.

169. *Head of divinity*, High-relief, Sandstone, Height 15.5 cm, Chien Dan style, 10th - 11th Century.

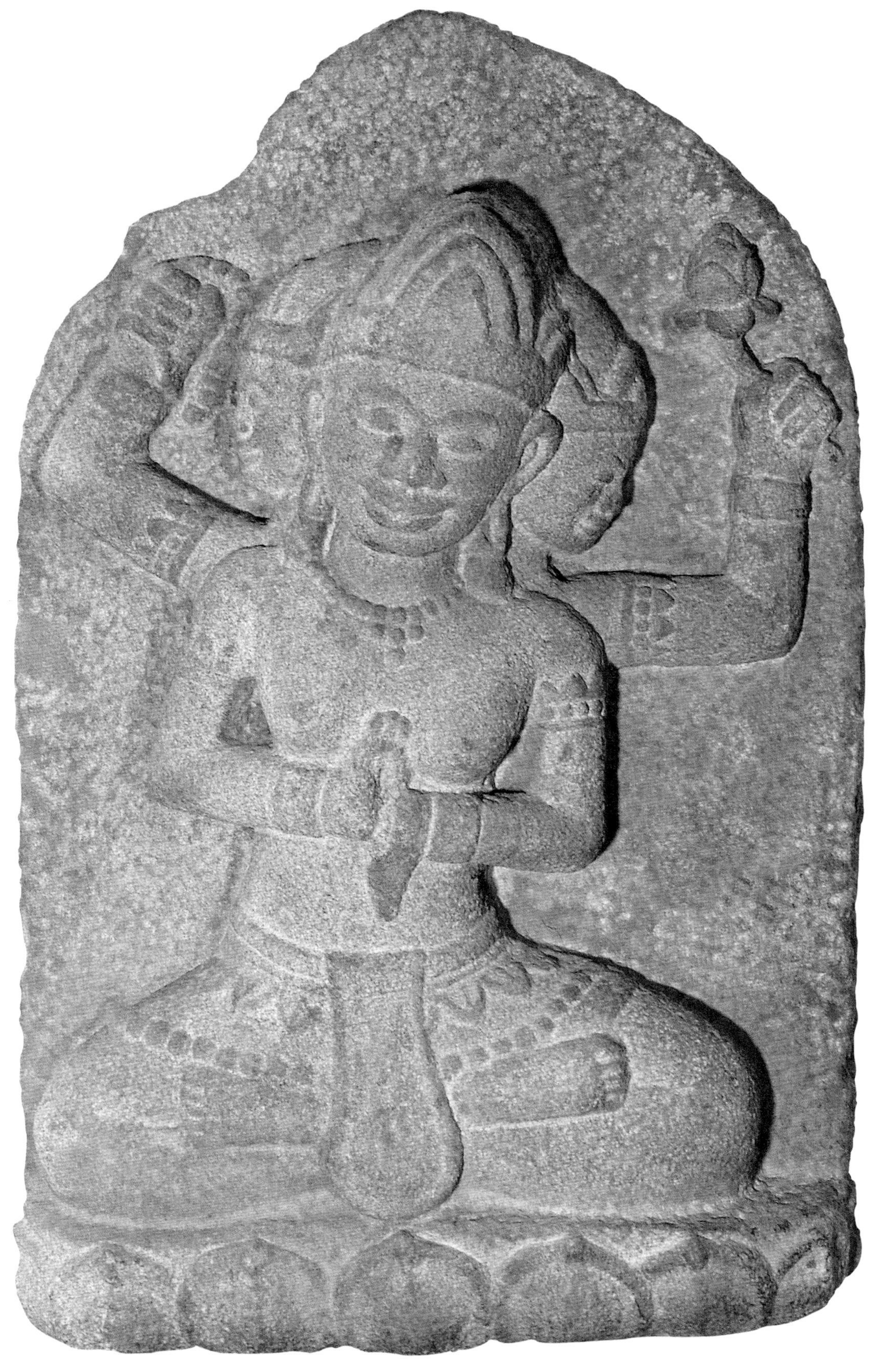

The divinity is holding in his four hands a rosary ("mala"), a vase with a spout and four books of the Vedas. He is seated in dyaasana on a base of lotus petals and is leaning against a stela. The representation of Brahma seated is very rare in Cham iconography.

170. *Brahma*, High-relief, Sandstone, Height 40 cm, Chien Dan style, 10th - 11th Century.

Following Page
171. *Sitting Lion*, Free-standing, Sandstone, Chien Dan Style, 10th - 11th Century.

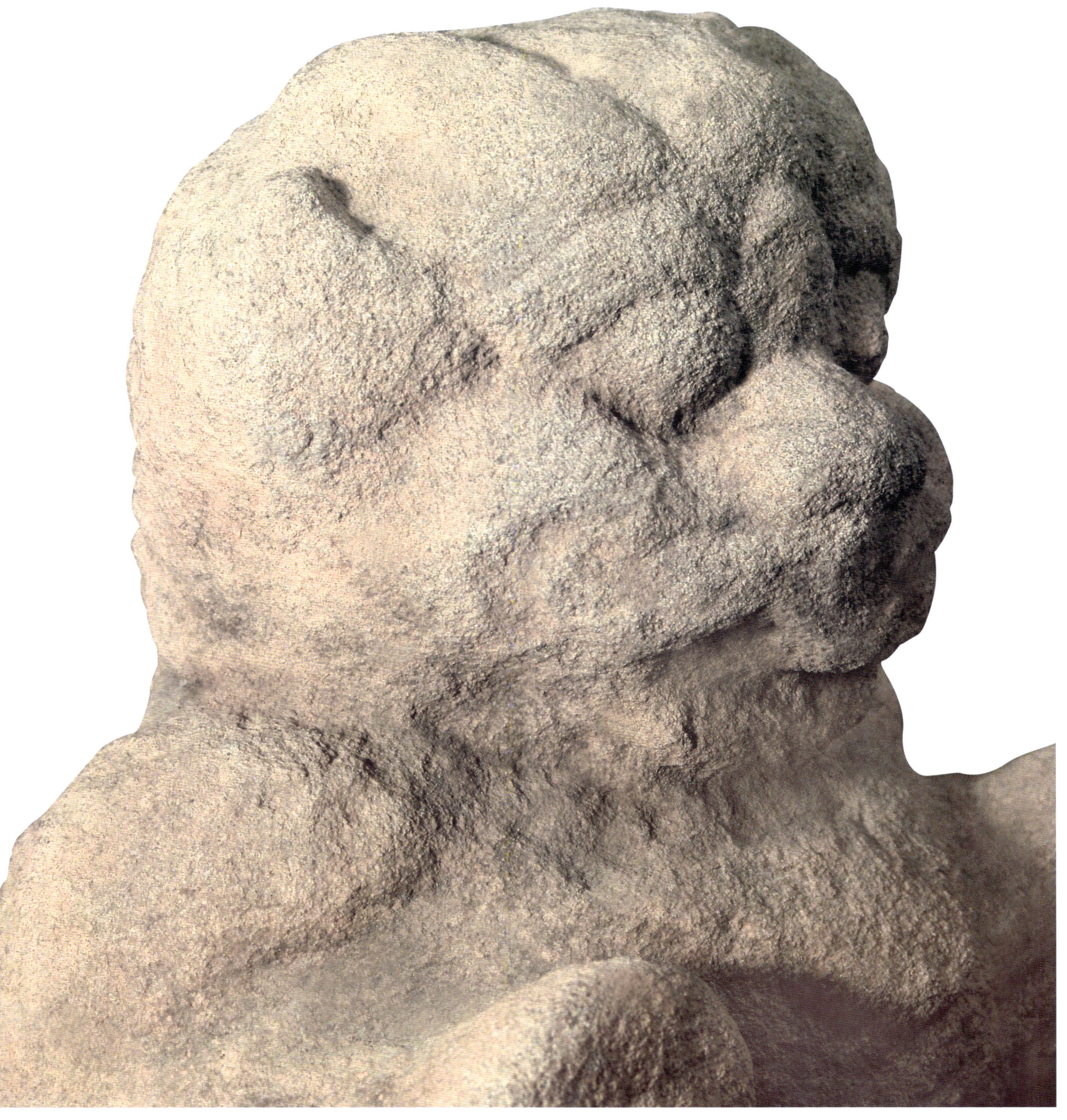

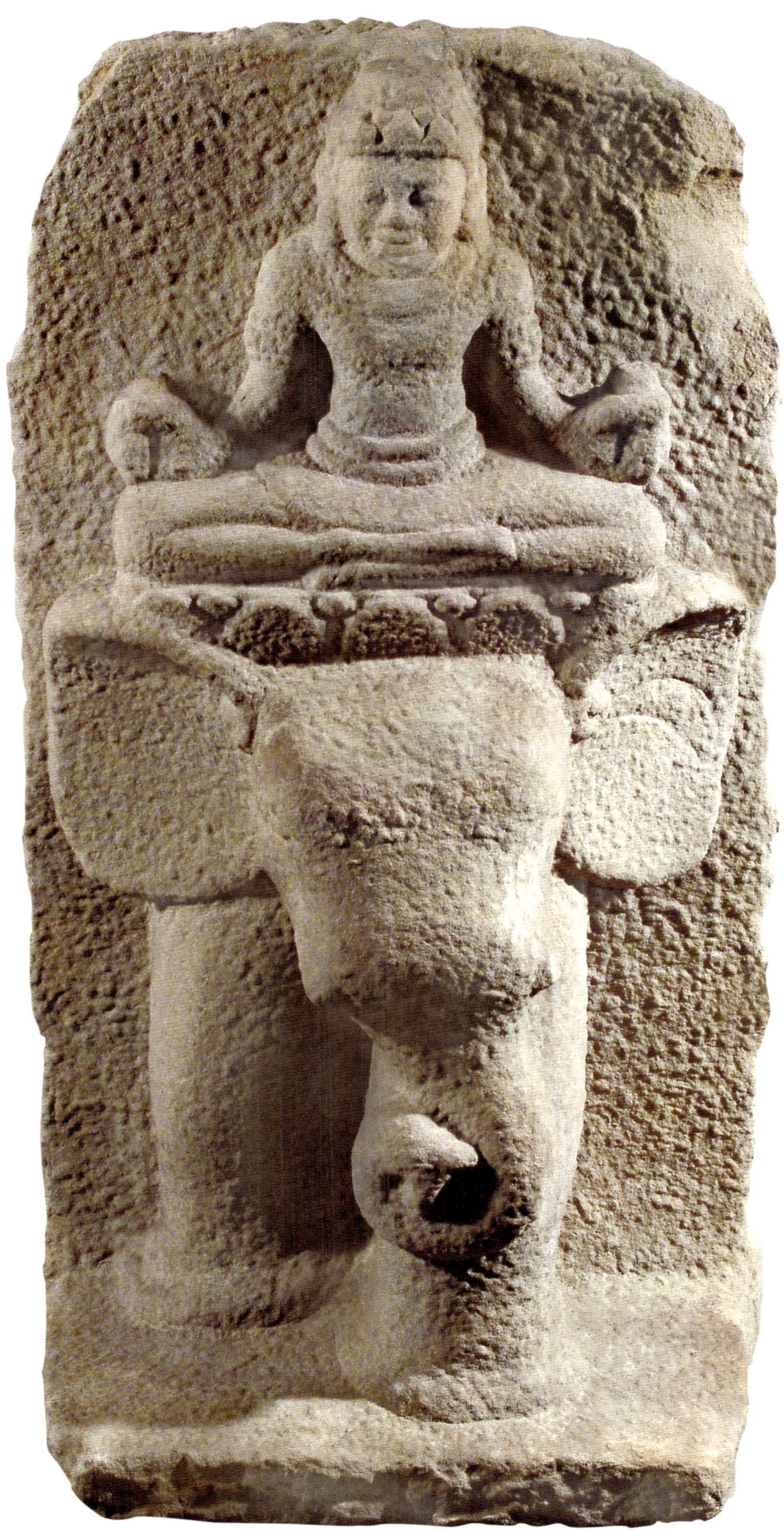

The divinity is seated, Indian style, on his mount Airavata.

172. *Indra on his elephant*, High-relief, Sandstone, Height 86 cm, Chien Dan style, 10th - 11th Century.

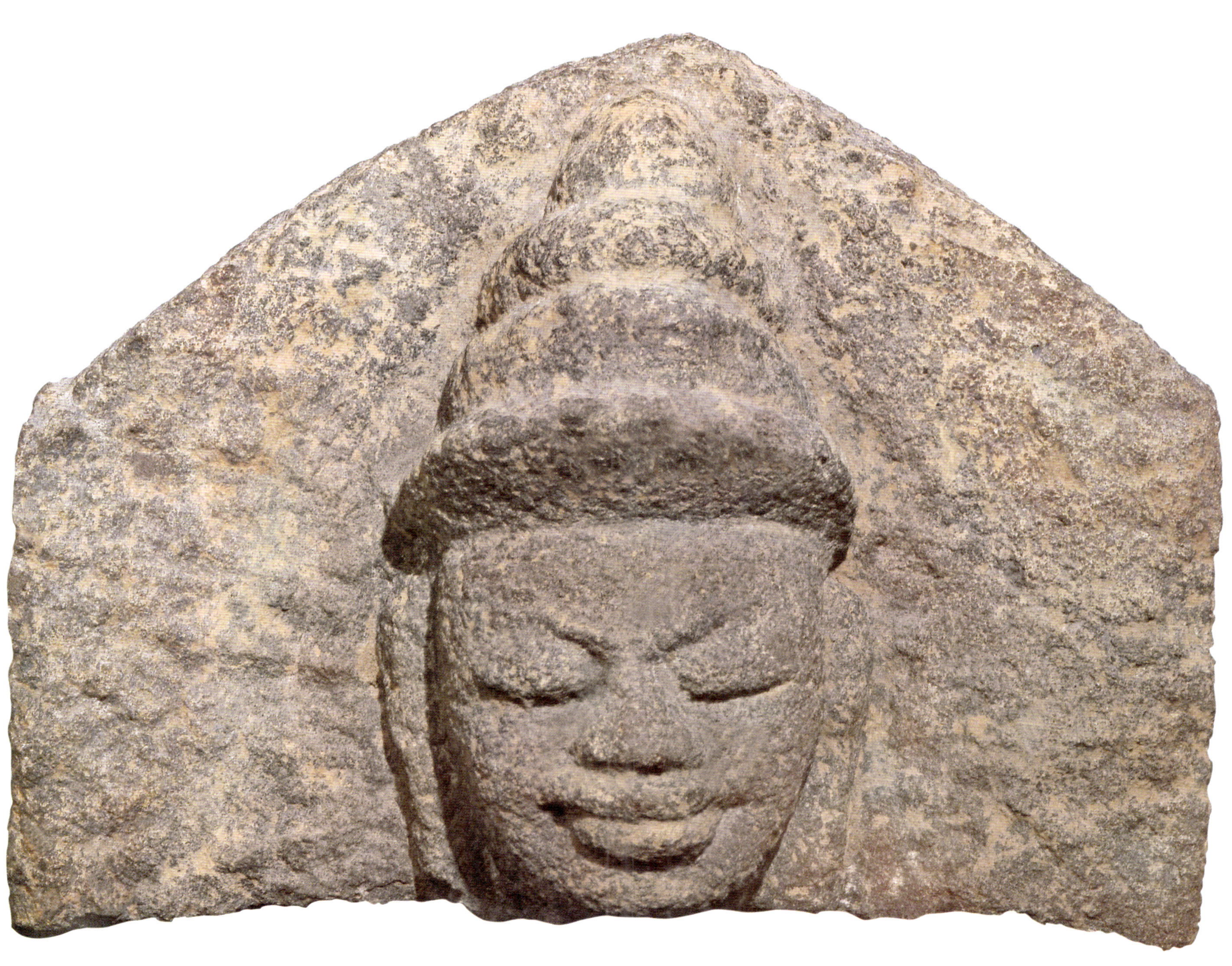

173. *Head of divinity,* High-relief, Sandstone, Height 20 cm, Thâp-Mam style, 11th Century.

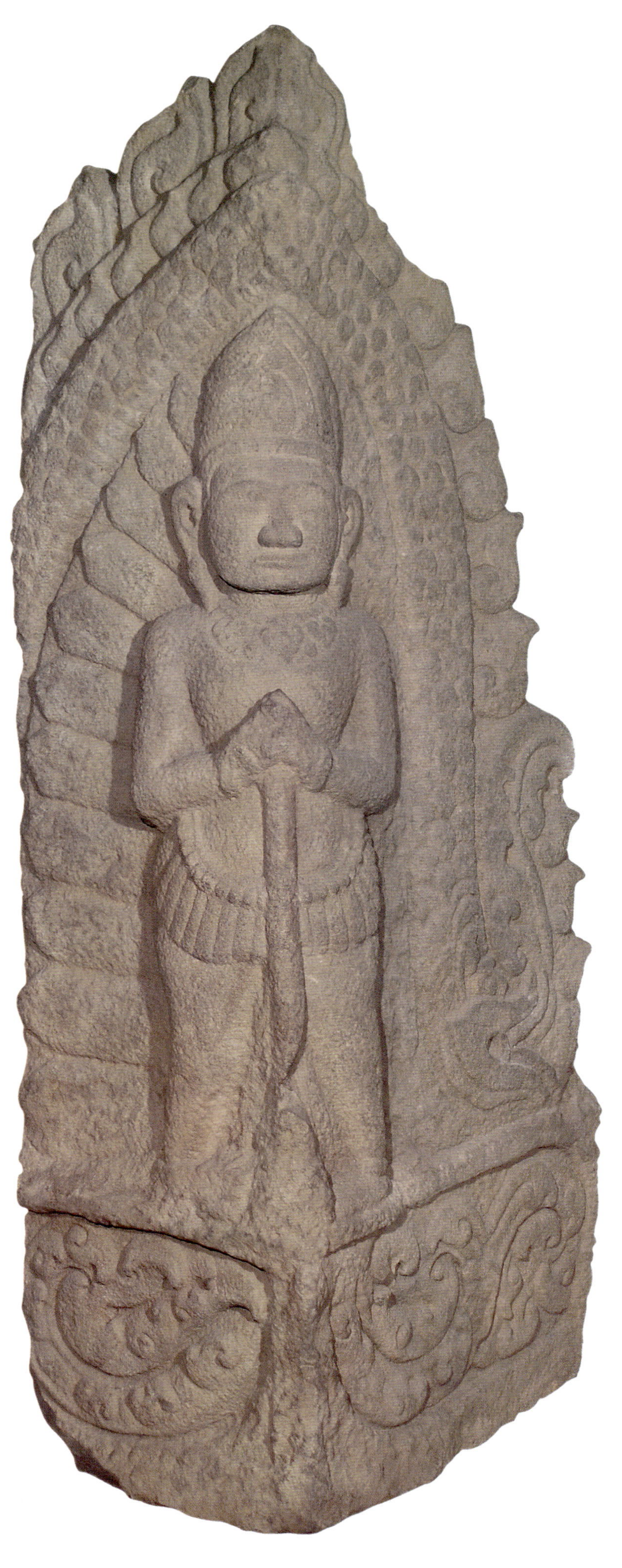

174. *Sage*, Bas-relief, Sandstone, Height 115 cm, Thâp-Mam style, 11th - 12th Century.

Following Page
175. *Sage wearing a mitre,* Nearly free-standing, Sandstone, Height 25 cm, Thâp-Mam style, 12th - 13th Century.

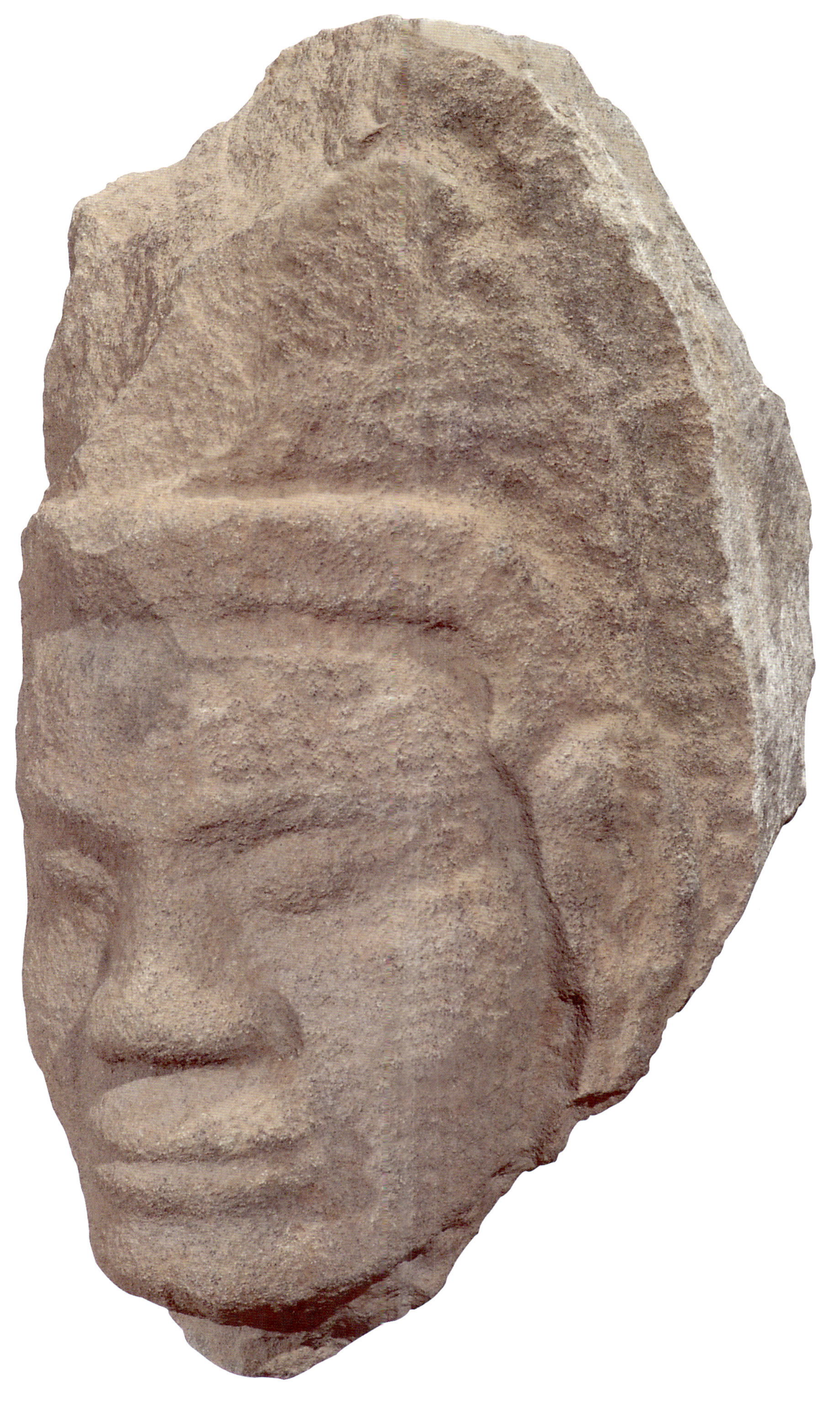

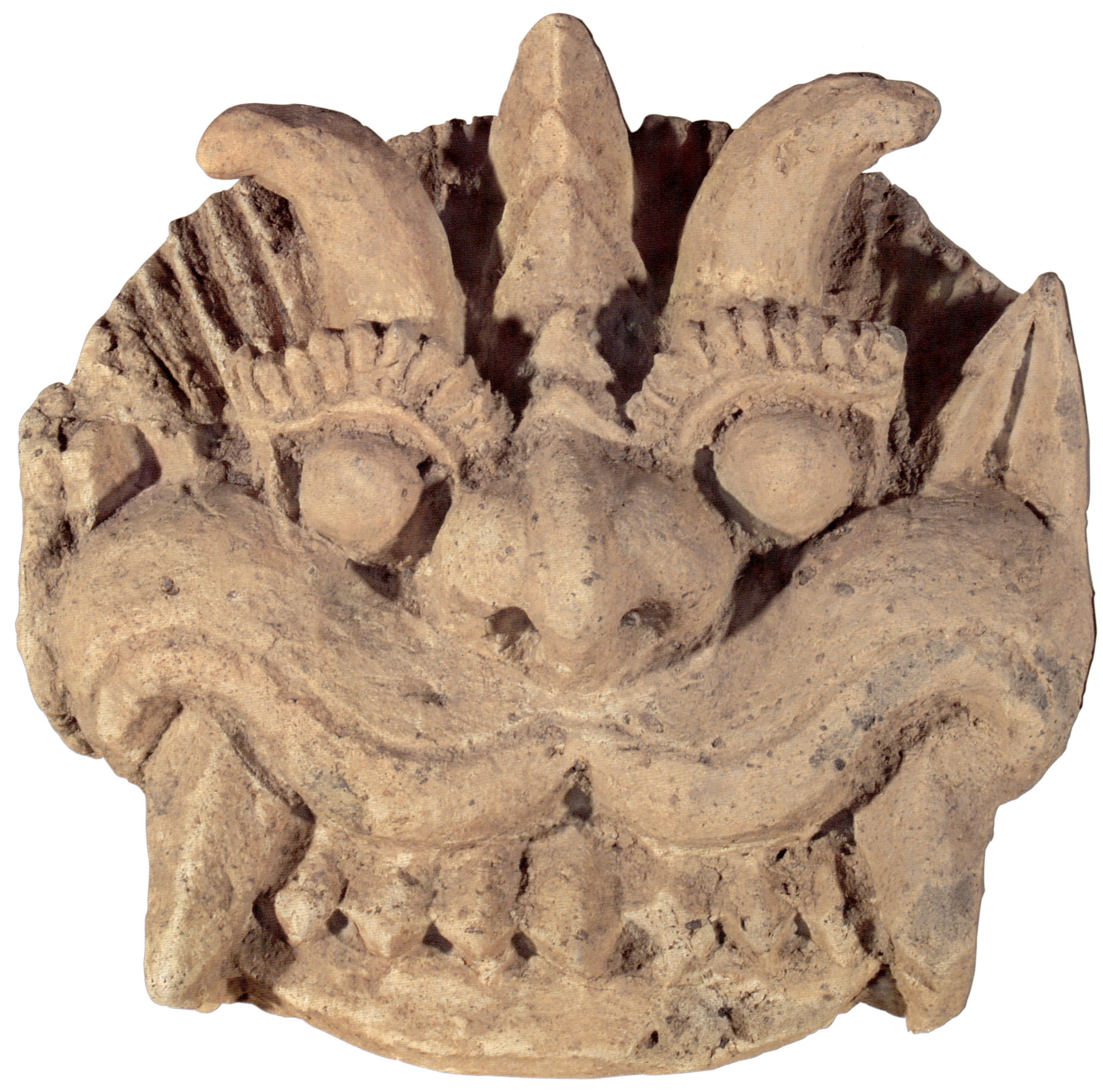

176. *Mask of Kala,* Bas-relief, Clay, Height 24 cm, Thâp-Mam style, 12th - 13th Century.

Following Page
177. *Mask of Kala,* Bas-relief, Clay, Height 24 cm, Thâp-Mam style, 12th - 13th Century (detail).

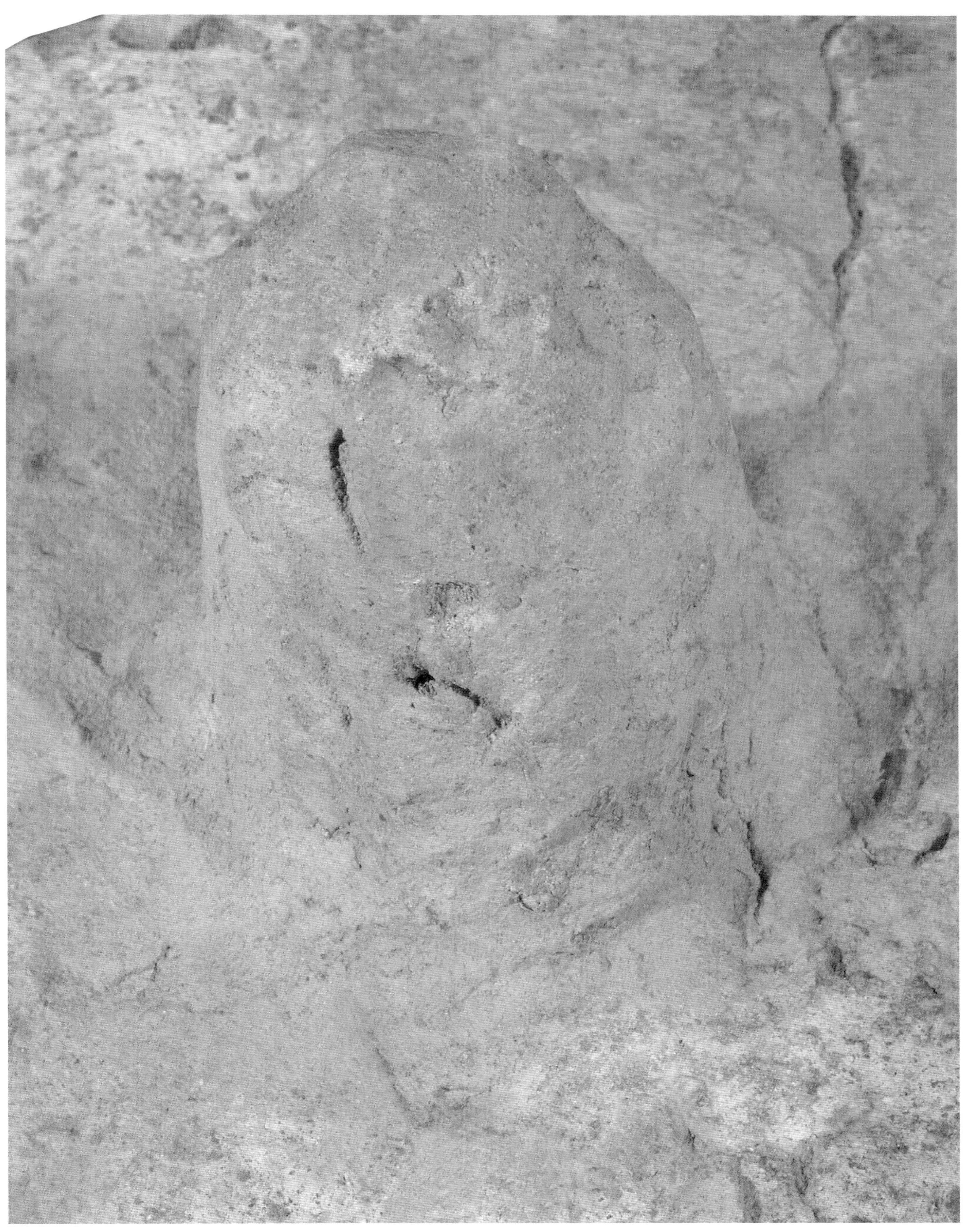

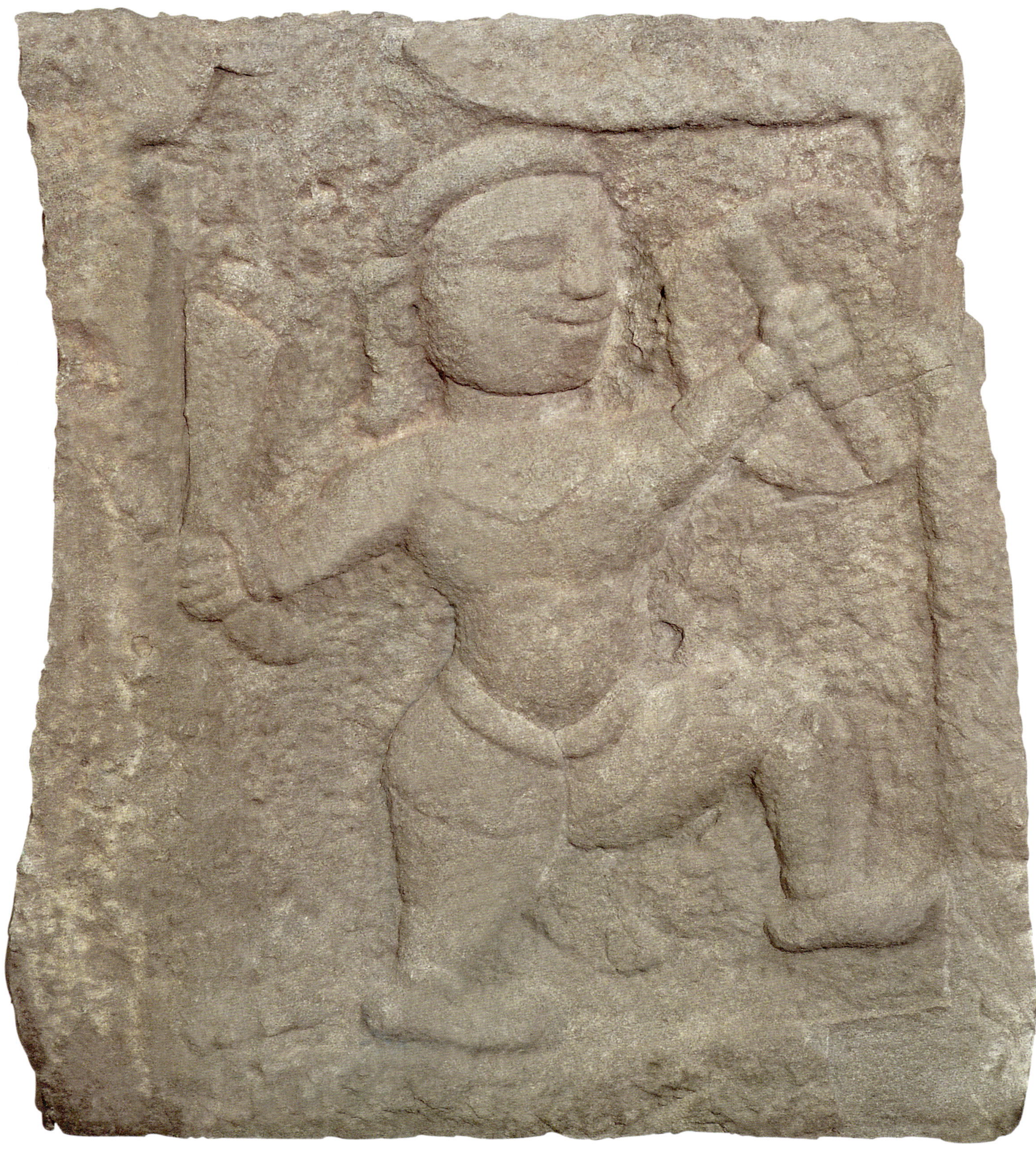

He is equipped with a shield and a "sabre" and has no armour. Chinese texts tell us that Cham soldiers protected themselves with armour made of woven reeds and were armed with shields, javelins and also halberds, bows and crossbows with which they shot poison arrows.

178. *Soldier,* Bas-relief, Sandstone, Height 42 cm, Thâp-Mam style, 11th - 12th Century.

Following Page

179. *Female dancer,* Bas-relief, Sandstone, Height 84 cm, Thâp-Mam style, 12th Century.

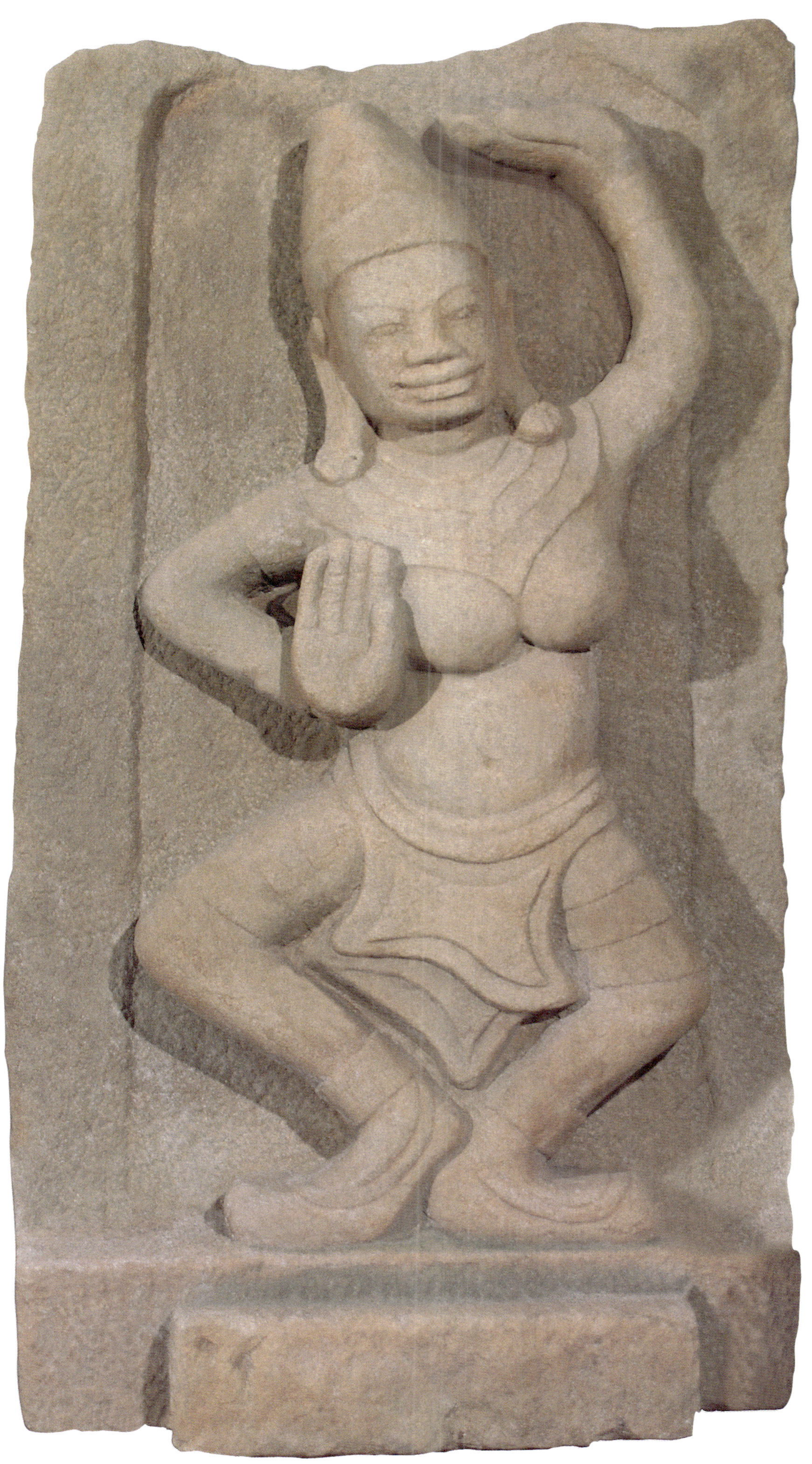

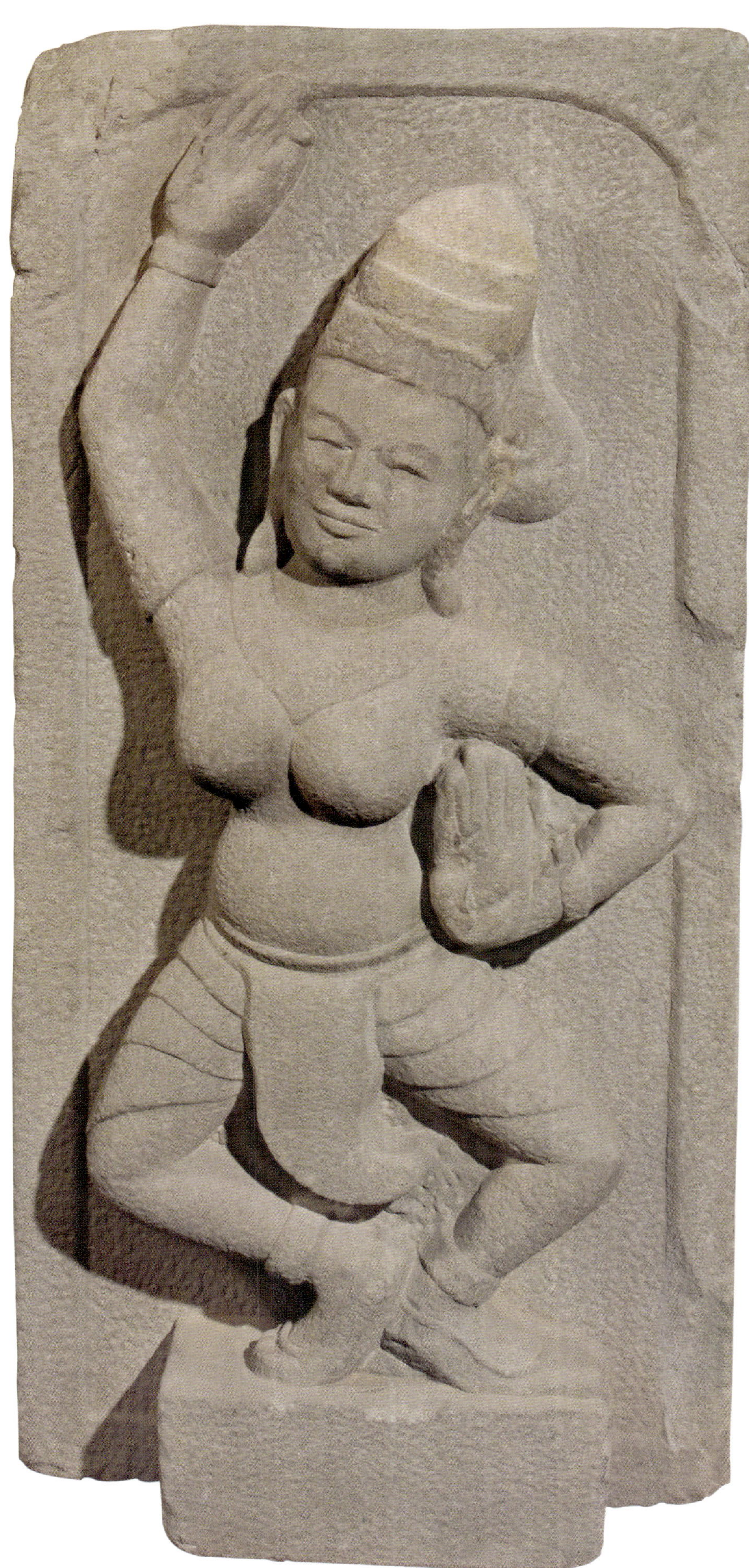

As with a good number of pieces of this model and from this period, this piece is unfinished, as can be noticed from the treatment of the fingers of the left hand.

This type of female dancer was probably part of a base. She is on tiptoe, the two first toes together, the others raised in a position called in “cinmudra” or “vyakhyanamudra”, which symbolises teaching through silence and contemplation. She is wearing bracelets on her arms and ankles; jewels hang from her ears. A complex code (several hundred mudras have been recorded) allows a dancer, with the hand only, to express many emotions or situations (such as the appearance of a god). It is always difficult to distinguish profane from religious in dance representations, to know whether there is a spiritual intention or simply harmony with the music. The Indian or Indianised world deifies music: Shiva is “king of dance” (Nataraja), Lakshmi is “mistress of the Apsara’s ballet”. The list of divinities associated with dance or music would be long. Two traits unify more than they separate the differences: dance must express a feeling (“rasa”) enriched by emotion (“bhava”).

180. *Dancer*, High relief, Sandstone, Height 62 cm, Thâp-Mam style, 12th Century.

As with a good number of pieces of this model and from this period, this piece is unfinished, as can be noticed from the treatment of the fingers of the left hand.

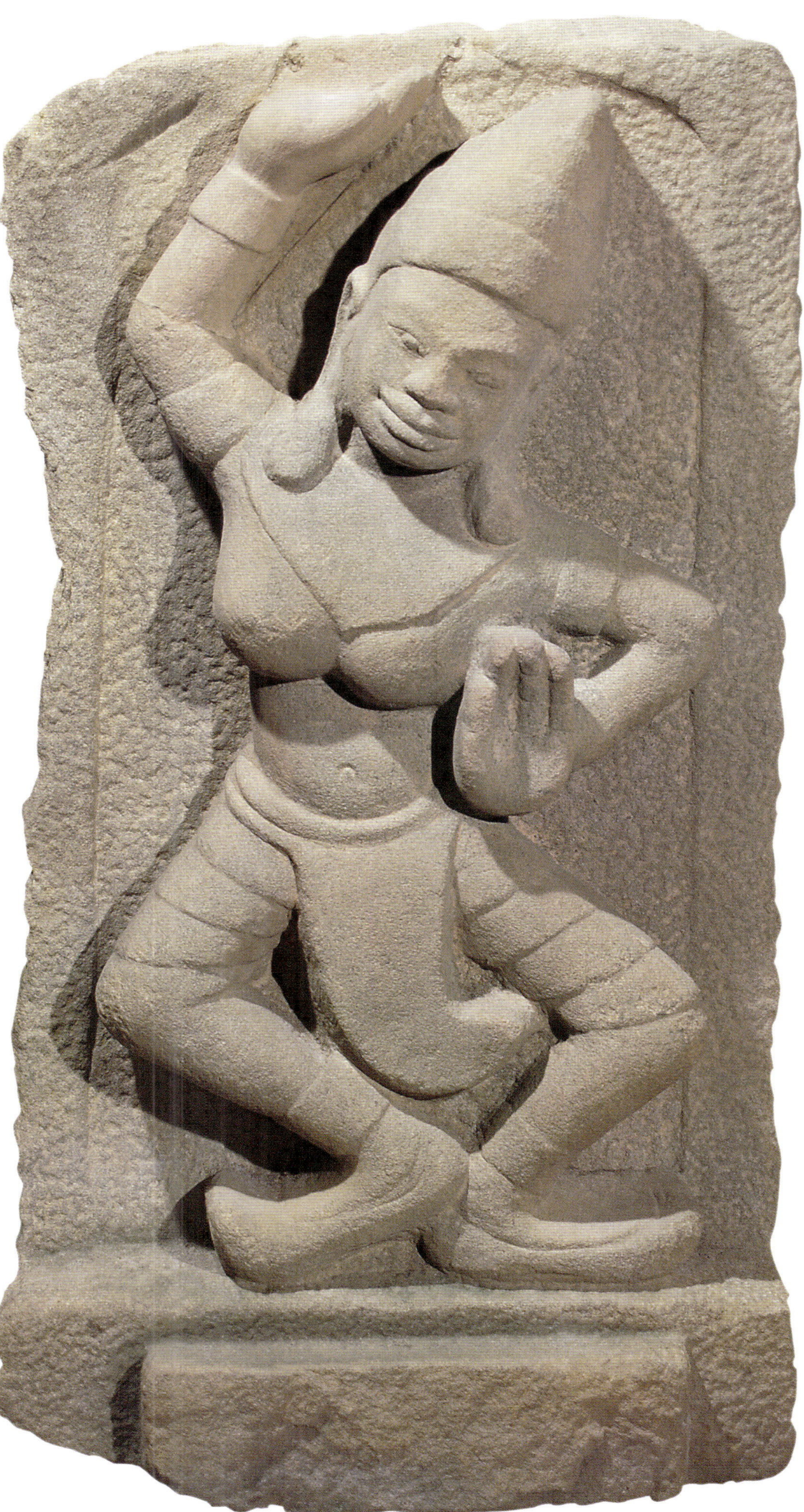

181. *Dancer,* High-relief, Sandstone, Height 70 cm, Thâp-Mam style, 12th Century.

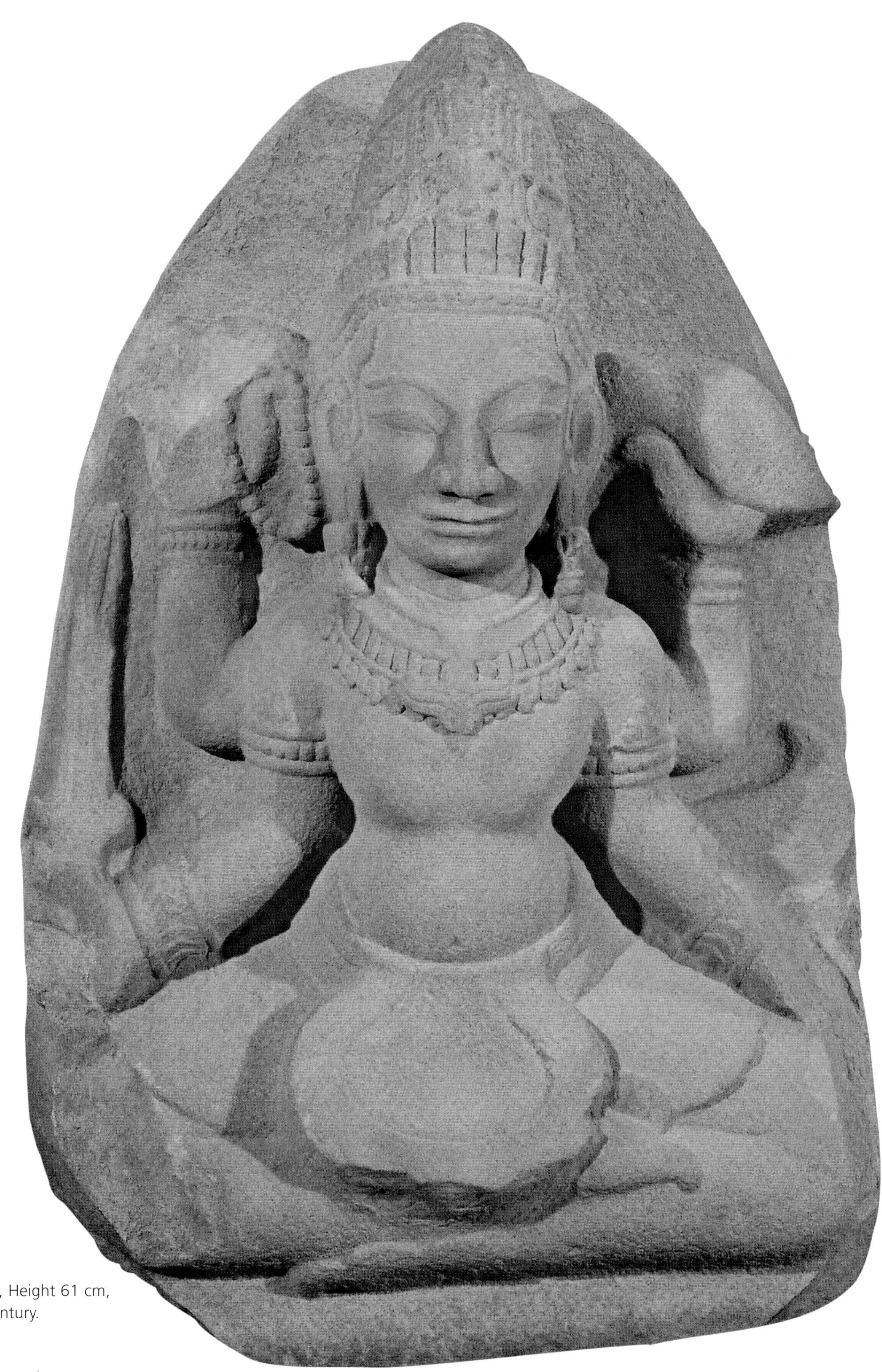

182. *Vishnu,* High-relief, Sandstone, Height 61 cm, Thâp-Mam style, 12th - 13th Century.

Following Page
183. *Dvarapala bust,* Free-standing, Sandstone, Height 50 cm, Thâp-Mam style, 12th Century.

As with a good number of pieces of this model and from this period, this piece is unfinished, as can be noticed from the treatment of the fingers of the left hand.

A dvarapala is a demi-god, guardian of the doors of Hindu or Buddhist sanctuaries. Statues nearly identical to this one, lacquered, are kept in the pagoda of Nhan Tap (Binh-Dinh). Another practically identical bust, though larger, (the head alone is 60 cm high) is kept at the Da Nang museum.

Notice the flower (a lotus) that marks the left breast, the naga head, the diadem of rosettes, the prominent eyes, the jutting upper lip, the wide nostrils, and the spiralling braid over the ear. The beard, moustache, eyebrows, all very neat, are many elements of a style at the pinnacle of perfection.

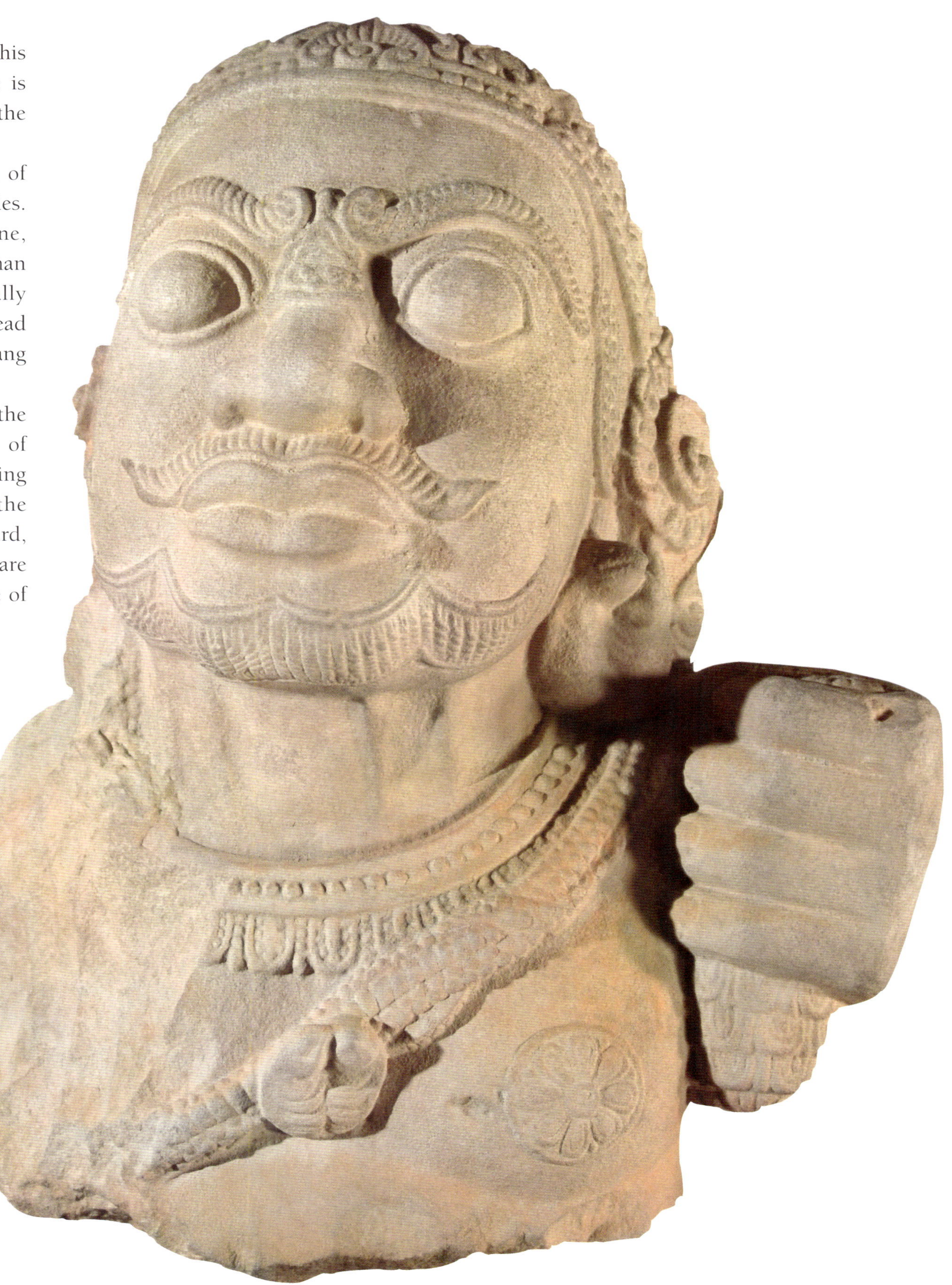

The Brahman is the officiant at sacrificial ceremonies.

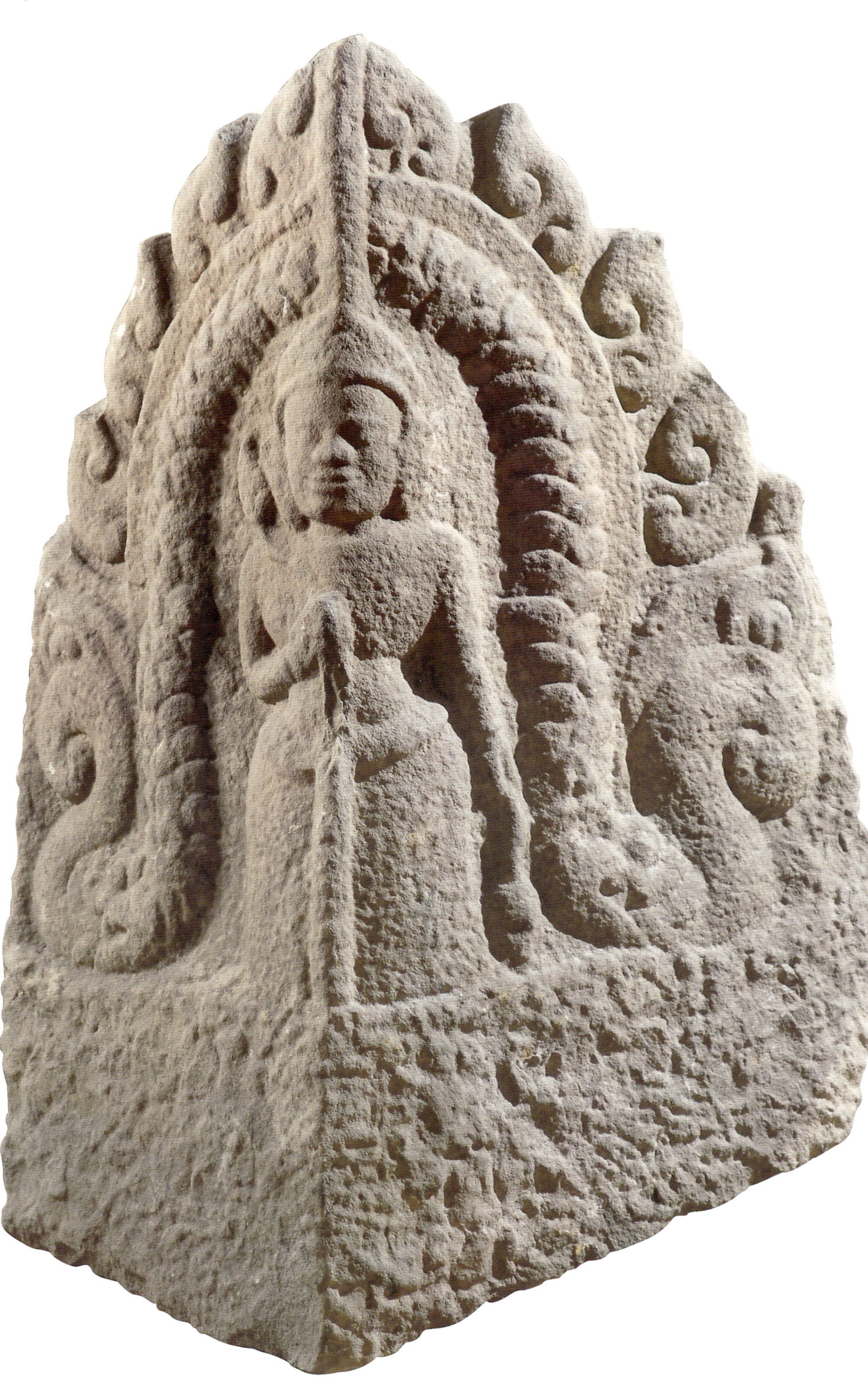

184. *Brahman*, Bas-relief, Sandstone, Height 80 cm, Thâp-Mam style, 11th - 10th Century.

Following Page
185. *Linga and its middle ring*, Free-standing, Silver and Gold, Height 26 cm, widest Diameter 21 cm, Thâp-Mam style, 11th Century.

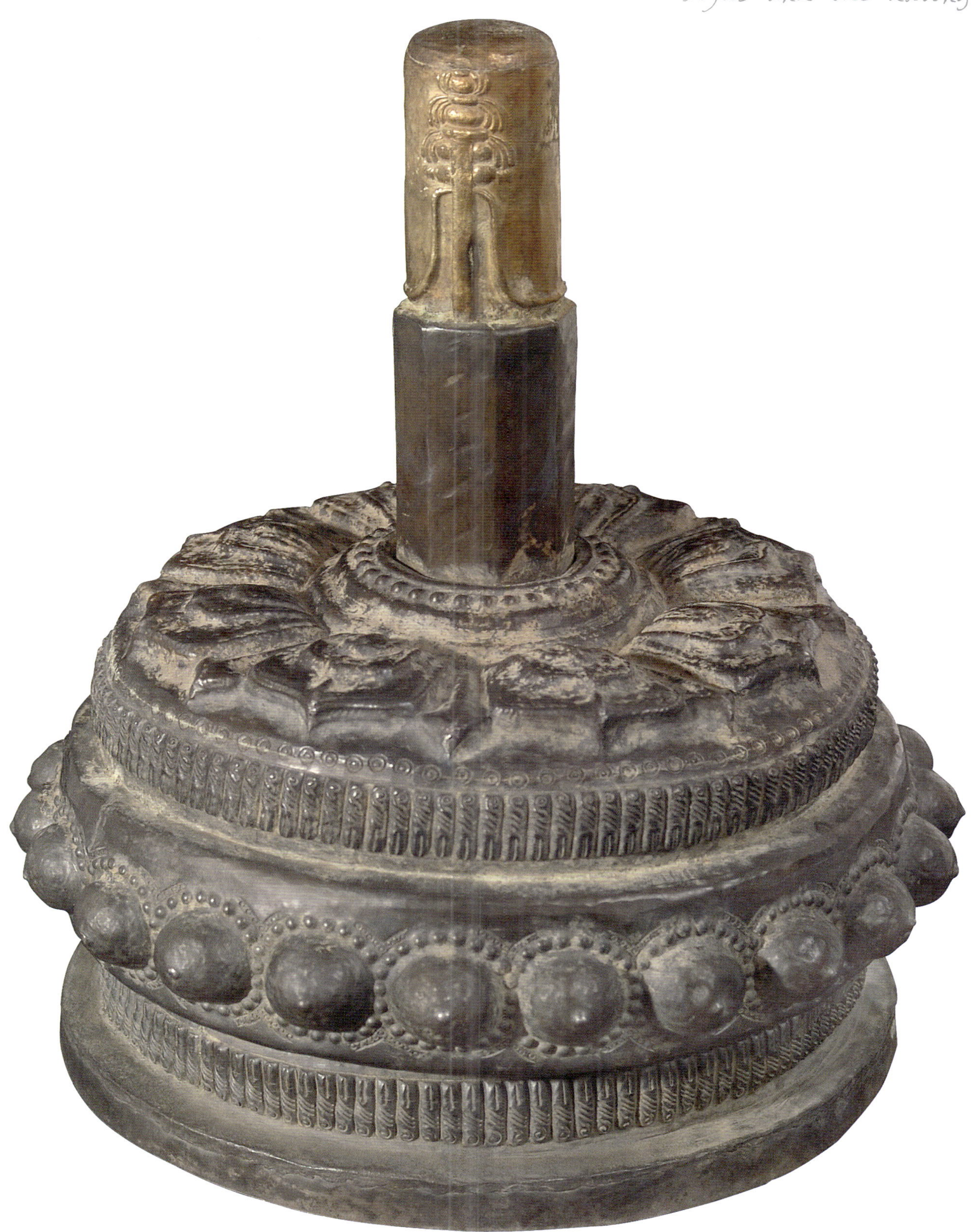

Only the Jatalinga ("linga with a chignon") is made of gold, the rest of this piece is in silver. The tray is decorated with lotus petals; the vertical strands above the breasts are characteristic of the early Thâp-Mam style, but they also appear in the Tra Kieu style. These breasts, here twenty-three in number, have generated hypotheses for researchers. One can refer to the Malayo-Polynesian context of the Chams and invokes the decor of traditional Jaraï houses on the high plateaux, where two feminine breasts are found. (Let us remember that the Jaraï are one of the "Malayo-Polynesian" groups in Vietnam. The other hypothesis refers to the evocation of the name of the mythical ancestor of the Indrapura kings: Uroja/Urah, meaning "breast, chest". Uroja was a goddess, also called Po Yan Ina Nagar, which translates into Cham as Po "his excellency", Yan "goddess", Ina "mother", and Nagar "country".

The sage ("rishi" in Sanskrit) is seated in dyaasana, dressed in a loincloth. Given large ears, he holds a rosary in his hands. The entire figure is inscribed in a recessed arcature. The niche could remind one of the caves where certain hermits isolate themselves in their quest for wisdom. The base has a tenon, allowing the piece to be set into the mortise of the structure of a temple.

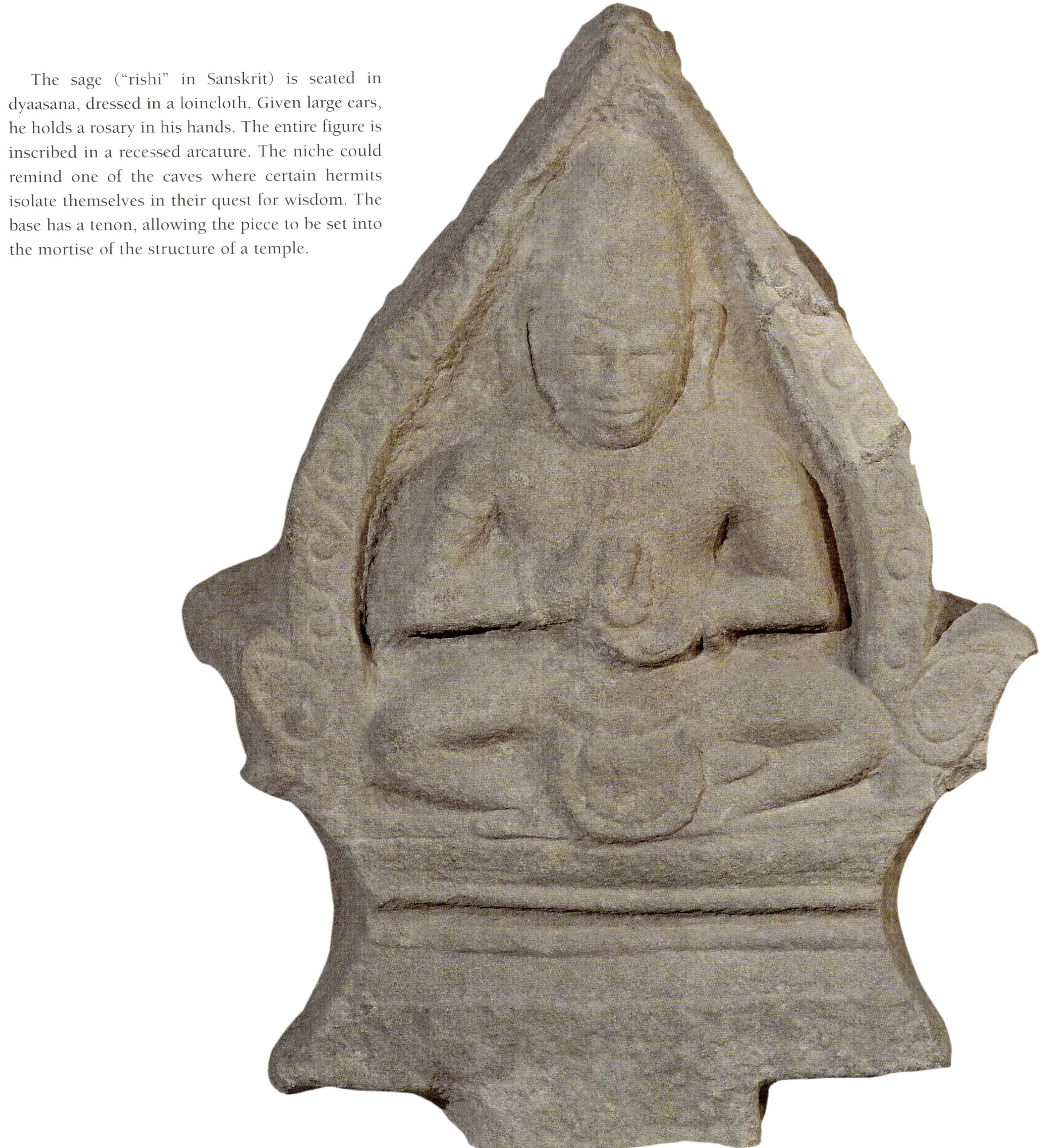

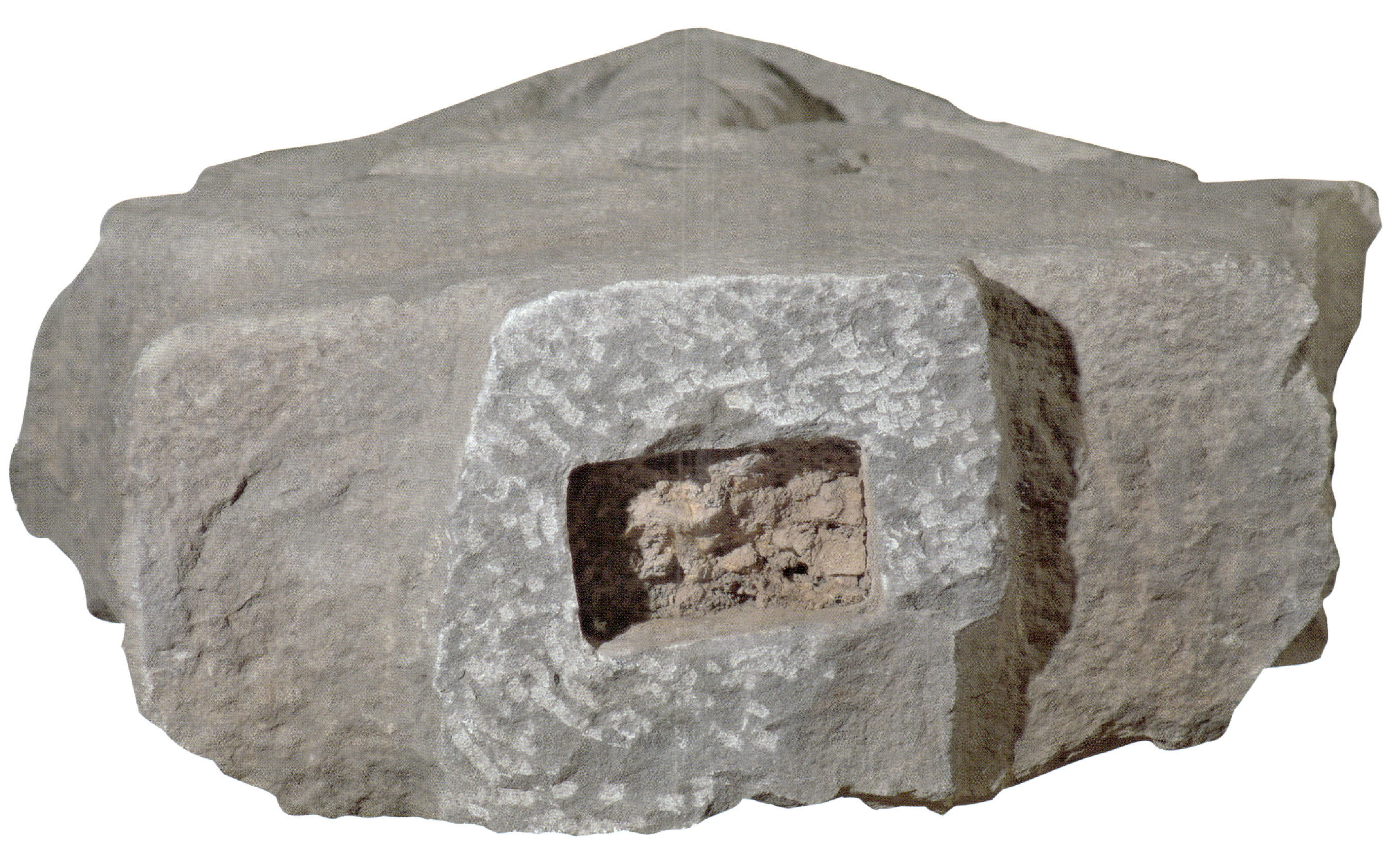

Previous Page
186. *Sage (Rishi),* High relief, Sandstone, Height 64 cm, Thâp-Mam style, 12th - 13th Century.

187. *Sage (Rishi),* High relief, Sandstone, Height 64 cm, Thâp-Mam style, 12th - 13th Century (view from underside with mortise).

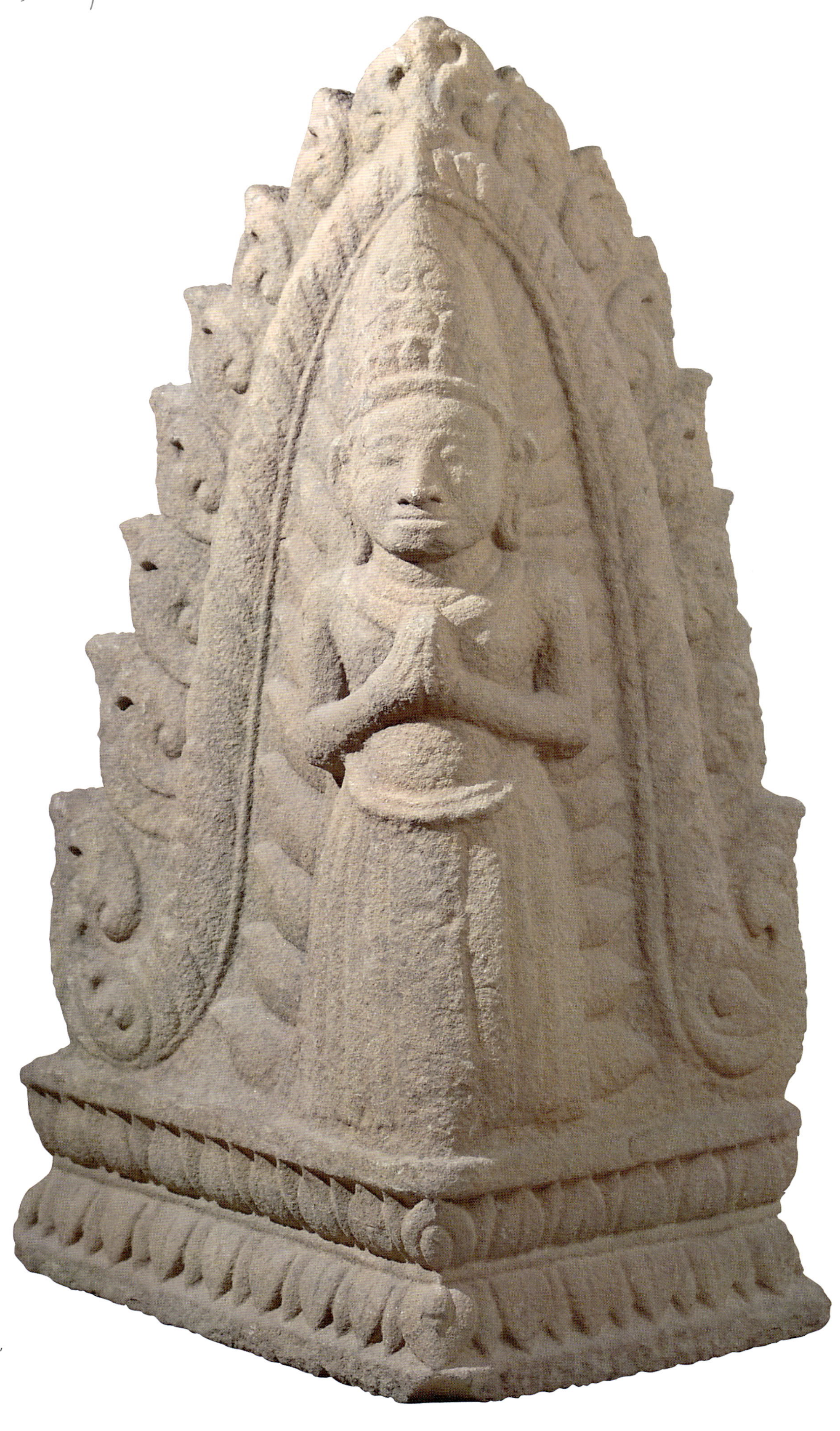

188. *Brahman*, High relief, Sandstone, Height 50.5 cm, Thâp-Mam style, 11th - 12th Century.

The facial features are massive and soft, with full lips, raised eyebrows that do not join, pupils that are clearly drawn. The conical hairstyle is decorated with the motif of vertical strands arranged in six concentric lines separated by a continuous line.

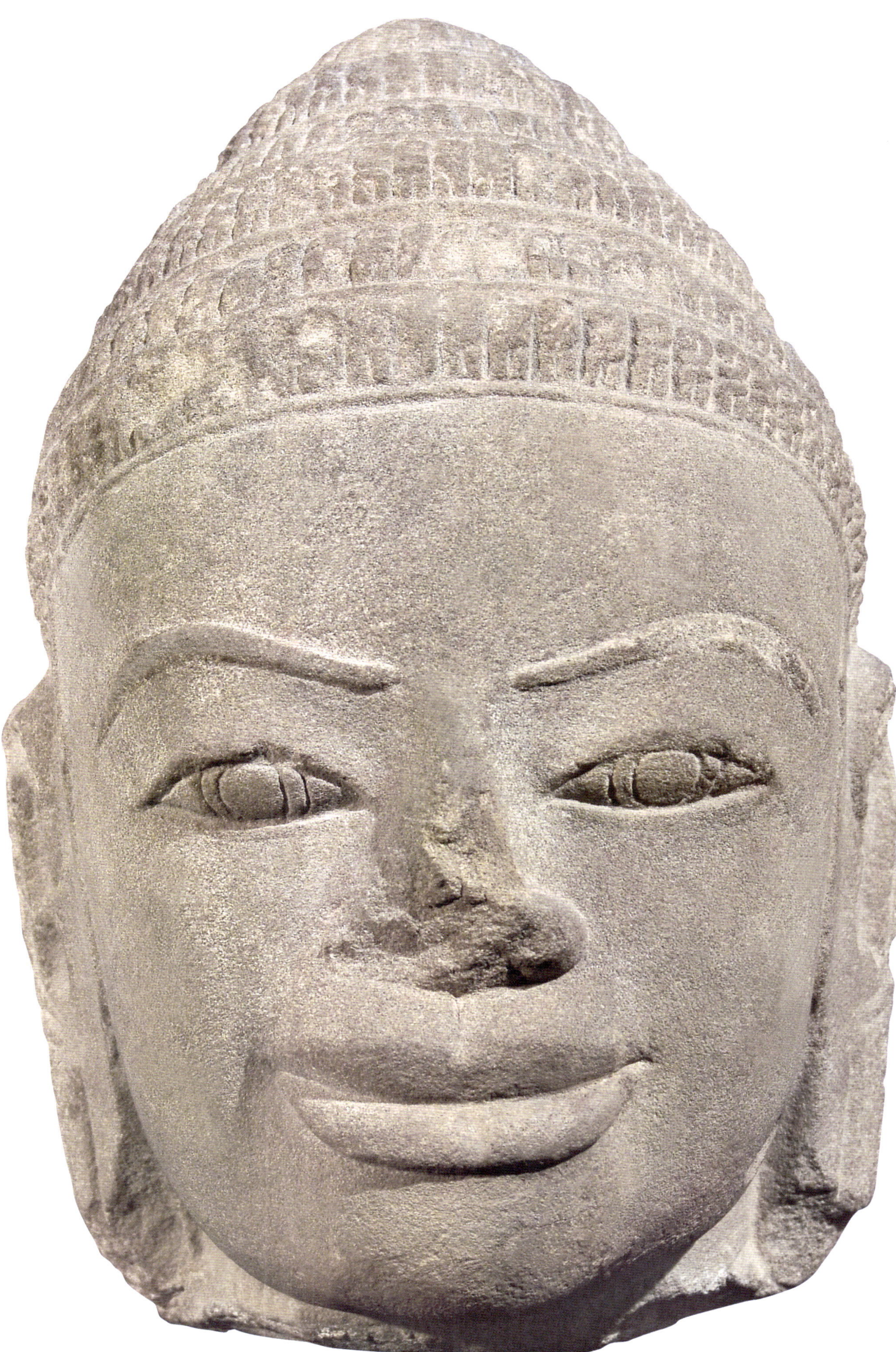

189. *Head of Buddha,*
Free-standing, Sandstone, Height 23 cm,
Thâp-Mam style, 11th - 12th Century.

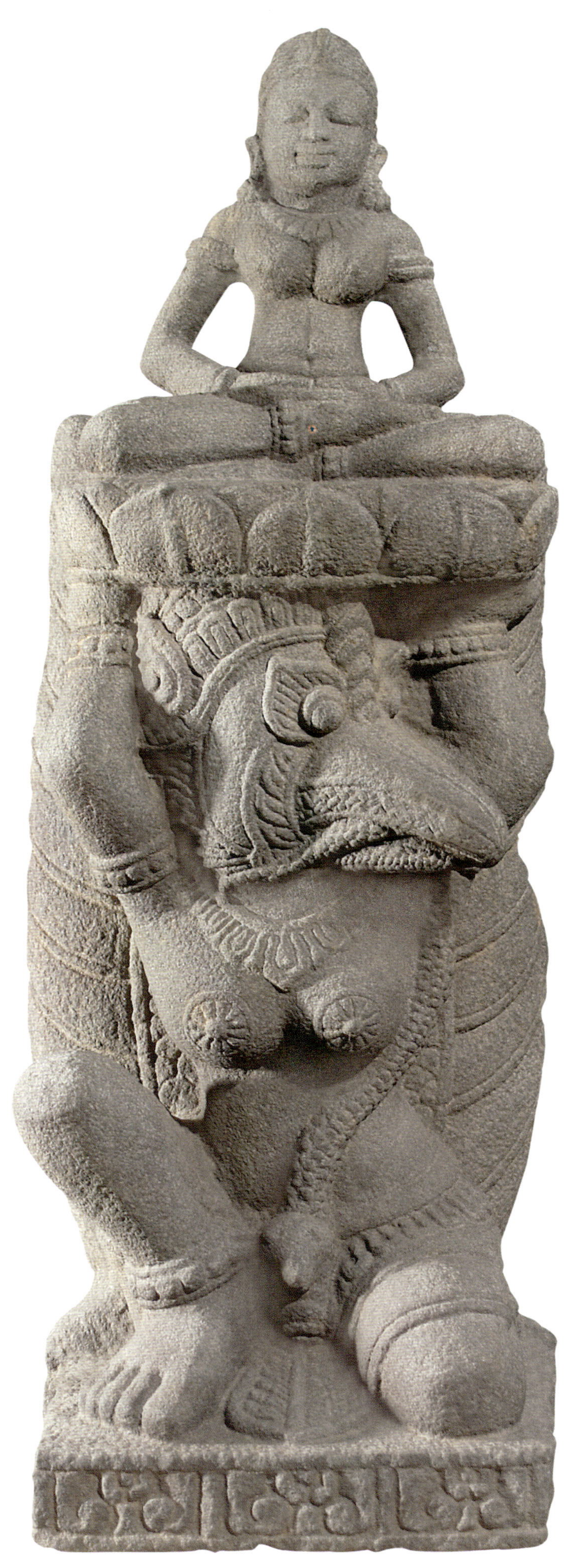

190. *Vishnu on Garuda*, Free-standing, Sandstone, Height 56 cm, 14th - 15th Century .

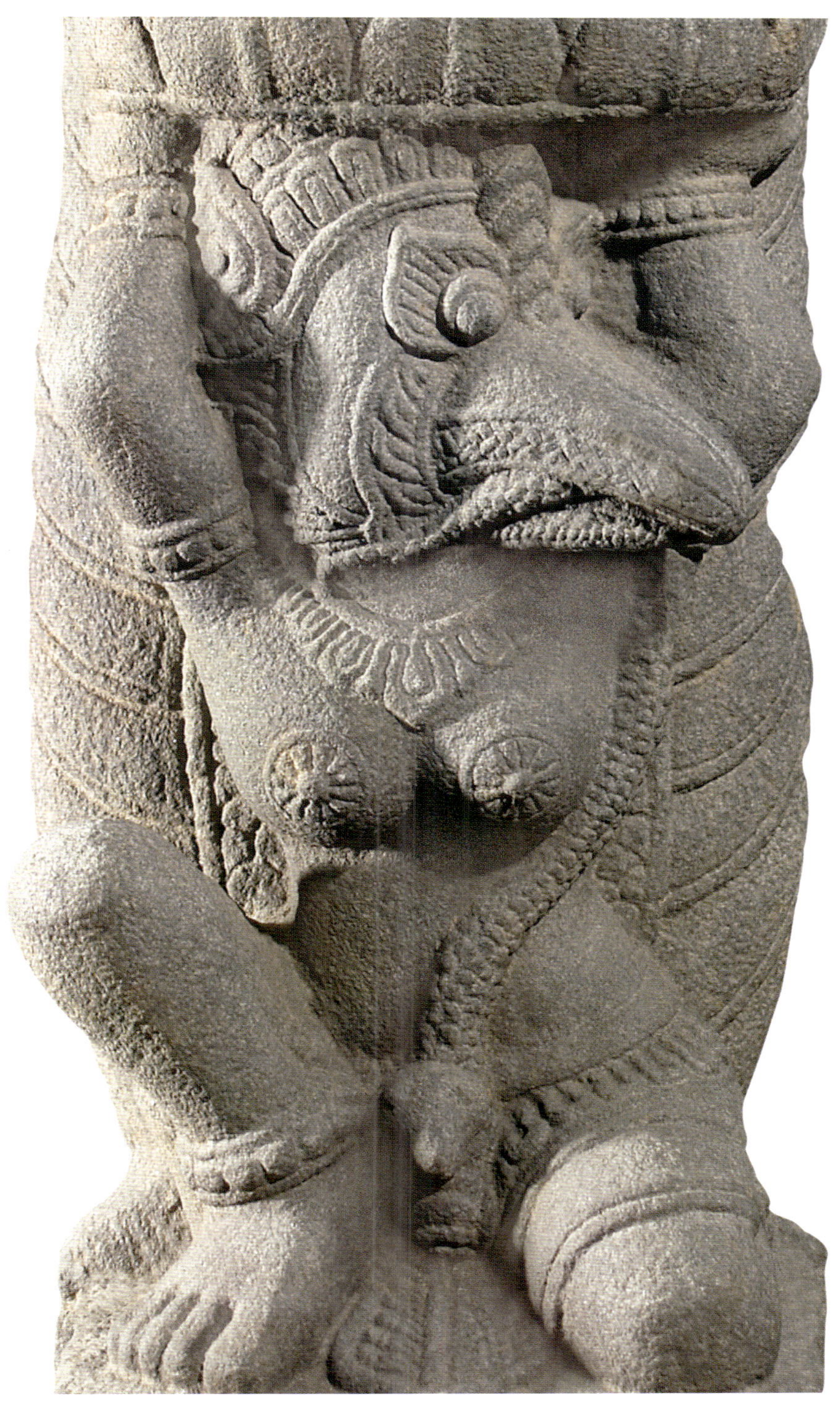

191. *Vishnu on Garuda*, Free-standing, Sandstone, Height 56 cm, 14th - 15th Century.

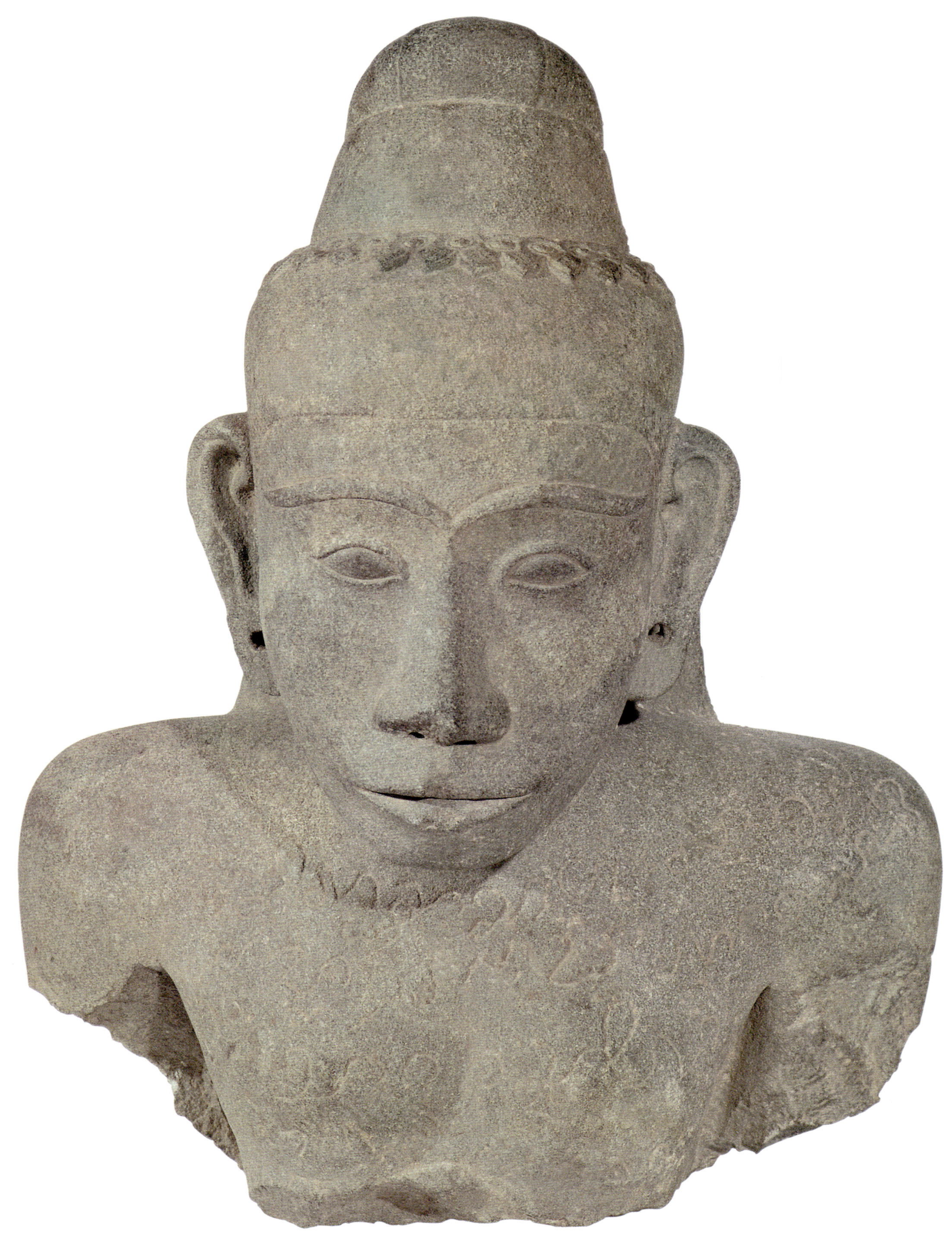

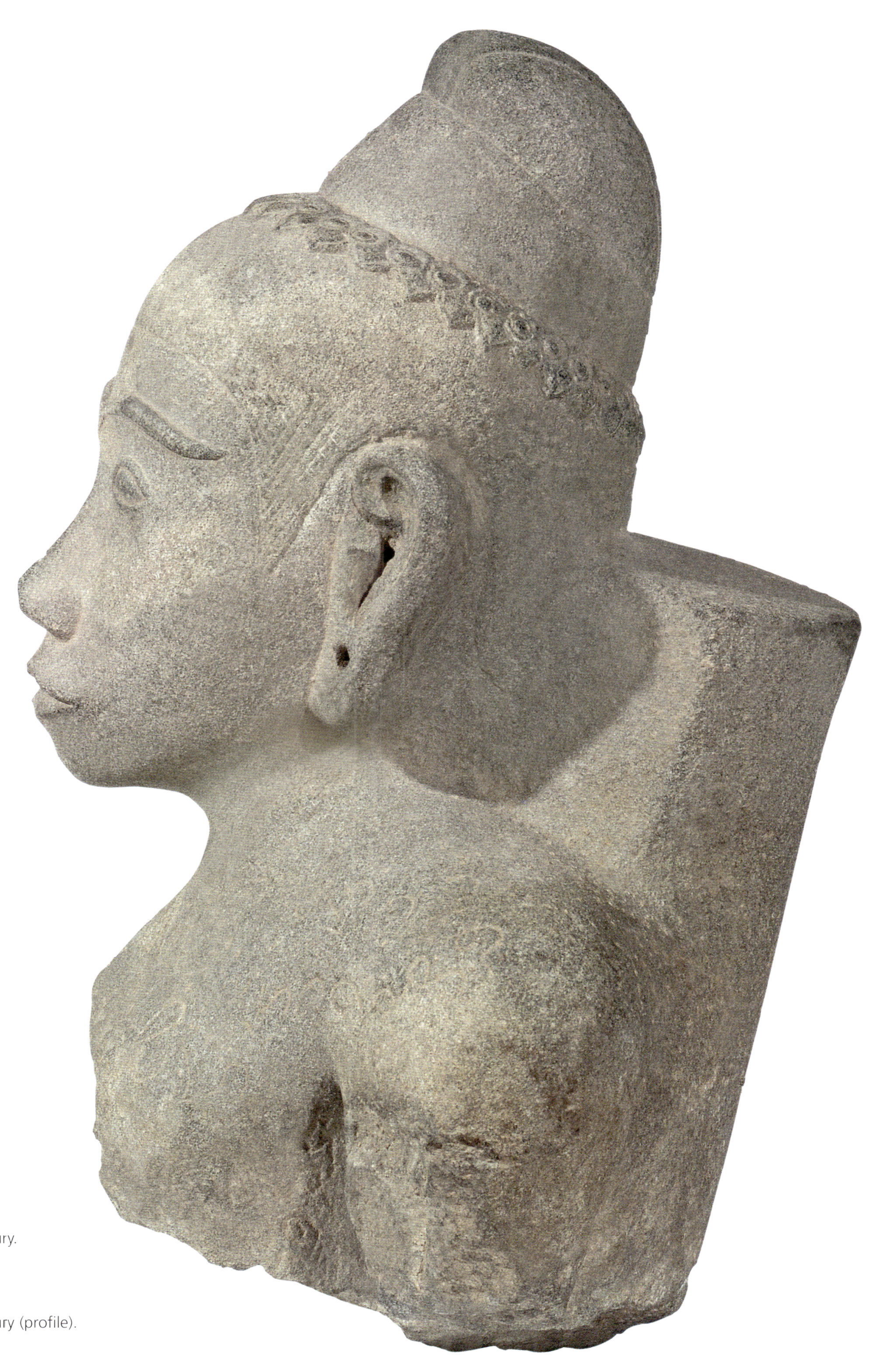

Previous Page
192. *Bust*, Nearly free-standing, Sandstone, Height 50 cm, Yang Mum style, 15th Century.

193. *Bust*, Nearly free-standing, Sandstone, Height 50 cm, Yang Mum style, 15th Century (profile).

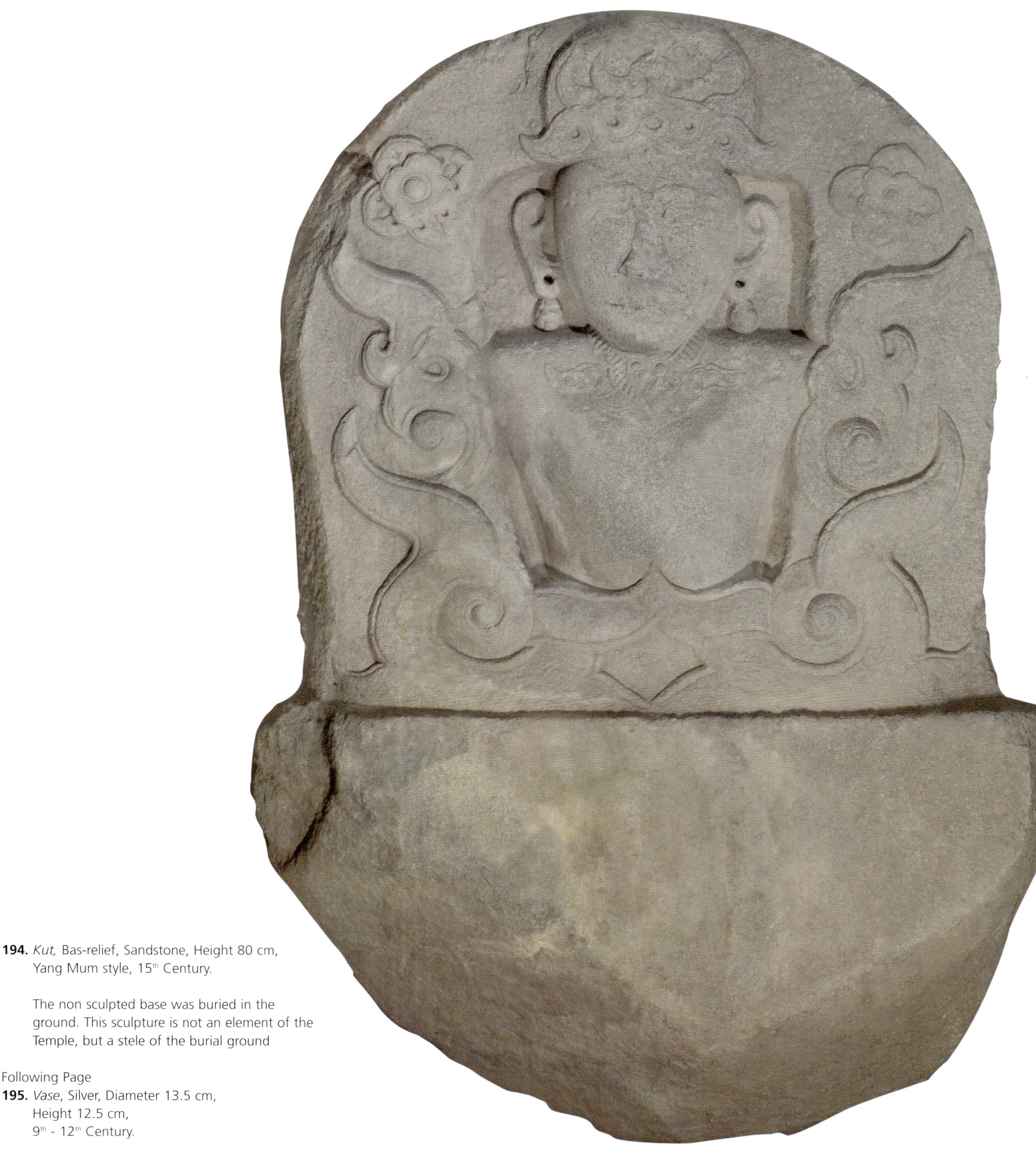

194. *Kut,* Bas-relief, Sandstone, Height 80 cm,
Yang Mum style, 15th Century.

The non sculpted base was buried in the ground. This sculpture is not an element of the Temple, but a stele of the burial ground

Following Page
195. *Vase*, Silver, Diameter 13.5 cm,
Height 12.5 cm,
9th - 12th Century.

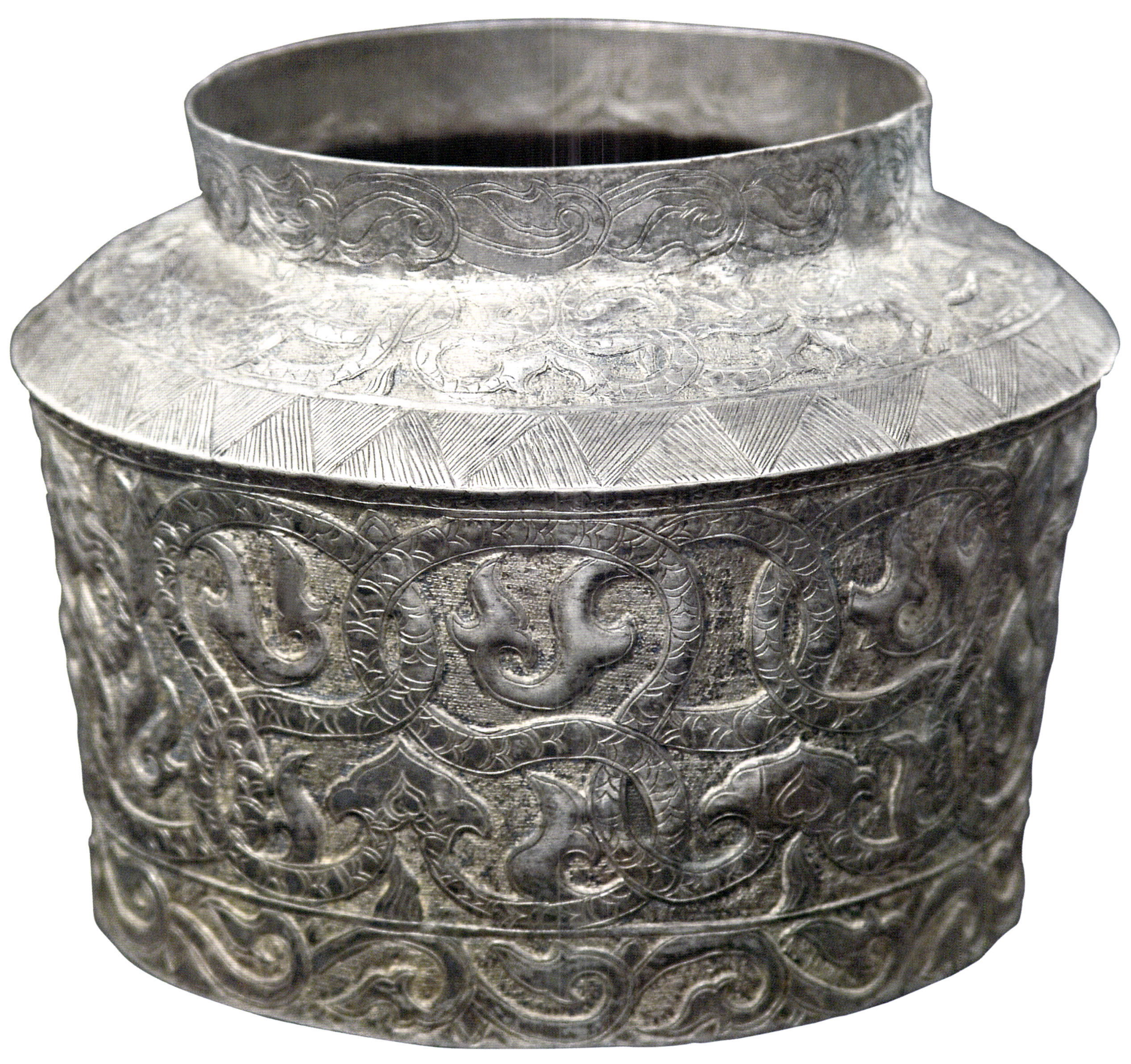

This type of object served in the worship of divinities. Its decoration, in relief, is a motif of stylised serpents and dancers. An inscription at the right south B2 foot of the main tower at Po Nagar in Nha Trang informs us that in 1050, the sovereign Jaya Parameshvaravarman renovated the temple that had been ruined in the wars against the Viets as well as civil wars. "He had the statue of the goddess Pu Nagara re-erected. He gave the temple fields, fifty-five Cham, Khmer, Chinese, Burman and Siamese slaves, fifteen pounds of gold and fifteen pounds of silver. For worship, he gave a vase encrusted with gold, a superb diadem ornament, a magnificent cord as a belt, a silver pitcher, a parasol of peacock feathers, a large silver canopy with beautiful gold vases, jugs, vases that could contain eight half coconuts, and large vases." (Maspero, p.13)

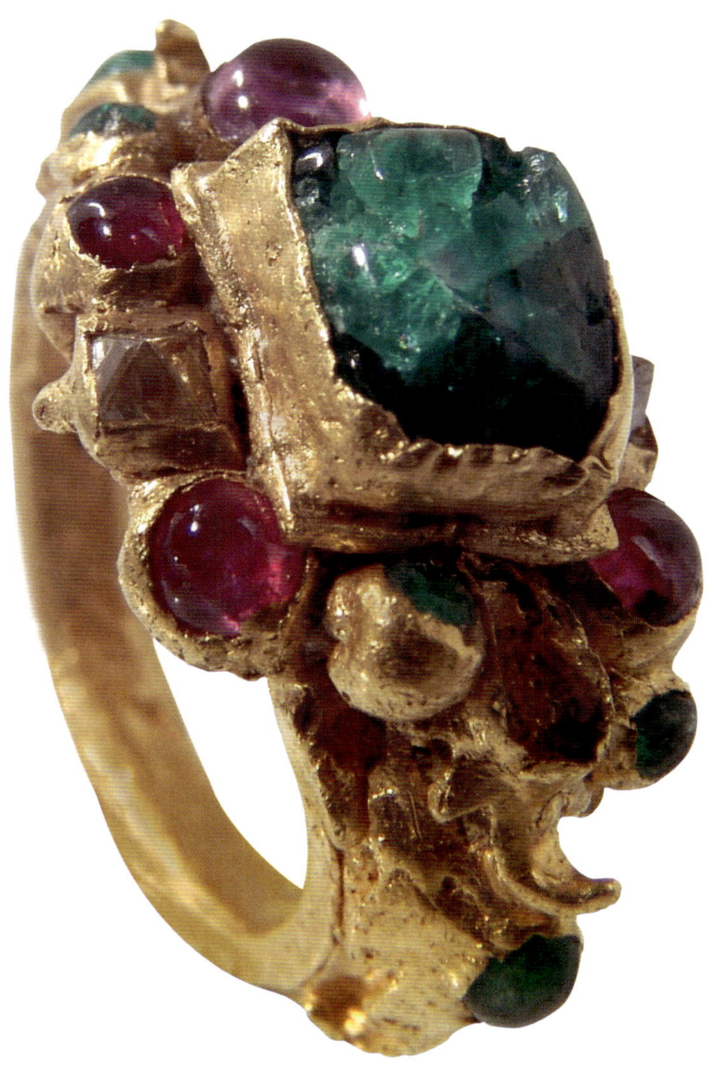

196. *Ring*, Gold, emerald, rubies and diamonds, Diameter 2.7 cm, 10th - 12th Century.

This ring is set with several precious stones: a large central emerald (about 5 x 6 mm) surrounded by six small emeralds (about 1.5 x 2 mm in diameter), five small rubies (1.5 x 3 mm in diameter – one stone missing), all cut in cabochon and two diamonds (about 2 mm). The central emerald is quite a deep green. It unfortunately has cracks running through it. The rubies are bright red with shades of violet. According to connoisseurs, these are stones of quality.

A gemmological examination took place mainly with a binocular microscope which allowed the study of the inclusions. The stones were illuminated by an optical fibre and, and although they were fairly inaccessible due to their closed setting, some information was retrieved as a result of this examination. The emerald is a transparent stone with many inclusions, mainly spots created during solidification, some solid inclusions (certain of which are whitish) and multiple open cracks (subsequent to the ring's fabrication – the stone currently only holding thanks to its setting. Inclusions with several phases, so typical of emeralds, are also present. They are biphasic inclusions (liquid and gas bubbles). The generally rectangular shape of some of the inclusions and their lineal orientation "in rows" might correspond to Indian origin. The problem is that Indian emerald lodes were only discovered in 1943. The rubies are fairly pure and contain few inclusions; some solid inclusions that seem to be negative crystals. They react strongly/very strongly under ultra-violet rays. With precaution, Burmese origin could be suggested. But, as for the emeralds, other means of analysis are needed.

The major interest of the ring, finely crafted with stones of value, resides in the presence of the two diamonds. And what diamonds! They are not cut; rather, they are in their natural crystalline form. Both are eight-sided, the most common crystalline form in which diamonds are found in nature – or "dominant form" – consisting of two pyramids joined at their bases. The two stones are perfectly transparent and have no inclusions visible under 90-fold enlargement. They are very pure. Their colour is difficult to ascertain due to the setting in yellow gold, but they could be qualified as practically colourless (lightly tinted yellow but white to the naked eye). The most extraordinary point is that they have eight perfect facets, pointed, with sharp edges, without chips or cracks, which is very rare in nature. The conclusion that must be drawn is that these two diamond crystals were chosen for their perfect shape, which corresponds to criteria for diamond appreciation in ancient India.

The main Sanskrit texts dealing with precious stones refer to a treaty known under the name of Arthasastra ("Teachings about profit"), which is attributed to Kautilya, minister under King Chandragupta Maurya (late fourth-early third century BCE) of which a part deals with precious stones. The objective of this work was to obtain a text that could serve as law and be used to calculate taxes on all products, with precise rules and criteria. The texts concerning precious stones reveal a profound knowledge of the subject. The diamond is presented as the "ultimate jewel" and elements to evaluate and estimate its worth are included. Depending on its weight – for diamonds of 0.50 to ten carats (those of over ten carats being reserved to the king) – the prices were set on the basis of a very precise "ideal" quality, any flaw decreased the stone's value and therefore the tax due. The "ideal" diamond is described as an eight-sided crystal, transparent and without any irregularity in the outside shape. Inclusions were accepted, as long as they did not mar the stone's sparkle.

The price of a ten-carat diamond, perfectly eight-sided and flawless, is set at 37.325 kg of pure gold (or 400 elephants). It is, however, practically impossible that such a stone would ever by found.

To evaluate a given stone, the shape was taken into consideration first and foremost: the eight-sided stone had to have six sharp points, eight flat and smooth facets, twelve straight and sharp edges. Next, description and visual qualities came into play: purity, transparency, sparkle, "fire", which means the dispersion of light as a perfect octagonal stone illuminates the surrounding space with all the colours of the rainbow. Finally, the importance of colour had to be taken into account. Although it was not considered a criterion of quality and estimation of value, it was significant with respect to caste: white reserved to Brahmans, red or yellow to Ksatriyas.

The texts also speak of the magical meaning of stones and the magical powers of the diamond are supreme in what a stone can bring: "luck, wealth, many children for he who wears a perfect diamond with pointed corners". It is also said that a woman who wants to have sons can wear "dull-edged or even triangular" diamonds that is to say of lesser quality, but still diamonds.

The origin of the diamonds in the ring is probably Indian because, until the discovery of diamond lodes in Brazil in the first half of the eighteenth century, India was the only producer. Another possible source of these diamonds would be Indonesia, but we lack information on them (Staf van Roy).

The ring itself is an alloy of gold (970 thousandths), silver (1.7%) and copper (1.2%). The overall analysis of the central emerald reveals, in the order of decreasing abundance, silica (Si: 31%), aluminium (Al: 8.7%) and about 3% each of sodium (Na) and magnesium (Mg). This analysis is compatible with the composition of an emerald, although the experimental apparatus was not intended to detect beryllium (Be), one of the chemical components of emeralds. Impurities which can characterise this stone are chrome (Cr: 2.1%), vanadium (V) and scandium (Sc), each at 0.14%; iron (Fe) in relatively high concentration – 2.2% – is also quantified. The ruby contains primarily a single element, aluminium (Al: 51.8%) that is included in the stone in the form of alumine (Al_2O_3). The aluminium is associated with 0.44% chrome (Cr), the chemical element responsible for the red colouring of the alumine. Trace elements are titan (Ti: 0.035%) and iron (Fe: 0.048 %). By comparing chrome and iron content with respect to data published in literature, the probable origin of the ruby can be situated in Ceylon (Sri Lanka)

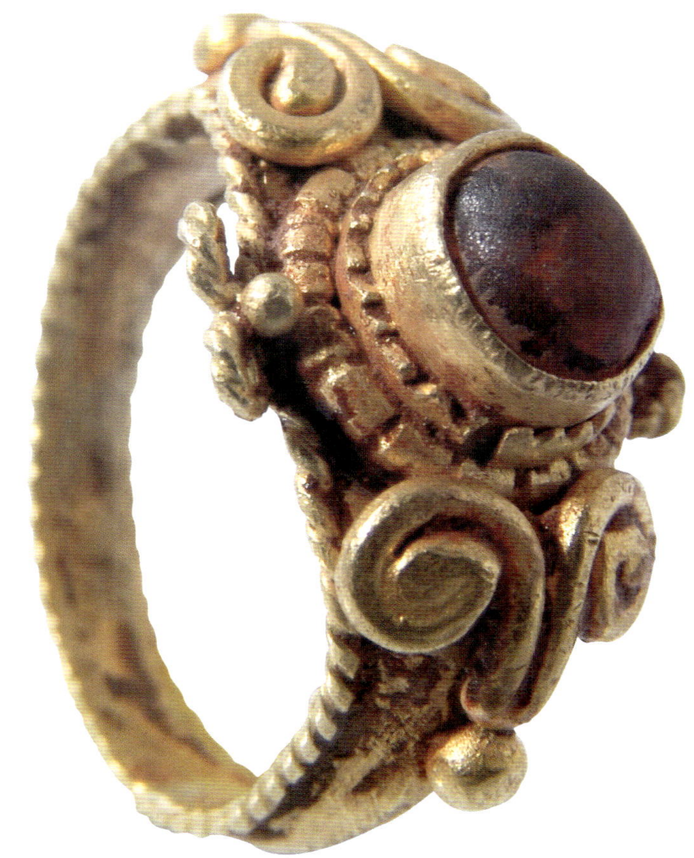

197. *Ring,* Gold, red glass stone, Diameter 2.4 cm, 10th - 12th Century.

The ring itself is constituted of 88.6% gold, 10.4% silver and 0.8% copper. The glass stone corresponds to a mixed silicate of 7.2% soda (Na_2O) and 4.1% potash (K_2O) stabilised by a very small quantity (1.4%) of lime (CaO). The silica (SiO_2) content, 77%, is exceptionally high whereas the concentration of lime seems too low to ensure the glass' stability. Lead oxide (PbO) is present (0.6%) without this being proof of intentional use; at this low level we cannot think this is leaded glass. The composition of this bead sets it apart from classic examples of ancient Indian glass, which is mostly potash: 13.4% K_2O for 3.1% soda (Na_2O) with 3.9% lime (CaO). Only the alumine (Al_2O_3) content, 1.8% in this stone, is in line with known data. As a criterion of identification of stones from South and South-east Asia, Glover and Henderson recommend situating the numerical relationship K_2O/Na_2O – 0.57 in our case – in relation to the CaO content. This red glass does not fall into the writings of these authors and probably is a result of local production. The red colouration comes from copper oxide (Cu_2O: 0.47%) that may be chemically fixed by a bit of iron oxide (FeO: 0.6%). This red colouration was developed in an oven maintained under reductive atmosphere.

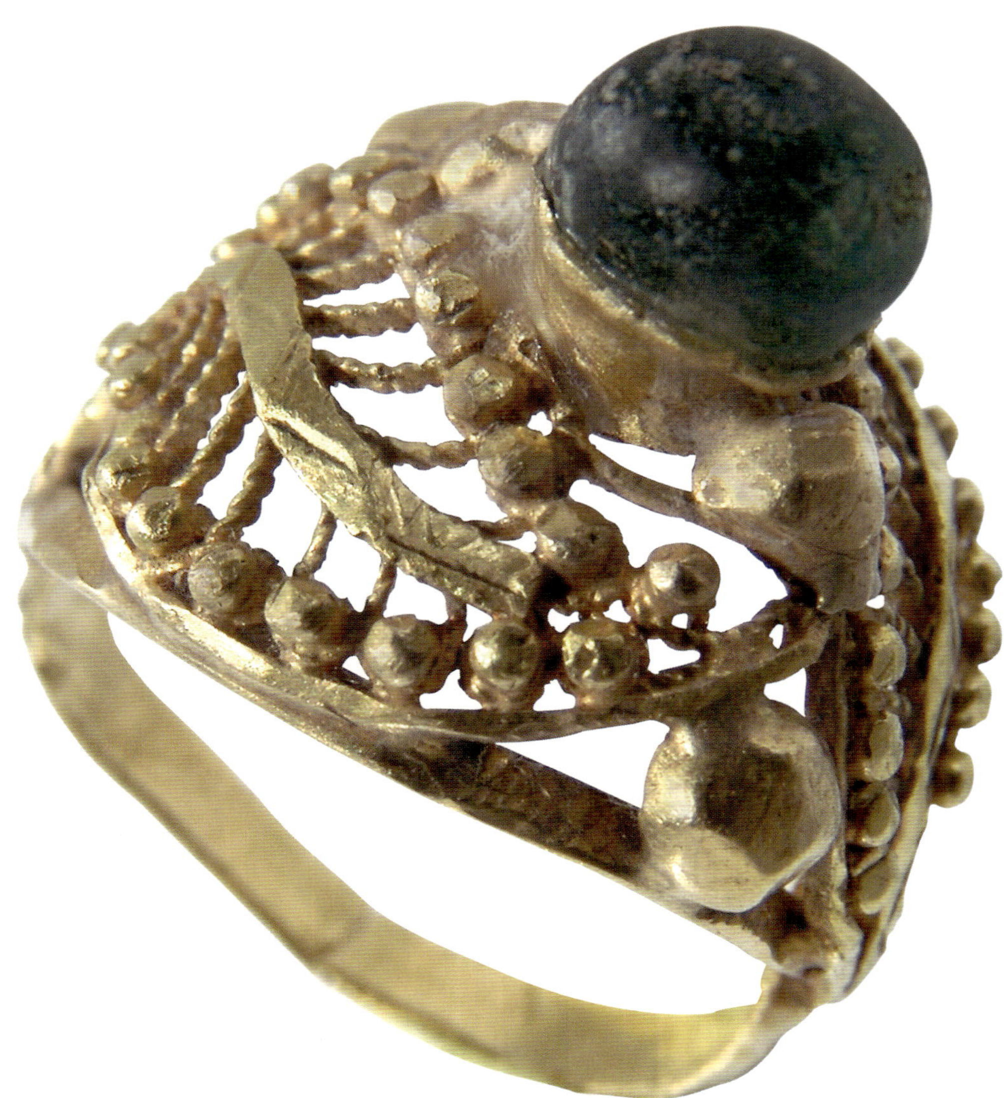

198. *Ring,* Alloy, green glass stone,
Diameter 2.05 cm, 10th - 12th Century.

The ring itself is an alloy of gold (975 thousandths) and silver. It contains no copper. The glass is typically high in soda (Na_2O: 12,6%) with 5.8% potash (K_2O). Lime (CaO: 12.1%) is the typical stabiliser; silica (SiO_2) content (60.6%) corresponds to the norms of ancient glass. This is glass made from plant ash, which usually gives a heightened presence of potash (K_2O) compared to soda (Na_2O). With a K_2O/Na_2O quotient equal to 0.46 and a high lime content, this glass does not belong to the Glover-Henderson *corpus*. The low copper oxide (CuO) content (0.15%) seems not to be able to explain the greenish colour, which would be the result of the addition, to the copper oxide, of manganese bioxide (MnO_2: 0.37%) and iron oxide (Fe_2O_3: 2.8%). This complex method of colouring was systematically used in Mesopotamia and in the Roman Empire.

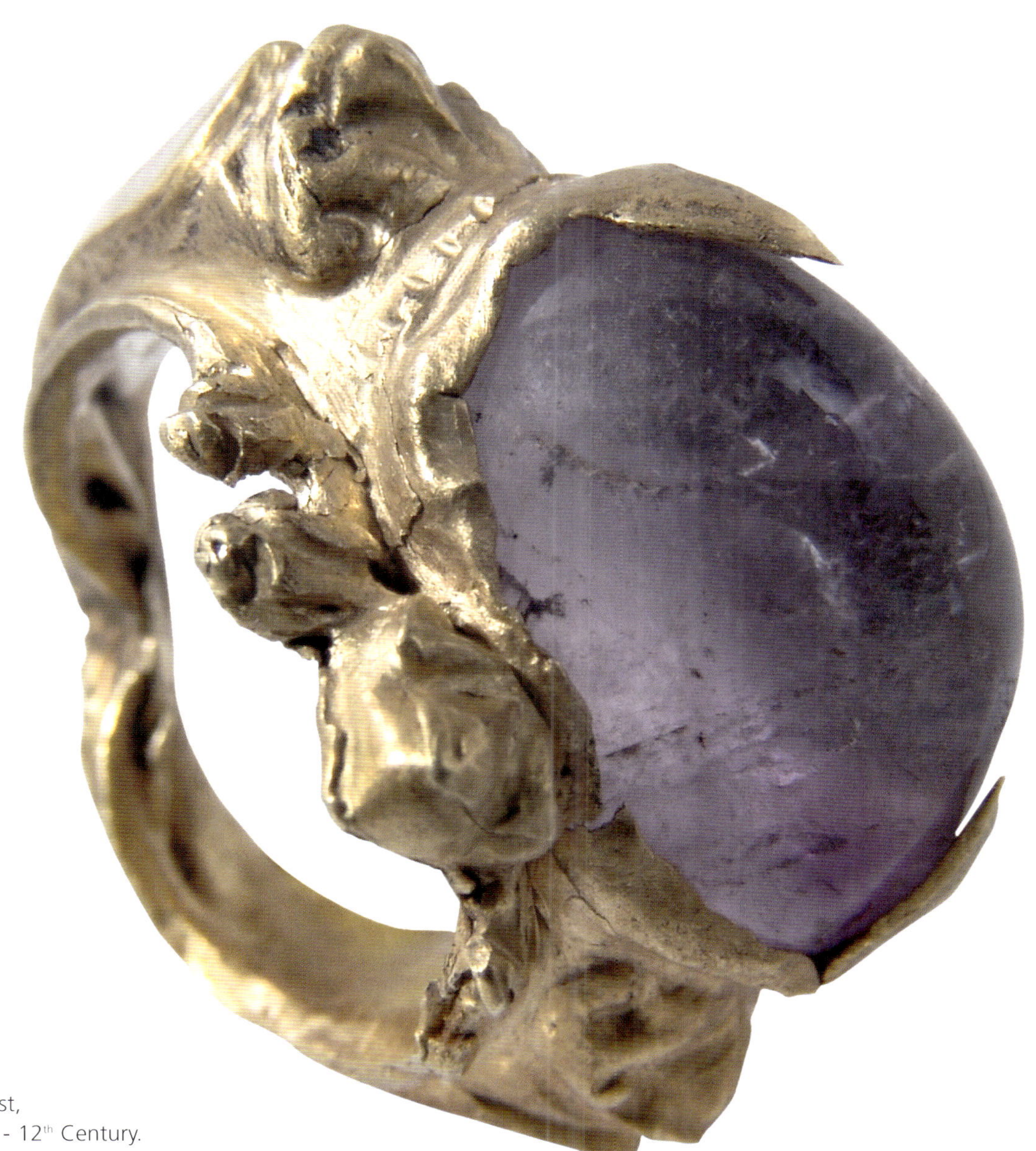

199. *Ring,* Alloy and amethyst,
Diameter 2.77 cm, 10th - 12th Century.

This ring, whose amethyst could not be analysed, is an alloy of gold (886 thousandths) and silver (104 thousandths) that contains only 0.8% copper. .

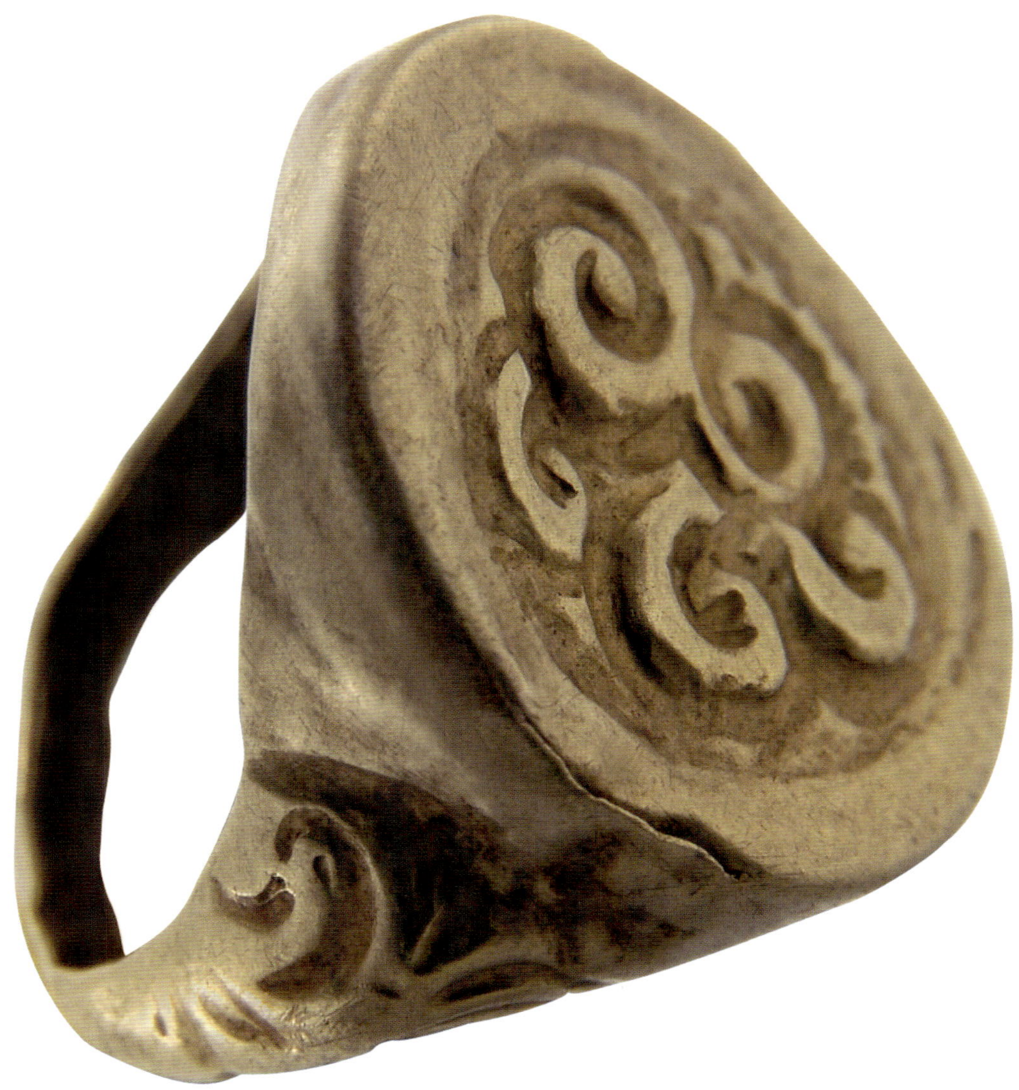

200. *Ring*, Alloy, Diameter 2.03 cm, 10th - 12th Century.

The embossing (8.32) is a three-part alloy of gold, silver, copper (composed of 80.4% Au, 15.6% Ag, 3.9% Cu) that is similar to the alloy of the ring itself (8.33), three-part alloy containing gold (79.4%), silver (19.0%) and only 1.3% copper.

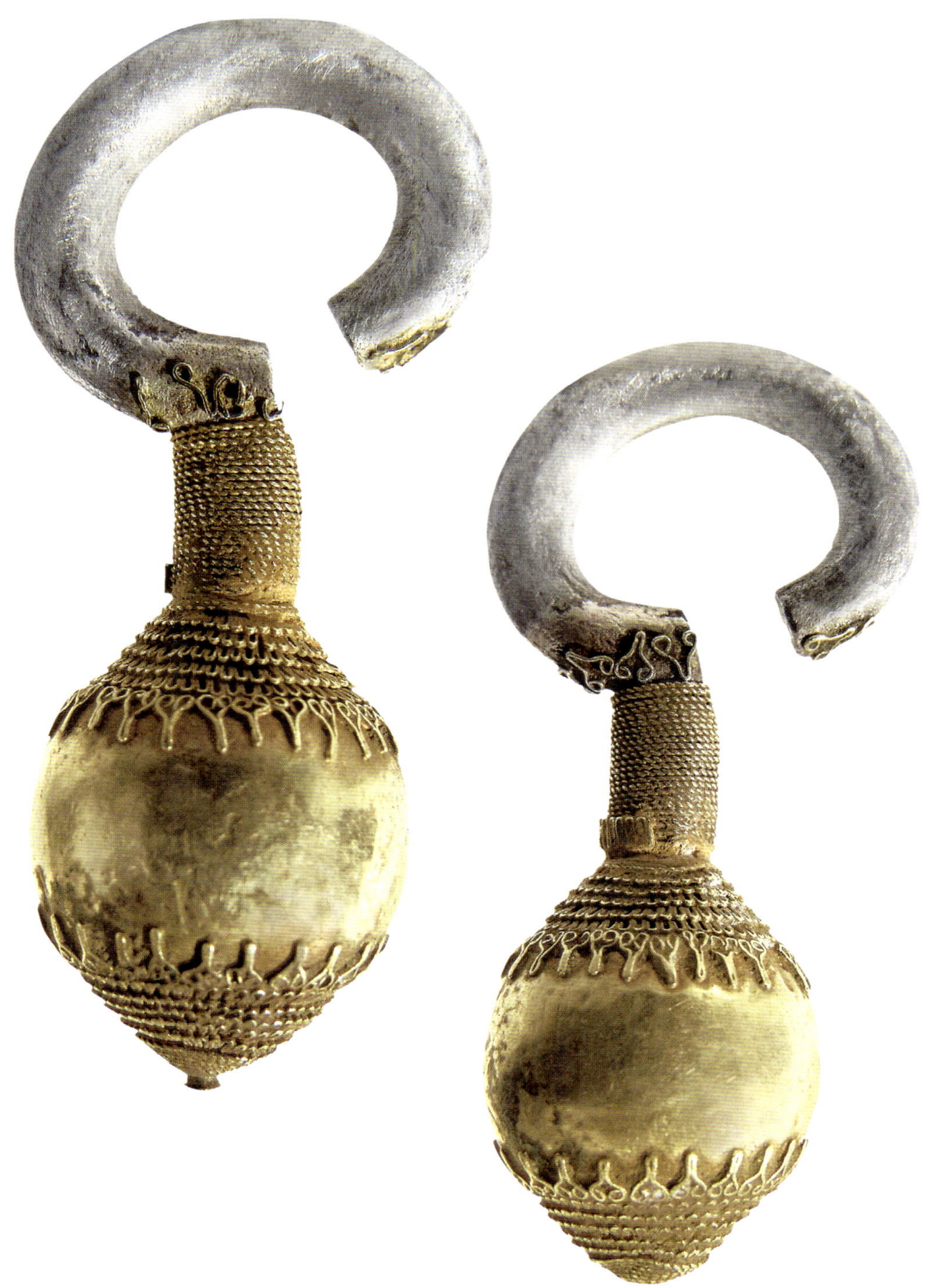

201. *Earrings*, Gold and alloy,
Length 4.6 cm, 10th - 12th Century.

The analysis of the earrings indicates that they are an assemblage of three parts made of three different alloys. Their spheres correspond to an alloy of gold (Au: 64.5%) and silver (Ag: 32.6%) with very little copper (Cu: 2.7%). The hooks are made of gold that is 980 thousandths pure. On the contrary, the threads are an alloy of gold (Au: 59.7%) and silver (Ag: 28.7%) with 5% copper. High iron content (Fe: 4.6%) seems abnormal in such an alloy. The iron could have been introduced accidentally during metallurgical processes or have been in the ores of the precious metals. A relatively high lead content (Pb: 1.9%) increased the malleability of the alloy and made it easier to put through a threader. Thus, the threader may be responsible for the presence of iron, as they were necessarily made of a hard metal.

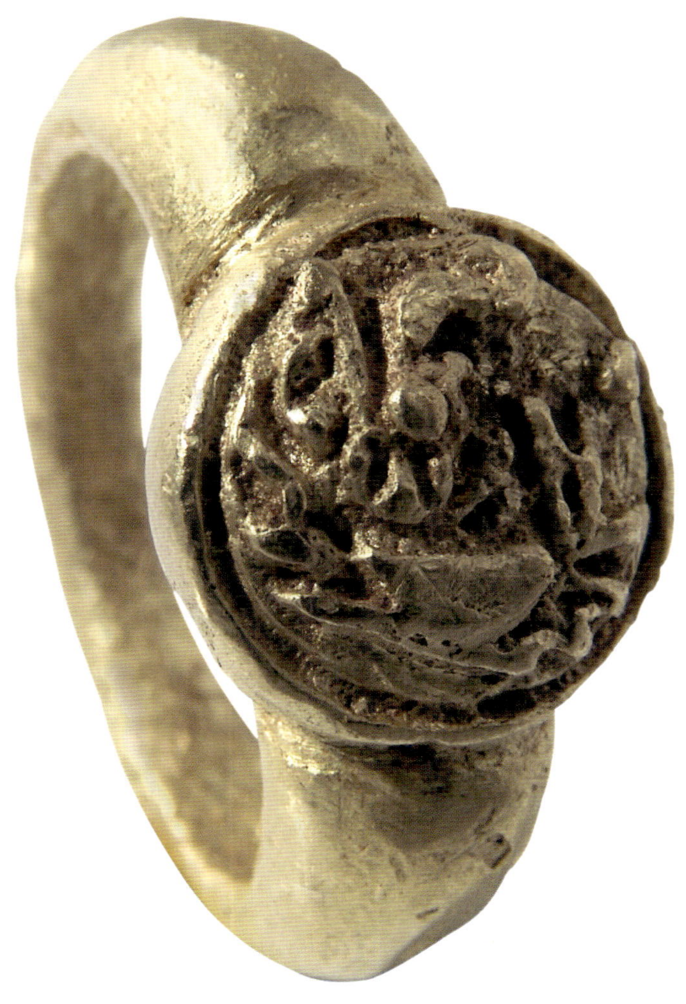

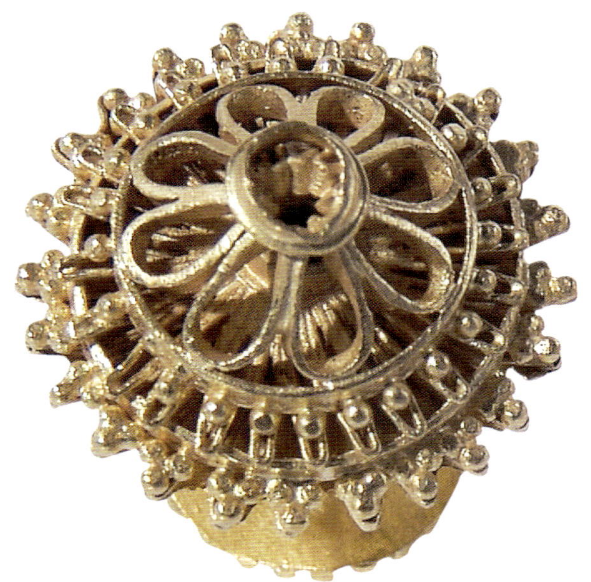

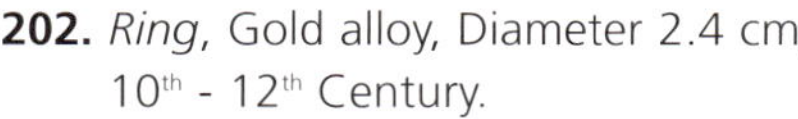

202. *Ring*, Gold alloy, Diameter 2.4 cm,
10th - 12th Century.

203. *Earrings*, Alloy, Length 2.22 cm,
10th - 12th Century.

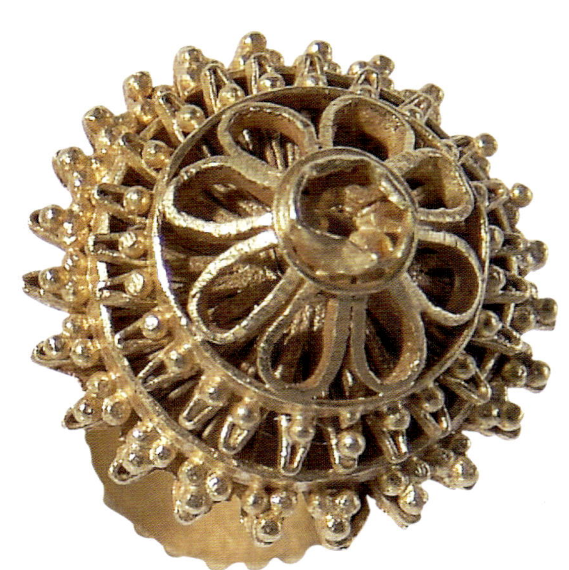

The collets of these filigreed earrings, the threaded posts and the backs were analysed separately; the same alloy was defined: gold (58.7%), silver (12%), copper (2.2%). Iron (Fe), with an average content of 0.055% was the only impurity present in the three elements. On the other hand, other earrings (not shown) revealed gold with a purity of over 995 thousandths.

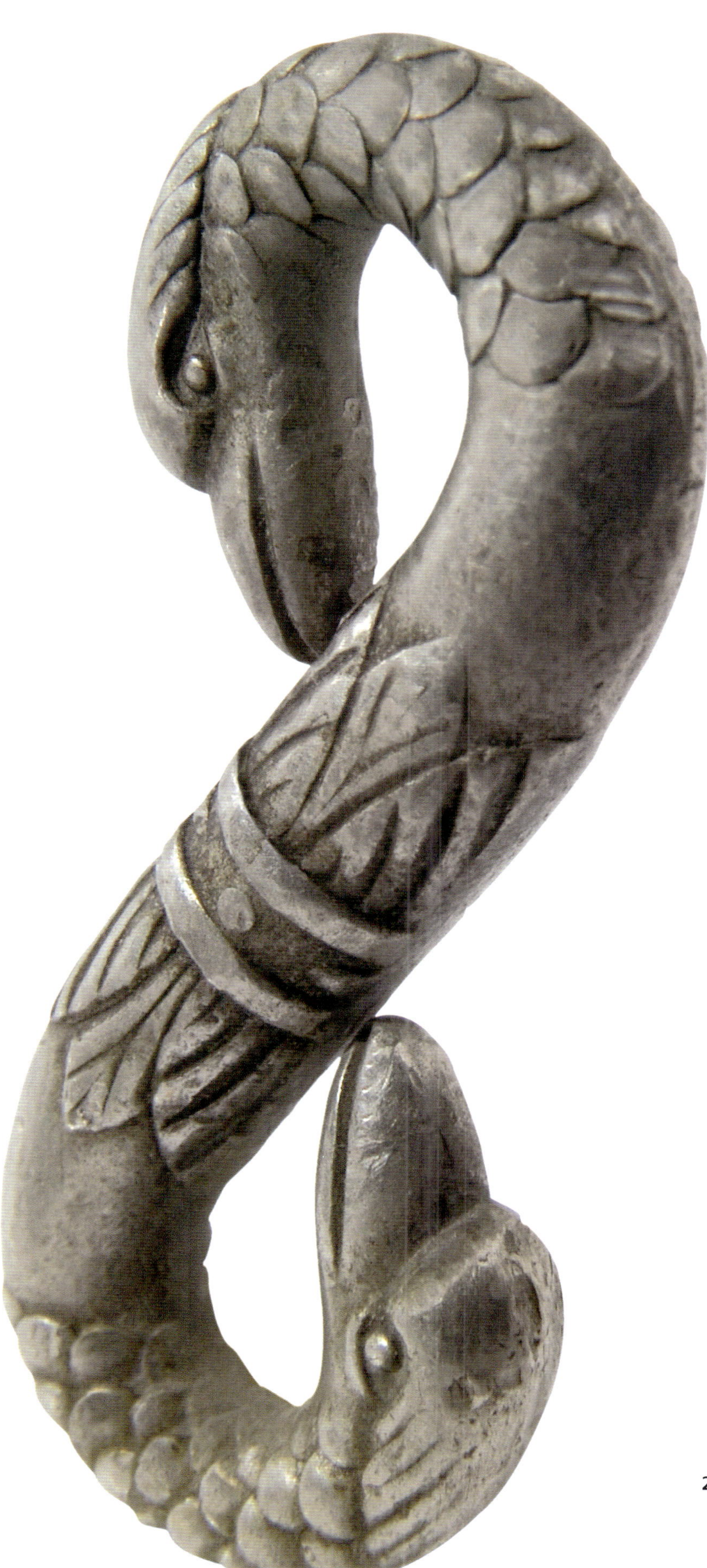

204. *Pendant,* alloy, Length 4 cm, 11th - 12th Century.

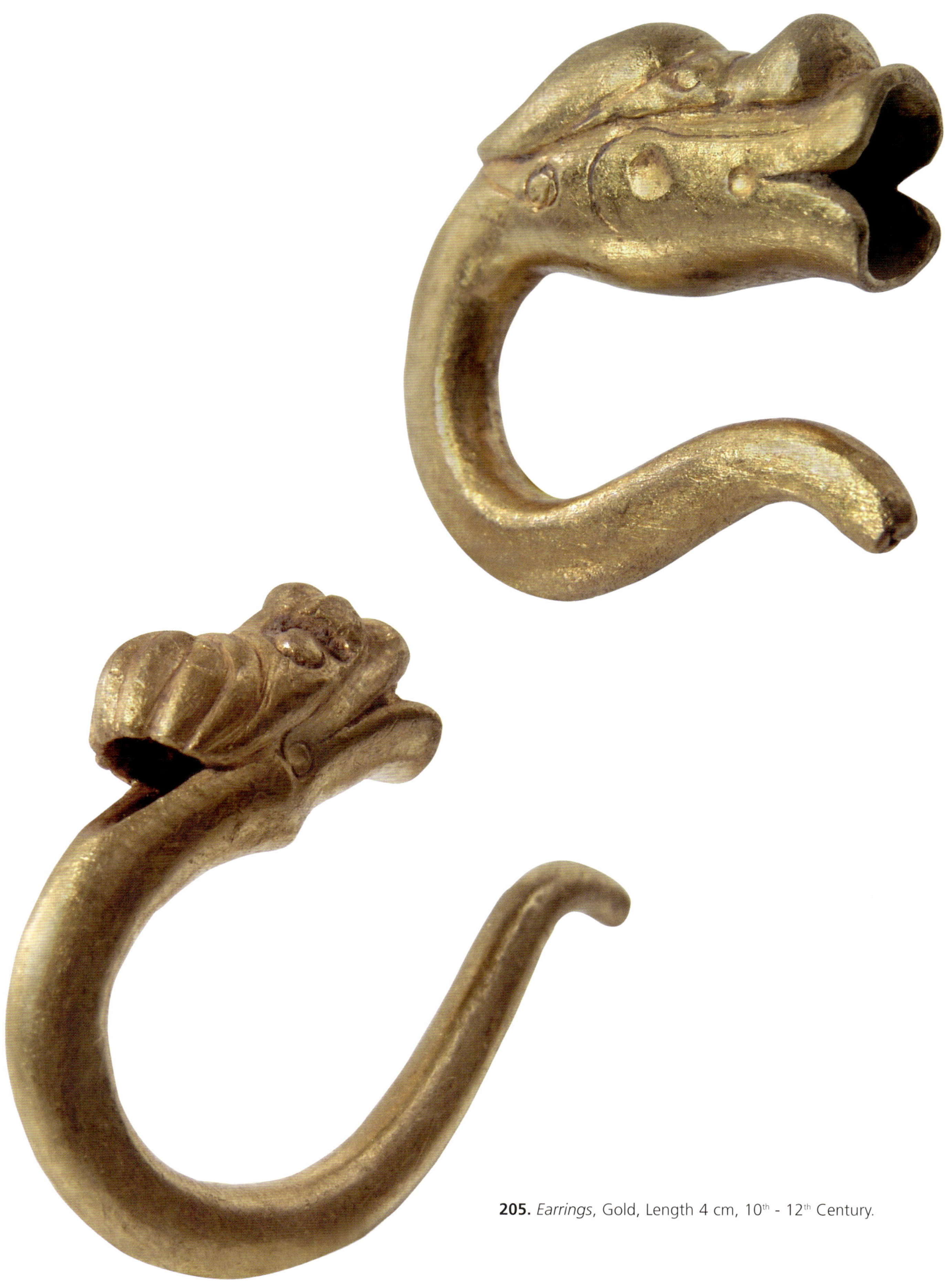

205. *Earrings*, Gold, Length 4 cm, 10th - 12th Century.

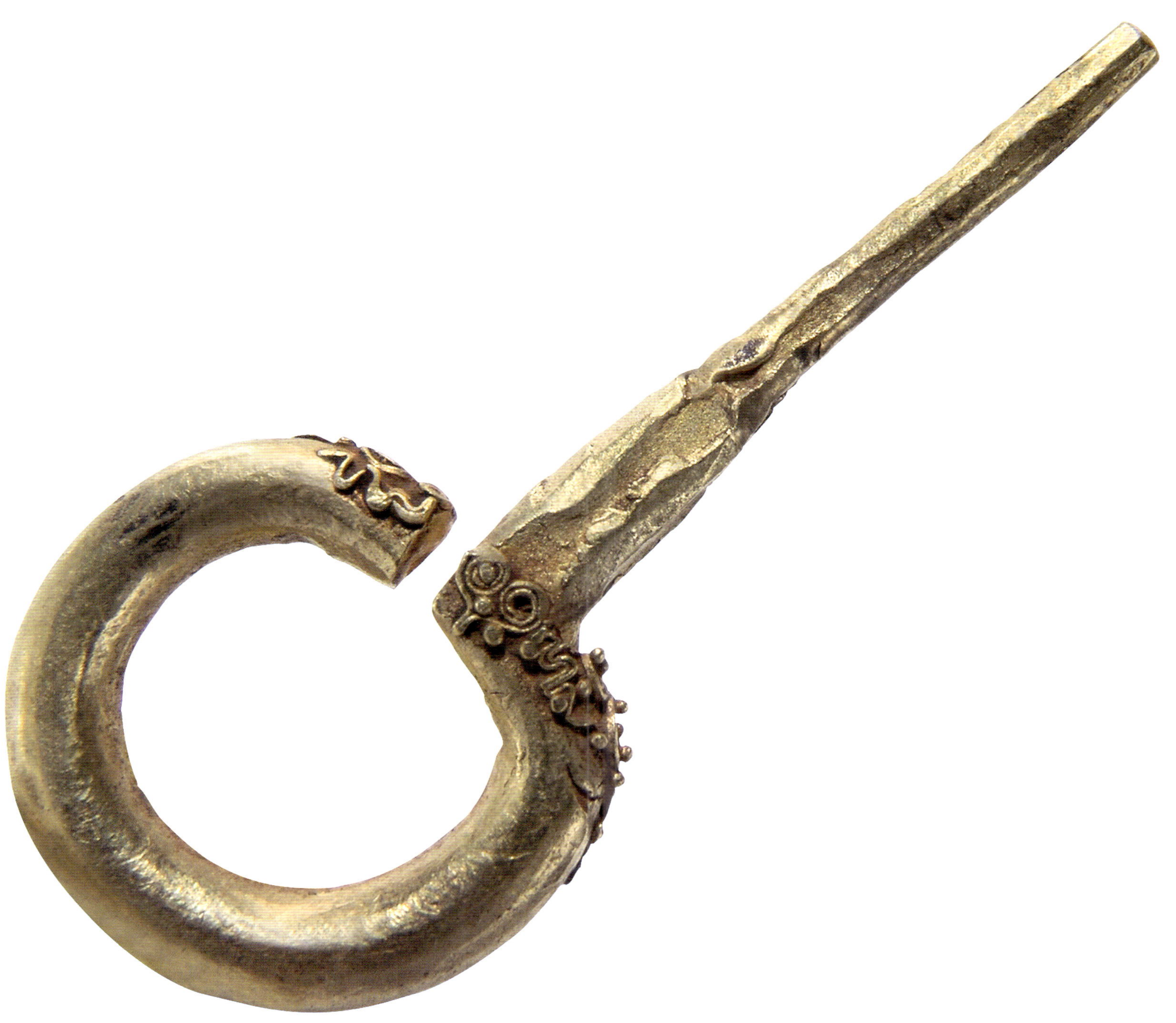

206. *Earring*, Gold, Length 4.4 cm, 10th - 12th Century.

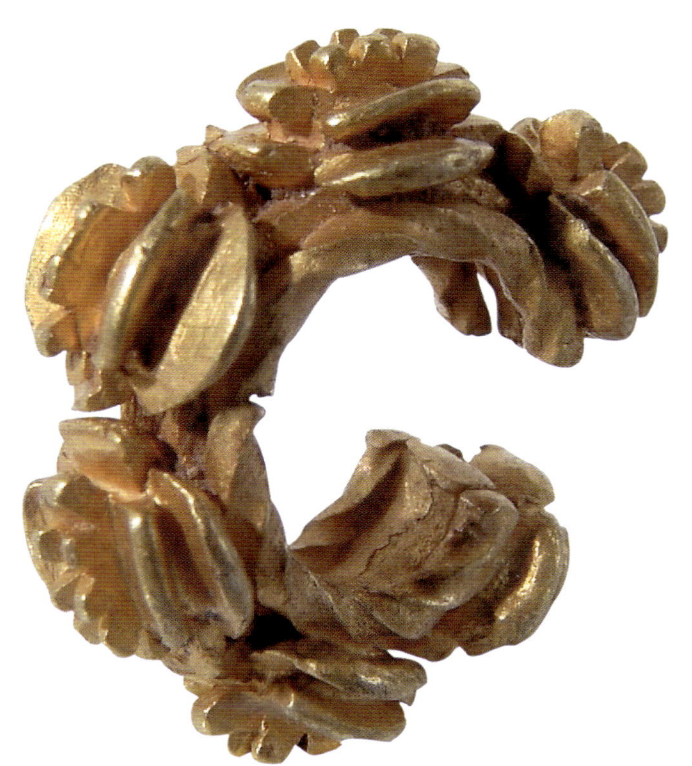

207. *Earring,* Gold, Length 1.5 cm, 10th - 12th Century.

208. *Golden pearl*, Height 1.7 cm, 10th - 12th Century.

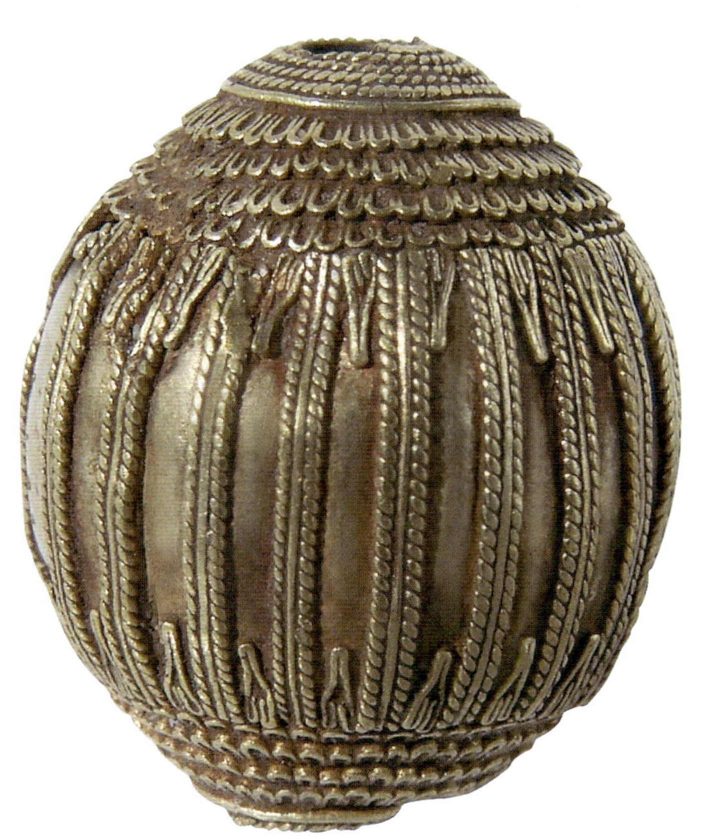

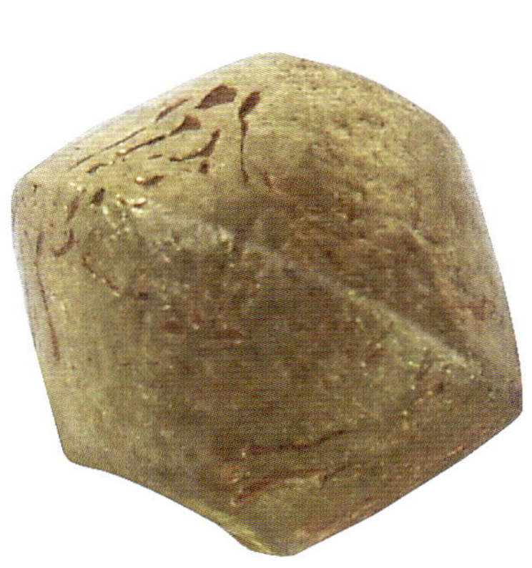

209. *Golden pearl*, Height 0.7 cm, 10th - 12th Century.

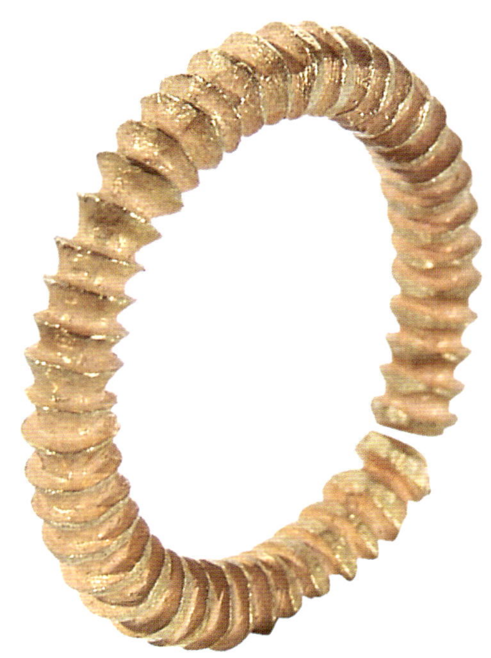

211. *Earring*, Diameter 1.5 cm, 10th - 12th Century.

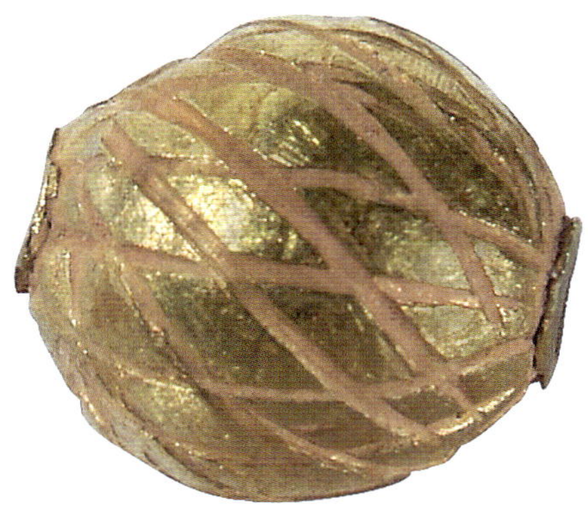

210. *Golden pearl*, Height 0.7 cm, 10th - 12th Century.

212. *Golden Pendants*, Total Height 1.5 cm, 10th - 12th Century.

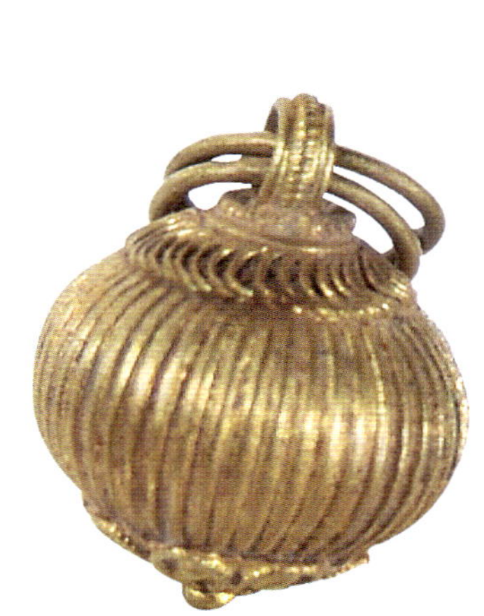

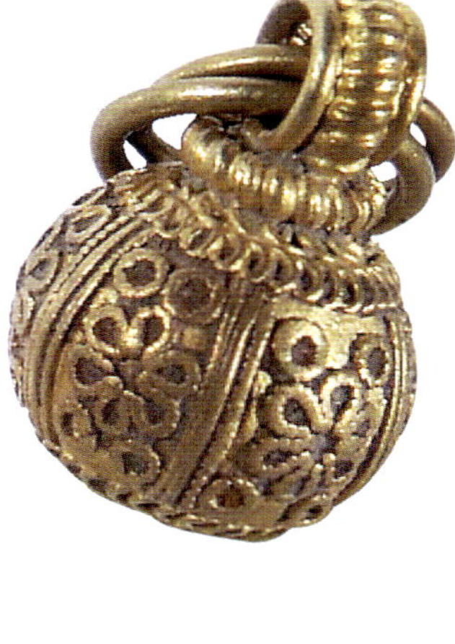

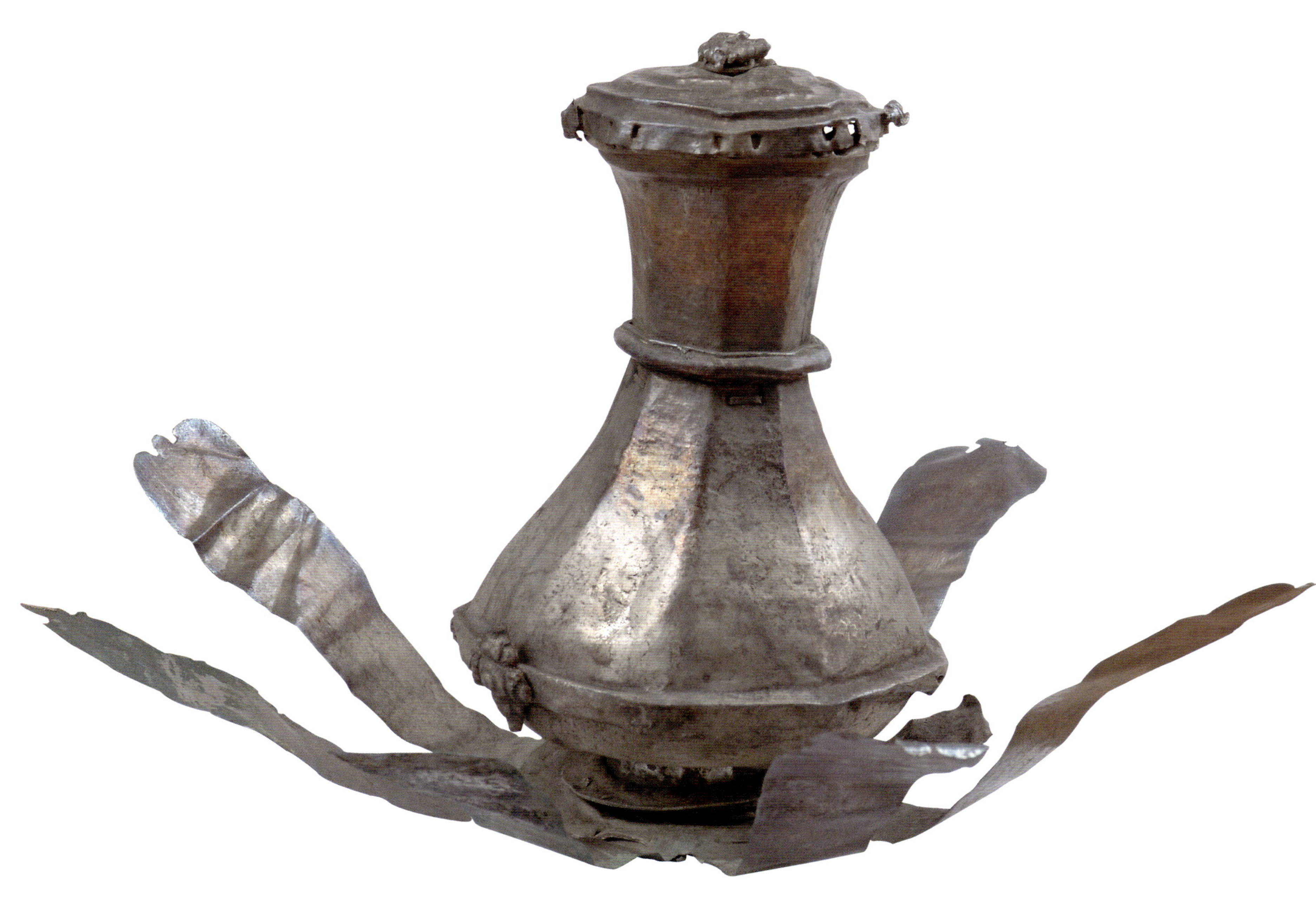

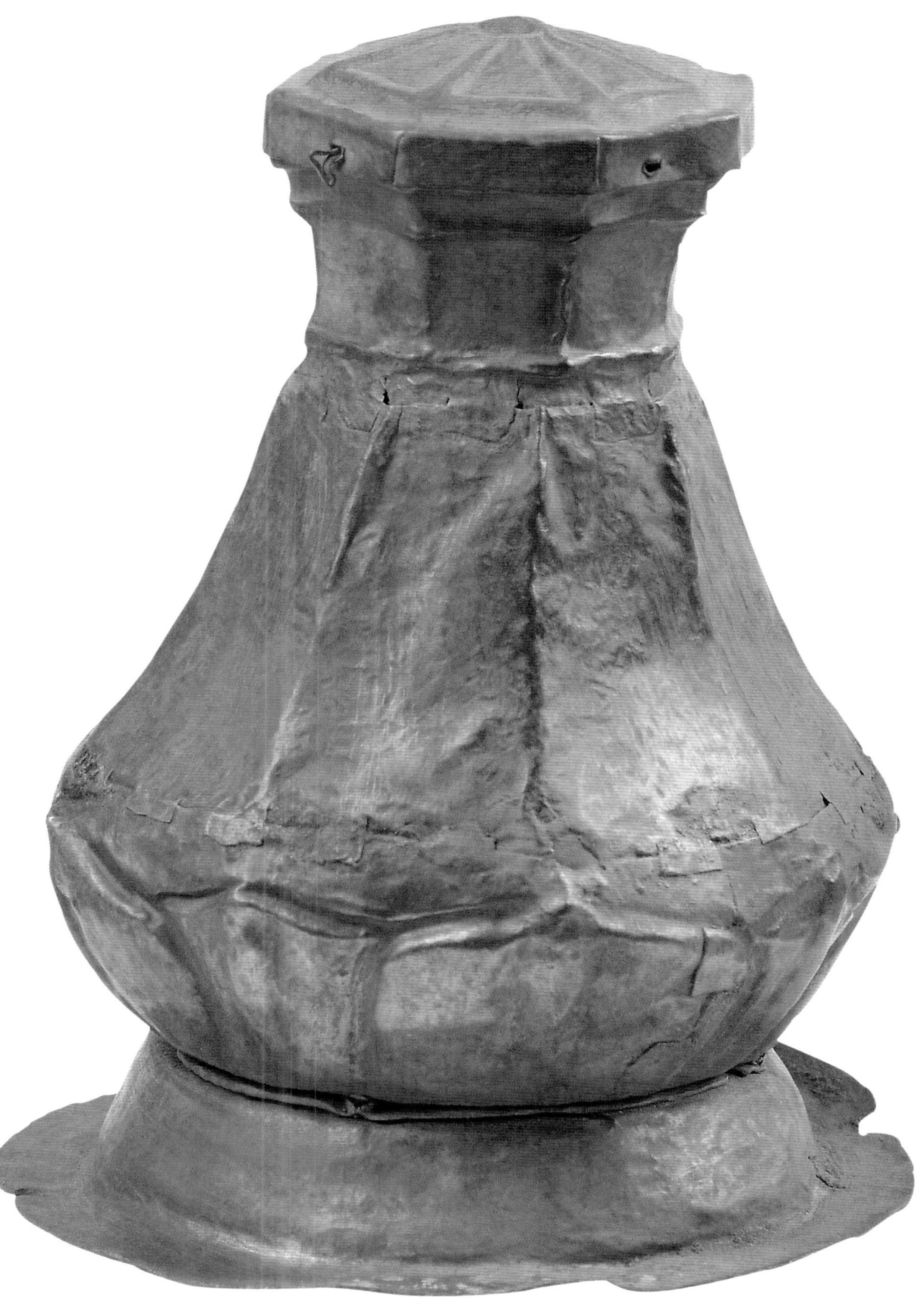

Previous Page
213. *Bottle with stopper*, Silver,
Height 17.5 cm, 10th Century.

214. *Bottle with stopper*, Silver, Height 16 cm,
10th Century.

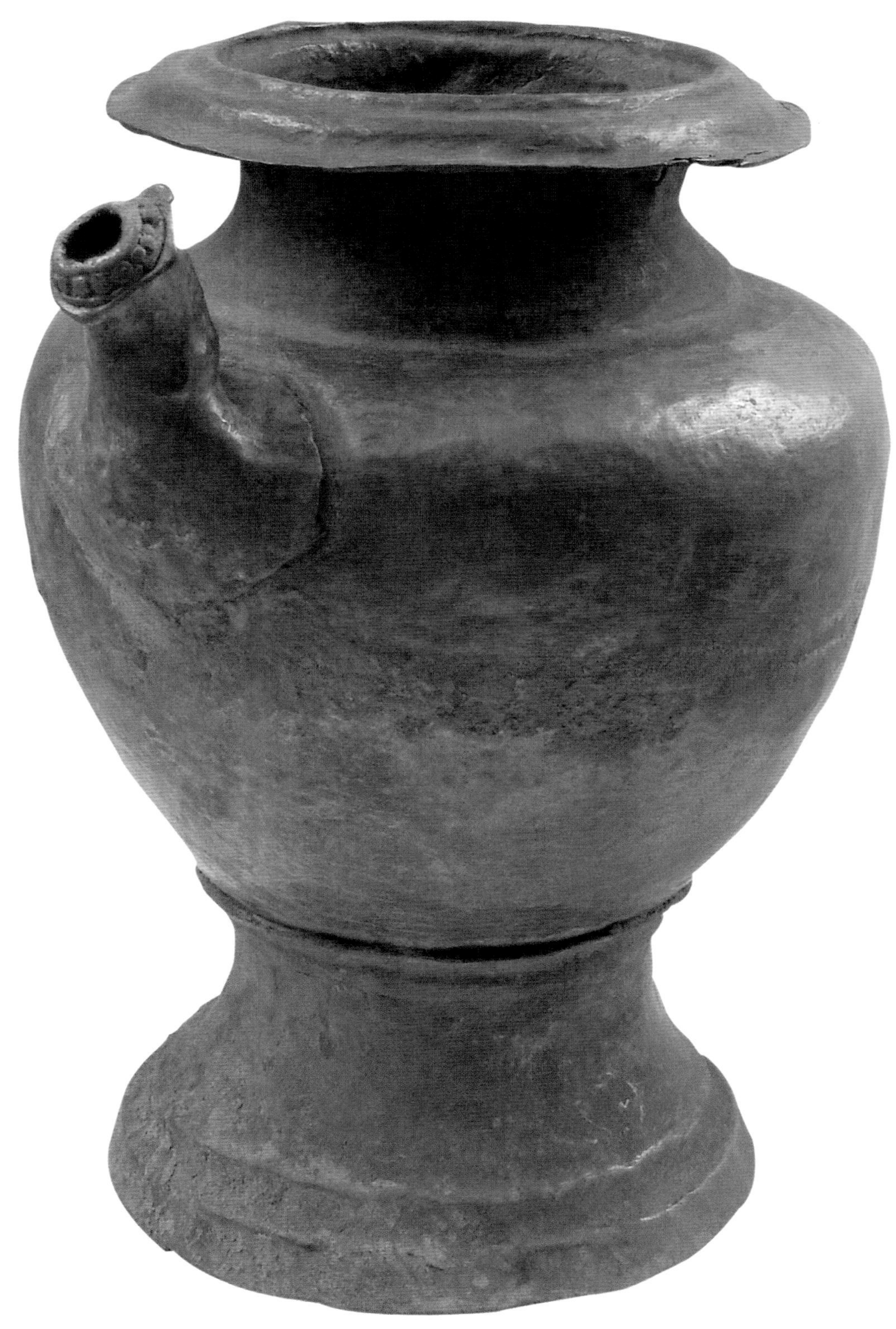

215. *Pitcher*, Silver, Height 16.5 cm, 10th Century.

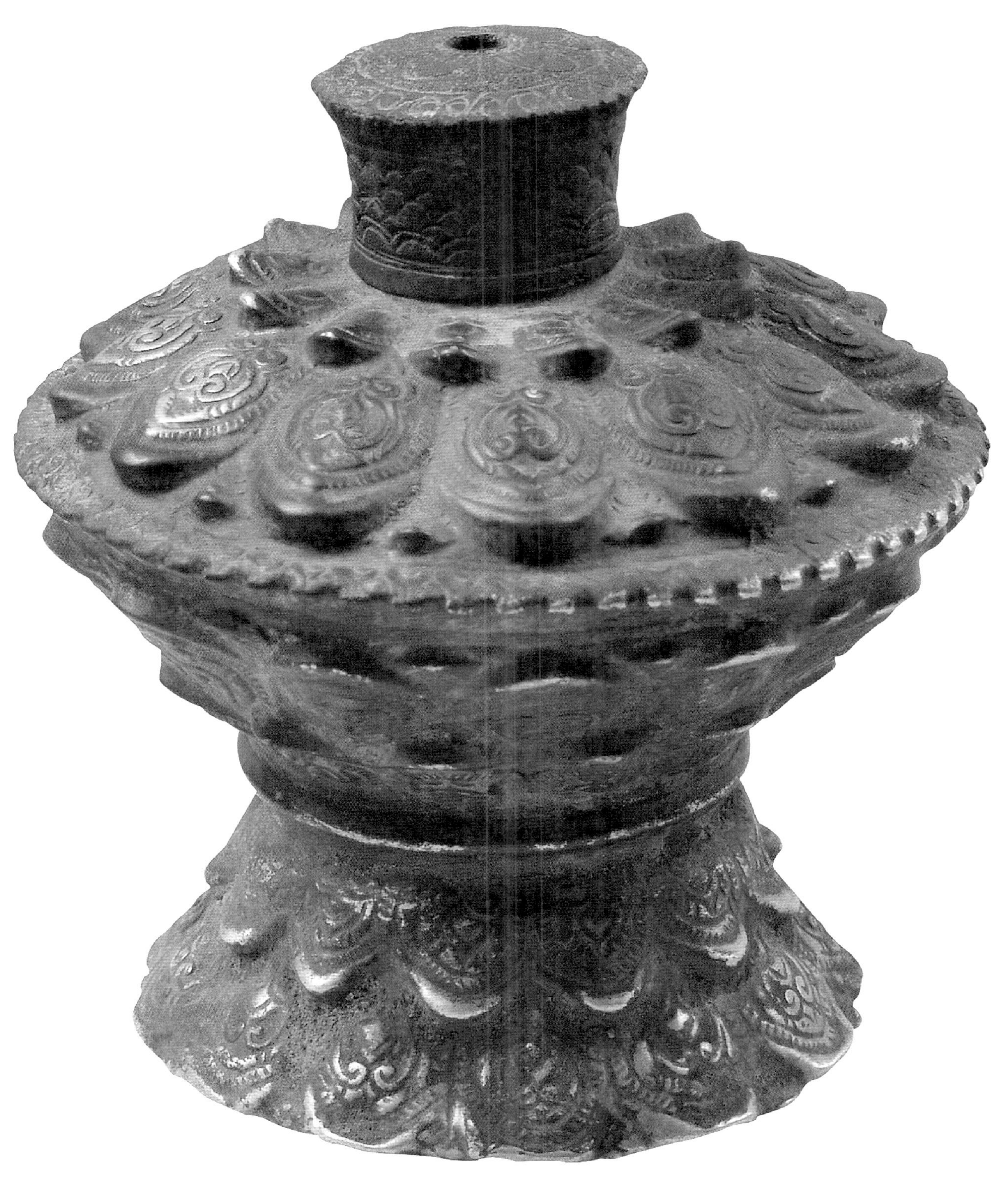

216. *Whitewash pot*, Silver, Height 9.5 cm, 14th - 15th Century.

Conclusion

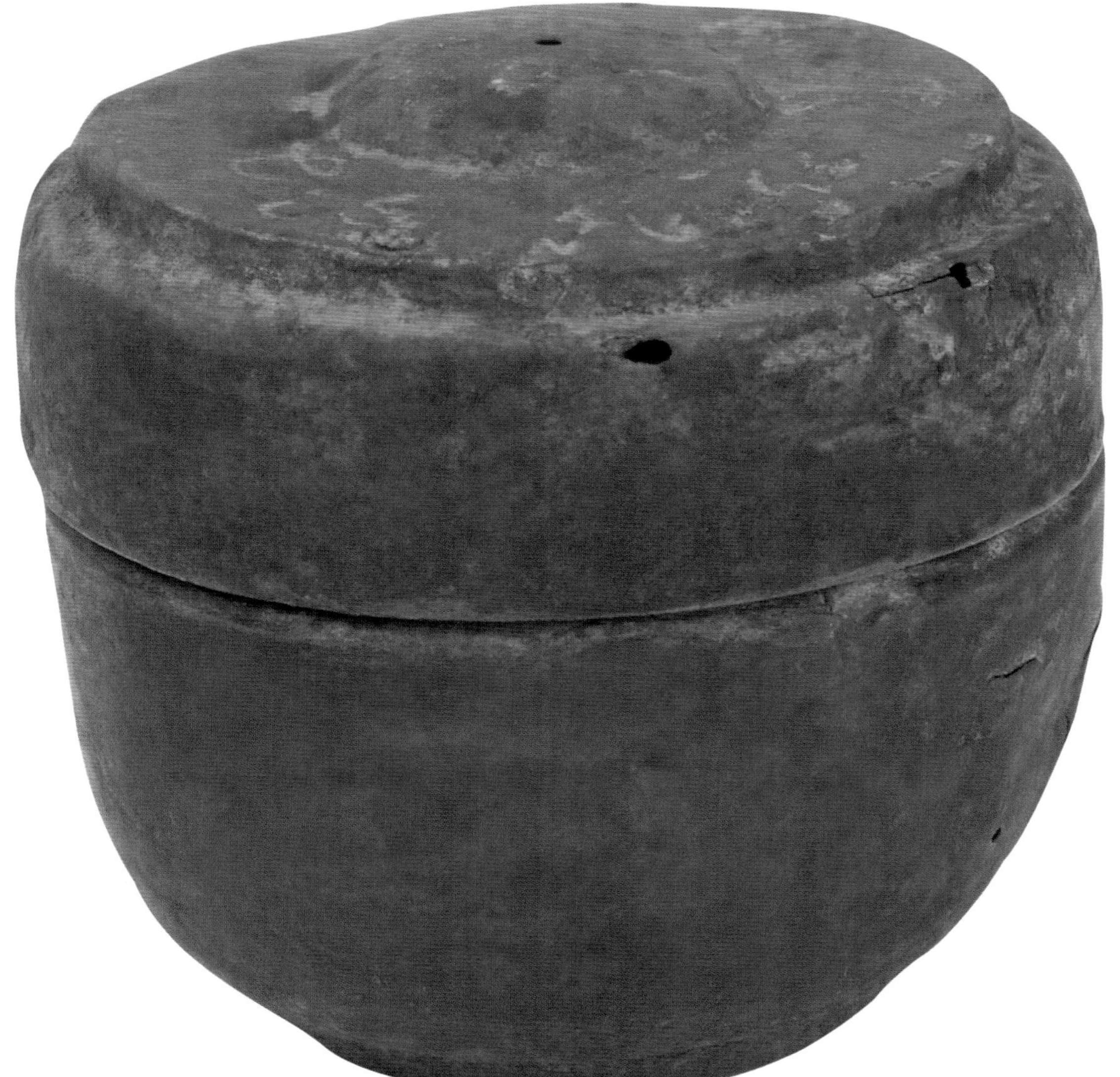

217. *Box with lid,* Silver, Diameter 5 cm, 10th Century.

Following Page
218. *Box with lid,* Silver, Diameter 5.5 cm, 10th Century.

At the conclusion of this work, a sensation of imperfection and incompleteness lingers. Despite this, to attempt to elucidate, even insufficiently, seems more honourable to us than to ignore. We have tried to return its splendour to Champa, via its sculptures, even if the homage was given to a departed people. Conscious of short-comings, approximations, even slight inexactitudes, we might, as an excuse, invoke the editorial constraints imposed, the conditions of urgency that impose furtive visits – which can rapidly appear to be intrusions – to collectors concerned with their tranquil wisdom. But we will not slip out from under any well-meant criticism; any constructive remark, any indication – documented, is encouraged. Our interest in the undisclosed, our desire to indicate new directions, our will to question more than to answer all appeal for a dialogue that must reveal itself productive. We have tried to show that, although all knowledge is necessarily rooted in givens, it must not content itself with conforming to them: rereading, reconsidering, rethinking, rewriting; such are the tools of knowledge offered to all without exclusivity. An idea is not an order and one is not born to individuality by gregariously becoming a vassal.

Lastly, we cannot finish without dealing with a question as old as art itself, which has been emphasised in recent years: Who possesses art in fact and by right? In the case of a past art, as Cham art is, who is responsible for its conservation, legally and legitimately? In recent years, the two notions of legal and legitimate have not come to interpenetration – as is their essence – but to discord. While the Occident has produced markedly few declarations concerning who does what in art, it has busied itself via two lobbies, only moderately actively it must be said, to bring shame upon the heads of private collectors, presented as odious predators feeding on exactions and augmenting their collections with "cultural orphans". It is true – we

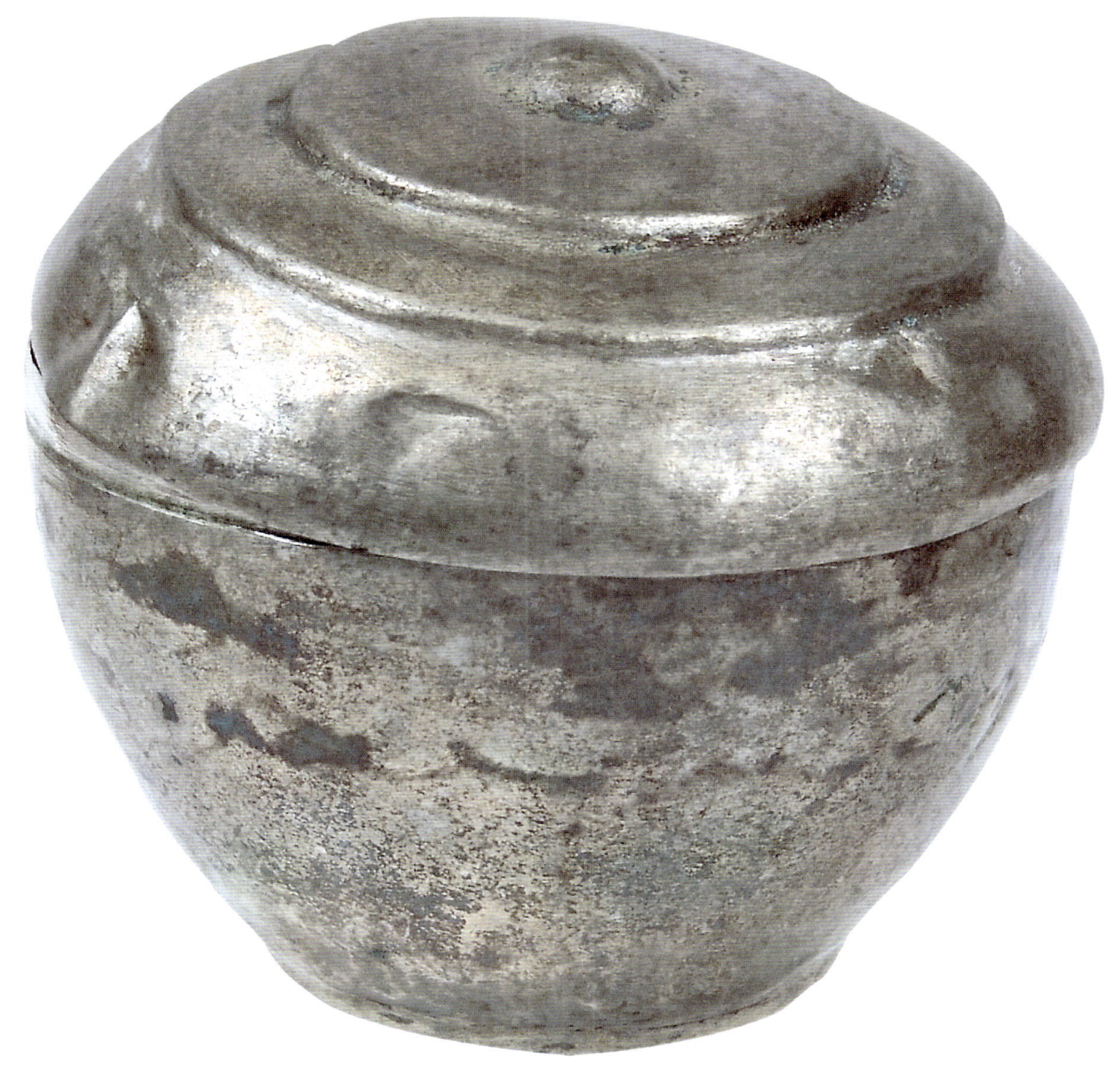

have constantly shown this throughout our book – that Cham sculpture is not fundamentally concerned by these recriminations. Certainly, the Occident at times calls upon itself, without raising its eyes to the horizon: thus, from time to time, the haunting problem of the pieces pillaged by the Emperor Napoleon I during his campaigns and kept today in French museums comes up in France. But, diversionary tactic or real issue, the debate today centres on objects of art called "Oriental". Two pressure groups, one influential and Occidental, the other discreet and Oriental, have joined forces to support a philosophy of the unfair: unfair possession of Oriental objects by the Occident, held to be proof of the exploitation of the former by the latter. The first group is made up of individuals that are at opposite poles structurally but who, for the sake of expedience, rally to a single line – one is tempted to write "string" – of thought: monopoly. These monopolists, by their very essence, are specialists and live only in defence of their monopoly. It is four-fold: social, cultural, economic, political; built on networks that are all adepts of one-track thinking and chronic inaction that aggregates in a syncretism of arrogance. The monopoly is political: no private property. Economic: no competition. Social: only the public sphere has the right to educate. Cultural: an art object in private hands has "lewd tones" to borrow a term from the public prosecutor Pinard who severely criticised Gustave Flaubert's *Madame Bovary* in 1857. Thus, dogma, exclusivity, Puritanism and xenophobia founded an ideology of exclusion and rejection. This ideology was adopted for purely political motives by a second pressure group, an Oriental minority this time, only too happy to contribute its stone to the wall of decolonisation. In the Occident, the art object of the twenty-first century has the status that a human being did in the nineteenth. Nevertheless, Vietnam has not fallen into its bottomless pit:

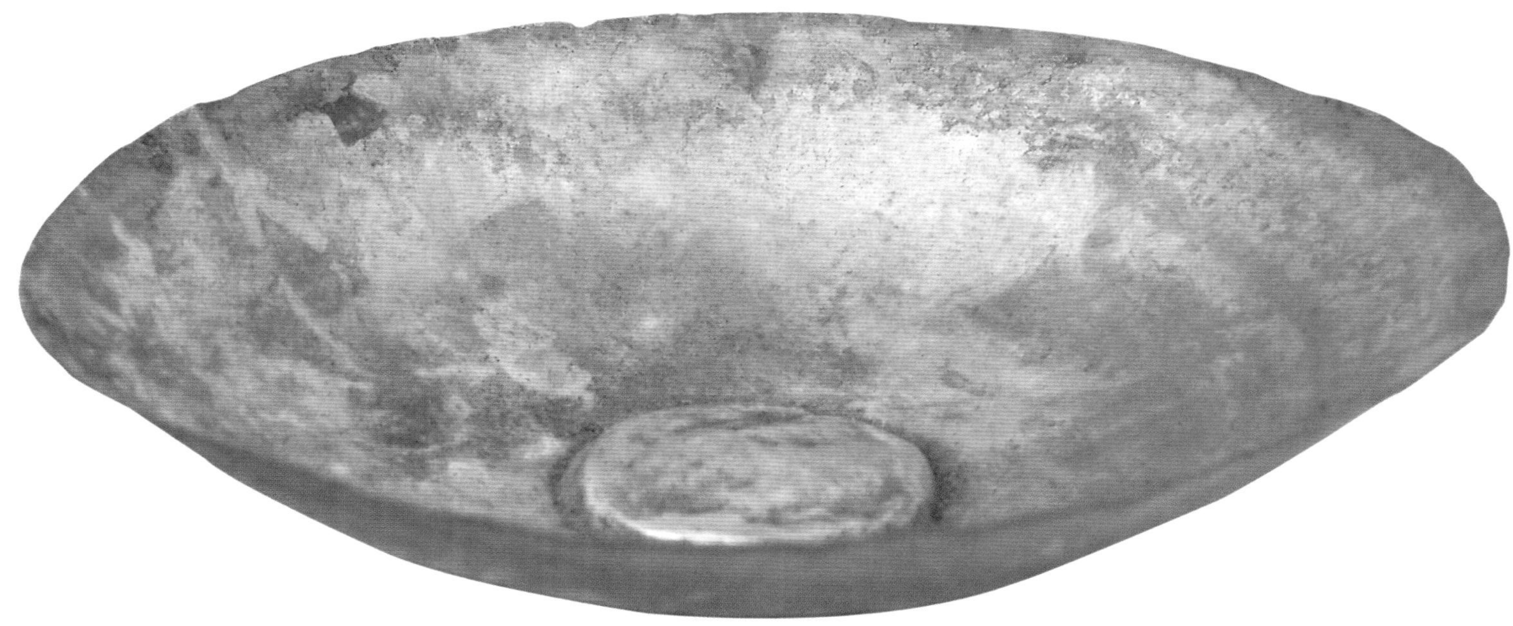

219. *Dish*, Silver, Diameter 9.8 cm, 10th Century.

Following Page
220. *Dish*, Silver, Diameter 9.8 cm, 10th Century.

Strengthened by and proud of its 3000 year-old culture, it has always favoured overseas exhibitions in which objects originating from Vietnamese soil, coming from long-established private collections, sang the praises of its culture and roots.

The splendid bodhisattva shown in the reference work of Jean Boisselier (1963, plate 50) was transferred to the Mallon collection at the beginning of the twentieth century, then exhibited at the Metropolitan Museum in New York, then the Museum for Volkerkunde in Berlin, and finally given by the Baron von der Heydt (1882-1963) to the Museum Rietberg in Zurich (*Treasures from the Museum Rietberg* 1980, p.69). It is one of Cham art's best ambassadors and does not deprive Vietnamese collections, which possess its double. By the same token, the kut shown (p.198), also illustrated in Boisselier's book (1963, plate 247), was part of a cemetery near Phan Ri and was given by former President of South Vietnam, Ngo Dinh Diem, to his special diplomatic envoy in 1962. It is the only kut in private hands, known outside the frontiers of Vietnam, which here again possesses numerous others. All of these pieces are not just survivors of history, but play a fundamental role in the explanation and promotion of an art that, without them, would be visible only in Vietnamese museums, by definition distant from the majority of the world's population, nonetheless avid for available knowledge.

The time has come to have a closer look at the Occident. In 1793, French revolutionaries undertook the devastation of, among others, Saint Anne's door of the Notre Dame Cathedral in Paris that included a group of sculptures representing the kings of the Old Testament, incorrectly identified by the revolutionaries with the sovereigns of the French *Ancien Régime*. Picked up out of the rubble, saved in extremis, the head of King David is today part of the collection of the Metropolitan Museum of New York (Harris Brisbane Dick Fund No.38.180). As Frenchmen, proud of our

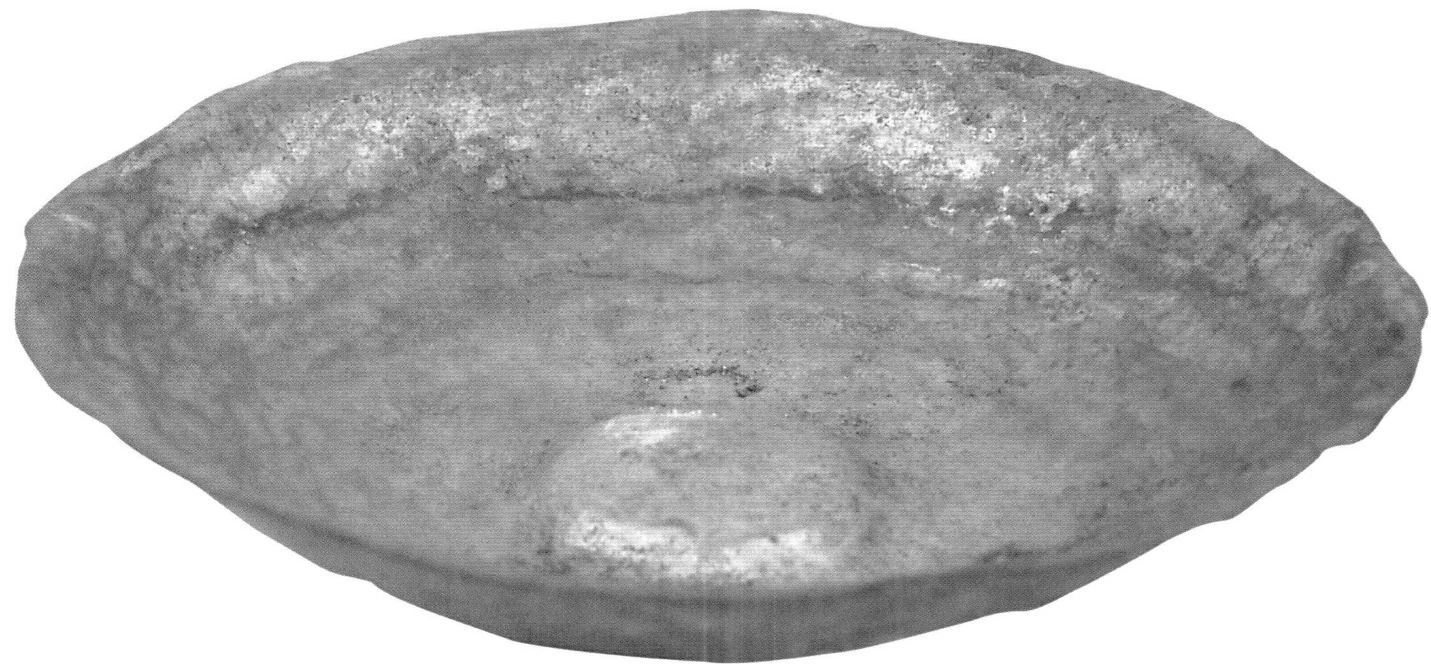

patrimony, we thank the Met for having acquired the head, for keeping it, and find no legitimate grounds to clamour for its return. This head is culturally French and judicially American, legally and legitimately. Public, it became private and yet it still belongs to the heritage of humanity. Nuances in time and place between private and public, national and local, international and universal can be understood. But, as current emphasis is after all on the search for origins, we cannot resist the temptation to question what appears to all as a symbol of friendship and respect between peoples: the famous obelisk on the no less famous Place de la Concorde in the City of Lights, Paris. Epitome of harmonious legitimacy: gift of Egypt to France, the khedive (Egyptian Viceroy) having offered it to Champollion himself in anticipatory thanks for writing a book on the history of Egypt. This being said, let us ask ourselves about the presence in Paris of one of the two obelisks from Luxor. What right had the khedive, who represented an occupying power (the Ottoman Empire), Albanian by birth, tobacco merchant by profession, to dispose of a consubstantially national symbol in this way?

We can see that if we wish to question the origin of all objects of art, it is necessary in the interest of all to impose a moratorium, coupled with a strict census and a new rule defining the circulation of pieces. This is simple and fair. A last detail: our private objects, buoyed by the increasing wealth of their countries of origin, are returning to them little by little, financed by new local collectors. In the past few years, thanks to the laws of the market, all the available patrimony of Asia is returning to that continent, with the gratitude of the new owners who are conscious of the fact that the Occident served as a sanctuary for over 150 years to pieces that the circumstances of history, particularly destructive as they were, would otherwise have led to their pure and simple annihilation.

The empty cage never goes in search of its bird.

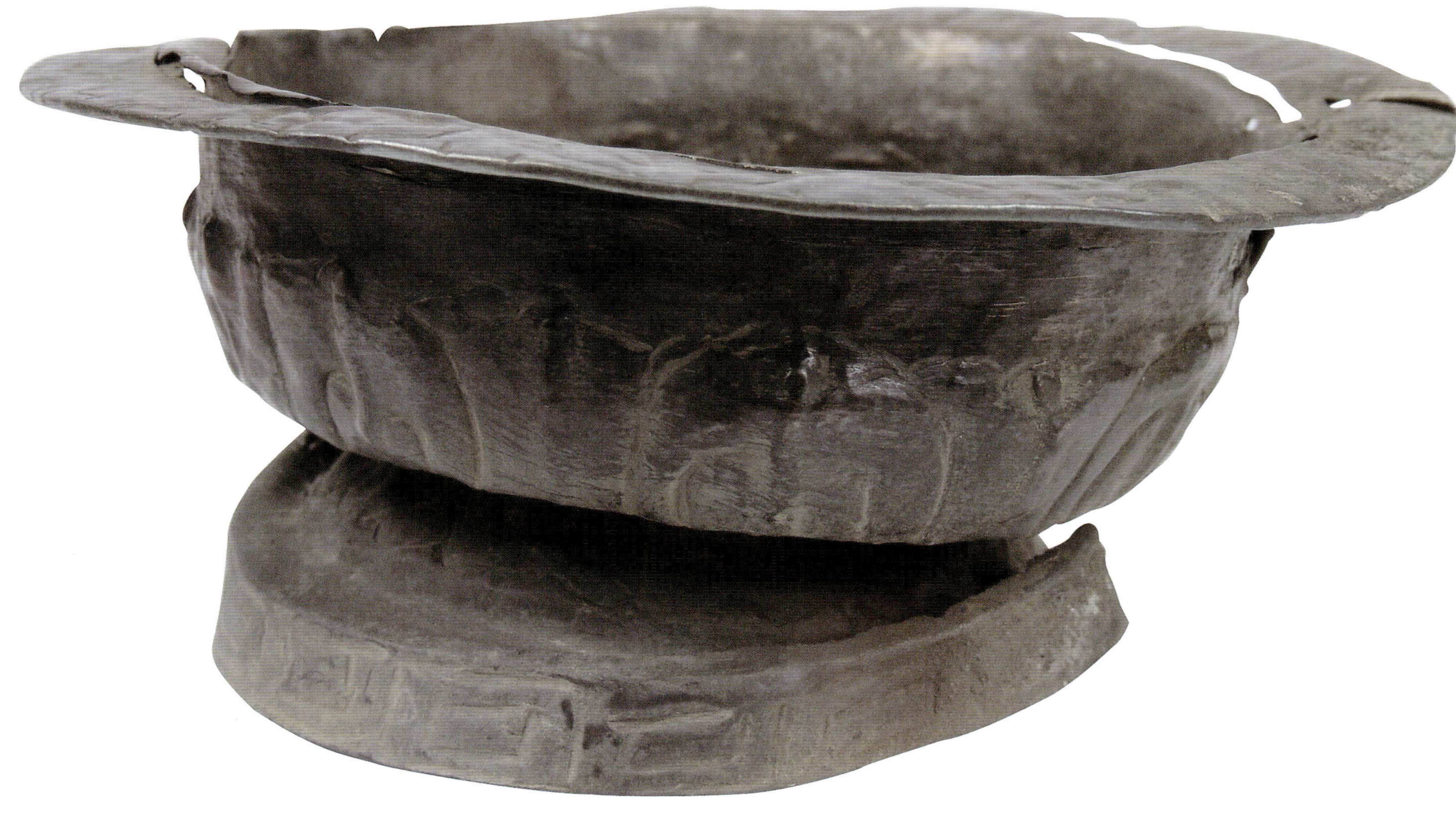

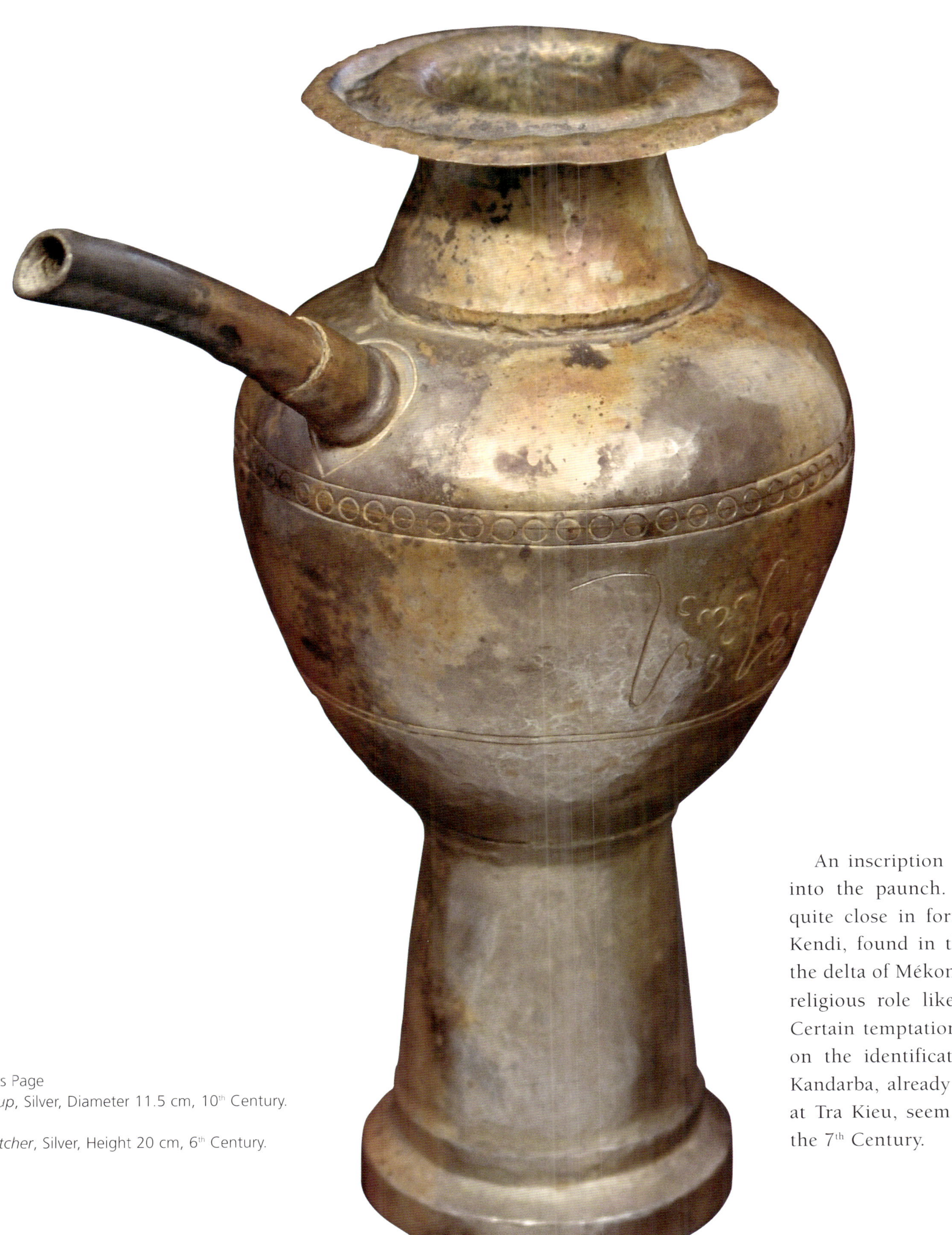

Previous Page
221. *Cup*, Silver, Diameter 11.5 cm, 10th Century.

222. *Pitcher*, Silver, Height 20 cm, 6th Century.

An inscription in Sanskrit is carved into the paunch. This type of piece, quite close in form to that of certain Kendi, found in the Oc Eo culture in the delta of Mékong, should have had a religious role like the previous ones. Certain temptations of dating it, based on the identification of the the God Kandarba, already found on the pillars at Tra Kieu, seem to date it at around the 7th Century.

Glossary

Except when indicated to the contrary, the following terms are words and names in Sanskrit with, if necessary, their English translation in quotes

Agni, "fire"
God of sacrificial fire and guardian of the South-East.

Airavata
The elephant that Indra rides.

Apsara, "from the water"
Celestial nymphs that spring from the churning of the sea of milk.

Amitabha "the Buddha of Limitless Life/Light"
Amitabha is a Buddha possessing many meritorious qualities.

Asana, "seat"
Originally, the asana was a Brahman ritual that consisted of offering a seat to the divinity invoked during the puja. Later, the term was applied to the seat itself (the actual seat and also the animal or lotus) in Hindu philosophy. By extension, the divinity's sitting position is also designated by this word.

Asura, "demon"
Opposed to gods (deva), particularly Shiva and Vishnu.

Avalokitesvara
Name of a bodhisattva symbolising Buddha's infinite compassion. Born from Amitabha's eye, which Buddha wears in his headdress, it is mostly found in the Dong Duong style (ninth and tenth centuries) in Champa. Also known as Laksmindra Lokesvara

Avatar, from **avatara**, "descent"
Divine incarnation. The god "descends" to earth to be incarnated.

Bhagavad-gita, "the song of the blessed"
Sixth book of the Mahabharata.

Bhagavati
One of the names of Shiva's "sakti". In Champa, it designates the principal divinity of the temple of Po Nagar in Nha Trang.

Bodhisattva, "being destined to enlightenment"
For the Theravada, this term designates the Buddha himself and Buddhas of the past before their enlightenment. For the Mahayana who were more prevalent in Champa, the bodhisattva purposely delays his enlightenment, out of compassion, to help other beings.

Bhumi, "Earth"
Earth made divine, Vishnu's second wife.

Buddha, "enlightened"
Historic figure, born at the frontier between modern Nepal and India in the sixth century BCE.

Brahma, "the absolute (made god)"
God of creation but secondary in Champa to Shiva and, to a lesser extent, to Vishnu.

Brahman
Member of the highest of the four classes of Hindu society, that of priests.

Brahmanism
Name of an Indian religion that followed the Vedic tradition, the earliest Indian religion (c. 1500 – 600 BCE) and preceding Hindu philosophies, be they sectarian (Shivaism, Vishnuism, etc.) or non-sectarian (Buddhism, Jainism).

Chakra, "wheel, disk"
Attribute of Vishnu.

Deva, "god" or "shining"
Divinity superior to men, in Hinduism. Celestial being, in Mahayanist Buddhism.

Devi
Usually a goddess.

Dharma, "cosmic law"
Moral law or doctrine.

Dikpala, **dikpalaka**
Name given to eight divinities who are guardians of directions: Indra (East), Agni (South-East), Yama (South), Nirriti (South-West), Varuna (West), Vayu (North-East), Kuvera (North), Ishana (North-East). When a dikpala rides his vahana, the term dikpalaka is used.

Dvarapala, "guardian of the door"
A dvarapala is a demi-god, guardian of the doors of Hindu or Buddhist sanctuaries.

Gajasimha, from **gaja**, "elephant" and **simha**, "lion"
Mythical animal with an elephant's head and the body of a lion.

Ganesha
Son of Shiva and Parvati. Parvati had made a small man out of earth whom she asked to guard her door. The man refused to let Shiva enter. The god decapitated him. Faced with Parvati's fury, Shiva ordered his ganas to find a head for his love's protégé. The ganas decapitated the first being they met, an elephant, and reconstituted a new being with an elephant's head.

Garuda, "wings of speech"
Mythical entity, half bird, half man, ridden by Vishnu and enemy to serpents.

Gopura
Monumental portal of a temple or city.

Guru or **gourou**, "heavy"
Spiritual master.

Hamsa (Sanskrit and Pali)
Celestial mythical goose or duck. Ridden by Brahma and Varuna, the guardian god of the West.

Hanuman
Name of the monkey hero of the Ramayana.

Indra, "master"
Vedic god of the storm and, later, king of the gods. His attribute is the Vajra, symbol of lightning. He usually rides an elephant.

Jata, **jatamukuta**, "chignon"
Name of Shiva's hair piece or bun. Symbol of Vayu, god of the wind.

Jati, "caste"
Social religious group often with professional criteria. Not to be confused with class ("varna").

Kailasa, "mountain of silver"
Mythical mountain in the Himalayas considered the seat of Shiva's heaven.

Kala, "black"
Head of a mythical animal resembling a lion. Usually a symbol of death.

Kinnari, **Kinnara** (Sanskrit and Pali)
Half-bird, half-human beings that play music to accompany the songs of the Gandharva and the dances of the Apsara. The word Kinnari is used for the feminine and Kinnara for the masculine.

Kirita-mukuta
Wrought and jewelled diadem.

Kosa, "sheath"
Object covering, in different forms, a linga.

Krishna, "the divine"
Avatar of Vishnu. Hero in the Mahabharata, particularly in the Bhagavad-Gita.

Lakshmi or **Shri**, "fortune" in the sense of good luck
Name of Vishnu's wife, born from the churning of the sea of milk.

Linga, "monkey"
Phallic symbol of Shiva. If a face is sculpted in it, it is called Mukhalinga, if it has a sculpted chignon, it is called Jatalinga.

Lokesvara, "lord of the world"
Represents either a Buddha or Avalokitesvara.

Mahabharata, "Bharavas' great gesture"
One of the two great Indian epics, with the Ramayana. Narrative (in more than 100,000 lines) of the great war that opposed the Pandava, allied with Krishna, and the Kaurava. Includes the Bhagavad-Gita.

Mahayana, from **maha**, "great" and **yana**, "vehicle", "great vehicle"
Constitutes with Hinayana ("small vehicle" in Sanskrit) one of the two main branches of Buddhism. Promotes the action and the existence of the Bodhisattva, beings that could attain nirvana but refrain from doing so, by compassion, to help their fellow man.

Makara, (Sanskrit and Pali)
Imaginary aquatic animal, composite of a crocodile and an elephant.

Mandapa, "pavilion"
Religious edifice with columns located in the temple's cultural centre.

Mohini
Vishnu's feminine form.

Mudra, "seal"
Canonical gestures that signify a "psychic state" (Albert Le Bonheur). Allow Buddha's expression to be "situated".

Mukhalinga, "linga with a face"

Mukhuta, "crown"
In Champa, as in the rest of South-east Asia, the name given to stiff diadems or divinities' headdresses.

Naga, (Sanskrit and Pali), "snake"
Multi-headed cobra. Symbol of waters in Indian mythology, Buddha's protector under the name of Mucilinda when the former, during the sixth week that followed the Enlightenment, nearly drowned during his meditation in the rising waters of Lake Mucilinda.

Nandin
Name of Shiva's (white) bull and mount.

Nataraja, "king of the dance"
Any of Shiva's dancing forms.

Pandit, from pandita, "traditional letter"

Parvati, "daughter of the mountain"
Shiva's wife, and Skanda's and Ganesha's mother

Prajnaparamita, "perfection of wisdom"
Mother of all Buddhas.

Rama, "charming"
Hero of the Ramayana.

Ramayana
One of the two great Indian epics with the Mahabharata, dedicated to the adventures of Rama, one of Vishnu's avatars. Attributed to the sage Valmiki.

Rishi, "wise"

Rudra, "screamer"
Vedic precursor and aspect of Shiva.

Sakti, "power"
Designates the god's consort, who is the personification of his power.

Sampot (Khmer and Thai), "cloth"
Designation of the clothing worn short in Khmer sculpture and by "abusive" extension to that in Cham sculpture.

Sarasvati
Brahma's wife-sakti, goddess of speech and knowledge.

Sarong (Indonesian)
Designation of long draped clothing in Khmer sculpture. Used essentially but incorrectly in Cham names for feminine clothes.

Shiva, "beneficial"
The destructive god in the Brahman trio. Cham sculpture is for the most part Shivaist.

Shri, "fortune"
See Lakshmi.

Skanda, "from sperm"
Son of Shiva, generally riding his vahana, a snake-killing peacock named Paravani.

Somasutra
Groove in the yoni.

Sugriva
Name of the king of monkeys, hero of the Ramayana.

Surya
The sun god.

Tara, "she who saves"
Feminine counterpart of Avalokitesvara, therefore also incarnates compassion.

Trimurti, "triple form"
Designates the three gods: Brahma, Vishnu and Shiva, all issuing from one supreme Shiva.

Uma, "light"
Shiva's wife.

Upanishad
Philosophical texts. The oldest can be dated to the end of the Vedic period (700 BCE).

Urna
Tuft of hair between the eyebrows. One of the distinguishing signs of Buddha or Buddhic beings.

Usnisha, "that which is at the summit"
Protuberance of the skull. One of the distinguishing signs of Buddha of Buddhic beings.

Uttarasanga
Large piece of fabric worn like a coat. It can cover one or both shoulders.

Varna, "class" in Sanskrit
The four classes; namely, Brahman (priests), ksatriya (warriors), vaishya (merchants), shudra (farmers and servants) date from an appearance initiated in Vedic times, the two first dominating the two others.

Vayu
God of wind and speech. Guardian of the North-West. Mounts, literally and figuratively, a horse.

Veda, "knowledge"
Set of four core texts: the Rig-Veda, "wisdom of verses", the Sana-Veda, "wisdom of songs", the Yajur-Veda, "wisdom of melodies", the Atharva-Veda, "wisdom of the Atharvan priests". Channelled to priests, who transcribed them, by the divinities – including Brahma – their origin goes back, for the oldest (the Rig-Veda) to 1200 BCE.

Vihara (Sanskrit and Pali), "place to stay"
Meeting room of Buddhist monks.

Vishnu, "he who penetrates everything"
God who ensures the maintenance of the world between its creation by Brahma and its destruction by Shiva.

Yaksha (masculine), **yakshi** (feminine)
Minor animist divinities integrated later into Hindu religions, where they are largely beneficial, and Buddhism, where they are mostly demonic. Represented with fangs and bulging eyes.

Yoni
Symbol of the vulva, always represented perpendicularly encircling the linga, which is vertical, and symbol of Shiva. One of its sides includes a groove (called a somasutra) that channels the liquids used during the ceremony (water, milk, etc.) to the exterior of the sanctuary.

Brief Chronology of Champa

Circa 220-230 C.E
Chinese texts mention a kingdom of Linyi, situated south of the Chinese command post in Rinan and enlarging northward into Rinan territory.

284
Embassy of Linyi at the Chinese court.

Second half of the third century
Inscription in Sanskrit at Vo Canh (in the Nha Trang region).

357
Northern frontier of Linyi (the capital of which is in today's Hue region) drawn at the Gate of Annam.

Late fourth century
Several inscriptions written in Sanskrit mention the foundation of the first sanctuary of My Son (dedicated to Shiva).

520
A king of Linyi bore the Sanskrit name Vijayavarman.

Sixth century
Gradual fusion of Linyi with a kingdom that would later be called Champa.

605
Chinese invasion.

658-668
Two inscriptions use the term "Champa" for the first time.

774
Sanctuary of Po Nagar (Nha Trang) burnt down by Javanese pirates.

Between 854 and 875 and the tenth century
Buddhist sanctuary Dong Duong founded. Time of kingdom's greatest expansion, regions – from north to south – with the following Sanskrit names: Indrapura (between the Gate of Annam and the Col of Clouds), Amaravati (Quang Nam and Quang Ngai, including My Son and Trà Kieu), Vijaya (Binh Dinh), Kauthara (around Nha Trang) and Panduranga (Ninh Thuan and Binh Thuan).

877
Transcription of the name Champa in Chinese: Tchan Tch'eng.

938
Ngo Quyen founded a state independent from China that became Dai Co Viet in 968.

950
Khmer raid on Kauthara.
982
The Viet king Le Dai Hanh attacks Indrapura.

995-997
Raids by Champa on Dai Co Viet.

1000
Transfer of the Cham capital from Indrapura to Vijaya.

1021-1026-1044
Viet attacks on Champa.

Eleventh century
First Muslim communities noted in Champa.

1043
Capture of Vijaya by Viet King Ly Thanh Tong.

1068
Champa attack on Dai Co Viet.

1069
The Viet king Ly Thanh Tong defeated Champa (Quy Nhon taken). Three northern provinces ceded by Champa to Dai Viet, as war damages.

1074
King Harivarman IV crowned. Closer ties with China.

1145
Khmer king Suryavarman II invaded Champa.

1177
Angkor, Khmer capital, taken by the Champa army.

1181
Jayavarman VII crowned in Angkor.

1190
Jayavarman VII freed his kingdom and captured Vijaya, the Cham capital.

1203-1220
After further battles, Champa is annexed by the Khmer kingdom.

1283
Mongol invasion.

End of the thirteenth century
Cham script replaced Sanskrit in inscriptions.

1306
Prince Harijit obtained the hand of the sister of the Viet king Tran Anh Tong in exchange for the cession of two northern Champa provinces (O and Ri).

Between 1371 and 1389
The lost provinces were reclaimed by king Che Bong Nga, who also carried out raids on the Viet capital Thang Long, later called Hanoi.

1471
Vijaya, the Champa capital, taken by the Viet: 60,000 killed and 30,000 made prisoner. The victorious Viet king, Le Thanh Tong, gave Bo Tri Tri, a military chief in Vijaya, the lands of Kauthara, Panduranga and the high plateaux of the west. The new kingdom received Chinese investiture in 1478.

1653
Another Cham defeat by Viet King Nguyen. Of Champa, only Panduranga remained.

1692
Further defeat: Panduranga lost its independence.

1802-1822
Po Sau Nun Can, a Cham and the companion in war of the emperor Gia Long, became leader of Panduranga (a "protectorate" of Annam).

1832
Death of Le Van Duyet. Vietnamese emperor Minh Menh erased the remains of Champa from the map.

1835
Death of Ja Tak Va.

Chronology of the reigns of Cham sovereigns, the construction of temples and their schools of sculpture

KING	Dates	Construction of temples and the creation of schools of sculpture
Bhadravarman I	late 4th century	Construction of a sanctuary dedicated to Shiva Bhadreshvra at My Son.
Sambhuvarman	?-629	Foundation dedicated to Lakshmi at My Son. Elaboration of the primary style
Vikrantavarman I and II	653- c.731	Elaboration of the My Son E1 style.
		Construction of My Son F1 and My Son C1.
Prathivindravarman	mid-8th century	774 - Destruction of Po Nagar in Nha Trang by the Javanese.
Satyavarman	after 750	784 - Restoration of Po Nagar
Indravarman I	?-802	
Harivarman I	802-c.820	Foundation of Senapati Par at Po Nagar.
Vikrantavarman III	mid-9th century	Erection of the Towers of Hoa Lai.
Indravarman II	c.874-c.890	Erection of Dong Duong style, My Son F3, A2, C7.
		Elaboration of the Dong Duong
Jaya Simhavarman I	c.897-c.904	Erection of My Son A12, A13, B2, E4.
Jayashaktivarman	c.904	
Bhadravarman II	c.905-917	Erection of My Son A10.
Indravarman III	918-959	Elaboration of the Tra Kieu style. Theft in 950
		of the gold statue of Bhagavami (consecrated in 918) by the Khmer.
Jaya Indravarman I	c.960-c.965	
Harivarman II	c.989-999	991 - Construction at My Son E of a Ishanabhadreshvara.
		Elaboration of the Chien Dan style.
Jaya Parameshvaravarman I	c.1044-1060	New dynasty claiming to be part of the Uroja line.
		The breast typically used as sculptural ornament.
Bhadravarman III	1061	
Rudravarman III	1062-1074	
Harivarman IV	1074-1081	Restoration at My Son and Simhapura.
Jaya Indravarman II	1086-1113	Elaboration of the Thâp-Mam style.
Jaya Indravarman III	1139-1145	
Jaya Harivarman I	1147-1166	My Son G1 founded, restructuring of Po Nagar in Nha Trang.
Jaya Indravarman IV	c.1166-?	
Jaya Parameshvaravarman II Ansharaja	1226	Restoration of temples.
Jaya Indravarman VI	1243-1257	
Indravarman V	1258-c.1285	
Jaya Simhavarman III	c.1285-1307	
Harijitatmaja (prince)	1307-1313	
«Troa Hoa»	1342-c.1360	
		Elaboration of the Yang Mum style.
«Che Bong Nga»	c.1370-1390	
Jaya Simhavarman V	1390-1401	
Indravarman VI	1401-1441	
	1446	First fall of Vijaya (taken by the Viet).
	1471	Vijaya's final fall.

Bibliography

Acharya P.K.,

Hindu Architecture in India and abroad, London, Oxford University Press.1946 *Actes du séminaire sur le Champa organisé à l'université de Copenhague,* Paris, Publications du Centre d'Histoire et Civilisations de la Péninsule Indochinoise, 1988

Arasse Daniel,

On n'y voit rien. Descriptions, Paris, Editions Denoël, 2000.

Aymonier Etienne,

Les Tchames et leurs religions, Paris, Leroux, 1891

Basham Arthur L.,

La civilisation de l'Inde ancienne, Editions Arthaud, Paris 1988

Baptiste Pierre,

« Asie du Sud Est », in *Arts Asiatiques*, Paris, 2001, pp. 112-113

Baptiste Pierre,

« Un grand chef-d'œuvre de l'art du bronze entre au Musée Guimet, grâce à une dation. Un bodhisattva cham du VIIIe siècle », in *La Revue du Louvre et des Musées de France* n 2, 2003

Barazer-Billoret Marie-Luce, Dagens Bruno,

Shiva libérateur des âmes et maître des dieux, Paris, Découvertes Gallimard, Religions, 2004

Barth A. et Bergaigne A.,

Inscriptions sanskrites de Campa et du Cambodge, Paris, 1885, n XX, pp. 191-198

Bhattacharya Kamaleswar,

« Précisions sur la paléographie de l'inscription dite de Vo-canh », in *Artibus Asiae*, XXIV, ¾ (1961), pp. 219-224

Bhattacharya Kamaleswar,

« Linga-Kosa », in *Artibus Asiae,* essays offered to G.H.Luce, 1966, vol. H : 6-13

Bezacier L.,

Manuel d'Archéologie d'Extrême-Orient, Première partie: Asie du Sud-Est. Tome II, Le Viêt-Nam. Premier fascicule: De la préhistoire à la fin de l'occupation chinoise, Paris, A. et J. Picard, 1972

Bezacier L.,

« Attitude inhabituelle commune aux arts cam et vietnamien du dragon, Makara et du lion », in *Artibus Asiae,* XXIV, ¾, 1961: 207-218

Boisselier Jean,

« Arts du Champa et du Cambodge préangkorien. La date de Mison E 1 », in *Artibus Asiae,* XIX, 1, 1956: 197-212.

Boisselier Jean,

« Un bronze cham inédit d'Avalokitesvara », in *Arts Asiatiques,* IV, 4 1957: 257-274

Boisselier Jean,

« Le Vishnu de Tjibuajan (Java occidental) et la statuaire du Sud-Est Asiatique », in *Artibus Asiae,* XXII, 1959,210-226

Boisselier Jean,

« Notes sur une statuette funéraire Tang représentant un danseur originaire du Champa », in *Artibus Asiae*, XXIV, 1, 1061: 5-10

Boisselier Jean,

La Statuaire du Champa, Recherche sur les cultes et l'iconographie, Paris, PEFEO, LIV, 1963

Boisselier Jean,

« Les sculptures de DONG DUONG du Muséum Rietberg de Zurich », in *Artibus Asiae*, XXVI.2 1963: 132-150

Boisselier Jean,

« Die Kunst Champas », Berlin, Sonderdruck aus der Propylaen Kumstgeschichte 1971, vol.XVI: 116-122, 286-295, fig.229-320

Boisselier Jean,

« Un bronze de târâ du Musée de Dà Nàng et son importance pour l'histoire de l'Art du Champa », BEFEO LXXII, 1984: 319-337, 5 pl

Boisselier Jean,

« Il Champa », Il Sud-Est Asiatico, Storia Universale dell'Arte, Torino, 1986: 293-327, illust.

Boisselier Jean,

« Le Champa », in Le Vietnam des Royaumes, Paris, Cercle d'Art, 1995: 49-75

Boisselier Jean,

« Le nàgaràja de My Son et les débuts de l'hindouisation du Campa », Studies and Reflections on Asian Art History and Archaeology, Essays honour of H.S.H Professor Subhadradis Diskul, Bangkok, Silpakorn University, 1995: 287-296

Bosh, FDK,

« Notes archéologiques. I. Le motif de l'arc-à-biche à Java et au Champa », BEFEO XXXI, 1931: 485-491

Bosh, FDK,

« Notes archéologiques. II. La lingodbhavamurti de Siva en Indochine », BEFEO XXXI, 1931: 491-496

Brocheux Michèle,

« Notes sur les deux bronzes chams inédits du Musée National de Saigon », BSEI, XII, 2:99-104

Cabaton Antoine,

Nouvelles recherches sur les Chams, Paris, PEFEO, Leroux, 1902

Cao Xuàn Phô, Pham Huy Thông,

Diêu Kbâc, Cham Sculpture, Hanoi, State Committee for Social Sciences of Vietnam Institute of Southeast Asian studies, Social Sciences Publishing House, 1988

Carpeaux Charles,

Les ruines d'Angkor, de Dong Duong et de My-Son, Paris, Auguste Challamet, 1908: 259

Claeys Jean-Yves,

« Introduction à l'étude de l'Annam et du Champa; les Chams; les Annamites », Hanoi, *Bulletin des amis du Vieux Hué*, 21, 1934: 1-144

Claeys Jean-Yves,

« Simhapura, la grande capitale chame (VIe -VIIIe siècles) », Revue des Arts asiatiques, VII (1931-1932), pp. 193-204

Clémentin-Ojha C., Manguin P-Y.,

Un siècle pour l'Asie, L'Ecole française d'Extrême-Orient, 1898-2000, Paris, EFEO, Editions du Pacifique, 2000

Coedès G., Parmentier H.,

Listes générales des inscriptions et des monuments du Champa et du Cambodge, Hanoi, EFEO, 1923

Coedès George,

« Le piédestal de Tra Kieu; à propos d'un article de M.J. Przyluski, « un chef d'œuvre de la sculpture chame: le piédestal de Tra Kieu » », in *Revue des Arts Asiatiques*, VI, 1931: 89 – 93

Coedès George,

« Notes sur deux inscriptions du Champa », *Bulletin de l'Ecole française d'Extrême Orient*, XII (8), 1912, pp.15-17

Coedès George,

Les Etats hindouisés d'Indochine et d'Indonésie, Paris, De Boccard ,1964

Coral Remusat, Gilberte de,

« Art cam, le problème de la chronologie », *Bulletin de la commission archéologique de l'Indochine*, Paris, Leroux, n 31-34, pp. 35-44, 1932

Coral Remusat, Gilberte de,

« Art cam, le problème de la chronologie », musée Guimet, *Catalogue des collections indochinoises*, Paris, musées nationaux, 35-44, 1934 (réédition de 1932 avec commentaires)

Coral Remusat, Gilberte de,

« Archéologie indochinoise », *Bulletin de la commission archéologique de l'Indochine*, 1935

Dalsheimer, Nadine,

Les collections du musée national de Phnom Penh, Paris, Ecole Française d'Extrême Orient, Magellan et Cie, 2001

Danielou Alain,

Mythes *et dieux de l'Inde. Le Polythéisme hindou,* Paris, GF Flammarion. 1994

Dupont Pierre,

« Tchen-la et Panduranga », BSEI, XXIV, 1, 1949: 9-25

Dupont Pierre,

« Les apports chinois dans le style bouddhique de Dông Duong », BEFEO XLIV, 1, 1950: 267-274

Finot Louis,

« La religion des Chams d'après les monuments », BEFEO 1, 1901: 12-26

Finot Louis,

« Note d'épigraphie XI, Les inscriptions de mison » BEFEO IV, 1904: 897-977

Finot Louis,

« Lokesvara en Indochine », Etudes Asiatiques, EFEO, XIX, XX, 1925

Finot Louis,

« Notes d'épigraphie I, III, V,VI, XI, XIV,XV, XIX », Bulletin de l'Ecole française d'Extrême Orient (1901-2020), 1 pp. 185-191; III, pp. 206-211 et 649-654; IV, pp. 83-115 et 897-977; IX, pp. 205-209:XV/2, pp. 1-19, 39-43 et 112

Frédéric Louis,

Dictionnaire de la civilisation indienne, Paris, Robert Laffont, 1987

Feray P- R.,

Viêt-nam, Paris, PUF, 2001

Groslier B.P,

Indochine, Carrefour des Arts, Paris, Albin Michel, 1960

Guillon Emmanuel,

« Champa », Dictionary of Arts, London, ed. Jane Turner, Mac Millan, 1996, Vol. 6: 417-433, illust.

Guillon Emmanuel,

Treasures from the Da Nang Museum, Vietnam, London, Thames and Hudson, 2001

Ha Van Thu ,Trân Hông Du'c,

Chronologie de l'histoire du Vietnam. De la tradition orale à nos jours, Hanoi, Thê Gio'i, 2000

Heffley Carl,

The arts of champa, Saigon, US Information service, Cultural Affairs, 1972

Higham Ch.,

The Bronze Age of Southeast Asia, Cambridge University Press (Cambridge World Archaeology), 1996

Higham Ch.,

Early Cultures of Mainland Southeast Asia, Bangkok, River Books, 2002

Hô Tân Tuân,

« Réexamen de la datation du piédestal de Trâ Kîeu exposé au Musée de sculpture Chame à Da Nang », Paris, Péninsule 32(1), 1996: 21-31,9 illust. (avec Hô Xuän Tinh)

Huber. Ed,

« Etudes indochinoises I, II, III, IV, VII, VIII, IX, X, XI, XII », Bulletin de l'Ecole française d'Extrême-Orient (1901-2012), V, pp. 168-176: XI, pp. 5-22 et 259-311

Hubert Jean-François

(Ed), *Le Viêt Nam des royaumes*, Paris, Cercle d'Art, 1995

Hubert Jean-François

(Ed), *L'Ame du Viêt Nam*, Paris, Cercle d'Art, 1996

Hubert Jean-François,

Hué (1930-1960), photographies de Loi Nguyen Hoa, Paris, Nouvelles éditions, 2001

Hubert Jean-François

(avec Catherine Noppe) (Ed), *La Fleur du Pêcher et l'oiseau d'azur. Arts du Viêtnam,* Tournai, musée Royal de Mariemont, La Renaissance du Livre, 2002

Hubert Jean-François

(avec Catherine Noppe), *Art du Viêtnam*, New York, Parkstone Press, 2002

Lafont P-B.

(Ed), *Histoire des frontières de la péninsule indochinoise. I. Les frontières du Vietnam*, Paris, L'Harmattan, 1989

Lafont P-B. et Po Dharma,

Bibliographie: Champa et Cam, Paris, L'Harmattan, 1989

Le Bonheur Albert,

« Champa », Paris, Encyclopaedia Universalis, Vol. 4. 1968: 133-136

Le Bonheur Albert,

« L'art du Champa », in *L'art de l'Asie du Sud-Est,* Paris, Citadelle et Mazenod, 1994 *Le Champa et le monde malais,* Paris, Publications du C.H.C.PI., 1991

Lefèvre Vincent,

« Le Champa », in *La Fleur du Pêcher et l'oiseau d'azur. Arts du Viêtnam,* Tournai, musée Royal de Mariemont, La Renaissance du Livre, 2002, pp. 125-144

Lemire Charles,

« Les tours Kiams de la province de Binh-Dinh (Annam) », Paris, Revue Ethnographie, VI. 1887: 383-394

Lemire Charles,

« Aux monuments anciens des Kiams. Excursion archéologique en Annam », in *Tour du monde,* LXVIII (1894), p.401-416 *Le monde indochinois et la péninsule malaise,* Kuala Lumpur, Publications du C.H.C.P.I, 1990

Lê Thanh Khôi,

Le Viêt-Nam, Histoire et civilisation, Paris, Editions de Minuit, 1955

Lê Thanh Khôi,

Le Viêtnam, Paris, Sudestasie, 1981

Lê Thanh Khôi,

Voyage dans les cultures du Vietnam, Paris 2001

Leuba Jeanne,

Un royaume disparu: Les Chams et leur art, Paris Bruxelles, Van Oest, 1923

Lê Xuân Diêm, Tu Kim Lôc,

Champa. Artefacts of Champa, TP Ho Chi Minh. 1996

Lombard D.,

« Le Campa vu du Sud », Bulletin de l'Ecole française d'Extrême-Orient, LXXVI (1987), pp. 311-317

Majumdar Rameo Candra,

Ancient Indian Colonies in the Far East, Vol 1: Champa, Lahore, Punjab, Sanskrit Book Depot, 1927: XXIX ,227

Manguin. P.Y.,

"L'introduction de l'Islam au Campa", Bulletin de l'Ecole française d'Extrême-Orient LXVI 1976, pp. 255-287

Maspero Georges,

Le royaume de Champa, Paris, Van Oest, 1928

Maybon Albert,

« L'art cham », Paris, in *L'art décoratif,* 1911: 157-172

Mus Paul,

« Cultes indiens et indigènes au Champa », BEFEO XXXIII, 1; 1933: 367-410.

Mus Paul,

« L'inscription à Valmiki de Prakacadharma (Trâ-Kiêu) », Bulletin de l'Ecole française d'Extrême Orient XXVIII 1 (1928) pp. 147-152

Ngô Vân Doanh,

Champa Orient Towers, reality and legend, The Gioi publishers, Hanoi, 2002

Ngô Vân Doanh, Nguyen The Thuc,

Champa sculpture, VNA Publishing House, Hanoi, 2004

Parmentier Henri,

"Les monuments du cirque de Mison", BEFEO IV, 1904: 805-896, cartes, illust.

Parmentier Henri,

« Rapport sur la création d'un musée cham », Paris, Bulletin de la Commission archéologique de l'Indochine, 1908: 89-94

Parmentier Henri,

Inventaire descriptif des monuments cams de l'Annam, Tome I. Description des monuments, Paris, Imprimerie nationale, Ernest Leroux, 1909

Parmentier Henri,

Inventaire descriptif des monuments cams de l'Annam. Tome II; Etude de l'Art cam, Paris, Leroux, 1918

Parmentier Henri,

« Catalogue du Musée Cam de Tourane », BEFEO XIX. 3, 1919: 1-114

Parmentier Henri,

Les sculptures chames au Musée de Tourane, Paris Bruxelles, Van Oest (Ars Asiatica IV), 1922

Parmentier Henri,

« Notes d'archéologie Indochinoise, I. Relevé des points cams, découverts en Annam depuis la publication de l'inventaire », BEFEO XXIII, 1923: 267-275

Patko Imre et Rév Miklos,

L'Art du Viet Nam, Paris, Aimery Somogy, 1967

Pham Huu My,

« Đọc lại nội dung Đai Thô Trà Kiệu (22.2) » (relecture de l'article « Le piédestal de Trâ Kiêu (22.2), Musée Cham-Dâ Nâng »), Tạp chí Khảo cổ học, in *Revue archéologique,* n°2, 1995: 84-88

Pham Huu My, Vuong Hai Yen,

Champa collection Vietnam Historical Museum Ho Chi Minh City, Bảo Tàng Lịch Sử VietNam, TP Ho Chi Minh, 1994

Pham Thuy Hop,

The collection of Champa sculpture in the National Museum of Viêtnam History, Hanoi, 2003

Po Dharma,

Le Panduranga (Campa). Ses rapports avec le Vietnam (1802-1835), Paris, Publication de l'EFEO, CXLIX, 1987 (2 vol.)

Po Dharma,

« L'Insulinde malaise et le campa », Bulletin de l'Ecole française d'Extrême Orient, LXXXVII, I (2000), pp. 183

Pratapaditya Pal,

Indian sculpture, Vol. I et II. A Catalogue of the Los Angeles Country Museum of Art Collection, 1986

Przyluski Jean,

« Un chef-d'œuvre de la sculpture chame, le piédestal de Trâ Kiêu », in *Revue des Arts Asiatiques*, VI, 1930: 89-93

Rawson Philip,

The art of South East Asia, London, Thames and Hudson. 1967

Renou Louis,

L'Hindouisme, Presses Universitaires de France, 1951

Schweyer A-V.,

« La vaisselle en argent de la dynastie d'Indrapura (Quang Nam Viet Nam). Etude d'épigraphie cam-II », Bulletin de l'Ecole française d'Extrême Orient, LXXXVI (1999), pp.345-355

Sharma Jagdish Chandra,

Temples Of Champa in Vietnam, Tháp Chàm ở Việt Nam, Nhà Xuất Bản Khoa Học Xã Hội Hà Nội, 1992

Stern Philippe,

L'Art du Champa (ancien Annam) et son évolution, Toulouse, 1942

Tarling N. (éd.),

The Cambridge History of Southeast Asia, Volume one, Part one. From Early Times to c. 1500, Cambridge University Press, 1992, 1999

Teston Eugène, Percheron Maurice,

L'Indochine moderne, Paris, Librairie de France, 1931

Tran Ky Phuong,

« Đọc lại nội dung Đai Thô Trà Kiệu, một kiệt tác của nghệ thuật Cham », (relecture de l'article : "un chef-d'œuvre de la sculpture chame: le piédestal de Trà Kiêu »), in *Revue Etudes des Arts*, n 2 (1983): 64-73

Tran Ky Phuong,

Les ruines Cham. A la recherche d'une civilisation éteinte, The Gioi Editions en langues étrangères, Hanoi.1993

Van Roy Staf,

« Une bague avec des diamants parfaits », in *La Fleur du Pêcher et l'oiseau d'azur. Arts du Viêtnam,* Tournai, musée Royal de Mariemont, La Renaissance du Livre, 2002, p. 151

Vatsyayan Kapila,

« Some dance sculptures from Champa », National Centre for the Performing Arts Quarterly journal, VII, 4, 1978: 1-19

Wales H.G. Quaritch,

« The Dong Son genius and the evolution of Cham art », JRAS, 1949, 1-2: 34-44

Waterston Richard,

L'Inde éternelle, Paris, Editions Albin Michel, 1995

Weber G., Martinot L., Guillaume J.,

« Les métaux précieux et bijoux du Champa vus par un cyclotron », in *La Fleur du Pêcher et l'oiseau d'azur. Arts du Viêtnam,* Tournai, musée Royal de Mariemont, La Renaissance du Livre, 2002, pp. 145-150.

List of Illustrations